CAMPING: Organization and Operation

JAY S. SHIVERS
University of Connecticut

PRENTICE HALL, ENGLEWOOD CLIFFS, NEW JERSEY 07632

Library of Congress Cataloging-in-Publication Data

Shivers, Jay Sanford.
  Camping: organization and operation / Jay S. Shivers.

  Bibliography.
  Includes index.
  ISBN 0-13-113630-5
  1. Camps—Management. 2. Camps–United States. I. Title.
GV198.M35S53 1989
796.54'068—dc19   88-2535
           CIP

Editorial/production supervision and
  interior design: Marjorie Shustak
Cover design: George Cornell
Manufacturing buyer: Peter Havens

 ©1989 by Prentice-Hall, Inc.
A Division of Simon & Schuster
Englewood Cliffs, New Jersey 07632

Printed in the United States of America

10 9 8 7 6 5 4 3 2 1

ISBN 0-13-113630-5

Prentice-Hall International (UK) Limited, *London*
Prentice-Hall of Australia Pty. Limited, *Sydney*
Prentice-Hall Canada Inc., *Toronto*
Prentice-Hall Hispanoamericana, S.A., *Mexico*
Prentice-Hall of India Private Limited, *New Delhi*
Prentice-Hall of Japan, Inc., *Tokyo*
Simon & Schuster Asia Pte. Ltd., *Singapore*
Editora Prentice-Hall do Brasil, Ltda., *Rio de Janeiro*

To RHO

Omnia vincit amor

Contents

Preface

Camping has been a part of human experience ever since humans learned to live in a hostile environment. By adapting to the outdoors and learning to obtain food, clothing, and shelter, early people used certain camping skills to sustain themselves. These techniques included trail blazing, water source discovery, and knowledge of animal migratory habits. This accumulation of knowledge contributed to their survival.

Outdoor education, the most ancient form of education, is any nature-oriented experience that involves contact with, appreciation for, or knowledge about natural phenomena. It is concerned with the full spectrum of nature, and includes such interesting topics as insects and plant species. Every science related to the outdoors is part of it. The ancestors of *homo sapiens* who learned to make and control fire, the camper who thrills to the starry night sky, and the spelunker who revels in the underground of a hidden cave—all have been caught up in outdoor education.

The transition from outdoor education to camping techniques, which are familiar to all those who participate in camping, did not occur quickly, nor have all the elements of survival been eliminated. Some of the basic camping skills involve the necessity of finding one's way in the wilderness; applying skills on the trail insofar as marking direction or shelter building is concerned; aquatics; adapting to small groups; and living in harmony with natural surroundings.

Modern camping developed out of the heritage of the pioneering spirit of this country, as well as through efforts of farsighted people who recognized the benefits of outdoor living for participants. Today, camping is an increasingly salient feature of contemporary life wherever it is practiced. Despite its narrow origin as a summer vacation for the young, camping now caters to all age groups, serving those who require special programs as well as those who can profit from being mainstreamed in spite of physical or mental disabilities. Camping programs are also conducted throughout the year. The camping institution is capable of satisfying the various recreational, social, educational, commercial, and conservation objectives of all campers. Camping is a complex, specialized, and professionally administered enterprise with a nationally recognized association, established by professionals, which maintains rigorous standards for operation of accredited camps.

This book's overall theme is to show both the diversity and the unity of camping. This book has two primary audiences: Camp administrators, and those who work directly with campers (either as counselors or program specialists, or in related services). If they have never been counselors or program specialists but have been employed solely for managerial skills, administrators will benefit generally from awareness of counseling techniques and program planning and implementation. After all, the camp exists to provide opportunities for campers. These opportunities are made available through counseling and programming, and the administrator should be familiar with these elements and understand what the staff is trying to accomplish. Similarly, counselors and program staff will be most effective if they understand the administrative framework within which they operate. Bridging the gap between these sometimes distant groups will contribute to better, more efficient camping operations.

Essentially, this book emphasizes large, residential camps for children and youth, although other examples are offered throughout the text. The content does have broad applications in all or most camp settings, but it is to the organized residential camp that attention is focused and from which experiences are drawn.

In their haste to discuss activities, too many contemporary texts ostensibly dealing with camp counseling neglect the details of everyday camp life and the dynamics of the counselor's role. This book attempts to offset that omission. It also offers a philosophical frame of reference for the values of outdoor education and of ecology, which is a vital concern of every educated person.

This book starts with an account of the history of organized camping in the United States. Part I of the book explores the problems of camp planning, administration, and operation. Differences among various types of camp sponsorship are based upon accountability, legal requirements, and fundamental philosophy, rather than management practices only. Part I explores and summarizes these differences and can serve as an administrator's handbook. More significant than the practices are the principles underlying them. Therefore, the book emphasizes the *why* as well as the *how* of camp administration. Rational action is likely when basic principles are understood and applied.

Part II of the book is an intensive treatment of the counselor's role in the camp. The various chapters discuss the dynamics of group living, counselor selection, orientation, qualifications, responsibilities, and conduct. Camper behavior, peer relationships, problems, and leadership are also emphasized.

Part III deals with nature-oriented and standard camp activities. Using the natural sciences as a point of departure for outdoor camp activities is stressed repeatedly. There is, to be sure, a place for indoor activities, spontaneous games, and team experiences, but primarily the camper must learn to be at home in the outdoor world. Survival techniques, exploration, nature study, camp crafts, and campfire activities are an integral part of the camp program.

Acknowledgments

This book is a labor of love. My personal views about camping, which pervade the book, are the outcome of my own experiences—not only as a camper from the ages of 4 to 13, but also as a counselor-in-training, counselor, waterfront director, and camp administrator. In addition to participating in a wide variety of organized camping situations, both resident and day, public and private, I have had the good fortune to share with my family the experience of tenting extensively throughout the United States and Canada, from Arcadia National Park in Maine to Yosemite National Park in California, from Banff National Park in the Canadian Rockies to Chaparral Park in New Mexico—and many of the wondrous places in between. The days on the trail, the evenings spent stargazing, my son's exuberance at mastering some new skill—all helped make this book possible. Now my grandson, the third generation, is being introduced to the camping experience by his father. I have complete faith in good camping experiences, and firmly believe that all children should be allowed, through camp attendance, to share in the magnificent heritage of the natural world around us.

In a world haunted by potential ecological disaster, among other obvious threats to tranquility, there is some comfort in the knowledge that it remains possible to fortify young children against the forces that tend to dehumanize life. The possibility lies in the intuitive interest of youngsters in nature, in their delight and fascination with the myriad sights and sounds discovered on the land, in the water, and in the sky. With regard to children's perceptive response to nature, Rachel Carson said, "If I had influence with the good fairy who is supposed to preside over the christening of all children I should ask that her gift to each child be a sense of wonder so indestructible that it would last throughout life, an unfailing antidote against the boredom and disenchantment of later years, the sterile preoccupation with things that are artificial, the alienation from the sources of our strength."

In the absence of good fairies, to whom may we look to cultivate, protect, and preserve an indestructible sense of wonder in our children? Parents and teachers must, of course, act decisively in its promotion; but experience indicates that they cannot usually effect complete success, particularly where deficiencies exist in the available resources or in the local environment. For the sense of wonder to develop fully, a child must live with nature. The opportunity to do so is now possible in thousands of camps throughout the country.

The kind of camping experience we seek for our children requires guidance by camp counselors who understand children and possess the knowledge and skills to make their experiences in the great outdoors rewarding. Good counselors function best in a well-organized and effectively administered camping situation. This is the responsibility of the camp administrators and, to a lesser degree, of the camp owner or sponsor.

I deeply appreciate those individuals whose assistance in the development of this book has been important: Dr. E. W. Niepoth, professor and graduate advisor, Department of Recreation and Parks Management, California State University at Chico; to camping professionals in Connecticut with whom I have exchanged ideas, anecdotes, and hair-raising stories; to former students who are now successful camp administrators; and to the many public and private camps whose contributions and valuable suggestions helped me achieve an accurate and more comprehensive picture of camping.

A special expression of gratitude goes to my son Jed Mark for his obvious enjoyment of all aspects of camping, which he is now passing along to his son, David Benjamin. Finally and always, particular recognition to my wife, Rhoda, for her continuous support, loyalty, and encouragement.

J.S.S.

Camping: Organization and Operation

chapter 1

The Camping Movement

A historical overview of camping in the United States provides a perspective on the initiation of the earliest organized camps. More important, such an overview provides information about the purpose of camping and the early concepts that influence today's camps.

THE CAMPING EXPERIENCE

Camping is living in or as close to nature as possible, in an environment untouched by urban culture, in which campers may have to fend for themselves. Camping need not be limited to one particular area, but may occur in solitude, without any permanent facility or boundary to prevent excursions into the wilderness. Campers may "pack-in"—that is, carry an entire supply of food, water, clothing, and shelter in a backpack. They may "live off the land," hiking without supplies and making do with whatever can be found or devised. Campers may use any mode of transportation to carry them and their supplies and still have all the fun of camping.

The value of a personal camping experience does not depend upon the method of transportation, nor upon encountering a variety of hazards—although this might make the experience more exciting for some people. Rather, the value derives from planning for, anticipating, and performing during the camping experience. Seeing new places or phenomena, revisiting favorite places, or coming upon memorable, awe-inspiring vistas—these and many other experiences are open to the camper. In whatever way campers attain something of value for efforts exerted, they do so because of the ability to participate in the unique process that, for our ancestors, was absolutely vital for survival. The capacity to live, work, and play in the natural environment has value for the camper, whether alone on a high ridge in dense snow, as a member of an organized camp in midsummer, or as a participant in the infinite variety of activities to which the camper may be exposed.

CAMPING VALUES

Camping has unique components that, when properly administered, can improve the quality of life for campers. Any well-conducted camp will provide the educational, social, and recreational experiences vital to the growth and development of campers. Moreover, the outdoor setting fosters appreciation for nature-oriented activities. If the camp's organizers are professional, it is likely that campers will come to understand their ecological role in nature and recognize the importance of the outdoors.

Outdoor Education and Camping

Outdoor education through camping attracts more than 120 million people each year. In the past, outdoor education taught people to appreciate and use natural resources; it must now teach them to use such resources wisely, so that they will be available for future generations. Education in conservation must be considered a part of outdoor education, and is one of the values to be instilled in the camper.

The enormous problem confronting those who are concerned with the protection and conservation of natural resources relates to the natural base that is the source of all material wealth. This finite resource is endangered by the increasing demands made upon it. No longer is there an open frontier capable of accommodating expansionist-minded individuals. Scientific management and technical processes must be devised to augment what still remains of our natural resources. Only the process of education oriented toward conservation and its manifold practices can ensure a sound future. One of the concepts that can be readily assimilated by young campers—the future protectors of the national heritage—is the value of conservation.

The major aim of conservation is to attain a balanced status between existing natural resources and potential consumers. It is apparent that the United States has not achieved this adjustment. Excessive consumption of depletable resources and pollution and despoilation of renewable resources is a salient trait of the American system. Unhappily, most American citizens neither understand nor recognize the outcome of such irresponsible behavior. It is thus essential to educate all citizens to realize and act upon the urgency of the need. To be sure, great strides have been made since the 1960s toward alerting citizens about ecological destruction. Even now, however, we suffer the effects of acid rain, strip mining, air pollution, water contamination, and a host of other resource degradations. The consequence of this ignorance has created a quiet crisis of our own making. It comes not with sound and fury, but rather with the slow strangulation engendered by polluted air and water. It is with us constantly, from the carbon

monoxide emitted in gasoline fumes to the tearing of the ozone layer covering our atmosphere. It has arrived insidiously and mounts daily. Young
campers, who are future voters, may become the cutting edge of a movement to preserve and protect the environment as a direct result of living at
close quarters with nature in an effective camp. While becoming aware of
nature, campers must also understand and respect the great treasures of
the oudoors. Camp administrators and counselors can be most influential
in teaching a responsibility that all citizens must share.

Among the benefits that may accrue from the camping experience are
the formation of lifelong interests based upon outdoor living and an appreciation of ecological balance and each organism's place in nature. Campers
can develop a sense of wonder at the detail and grandeur of the natural
landscape, the vastness and beauty of the night sky, the intricate designs
formed by light and shadow, or the form of habitats of creatures great and
small. Campers gain a great deal of information, the value of which is
lasting.

Relationships and Associations

Camping thrusts youngsters into small-group living situations that
force them to take stock of themselves and the others with whom they come
in contact. Although some camps cater to a homogeneous collection of
campers having the same social, ethnic, religious, or economic background,
it is more likely that the camp will be heterogeneous. Individuals of different backgrounds will be constant companions, and each camper must learn
to accept the foibles and the attributes of those who constitute the group.

All campers bring their experiences, habits, strengths, and weaknesses
to the group situation, and each will have to learn the give and take of small-
group life. Naturally, counselors can ease the way so that good relationships
develop and divisive episodes are minimized.

The camp can promote a sense of autonomy among campers who are
overly dependent on their home environment. Campers are taught to be
independent. They must participate in discussions about proposed activities, responsibilities, chores, and other topics that arise in the course of
daily living. Rules and regulations that promote campers' safety and health
must be understood and obeyed. Campers learn to (1) cooperate and shape
decision making as it pertains to group living arrangements or camping
activities, (2) participate in the democratic process of majority rule, (3) listen
to all sides of an argument before reaching a conclusion, and (4) discuss
differences of opinion and compromise in order to resolve conflicts. The
development of a *modus vivendi* that will provide the camper with lifelong
skills for coping with problems and stress can be the most significant lesson.

The Camping Program

Obviously, the camping program is the reason for going to camp. The
learning of new skills, the practice of old skills, the development of knowledge, and the formation of attitudes about others, as well as the camp activities, provide the most important package of values to be assimilated. Partici-

pation in every facet of camping brings to light previously unrecognized talents or interests, encourages a wider appreciation of one's own skills and capacities and those of others, opens the panorama of outdoor living, and promotes enjoyment through participation. The camping experience proceeds under the supervision of professional staff who are involved with the health, safety, and well-being of each camper. The learning that is accomplished in camping is underscored by fun, which succeeds in focusing the camper's attention. Outcomes of the camping experience include (1) improved mental and physical fitness, (2) good health, (3) an appreciation for outdoor living, (4) a foundation for lifetime recreational involvement, self-expression, self-realization, and self-actualization, (5) contact with varied opinions and value systems, and (6) the dynamics of group interaction in the democratic process. The camp should be designed such that these values are a natural outgrowth of daily participation.

THE ORGANIZED CAMP

Organized camping provides the camper with the practical conditions for combining outdoor education, conservation education, and recreational experiences in a place that encourages self-expression, exposure to nature, physical development, good health, and the acquisition of appropriate skills. Three elements are basic to the description and definition of organized camping. First, the camping experience occurs in a permanent facility with suitable space and structures. Second, guidance and directed learning experiences are offered by qualified counselors. Third, all camping activities are oriented toward group need in a democratic context. The distinctive feature of organized camping in this sense is that it is a habituation of social living in an outdoor environment.

Organized camping began as a movement. A movement is best characterized as an ameliorative effort to overcome a social problem. From a position of concern, directed efforts are made to overcome whatever disintegrating conditions exist. Deliberately arranged programs must follow logically over an extended period of time. Assigned values and selected criteria indicate the fulfillment of the movement. Ultimately, the goals of the movement are realized and the criteria are satisfied. Once objectives have been obtained, a movement becomes institutionalized.

The growth of organized camps can be understood from the material offered in subsequent pages. Organized camps were initially developed in an attempt to provide healthful outdoor living for children who were cooped up in classrooms all winter long. In some instances, it was the effort of a few individuals who recognized that children's needs might be better served in the wholesome refreshment of an outdoor environment as opposed to the stifling city atmosphere.

No longer a movement, camping is an established, organized institution in the United States and in other countries. Camping has succeeded in becoming institutionalized without dilution or slackening of standards; rather, higher standards have been defined and increasing excellence has been achieved.

Most movements die when their aims are achieved. They are generated solely to solve an immediate problem, and when the problem is solved they lapse. Because it appeals to each new generation, however, camping is self-perpetuating. There remains a bridge between those who have camped before and the new summer breed, or those whose interests reflect other seasonal orientation. This consistency is mirrored in the growth of new camps as well as in the endurance of those that have been able to build traditions.

The First Camps

In the spring of 1861, Frederick William Gunn, headmaster and founder of the Gunnery School for Boys in Washington, Connecticut, decided that he would devote a part of the school year to an outdoor experience for his students; thus was born the first school camp. Two weeks were spent at Milford on the Long Island Sound, where the boys fished, swam, sailed, and hiked. The trip was a great success and was repeated, for longer periods, for the next 18 years. A new camping site was later selected at Point Beautiful on Lake Waramauge. Gunnery Camp, established as an integral part of the school curriculum, was the initial effort from which sprang the many types of camps we know today.

The first private camp was started by Dr. Joseph T. Rothrock, a physician. His camp, established in 1876, was founded primarily for the benefit of boys in poor health. Rothrock's camp in the hill country of Pennsylvania was a tent community. There his pupils engaged in outdoor living, took part in physical fitness activities, and continued their schoolwork. The camp was short-lived, however; financial support failed to materialize, and Rothrock abandoned it after the first year. Although others tried to revitalize it, lack of proper financing remained a problem and forced the final closing of the camp.

The Reverend George W. Hinckley founded what is considered the first sectarian camp in 1880. With seven young members of his congregation, he took a brief trip to Wakefield, Rhode Island, where the boys were able to fish, participate in various games, and camp out. So successful was this first effort that Hinckley decided to establish a permanent camp in Maine. It was well organized and included religious services, educational activities, and various recreational experiences.

The first commercially successful camp was founded by Ernest B. Balch. Balch took over what he thought to be a deserted island in Asquam Lake, New Hampshire, in 1881. He finally purchased the property and named it Camp Chocorua. Balch recruited campers from wealthy families and set the trend in private commercial camps for many years. His camp was staffed with apparently qualified counselors. The first camp to require uniform dress, it was organized to provide for the physical and spiritual needs of the campers. Competitive activities made up a great deal of the summer schedule, and merit awards were presented. Camp Chocorua flourished until 1889.

Although other camps were established during the next few years, it was not until Sumner S. Dudley organized the first agency camp that the camping movement really gained momentum. Dudley had been associated with the Newburgh, New York, Young Men's Christian Association (YMCA) and initiated its camping program when, in the summer of 1885, he took several members of the organization on a short fishing trip to Orange Lake, near Newburgh. This camp became the oldest continually existing camp in the United States, and is still operating under the auspices of the state executive committee of the New York YMCA. When he died in 1897, at the age of 43, the camp was named Camp Dudley in his memory.

In 1888, Dr. Luther H. Gulick and his wife opened a camp for girls on the Thames River in Connecticut. Another camp, Camp Arey, established in Rochester, New York, in 1892 allowed girls for periods of one month only. In 1902, Laura Matoon began Camp Kehonka for girls at Wolfeboro, New Hampshire, on Lake Winnipesaukee. The first girls-only camp was followed in short order by the establishment of several camps for girls as well as boys.

STAGES IN THE DEVELOPMENT OF ORGANIZED CAMPING

The growth of organized summer camping can be seen in the rapid development of newly established camps, in the expansion of camp seasons, and in the stimulating variety of programs offered to campers. From the beginning of the movement until the present, camping proponents have been attracted to organized camping for numerous reasons, not the least of which being the provocative experience of outdoor living. The pioneers of the camping movement stressed the values that could accrue to children living in nature. The objective of camping has always been to offer something of value to the camper. During the early days it might have improved physical or spiritual well-being. Perhaps the idea of merely changing the environment from city to country served to motivate these efforts. For whatever reasons these innovators were drawn to the idea of organized camping; they were deeply concerned with the need to discover ways by which the fundamental gains from camping could be achieved. Before human and group dynamics became the special province of psychologists and clinicians, certain camping administrators were investigating the important relationships of elementary camp organization. Examination of the methods of the democratic process within the camp structure has been of significant concern since the 1920s.

Throughout the development of the camping movement, administrators and their staffs have been primarily motivated to maintain a high degree of personal rapport and good human relations. Without the qualities reflected in the happy outlook of a secure individual, organized camping can lose much of its flavor. Modern camps are an amazing complexity of public relations, culinary arts, planning, construction, maintenance, logistics, health services, administration, and transportation. Nevertheless, camp administrators have retained the ideals and standards that gave rise to the camping movement. Camping is primarily concerned with camper enjoyment of outdoor living and group participation. This dedication to the preservation of the camping aim has set the tone of the field throughout its history.

Before arriving at its present condition, organized camping passed through four stages of development: the hero stage, the individual-needs stage, the custodial stage, and the social-group stage. As with all social movements, one stage cannot always be clearly differentiated from the next. Even specialists in the field, while able to identify the periods, have varying opinions on practices, administrative techniques, and program orientation.

The Hero Stage (1861–1912)

The pioneers of the camping movement were people of truly heroic proportions. They were far-sighted individuals whose vision and capability allowed them to look beyond selfish interests and invest in the future by encouraging the growth and development of younger generations. They believed in developing strength and health through close contact with the outdoors. Rugged individualism appealed to them. They envisioned children growing up to appreciate and value the gifts of nature. Early camping embodied a "back to nature" concept that was closely linked with sectarian values and camping for its own sake. There was no attempt at directed learning. The ideals and objectives of these principled innovators were to be emulated. Strength of character, integrity, selflessness, and high moral standards were thought to be all that was necessary for the successful camping expedition. If a better life through better environmental conditions was the objective at this initial phase, the movement almost achieved the goal. There was little organization and minimal financial support for the ventures, however, and these factors contributed to the inability of some early camps to survive beyond the first session.

The first camps focused on the visionary, or hero. He was an individual with the ability to dominate the conscience of those around him. He stood for moral and physical courage. His actions enabled others to throw off their anxieties and approach the unknown with a sense of excitement and adventure. He was idolized by the boys who camped with him. He was the translator of the dream, a man who would share every hardship, more than uphold his part of the burden, and exercise constant vigilance for the welfare of his charges. He earned his influence with those for whom he was responsible. Initially, camps were fishing and boating expeditions, with a combination of work, in setting up a base from which the boys could live, and recreational activities. The trips were relatively short and therefore all the sweeter. The hero phase required men of heroic proportions. Because they were few and far between, camping did not expand dramatically during these years. By 1900 there were fewer than 100 established camps in the United States.

The Individual-Needs Stage (1912–1930)

In its next stage, organized camping focused upon the promotion of activities that could meet each camper's individual needs. There was something for each camper, and permissiveness took the place of regimentation. Many new camps opened during this period. Attempts were made to follow new ideas from the field of education. Program offerings were broadened, and camper selection of activities was encouraged. The atmosphere of choice and flexibility permeated the camping environment, and the previous emphasis on strenuous physical exercise and "roughing it" was replaced by an effort to provide more comprehensive and varied recreational experiences, including the arts.

The Custodial Stage (1930-1950)

Each stage of the camping movement has contributed to the general success of the field. The transition from one stage to the next has usually enhanced, rather than obliterated, that which came before. The concepts of high morals, good character, courage, and resourcefulness are the standards of today's camps, just as they were 100 years ago. Camps still attempt to meet individual needs. The camps of the Depression years and the years preceding and following World War II are best viewed as prescriptive or instructional in their orientation. Some of these features linger. The practices of those 20 years were both negative and positive.

Research on camping practices conducted in 1930 revealed few commonly held standards. While some camps were excellent, the environment of others was deleterious to health and welfare. As a consequence, camp staffs were enlarged to include resident physicians, nurses, and dieticians. More highly qualified counselors were required. But, as is often the case, these remedial measures brought forth an overcautious and sometimes restrictive attitude. With camp administrators vitally concerned for the health and welfare of their charges, everything became regimented. Emphasis was on routine necessities. Specific rules, regulations, limitations, and stringent controls were adopted, ostensibly for the protection of the camper. However, such regimentation probably made administration of the camp much easier. Although there is little question that these practices were necessary, the tendency to overregulate and to forget the real reason for coming to camp was prevalent.

Perhaps most important during this period was the attempt on the part of the camps to teach a variety of skills. Instructional preparations were emphasized as never before. Specialists were on hand for major and minor sports skills, and achievement awards were coveted. Although all camps were not characterized in this way, enough of them were like this to allow classification of this period as the custodial stage. There is nothing inherently wrong with instruction; it is usually essential if the individual is to learn a skill that will enhance participation in an activity. Too often, however, camp administrators were willing to ignore the needs of the campers in order to be able to claim that all their campers learned a skill, and thus to ensure the camp's financial endowment. Regimentation and custodial care to facilitate administration, coupled with instruction to enhance the financial balance sheet, left much to be desired of many camps. Each day was designed to be full of activity; there was no choice for the camper. The program was scheduled according to the staff employed by the director. There was much to do. One had to sing, to invent new words to familiar tunes. One had to present a skit or play—and one was a slacker or quitter if one didn't participate. One had to go to religious services; it was not only expected but mandatory. One had to attend campfire ceremonies. One had to go hiking. One had to take a nap at a specified time.

The years preceding and following the war encouraged this attitude in camps. The atmosphere was charged with the possibility of war and the aftermath of the Depression. Regimentation of even the simplest pleasures was encouraged. It was dangerous to be a nonconformist. It did not matter so much which camp the youngster attended as long as the parent could say that the child was at camp. One might wonder whether many of the children who were sent to camp at this time were sent to get them out of the way. The world was in turmoil, and old standards were dying. Camps merely reflected what society had made of itself: a bloodless, mechanistic, materialistic culture confined to routine endeavors.

The numbers of children attending camp decreased during the war years. Many camps closed because staffs could not be recruited. But there were other reasons as well. Children came to camp with the idea that it was going to be fun. It was supposed to be a vacation, a time for having fun, learning new things, and meeting new people. If these expectations were not fulfilled, the child would refuse to go to camp. Camp clientele lists were decimated as children refused to attend a particular camp that just wasn't enjoyable. "They make you do everything you don't like to do" was a frequent complaint. Camp directors realized that current practices would have to change.

The Social-Group Stage (1950–1960)

A group-dynamics and social-group concept characterized the level of the camping movement which was, in fact, the institutionalized stage. Camping had matured to the point at which its original aims and standards had been all but accomplished. There now remains the perpetuation of the institution of camping for the benefit of those who participate. Social awareness, group participation, and democratic fundamentals of social responsibility are at the center of camp philosophy. There is recognition of individual needs, awareness of the health, education, and welfare of all campers, and an understanding of social-group requirements. The realization has also grown that the "fun" factor needs to be cultivated.

Group living in the outdoors provides a foundation for democratic action and fosters a belief in individual freedom and responsibility. The valid aims of camping are inextricably bound to a logical recreational camp program. In this era of camping, the well-developed program, based on the philosophy of democracy, gears the camp to the tenor of the times. That is, it recognizes the need for relaxation in a world of speed and stress. It emphasizes the promotion of the health and well-being of each camper. Health in all of its facets deals with mental health as well as with positive character traits. The ability to adjust to one's surroundings and one's peers is enhanced by group life at camp. At this institutionalized stage, camping provided recreational opportunities, a leisurely existence, the stimulating scope of outdoor adventure, and a vital concern for camper safety. It also encouraged and enhanced democratic conditions, strengthened creative group efforts, built positive physical and mental health habits, and enriched the life of each person who pursued happiness through its nature-oriented structure.

Contemporary Camping (1960–1988)

In 1952, approximately 12,600 organized camps were operating. Almost 4 million campers had participated in some organized outdoor living experience. In 1970, the number of established camps expanded from 15,000 to 20,000, serving almost 6 million children during the summer.

By 1987, 55 million people participated in some form of camping. Of these, about 5 million youngsters attended more than 6,000 residential camps, while several million persons were involved with day camping or other seasonal and special-interest programs. Recently, however, the number of residential camps serving youth has dropped radically. Approximately 4 million children form the current client pool.

The stock market plunge of October 19, 1987, created doubts about America's economic future. This downward trend tends to impinge on the commercial camping field and finds outlet in a decreasing number of young campers attending. However, with a restored economy, the camping market should be able to tap a larger share of the potential campers among school-aged children.

The potential of youth camping is restricted only by economic factors and by the number of school children available to go camping. There are now more than 40 million school-age children in the United States. It is estimated that 10 percent of all school children now participate in some camp experiences. As the information disseminated to parents about camping values increases, they will assuredly make every effort to provide the means for youngsters to take part in some type of camping program. Elder hostels, cruises, and off-season camping are attracting adults as well as youth. Approximately 11,000 camps of all kinds serve the needs of those who attend.

More than 15,000 employees find full-time positions in the camping field. During the peak summer season, an additional 200,000 are employed. Most of those who seek summer employment are high school and college students or university graduates. Camps vary in size, scope, auspice, and orientation. Some camps care for fewer than 10 campers. At the other end of the scale are those camps capable of ministering to many hundreds of campers, with a few offering camping experiences to more than 1,000 campers. The typical camp, however, is geared to accommodate between 75 and 200 campers during the average summer season.

PROFESSIONALIZING THE CAMPING FIELD

Camping was started because of the vision of a few men and women, and its development and expansion came about because of the widespread disparity between camps and the lack of common standards, which was of concern to farsighted administrators. In the early days of the movement, camp directors were responsible for its maintenance, staffing, and support. Unfortunately, few administrators were capable of carrying such a complex function; consequently, standards of health and programming were inconsistent.

It is perhaps more accurate to state that no standards for the care of campers existed during the formative years of organized camping. Each camp confronted its own problems and treated them in whatever manner it deemed proper. It is not surprising, therefore, that camp environments ranged from execrable to excellent. There was no formal association of camp administrators or of sponsoring agencies. Growing awareness of the need to discuss mutual problems and potential solutions finally led to a series of informal meetings between camp directors. The first meeting was held in Boston in 1903. These meetings continued sporadically, but by 1910 the leaders of organized camping were forced to band together for the mutual protection of their clients and themselves. Because camping was new, the unscrupulous as well as the altruistic opened camps. Some poorly operated camps spread serious epidemics among their campers. In others, poorly qualified and motivated staffs offered the children nothing.

In order to save the movement from deteriorating into a commercial trap, the Camp Director's Association was organized. The National Association of Directors of Girl's Camps was begun in 1916. The Midwest Camp Director's Association followed in 1921. The Pacific Camping Association was established in 1923. The three initial groups united in 1924 as the Camp Directors' Association. At the 1935 national convention in Cleveland, the name of the organization was changed to the *American Camping Association* (ACA). It included not only camp administrators, but any individual, organization, or agency with an interest in camping. In 1941, the association was enlarged again to include the Pacific Camping Association, thereby becoming a true representative of all those interested in the camping movement in the United States. Other organizations have been formed to account for specialized, group, interest, or regional needs, but the ACA has indeed become the main instrument through which the camping field has progressed. Today, the ACA is the chief advocate of organized camping in the United States and represents nearly all camping elements in its membership. It is a nationwide, nonprofit, nonsectarian organization whose chief objective is to enhance organized camping for all who participate.

The ACA consults for a number of public and private agencies on issues of camping practices. It guides and advises institutions of higher education in carrying out environmental studies. The ACA also provides leadership-preparatory syllabi in camp counseling and administration. Further, the ACA also developed the first national program for certifying camp directors, camp ecologists, and outdoor living skills specialists.

The efforts of the ACA to upgrade camping are illustrated by the variety of services offered by the association. In 1948, and again in 1950, the ACA adopted national standards for personnel, programs, facilities, management, and health and safety procedures. Camps that desire certification from the ACA, indicating to prospective clients that high standards are maintained, are visited and rated by ACA specialists. If the camp meets the standards, it is entitled to advertise its rating. Some 2,000 camps are currently accredited by the ACA.[1] The visitation program has taken the camping movement a matchless step forward in its professional thrust. Other ACA services include developing public relations and education programs about camping values and good camping practices, encouraging research, lobbying for legislation favorable to camp interests, performing consultative services, developing leadership courses, providing a placement center for camp personnel, and conducting conferences, workshops, and institutes. Naturally, it is concerned with the transmission of successful practices and methods of camp management. It continually attempts to raise the criteria by which camps operate. It stimulates professional conduct in the administration of camps and calls for counselor preparation for optimum quality and effectiveness.

As the camping field has continued to professionalize, administrators have realized the necessity for additional study and research. Many new features of organized camping have been developed. Relationships with public agencies, development of community plans for camping, education and recruitment of personnel, and promotion of health and safety are acknowledged as continuing problems for administrators. Inevitably, professionalism is reflected in participation in the national organization.

As with other vocational endeavors that answer certain social needs, the field of organized camping has come to maturity with its acceptance by institutions of higher education. More than 300 colleges and universities offer courses in some phase of outdoor education and camping. Many of these courses are integral parts of professional preparatory programs in such fields as recreational service education, physical education, conservation education, and natural resource management. The many colleges that recognize the need to prepare students for employment in the field of organized camping provide courses in counselor education, camp administration, food services, and camp site planning, as well as a variety of outdoor recreational and nature-oriented activities for future counselors and directors.

TYPES OF CAMPS

Countless organizations have become aware of the value of camping. They recognize that camping can forward their aims and philosophies while serving the individual camper. Camps are therefore established to meet the objectives of the group or agency that sponsors them. They may be classified as public or governmental, quasi-public or institutional, and commercial, private, or agency.

---

[1]American Camping Association, *1980 Parents' Guide to Accredited Camps.* (Martinsville, Ind.: ACA, 1980), p. 24.

Public or Government Camps

These are camps created by any agency acting for the body politic. Supported by tax funds, they are controlled by government. These camps are designed to provide camping experiences to the public. They are generally free of charge or have a nominal fee attached for users. Youngsters under the age of 16 are usually accommodated. Public or government-controlled camps may be organized by municipal recreational service departments, park commissions, school systems, welfare departments, hospitals, and other federal, state, county, or local institutions.

Quasi-public or Institutional Camps

Camps sponsored by community organizations, and sometimes officially attached to a public agency, are considered quasi-public. Such organizations are not tax supported per se but may draw some revenue from public funds as well as from voluntary contributions. Such camps may be organized to care for a specific segment of the public or to meet community needs. Included in this classification are camps sponsored by American Red Cross chapters, police or fire department athletic leagues, neighborhood or social settlement houses, United Funds, 4-H Clubs, and similar agencies.

Agency or Institutional Camps

Youth-serving organizations have been involved in camping since the earliest "fresh-air" funds were inaugurated in cities during the 1920s. Agency camps tend to use the camp as an extension of their year-round services originating at the agency center, which is usually in a city. The camp is but one branch of a multifaceted organization designed to further a particular ideology or value system, or to reach a targeted population in order to enhance their quality of life. Because of the expense and the large population waiting to attend these camps, the camping season may be limited to one or two weeks. Nevertheless, they serve the important purpose of enabling children to leave the city environment for a brief period and exposing them to new and exciting experiences. Some of these camps offer the same kinds of activities that the agency provides throughout the year. The staff generally consists of the same personnel who operate the agency's city center, augmented by additional specialist personnel employed for the summer season.

Agency camps can receive some public support, although they may not be formally or officially associated with a public enterprise. These camps may receive public donations through the United Fund and other philanthropies. In some instances campers may have to pay a small amount of the total fee in order to be accepted. In other cases, for those unable to pay, the fee is offset by a stipend.

Included in this category are the camps run by churches, synagogues, labor unions, fraternal and benevolent orders, civic clubs, the Boy and Girl Scouts of America, the Federated Boys Clubs, the Catholic Youth Organization, settlement houses, the Salvation Army, the Jewish Welfare Board, the Protestant Welfare Council, the Young Men's Christian Association (YMCA), Young Women's Christian Association (YWCA), Young Men's Hebrew Association (YMHA), Young Women's Hebrew Association (YWHA), Camp Fire Girls, the Grange, and numerous other associations.

Commercial or Private (Independent) Camps

Camps in this category are formal organizations designed to meet the specific needs of clients who pay a set fee for the privilege of coming to the camp. Camp activities are usually conducted in relatively luxurious surroundings, with the added attraction of celebrity instructors or directors, and tend to be operated so as to please the most demanding taste and afford the greatest enjoyment to the participant. Naturally, commercial camps are operated for profit. The physical plant and the caliber of the staff requires high-paying patrons. These camps typically draw their campers from upper-middle- and high-income families. Such camps usually also recruit campers from all parts of the country, thereby providing a mixture of backgrounds and experiences that enhance camp life.

These for-profit camps are in the business of offering specialized instruction, excellent facilities, well-trained personnel, and comfortable accommodations. This does not mean that there cannot be poorly managed expensive camps. These camps range from those whose operation is negligent to those long-lived camps that have a tradition of excellence in all departments. Except for those few camps that put monetary gain above all else, most private camps have committed themselves to the provision of superior services.

TYPES OF CAMP ORGANIZATION

Camps may also be classified according to organization. The sponsoring group chooses the type of camp that will best meet the needs of its members.

Resident Camps

A resident camp has a fixed site and permanent facilities. The camper lives at the camp for varying periods and receives shelter and counseling in carrying out a planned program of nature-oriented activities. Resident camps are characterized by structured groupings and camper periods of occupancy.

For many years, centralization seemed to be the key to accommodating the upsurge of campers in individual camps. Rapid expansion of camp facilities, staff, and program was required to keep pace with increased enrollment. Centralized structuring was considered the best way to handle large numbers of youngsters who might or might not have had previous camping experience. Characteristically, camps were constructed around one or two core facilities. At the hub of the camp were placed the dining hall, recreational center, administration building (if the camp required one), and perhaps athletic fields, with cabins or other shelters radiating from this point. All activities took place within the core. All campers were fed at the same time, activities were scheduled and strictly followed, and all groups participated in all camp activities, regardless of heterogeneity. The rigidity of facility structure was carried over into programming. Camps were designed more for ease of administration and accountability than for appeal to the camper. Centralization was regimentation, with all permanent structures neatly oriented around or aligned with a midpoint. Even today, military bases are laid out in this pattern and are called camps.

Camp administrators were quick to recognize the drawbacks of centralization. They realized that the reason for coming to camp was to get away from strict routine and conformity. To overcome the centralized structure, progressive camp administrators experimented with small-group structures and decentralization. Unit living and programming now characterize the typical camp. There remain some camps whose sponsoring agency desires the centralized structure, but this form is disappearing.

Decentralization consists of separate homogeneous groupings and small living units that stay together for the entire camping season. Facilities are thus widely scattered on hundreds, and even thousands, of acres. Living units called bunks, cabins, villages, tribes, clans, or communities accommodate 8 to 10 campers living under the immediate supervision of a qualified counselor. Each unit may do its own activity planning. A unit may cook its own meals at least once each week throughout the camping season. Programming is carried on by age group, although there are all-camp functions that every unit attends. Thus the decentralized camp offers satisfaction of individual needs, special attention to problems that arise, small-group initiative in planning activities on a daily basis, and a careful mixture of large-group special events.

Duration of camper occupancy also characterizes resident camps. It is not unusual for private and quasi-public camps to have two sessions operating at the same time. If this is the case, the divisions are between campers who remain at camp throughout the summer season and campers who attend the camp for only one or two weeks. Depending upon the capability of the camping facility to accommodate campers, permanent and temporary campers may be segregated in living quarters, have their own separate activities, and associate infrequently, or they may be integrated. Whether of a temporary or permanent designation, the camper is a resident and participates to the fullest extent in every aspect of the program.

Day Camps

Day camps are established within easy commuting distance of the campers' neighborhoods. Children walk or are transported to the camp in the morning and return home before the evening meal. Generally, the only meal eaten at a day camp is lunch, which may be brought from home and supplemented by the camp with a beverage and a dessert. The day lasts from 5 to 6 hours, usually at least three days a week. Most day camps have a two-week session. Fees are nominal; some agencies do not charge those who cannot afford to pay.

Day camps may have no permanent structures, but rely upon temporary shelters such as quickly erected tents. Of course, there may be constructed facilities, including sanitary facilities, swimming facilities, and a shelter that can serve as a recreational hall during inclement weather. Although it may seem contradictory, some day camps do offer at least one night during the week when overnight accommodations are arranged so that campers will have the benefit of the continuity of a camping experience. The camper sleeps with his group at the camp facility, participates in evening activities around a campfire, and eats evening and morning meals that are cooked out.

The day camp should stress outdoor living and camping-oriented activities, such as nature study, crafts, cooking out, hiking, specimen collecting, rock hounding, and climbing. Camper–counselor ratios should approximate those of the resident camp. The camper is part of a particular unit, and should have the same counselor each day.

Special-Interest Camps

Special-interest camps may be residential, day, or a combination of both. Characteristically, however, specialized camps always have one chief objective. They are concerned with the development of a particular skill or talent, or with assimilation of knowledge in one given subject or area. They may emphasize meeting unique or unusual limitations or needs. The distinguishing feature of the specialized camp is that it provides a natural, enhanced environment in which a specific interest or need may find fulfillment.

Among special-interest camps are those that cater to sports, particularly tennis, basketball, baseball, small-craft handling, riflery, archery, horseback riding, and aquatics. Some camps promote the performing arts, and there are now camps that cater to children and adults who want to learn about computers.[2] Some camps specifically minister to the aging, ill, or handicapped. There are camps that specialize in caring for children afflicted with cardiac problems, tuberculosis, blindness, cerebral palsy, mental retardation, diabetes, epilepsy, orthopedic problems, deafness, muscular dystrophy, rheumatoid arthritis, and multiple sclerosis. Despite the special camp's concern with individual problems or interests, it is first a camp—with all the values, leadership, facilities, and activities implied by that term.

Pioneer Camps

Pioneer or wilderness camps are never constructed. The salient feature of the pioneer camp is that it is remote. This may be the only *real* camp in the most valid sense of the word. Pioneering or wilderness camping is outdoor living in its basic form. It is primitive; campers must forage for themselves. They learn to live off the land, accommodate to the environ-

[2]P. Elmer-DeWitt, "Mixing Suntans with Software," *Time* (August 22, 1983), 61.

ment, select sleeping sites with an eye toward possible flooding if it rains and warmth if the weather turns cold. All meals are cooked out. All activities are bent toward immediate survival. The camper's concern is with reaching daily objectives.

This by no means implies that pioneer camping is a life-or-death situation. It is one of the most fascinating kinds of organized camping. Pioneer or wilderness camps can be organized by resident camps or initiated by individuals and private groups. Some pioneer camps are established for older and highly skilled campers. The pioneer camp is often a small operation of an established residential camp with a skilled counselor-guide in nominal charge. The campers are transported to a jumping-off place and then either pack-in or secure suitable transportation by canoe, horse, mule, or, if possible, wheels. There comes a point at which the only transportation will be on foot. The campers must then pack their supplies, shelter, and sleeping equipment on their backs.

The pioneer camp is chiefly characterized by temporary quarters and continual movement within a demarcated area. Most pioneer camps operate for not less than one week; they may extend for the entire summer period. Naturally, the maturity and skill of the campers will play a significant role in the organization of such camps.

Rarely, the pioneer camp may have a relatively permanent base. The campers select the camping site, construct shelters from the natural materials found at the site, or erect tents or shelter halves that they have carried, and then forage from the base camp. Permanent pioneer camps may be situated on lakes or mountain streams, or may be located so as to offer protection from the elements through rock formations. Such camps are designed to test the endurance, skill, and knowledge of campers who enjoy living under these conditions. The pioneer camp may be part of the program of activities organized by a home or resident camp, but it is usually an organized form of camping significantly different from the better-known types of camping experiences.

Trip Camps

Trip camps have no permanent structure or accommodations; rather, they are organized around continual movement of the camper from place to place. Designed to allow the camper to travel through a given geographic area or from one region to another, trip camps offer transportation by foot, canoe, horse, bicycle, automobile, train, bus, or even ocean-going vessel. Trip camping is usually reserved for the mature and skilled older camper who can handle an ax, lash tent poles, feel at home where there are no trail markers, or climb a mountain.

Unlike the pioneer camp, which has no destination and may be confined to a particular region, the trip camp may travel cross country or intrastate and has a predetermined destination. Perhaps the most illustrative trip camp is the youth hostel. These hostels, developed in Europe during the 1930s, provide lodging to bicycling or hiking groups. Stopovers are located a day's journey apart. The journeys are simple, low-budget trips under competent supervision and may be coeducational. Hostels are permanent structures that can accommodate a group belonging to the association. Facilities include room, cooking equipment, and sanitary facilities. Members of the youth hostel must travel on foot or bicycle, by horseback, or on small hand-powered crafts.

Trip camps require scrupulous planning, particularly if the country to be traveled is harsh. Some camps have limited time schedules. The trip camp undertakes responsibility for the destination, means of transportation, and length of the trip.

Camping Today

There are hundreds of specialty camps where participants can concentrate on space exploration, astronomy, art, crafts, computers, gymnastics, almost any competitive sport or game, and many other interests. There are an even greater number of traditional camps, which focus attention on outdoor activities and living skills, the experience that initially gave rise to the camping movement. The year 1987 saw renewed interest in wilderness travel, pioneer camping, rock climbing, white-water canoeing, and horseback riding.

Camping can be an enriching or a disappointing opportunity for the camper. If satisfaction and learning is generated by life at camp, then the participant has a rewarding experience. If the individual has been demoralized, frustrated, or ill-treated, then the experience will forever after be looked upon as an unmitigated disaster. For the most part, camp personnel make the difference. Highly motivated, well-prepared counselors and other specialists can make the difference between success and failure, both of the camp and for the camper.

The camp experience can be very positive, but not necessarily inexpensive. Even agency or nonprofit camps now charge from $20 to $25 a day, although there are scholarships available to those who would be denied the experience if financial assistance were unavailable. At the upper end of the scale, depending upon activity focus and instruction by celebrities, the daily charge may be almost $55 a day. Indeed, some camps add separate fees for each activity over and above the price for entry.

Variations on a Camping Theme

The uses to which a modern camp may be put are limited only by the ingenuity and marketing skills of the camp operators. The traditional summer camp, which makes intensive use of the camp's physical plant for only two or three months of the year, neglects other significant opportunities that can be employed to enhance the balance sheet.

Winter and weekend camping operations offer many remunerative options to the camp operator and provide extended camping experiences to young and older campers alike. Elder hosteling, for example, is becoming increasingly popular among older adults, both during and after the regular summer season. Contact with school systems may enable the camp to access campers for weekend and winter programs through coordination with such curricula specializations as biology and physical education.

The camp that is located close to a big city can be used as a site for meetings and conferences for business, professional, or social organizations. Easy access to the camp from large urban centers may not be a critical requirement. In fact, remoteness from urban amenities and the need to travel to reach the camp may be the attraction that generates additional use as a retreat, conference site, or off-season vacation spot. Any and all of these possibilities offer excellent potential for making the camp a profitable one.

chapter 2

Elements of Camp Management

The founding of the camping movement, an innovative concept originated in the United States and exported to the rest of the world, was discussed in Chapter 1. A positive camping experience can be ensured through the efforts of competent management. With this objective in mind, organized camping reaches its highest achievement. To realize the purposes for which camps are established, certain administrative procedures must be initiated. These become the reference points around which natural, human, and financial resources combine to enhance the camper's life. Only as these elements are coordinated and controlled will the outcome coincide with the objectives espoused by the camping movement.

CAMP ADMINISTRATION

Camp administration is concerned with providing outdoor and nature-oriented experiences through the employment and direction of specialized staff, supported by an optimum environment and appropriate facilities. Administration is fundamentally engaged in maximizing camping experiences without neglecting the health, safety, and public relations features that ensure the success and prosperity of the camp.

Administrative Functions

The organization, initiation, performance, and maintenance of program, leadership, group effort, and supply operations are integral to administration. Camp administration must be aware of the techniques and responsibilities necessary to execute its mission. Camp administration uses methods common to every administrative situation. Administration of the modern camp includes the following functions:

1. Establishment, either by incorporation, charter, or contractual agreement, of the camp's existence.
2. Initiation and execution of value judgments designed to guide the development and regulate the conduct of the camp; in other words, the enactment of policies that give a frame of reference to the operations of the camp.
3. Inauguration of fiscal management techniques and revenue sources for the support of the camp.
4. Establishment of personnel management practices and policies designed to recruit, educate, and retain the most highly qualified and competent staff possible. Assignment of duties and responsibilities with concomitant authority to carry out imposed obligations.
5. Arrangement of comprehensive and varied nature-oriented opportunities to enable all campers to fulfill their capacity to participate. Promotion of stimulating activities designed to satisfy the interests, needs, and abilities of each camper.
6. Property acquisition, development, and maintenance.
7. Public relations, whereby information about the camp and its value to campers is routinely disseminated. (A well-directed public relations program can do much to build staff morale, camper enthusiasm, parental support, and financial success.)
8. Establishment and maintenance of comprehensive records and reports dealing with every facet of camp life. (The necessity for newly organized camps to develop records and report forms is well known. Records and reports will reveal every aspect of camper background, camp program, personnel, property, and legally required accounts.)

The relative amount of time and concentration spent by administrators on these functions varies with the camp sponsorship, the physical resources, the range of the program, the number and quality of personnel, and the campers' individual needs.

CAMP ORGANIZATION

The structure of the camp is determined, as we have seen, by the nature of the sponsoring group. Operationally, however, organization is the methodical cohesion of interdependent units to form an integrated entity through which control, direction, and accord may be effected to reach a goal. Because the interdependent aspects of the camp involve people as well as functions, organization includes both structure and personnel and therefore divides the work to be performed, establishes procedures for routine practices, creates policy, organizes communication, and provides in-service staff development.

Organization is normally thought of as that phase of administration most amenable to systematic treatment. But since structure varies based on the nature of the camp and its sponsoring group, each factor must be humanized. While organizational relationships in any camp can be diagramed, they reflect human relations and a need for flexibility that can hardly be permanently fixed. An attempt to formulate certain operational procedures of organization that are flexible and that may apply to most camps is offered here.

A combination of factors determines the most efficient and effective organization for the camp. Insofar as they can choose, it is the function of administrators to appraise each factor and compare it to the others so that radical effects will not distort the purpose of the structure. This responsibility is paramount in the case of newly established camps, but it remains in long-lived ones as well. Because the administrative process is perpetual and dynamic, modifications will be necessary. The organization must undergo periodic evaluation. It is not sufficient to consistently orient the camp's structure toward its initial goals. On the other hand, early objectives can be lost as administrative and other factors begin to weigh on the operational aspects of the camp.

Size and the disparate functions of camp personnel are two of the major reasons that organization is needed. In the small camp, each employee may have several responsibilities and may reasonably be expected to fill in for an absent member if necessary. In the largest camps, however, the administrator must scrupulously evaluate each phase of the organization, examine all operations, and separate the efforts of the staff to ensure continuity, efficiency, and smooth management. Division of the work to be done at each level must contribute to the harmony of the entire organization. Just as there is division of functions, there must be planned integration of functions, culminating in the production of optimum camp services for the benefit of the campers and, incidentally, the camp. The group spirit of the camp depends on the careful balancing of the qualities and expertise of each with the coordinated efforts of all. It is the chief function of the administrator and all supervisory personnel to indoctrinate employees to be cooperative members of a team effort and to grant them initiative in exercising all the individual talent or potential they possess.

There is no one organizational plan for camps, but the diagrams that follow may be helpful in understanding positions, functions, and lines of responsibility. The typical camp has four levels of hierarchy: (1) executive, or policy-making, (2) administrative, or middle management, (3) supervisory, and (4) functional (Fig. 2-1). Within these levels there may be further division on a program or specialty basis.

To a greater or lesser degree, depending upon the size of the camp and the number of campers accommodated, all camps are organized according to these functions and subdivisions (Fig. 2-2). In large or elaborate camps, specialized facilities may call for managers, but few camps either have or require very specialized areas. In any event, specialists of various kinds may be fitted into the organization at the supervisory level. Because small camps expect personnel to double up in their functions, they may not require these line and staff combinations. Thus, unit supervisors may also be specialized program counselors. In small operations, the camp director

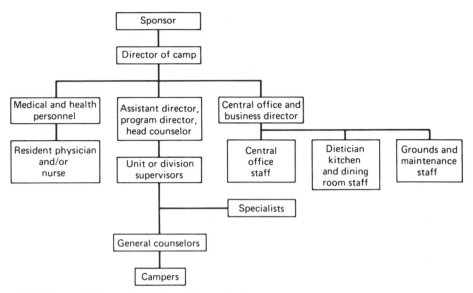

FIGURE 2-1.   Typical line and staff organization chart.

may combine the functions of business manager and program coordinator. Sometimes, although rarely, the camp nurse may assume dietician responsibilities, but this practice is not recommended. In many situations, kitchen or dining room staff may also function as part of the maintenance and grounds-keeping staff. The organizational development will reflect the size of the camp and the administrator's recognition of the camp's mission.

Formation of Organizational Groups

Camp employees are part of a social situation from which friendships and acquaintanceships are derived. The behavior of individuals in groups

FIGURE 2-2.   Variations of camp organization in a small private camp.

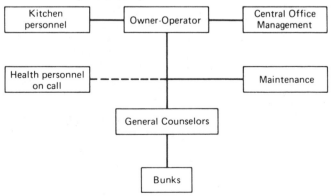

is usually modified by group expectations. Very large camps contain many groups, and much of the success of the camp will depend on interaction among the groups. Generally, members of homogeneous groups will share values and tasks. These groups affect employees' behavior and hence the outcome of the camp experience for the camper.

One of the problems in describing camp organization is the lack of uniform terminology designating the parts of the camp. Here, we will use commonly understood terms. The overall organization is called the *camp*; subdivisions of the camp are *departments;* and subdivisions of departments will be called *units* or *divisions.* The term *bunk* designates the smallest subdivision recognized in the supervisory structure; it generally refers to the small group of 5 to 10 campers assigned to one counselor.

Counselors play perhaps the most important role in any camp organization. They are the functional, face-to-face employees on whose shoulders rides the effectiveness of the camping experience. Nevertheless, all employees and owners who are part of the organization make their unique, important contributions to the overall outcome of the experience. In terms of duties or responsibilities, supervisory and administrative employees do not carry out the function for which the camp was established; however, they do assist in ensuring that the counselors are as productive as possible.

Individuals who become part of an organization must either identify with the working group or accept the indifference, and sometimes the hostility, of that group. Those who cannot accept the group's concepts, disciplines, or mores will be ostracized. Their working relationships will be unpleasant at best. Either individuals become assimilated or the group will attempt to bring them into disrepute and thus succeed in their removal. This is noticeably true for counselors and other employees of various divisions. Long-established camps may have staff personnel that return year after year. Nevertheless, there will always be new employees. The "old-timers" usually set the tone for employee relationships within each department. When the camp is newly established, the divisional supervisor is in the best position to influence group values and conduct.

Division of Functions

The camp's responsibility to the camper necessitates specialization, or divisions of functions, to ensure that its chief aim is carried out (Fig. 2-3). A number of employees must be hired and assigned to various positions. Each of the employees then specializes in performing that part of the responsibility which leads to the success of the camp's mission.

Organizational Subdivision

The division of work in any organization is rarely fully planned in advance. Normally, camp organization is thought of in single units and expands by repeated subdivision whenever indicated. When a camp is established, the sponsoring agency appoints a camp director. If it is a private venture, the camp director may be the owner. In either case, the chief executive will soon find it necessary to consult others to determine the best meth-

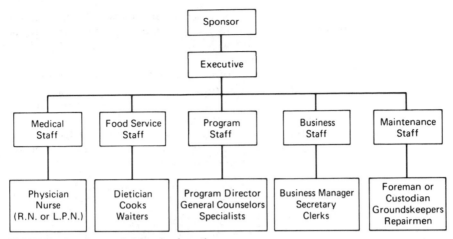

FIGURE 2-3. Camp division by functions.

ods by which to get underway. As problems are identified, someone from the original consulting group or from the outside will be assigned to solve them. These people may in turn call on others for advice or technical services. In this way the original group is subdivided into secondary units that may be further divided as the situation changes.

The process of subdivision is controlled by the conflicts that occur and the manner in which individuals involved in the organization react to these confrontations. Over any long period of time, specific situations will require the assignment of a specialist. As the camp grows, there will be new areas for subdivisions. When agencies create a camp with predetermined structure as the result of having examined existing camps, however, the subdivisions are already included. But usually specialties are added as the need for them arises.

The arrangement of administrative, supervisory, and program personnel must be integrated if the experience is to be of value to the camper. To achieve this, each worker will need to know what others in his division are doing so that he may coordinate his efforts with theirs. Traditionally, a supervisor is selected to coordinate efforts and to relate the activities of each person to those of the others in the division. The supervisory process is perhaps most significant in effecting outcomes of values. The supervisor must recognize, for instance, that when a unit becomes so large that supervision is hindered, it is necessary to break it down into groups small enough to be effectively coordinated.

HIERARCHICAL DIVISIONS

The executive, or policy-making, level consists of representatives of the camp sponsor and the camp director. Policy, which outlines the conduct of the camp, is designed to carry out the wishes of the sponsor, but it is also of primary importance in setting the camp's operational standards. Policies are designed to promote the health, safety, and well-being of everyone at the camp. They reflect the camp's attitudes, philosophy, setting, and objectives. Behavior of employees and campers alike is subject to policy.

Policy making is handled by a committee for the sponsors, all of the sponsors (this is unlikely, unless it is a commercial venture with one or two owners), and the camp director, if he is a separate employee. While the camp director helps make policy and advises on it, he is employed to execute policy. He may, however, shape policy in terms of his expertise, immediate knowledge of a particular situation, or intimate relationship with the needs and problems that confront the camp.

Management Level

Positions on the administrative level may carry either line or staff identifications but are usually associated with the direction of a particular function and the staff assigned to it. *Line* employees are directly responsible for carrying out the program function of the camp. *Staff* employees are not directly involved in program work but, as a consequence of special skill or knowledge, provide technical aid and advice to line personnel in order to make the line more efficient and effective.

Administrative-level personnel have usually been concerned with the execution of policy and the manner in which daily assignments are handled. Consequently, middle-management personnel deal with tangible subjects directly related to the production of output necessary to operate the camp program. Regardless of title, administrators perform identical functions at the same level within the camp. Some may be concerned with staff, such as personnel, fiscal, or office management; others may be responsible for giving direct assistance to line employees. Others may be called upon to act in the absence of the camp director.

The association and rapport between the executive and the administrative level must be one of close cooperation and support. The administrative person is responsible to the executive for the daily management of her particular part of the camp operation. Administrative personnel are important both to the chief executive and to all other personnel. With administrative support, well-coordinated efforts can be expected. Without administrative backing, little is accomplished.

Department Level

The administrative level is concerned with the routine, daily management of camp affairs. Middle management deals with departmental functions. There may be two or three departments, depending upon the specialties needed. Normally, at least two departments assume responsibilities on which the large modern camp operates. These relate to program and to central office or business practices. If the camp has the services of a resident physician, then health becomes the third department. If the camp owns extensive properties, a fourth department may be created for maintenance;

however, this function is almost always included within central office administration.

Central Office Function

At the administrative level, certain functions are related to the overall operation of the camp even though they are not directly involved with camping. These staff duties have to do with technical assistance in conducting the camp. Some of these services are situated in a central office, where they are accessible to all for whom they are pertinent. Other central office operations are delegated through divisional status and have facilities from which they perform outside the central office. The extent and specialization of the central office staff is determined on the basis of the number of campers and personnel. It administers business transactions, personnel classification, office management, accounting, and data recording.

Business Manager Function

In small camps, the director-owner may perform the duties of the business manager. The danger inherent in such practice is that the details of managing the office; purchasing and dispensing supplies, equipment, food, and materials; keeping records; and maintaining the building, grounds, and equipment may prove too much of a burden. The director may then be forced to relinquish his primary function—that of directing camping activities through his staff of counselors. Large, modern camps invest in a business manager.

Divisional Levels

Included within the range of responsibilities assumed by the business department are the divisions that manage maintenance, kitchen, and dining room personnel (if the camp requires waiters). Insofar as maintenance of the physical plant is a part of standard procedures, cleaning services (where appropriate), landscaping, and the repair services are necessary for maximum operation. Safe use of all vehicles and tools, and enhancement of all structures, facilities, and areas are mandatory if the camper is to enjoy optimum satisfaction from participation at camp.

Personnel Function

The direction of sound personnel practice has tremendous influence on the success of any camp. Personnel records and reports must be updated so that the highest staffing standards can be maintained.

Fiscal Function

Fiscal management is essential to the operation of all camps. Whether the camp sponsor wants to make a profit, wants only to break even, or is unconcerned about money matters, there remains the necessity of financial accounting as required by law. The custodianship of the funds deposited by campers and of the records of purchases, disbursements, receipts, and vouchers requires control to ensure accuracy and honesty.

Office Function

Office and clerical management refers to the recording, filing, stenography, and supply and inventory keeping that are part of all soundly arranged business offices. These functions are performed whether or not the specific activities just listed take place. They are necessary even if carried out on the most perfunctory level. Large camps dealing with hundreds of campers and many staff specialists generally require an effective central office work force. Smaller camps may assign one or two staff members to this task.

Food Service Function

The central office also supervises the kitchen and dining room staffs in the purchase of supplies, materials, and equipment. With the exception of waiters, specialists are employed to supervise and prepare food at camp. A dietician may be hired to develop menus and to ensure the preparation of nourishing, tasty, and attractive meals. Within this division, there may be a head cook and other subordinates. Food preparation and service can be one of the most important functions of the resident camp; it contributes to the health and morale of campers and staff alike.

Program Department

The single most important function of any camp is carried out by the program department. This department may be administered by the camp director, an assistant director, or an individual variously identified as the head counselor or program director. It is the responsibility of this department, through its subdivisions and counselor staff, to promote the greatest possible variety and broadest possible range of nature-oriented and camp-based experiences. The program department is directly involved with the health (exclusive of problems that are more properly dealt with by medical specialists), safety, welfare, skill development, instruction, participation, and daily-living experiences of all campers. It is through this department that the entire camping season is interpreted. So vital is this department to the success of the camp that camp directors leave nothing to chance in recruiting the most highly qualified and competent counselors available. Clearly, the program department is supported by all other activities of administration; these other administrative functions would be meaningless if there were no program.

Program Units

The subdivision of the program department is the unit. Depending upon the number of campers and the extent to which the camp is centralized or decentralized, the breakdown into units and then bunks will prescribe the counselor–camper ratio and the supervisor–counselor ratio. For each 300 campers it is probably best to have 40 general counselors. Each counselor would be responsible for one bunk of 5 to 8 campers. With 40 bunks, at least 4 unit supervisors, responsible for 10 counselors each, would be needed. Added to this would be other supervisory specialists—perhaps a waterfront or aquatic director, an arts-and-crafts specialist, and a nature-science specialist. It is to be expected, when other activities are to be taught, that the general counselors possess the necessary skills. The general counselors are assigned to bunks and can also be used for instructing in specific motor skills. Thus, in addition to their bunk-counselor responsibilities, general counselors may also teach or assist in teaching riflery, archery, tumbling, horseback riding, or tennis.

Specialists

Some large camps employ specialists in a wide range of activities. These individuals are not given general counselor duties, nor are they assigned to bunks. Specialists, in this instance, devote their time to instructing campers in particular skills. It is not unusual for a camp to have an expert in dance, dramatics, music, crafts, nature, tennis, sailing, archery, riflery, riding, or other activities. In special camps, specialists may be engaged to teach more restricted subjects. In a general music camp, for example, instructors of all instruments are employed to teach whatever type of music the camp offers. In band camps, only band-instrument instruction is offered. The same holds true for a general sports camp or for a camp solely devoted to basketball, baseball, or swimming.

Health Department

If the camp has a health department, the resident physician or nurse reports directly to the camp director. Managerial functions relate strictly to the operation of the dispensary or infirmary. Large camps may have both a resident physician and several nurses, either registered nurses (RNs) or licensed practical nurses (LPNs). Smaller camps may have a resident nurse with clearance from a local physician or treatment center. All resident camps are wise to make provision for any medical problems that may arise. Although camps are conducted in the safest and most healthful way possible, certain hazards must always be taken into account. In addition, health and medical forms originate from this department.

CAMP PERSONNEL

Following is a list of positions often found in camps:

Animal husbandryman	Cook	Mechanic
Bookkeeper	Dishwasher	Secretary
Caretaker	Driver	Waiter
Clerk	Groundskeeper	

The kinds of personnel required for camps and the credentials and experiences described here meet or surpass the standards set by the American Camping Association.[1]

The personnel employed by any camp are engaged in one of three separate but interdependent activities: (1) organization, leadership, supervision of camping experiences; (2) business operations, including plant maintenance, accounting, and dietary; and (3) health and safety services. Employees in the last two categories are recruited from the general labor market; their skills are the same as those of personnel employed in a business organization or hospital. Their preparation, therefore, is not necessarily oriented to camping. If the camp administration wishes to orient these employees to the camp environment, it must provide in-service training.

In the following pages, generally used titles and the functions usually assigned to each position are given. Job descriptions are included in describing the three highest positions. See Chapter 6 for information on the qualifications and duties of counselors.

Camp Director

The camp director is the chief executive officer in charge of the camp, including all employees and campers. He is usually responsible to a committee of the sponsoring agency but may be responsible to the owner if the camp is private. In some camps the director is the owner. Ultimately, all camp directors are responsible to their clients. The camp director may also be the program director.

Background.   The camp director should be at least 25 years old (preferably older) and a graduate of a recognized college or university. His major study should have been in outdoor education and camping, conservation, natural-resource management, education, sociology, psychology, business administration, or recreational-service education. His experience should include at least 5 years of professional employment in the camping field, with at least one in administration. Successful employment in related fields in formulating agency programs, supervising personnel, directing activities, planning and managing facilities and their use, and sound knowledge of public relations is necessary. His knowledge of the camping field, including its philosophy and objectives, must be broad. He should also have knowledge of personnel management, fiscal management, and human dynamics as applied to the camp setting. Graduate study or completion of degree requirements is preferred, although not essential.

Responsibilities.   The camp director is charged with the general organization, administration, control, and leadership of the entire camp. He exercises all necessary authority in management and policy execution. He is immediately associated with the direction of personnel practices, fiscal

[1]American Camping Association, *Camp Standards with Interpretations for the Accreditation of Organized Camps* (Martinsville, Ind.: ACA, 1984). See also *Update on 1985 Standards with Interpretation.*

control, and program planning. He is concerned with the recruitment, orientation, development, and supervision of all personnel. He generally plans the work of his subordinates, sets the objectives to be obtained, creates the philosophy and tone of the work atmosphere, and provides information needed to facilitate the work and aims of the camp. He is ultimately responsible for the character and performance of all employees. Since the essence of camping is the program, the director's main concern is the initiation of healthy, wholesome outdoor experiences to provide opportunities for satisfaction, individuality, development, and happiness. To this end, therefore, he translates the agency's philosophy into tangible activities and balances a variety of nature-oriented and recreational opportunities to effect optimal achievement.

The camp director is responsible for fiscal control and administration. It is upon his estimate of campers to be served, personnel required, supplies, materials, and equipment to be purchased, and contingencies to be faced that financial support will be based. Although he remains responsible for this function, he may delegate authority to experts for the establishment of techniques and procedures in executing fiscal control. He generally supervises the financial transactions of the camp.

Another responsibility is to keep data relating to all personnel and campers. Forms must be devised for the handling of camp business and records in order to ensure continuity of the camp and to facilitate the best possible program.

As the highest authority of the camp, the director is immediately concerned with the health, safety, and well-being of each person associated with the camp. For this reason, no decision affecting the welfare of any individual may be implemented without his knowledge and approval. Problems of behavior, health, and program may be handled by competent personnel at lower levels, but serious problems may eventually have to be solved by the camp director.

Assistant Camp Director

The assistant camp director may also be called the program director or the head counselor. In the absence of the camp director, she performs the director's functions. This person is in charge of all counselors and is specifically responsible for the day-to-day program of activities. She is responsible to and reports to the camp director.

Background.   The assistant camp director should be at least 23 years old and a graduate of an accredited college or university. She should have thorough knowledge of the principles and practices of camping, and familiarity with the camp's facilities, areas, staff requirements, and program. Skill in staff supervision, with the ability to guide, direct, and lead the work of employees, is essential. She must have the ability to work cooperatively with associates and subordinates; those who work with and for her should want to emulate her. She must have skill in communication so that she can interpret the efforts being planned and organized by her department. Her experience should include several years of successful employment in camps, with at least two years of supervisory experience.

Responsibilities.   The assistant camp director, program director, or head counselor is in complete charge of the program department. She manages its daily operation and has wide decision-making discretion. She participates in the formulation of policy. She may make recommendations for improvement of various aspects of the camp. In the absence of the camp director, she will probably be called upon to function as acting director.

The assistant supervises and manages all staff personnel associated with the program department; she is responsible for all phases of the camping program. She is required to familiarize herself with current programming methods and to use those techniques where applicable. She may be asked to supervise and direct the in-service development program for the counselor staff. As the second-highest executive in the camp hierarchy, she will resolve most of the camp's problems. She will be in direct contact with all operational aspects of camp life. In rare cases, she may also serve as the budget officer for the camp.

Unit Supervisor

The unit supervisor is in charge of a unit or division of the program department and is responsible for the counselors and campers residing in the bunks of his jurisdiction. He reports directly to the assistant camp director.

Background.   The unit supervisor must be at least 21 years old and a graduate of an accredited college or university with a major in any field related to recreational programming. He must have the ability to organize groups for effective work—that is, to explain, define, and interpret objectives to the personnel in his jurisdiction. A special skill or technical ability will probably be combined with his general knowledge of all phases of the camping program. While working harmoniously with his colleagues, he must be capable of identifying and reducing potential frictions and of seeing that all work assignments are carried out promptly and with maximum benefit to the camper. He should have at least 3 years of successful experience in camping, with at least one in some supervisory capacity.

Responsibilities.   The unit supervisor acts on all policy statements initiated by or through the camp director. Under the general supervision of the assistant director, he assists in planning the work of general counselors, offers technical help in implementing the program, interprets camp policy as it affects his division, and attempts to improve all program experiences. He must exercise leadership in carrying out his responsibility, as he will be asked to handle difficult counselor–camper relations, to provide technical assistance to counselors, and perhaps to act as a specialist in an instructional area. He requests supplies for the safe and sure handling of the program. He is responsible for all records and reports to be obtained from counselors assigned to him. Acting as line supervisor, he also has specific responsibility for the campers assigned to his unit.

Supervisory Specialists

These employees are experts in specific camp activities. There may be, for instance, aquatic, nature-study, or arts-and-crafts supervisors. Such specialists are responsible for carrying out their programs in relation to the overall program of the camp. They are particularly responsible for their facilities, equipment, and supplies. They report directly to the assistant camp director.

Counselors

These employees exercise general and specific supervision over the activities of each camper assigned to the bunk. They fall under the close direction of unit supervisors. All aspects of the camper's life at camp concern them; their time is spent in direct contact with their assigned charges. They are relieved only when designated as being off duty.

Specialists

Specialists are instructors in specific activities. Their duties are largely restricted to organizing and teaching individuals or groups, although specialists may be general counselors who spend part of their time as instructors.

Business Manager

The business manager supervises the business office and handles all bookkeeping, accounts, transactions, purchases, and disbursements. He can also direct or supervise the dietician and the plant maintenance division. His duties include arranging transportation and supplies for the camp. He reports to the camp director.

Plant Maintenance Supervisor or Custodian

Under the supervision of the business manager, the plant maintenance supervisor is in charge of all camp property. His duties include keeping central buildings clean, maintaining the grounds, repairing buildings and equipment, setting up equipment needed for daily activities, marking fields and courts, and supervising groundskeepers, drivers, and other members of the maintenance crew.

Dietician

Also under the supervision of the business manager, the dietician plans and orders supplies for meals. Other duties include preparing menus, checking and issuing receipts for incoming food supplies, assisting in inventories of food supplies to be taken on excursions, discussing various aspects of food preparation and service with counselors, and working with camp medical authorities in maintaining sanitary kitchen conditions. The dietician supervises all kitchen and dining room staff and prepares accurate statements of costs, including supplies, labor, and utilities.

Physician

The physician can be either resident or on-call. She performs all necessary medical functions and thus is charged with prescribing and executing medical treatment for any injury, illness, or disability. She reports any unusual health incidents or hazards to the camp director, to whom she is directly responsible.

Nurse

A resident nurse is a necessity for any resident camp. The nurse should be registered, although LPNs are recognized as being competent in following a physician's orders. In the absence of a resident physician, the nurse is the only competent medical authority at the camp. Acting under the standing orders of a physician, in the event of illness or accident, the nurse performs those immediate remedial measures necessary to safeguard the life and welfare of the camper. The nurse routinely assesses campers for any signs of health deterioration, parasitic infection, or disease. The nurse reports to the resident physician or to the camp director.

chapter 3

Operating the Camp

Camp operation includes all the activities and responsibilities that must be carried out if the camp is to function successfully. Operation includes duties that can be categorized as fiscal management, personnel management, program development and supervision, logistics (supply), camper recruitment, maintenance management, and such diverse elements as public relations and camp promotion, transportation, food services, health services, risk management, and related components.

Operations can be classified into the following groups: business-related components, physical property-related components, camper-related aspects, and program. All business-associated functions deal with financial matters, including budgeting, accounting, ordering, purchasing, and record keeping. Property-related matters can include planning and development of the camp, property-maintenance procedures, safety and emergency procedures, central storage, and procedures for responding to work orders. Personnel, health, safety, and food services—to the extent that these areas require supplies, materials, and equipment for which money must be expended—all monitored by fiscal services but are basically part of camper-related matters. Camper recruitment, housing, transportation, public relations, counselor orientation and training, health services and food services are directly concerned with camper welfare but may have significance for camp employees as well. Finally, program development and execution is the heart of the camp's existence. The program contains all the planned and extemporaneous activities in which campers engage.

Responsibility for operational control resides with the management of the camp, whether they are professional employees, sponsors, or owners. The ability of the camp director to administer the various functions necessary for camp operation depends upon the size of the camp in terms of number of campers served, the number of personnel, the number of departments into which operations are divided, and the extent of camp property. The smaller the camp, the more likely it is that owner-operators will directly manage it. The program is the direct responsibility of the camp director, who is also charged with staffing for all departments. All program personnel, whether general counselors, specialists, or supervisors, are interviewed and employed by the director. (A complete description of personnel duties and responsibilities is provided in Chapter 2.)

Although this chapter introduces the topic of operations, it focuses primarily on finance, purchasing, the physical facility, insurance, and public relations. All such specialities related to camp operations cannot be treated in one chapter. Therefore, other operational elements will be introduced and explained in subsequent chapters.

THE BUSINESS OF CAMPING

Sound business management is the sine qua non for successful operation of any camp. The financial underpinnings of the camp must be adequate and secure, and the methods for allocation of funds and for their receipt and deposit must be accurate and accountable. Finally, in today's competitive market, the camp must be run in a cost-effective manner so that the greatest good for the campers will be forthcoming at the least cost. Surely expert advice and counseling on matters of fiscal management is a wise investment. In the same way that specialists are sought to direct the other enterprises of the camp, the business aspect of camping requires the expertise of no less than a financial or business manager. But financial competence is not the only requirement for the management and operation of a camp. Other factors, the details of which are vital to the success of a camp, must also be considered and acted upon.

FINANCIAL SUPPORT

In most privately sponsored residential or day camps, camper fees are the chief source of revenue. The fee is based on several factors, not the least of which is the owner's desire to make a net profit on his original investment. Many owner-operators of camps are able to live quite comfortably on the proceeds of the summer-camp income. The fee is set by operational costs involved in feeding, housing, and supervising a camper for a specified period. The fee is more accurately determined if careful attention is given to such diverse items as the accounting system used, overhead costs, ratio of campers to counselors and specialists, and budgeting procedures.

When camps are operated as a business venture and profit motives are the owners' concern, the fees will be set according to what the camper traffic will bear. Hence, fees are set in accordance with the cost of maintaining and supervising the camper, plus a net profit. When camps are operated primarily as a public service or as a philanthropic venture, then fees are set according to what each camper can afford to pay, despite the actual cost of operation. These camps may pay their employees lower wages and have more rustic permanent quarters. Many hope to make up any monetary deficits through donations, gifts, bequests, or other endowment income. Other income may come from sales of camping supplies and equipment to campers, from additional fees charged to campers who desire specialized activity not generally offered as part of the program, or from sales of candy and other personal items. Camper fees for residence should be collected prior to the opening of camp.

Fiscal Management and Accounting

The financial elements of management include responsibility for the control of all activities concerned with the apportionment and distribution of money. Camp administrators must organize the accounting and budgetary procedures necessary for integrated performance. Fiscal management requires the collection of information associated with financial engagements generated by whatever transactions are necessary to support camp operations. Fundamentally, fiscal management will be involved with personnel practices, accounting practices, and budgeting.

Budgeting.   The essential activities of budgeting are planning, coordinating, and direction. Planning deals with the identification of organizational aims, including a description of resources required to fulfill the objectives and the creation of a policy for obtaining and using them. The budget is a statement of this policy in fiscal terms. Coordination is the smooth combination of the various parts of the organization to produce an efficient and effective result. Direction ensures that the functions of organization are performed in ways that use the resources at an optimal level of effectiveness and for profitable cost–benefit ratios.

The budgeting process.   The initial step in any budget-making process is the designation of performance classifications. Performance categories are developed to determine volume and achievement. In this way, the output of the various activities is brought into congruence with the organizational goals.

Performance categories are units of measure; they are detailed descriptions of the functions, subfunctions, activities, and subactivities of the camp. Examples include the following:

1. Administration and business management
2. Construction, planning, and development
3. Plant maintenance
4. Facility operation

This breakdown of categories is not itemized; each could be further subdivided. At the cost level, units of measure are associated with work-performance units. They are designed to assist the administrator in budgeting for and regulating the resources employed in camp operations. Budgeted performance is developed for each cost center and is used to generate a position for the wages and salary expenditure budget and the materials, supplies, and equipment expenditures budget. These budgets offer expenditures specifically associated with units of measure. Once budgeting performance statements have been completed, the expense outlook of the operating budget can be started. The performance budget emphasizes what has been accomplished rather than the line-item unit that has been purchased in order to finish production. Thus, instead of budgeting for tents, canoes, bows, paint, or clay, the performance budget accounts for the number of discrete recreational activities that previous experience suggests will be performed as an outcome of having materials, supplies, and equipment available.

A budget should be prepared so that the document can be used both for financial control and as a basis for planning, policy making, and general administration. These needs can be fulfilled if the accounting procedures reflect the camp's organization. The budgeting process should be identical to the performance and goals of the camp. It is vital to the success of the budgeting process that the items to be evaluated are those which indicate the work to be performed or the services offered. The production of line-item categories is not merely a waste of time; it has no relation to what is being performed with campers at the camp. The fiscal control lost through minimizing the number of object-classification accounts is more than offset by the greater number of activity accounts.

Object classification is a budget type whereby all proposed expenditures are classified. Under a number of major functions, expenditures are made for similar objects. There are expenditures for personnel services, supplies, materials, equipment, purchase of property, and so on. A high degree of standardization in the classification of objects of expenditure is possible, permitting comparison of expenditures for like objects to be made within the various camp departments. A simple expenditure classification by objects may contain the following:

    1000.   Services, personnel
    2000.   Services, contractual
    3000.   Commodities
    4000.   Current charges
    5000.   Current obligations
    6000.   Properties
    7000.   Debt payment

The code numbers that appear opposite each segregation in the classification of expenditures are for convenient identification of each item. Use of the code renders unnecessary the writing out of the property segregation to which any item may be charged. The term *line item* is sometimes used to denote the object-classification budget format.

Budgeting schedule.   The budget-making period will coincide with the yearly calendar if the camp is a full-time business or is part of an agency's year-round program. First, the camp programs are developed by the heads of the various departments, particularly the head counselor or program director, who must specify the components required to satisfy the camp's objectives. To finance the entire service, estimates are obtained in order to carry out the desired goals in relation to types of activities, personnel, materials, supplies, and equipment needed.

Budget estimates.   At some point, preliminary calculations must be made for the coming season and the fiscal year. These are based upon the continuous cost extracts that the camp administrator reviews. All line personnel should have some input into the budget-making process so that they are aware of the overall camp needs as they relate to their particular departments. After such estimates are collected, some discussion justifying the introduction of new activities beyond those that had previously been included in the camp program should occur. Salaries and wages will probably include cost-of-living increments, and it is probable that budget estimates will show rising costs beyond the camp's control. The mere maintenance of adequate services requires a larger budget than had been previously recorded.

Budget review.   The detailed estimates from the various camp departments are collected for summarization and review. Allocations are considered and the budget is prepared. All factual bases for increments are included. These should be stated in terms of the camp's goals. Highly specialized activities require analysis and research if support is expected. There may be the need for experimenting with innovative activities or with those that call for the employment of specialists—a mountaineering instructor or a white-water canoeing expert, for example—if that is how the camp projects its offerings for the new camp season.

Budget submission.   The completed budget is assembled and submitted to the sponsoring authorities or to the owners (if that is appropriate) for examination, amendment, and approval. To be sure, whenever any question of cutting activity proposals arises, fiscal planning must call upon those specialists who first suggested the cut for defense of the proposal. Realistic budgets are based upon the program supervisor's judgment of the optimal program that can be accomplished during the camping season. The budgetary process also incorporates routine information dealing with the camp's adherence to budget. Thus, the camp administrator is constantly apprised of the amount of money expended, together with the budget figures for the same period, adjusted to the actual level of activity experienced. Any variations are noted and explained. When this procedure is carried out continually, the budget procedure will become more accurate and control will be more effective.

After a camp has been in operation for at least one season, it may project a budget based upon the number of campers who return for a second year. When the camp administrator has a clear picture of how many campers are returning for the new season, he will be able to predict with greater precision the capital that the returnees will bring. By concentrating on promoting the camp and recruiting new campers to fill the available spaces, the administration will have a sound basis for determining the total expected income from camper fees and secondary sources.

Budget classifications.   Once collected, the data must be organized so that expenditures can be accounted for and proper records maintained. Most camps prefer to classify camp expenditures on a program or departmental system. Thus, the camp's departments are broken down into the components which together make up the camp operation. Such a classification might include administration, health services, food services, maintenance, and program. Each of these categories are subdivided; if necessary, the subdivisions may be further divided.

Administration may be subdivided into such classifications as insurance, public relations, communications (including all mailings), overhead, salaries and wages, transportation, power, maintenance, office machines, supplies, materials, and equipment. Each of these classifications is given a budget code so that expenditures can be credited to the function or element that generated the cost. In like manner, all of the major categories are ramified in order to determine which activities are producing the greatest interest among campers and which are being called upon to meet camper needs. On this basis, the budgeting system can be arranged. Of course, other combinations and emphases are possible; the choice depends upon the camp administrator's orientation and the information she requires for assessing the effectiveness of camp operations. More important, the budget should accurately reflect those elements of operation that are adequately financed and those that will require infusions of funds due to exigencies or because some cost centers were not properly allocated. In either instance, funds may be transferred on demand.

PURCHASING

Purchasing procedures are routinely taken care of when budgeting methods are employed. The budget is used as both a guide and a barrier to major error by those who handle the purchases for the camp. Supply requisitions and expenditures can be accounted for and appraised when comparisons are made between the approved budget and the camp's operation. Supplies, materials, and equipment are produced on a scheduled basis. All needs are anticipated, approved, and usually satisfied long before a shortage arises.

All supply items should be recorded on a supply inventory sheet that is issued to each of the departments. Since the inventory is recorded in the accounting system in the same way, all issuances can be appropriately charged and control can be ensured by providing the camp administrator with a detailed monthly breakdown of actual expenditures as they are incurred throughout the season or annually. Information about supplies should be provided by the camp's business office on official forms before they are sent to the administrator. Information given should include the following: (1) the supply account name; (2) the previous year's actual expenditures; (3) the current year's actual expenditures to date; (4) the current year's estimated expenditure; and (5) the sum requested in the budget for the coming year's expense. Obviously, the fourth and fifth items require the camp administrator's input.

Commodity Purchasing

The camp administrator should consult staff specialists before purchasing any equipment for use in the various functions of the camp. Camp personnel will have specific information about the needs of the various departments or activities that require supplies, materials, or equipment to carry out their respective functions. In addition, the specialists will probably know about commodity specifications and about how such commodities will be used. The administrator may have far more experience with purchasing than do other members of the camp staff, although a staffer specializing in a technical activity may have detailed knowledge that comes only after prolonged investment of time and energy.

Purchasing Policy

After material needs have been determined, a purchasing policy must be developed. It is not necessary to buy the most expensive merchandise to be assured of quality material, but it is likely that higher-priced items will be more durable, work more effectively, require less maintenance, and have a more attractive appearance. Among the factors that should be considered in the development of a purchasing policy for the camp is the need to set minimum specifications for durable goods. This is particularly true when bulk buying is required. With standardized items, parts can be more easily replaced when necessary, the quality of material used is maintained, and repairs can be made efficiently. Purchases should be made as need arises. The budgeting procedure will probably not permit expenditures that exceed encumbrances; however, sound purchasing policy should prohibit reckless buying.

Ordering

Early ordering will probably provide several advantages to the purchaser. Early delivery follows early orders and allows complete inspection of all supplies, the marking of equipment, and proper storage of materials. Ordering early offers the opportunity to examine the merchandise and permits adjustments in quantity.

Bulk Buying

Purchases should be made from established firms with reputations for sound consumer-service and readiness to guarantee their products. Discounts are often obtainable with bulk buying. When purchasing items that have a limited life and are used quickly and needed continually, it may be wise to request bids from several suppliers.

Central Stores

If the camp is large enough, it will probably have a purchasing officer, responsible to the camp administrator to supervise the central-stores department. Generally, the supplies maintained by the central-stores department or office are used by all segments of the camp. Bulk buying, standardization of commodities, procurement on bids, and other facilitating methods enable materials, supplies, and equipment to be routed through central stores for distribution after checking. Furthermore, discounts can be obtained for large-quantity orders.

Storage

A central-stores department should have the space required for storage of the various commodities that are used in camp on a daily basis. For example, craft supplies and athletic equipment must be stored in an area that provides the proper temperature, humidity, ventilation, and light. Storage of other commodities, such as paper goods, photographic equipment, leather goods, and paint, should be planned with their potential for dangerousness and rapid deterioration in mind.

Routing

The movement of all supplies should be in a direct path from the camp receiving office to the storeroom for checking, marking, and appropriate care. From that point, needed items are transferred to the various line departments as requests are made and filled. A perpetual inventory system will enable staff to replace items when necessary and to determine which items are not being used. Stocks that have become obsolete should be removed from central stores and returned for credit. Unused or deteriorated equipment should be destroyed or disposed of for the salvage value.

Issuance

Stored items should be grouped for easy access and dispensing. Recreational goods can be classified as follows: art, craft, photographic, paints, ceramic, fibers, athletic, and office. Such classification is effective when particular days are designated for the requisitioning of supplies, materials, or equipment for specific activities. The issuance of stores to the various departments necessitates the preparation of the requisition and the practical routine of handling goods for delivery.

Requisition forms, which should accompany any demand for items from the central stores, contain spaces and headings for date, function, item and quantity requested, and signatures of those who fill, file, check, and receive the order. All material, supplies, and equipment should be ordered in specific units of issue designated by the central-stores requisitions. The camp program or activities department should be assigned a regular order day. Emergency needs, which should be minimized, may be filled by special request and administrative approval.

Issuance and Exchange of Supplies

Every camp, regardless of size, should have a set of policies dealing with supply items. Items that are relatively durable or nonconsumable, such as paint brushes, tools, athletic equipment, tents, or sleeping bags, should be replaced when they have been found to be unfit for use. Redemption of items by central stores will probably prevent the discarding of half-used equipment; exchange of certain items for repair or replacement may be on a one-for-one basis. Capital equipment—that is, items that are long-lived and expensive—should be maintained in order to enhance durability. Items of this nature are not expected to be replaced periodically and are almost never stored; rather, they are constantly used within the program of activities. Such items as sound systems, lighting equipment, kilns, potter's wheels, and looms require considerable financial outlay and are purchased in single units.

Breakage

Breakage slips should be made in duplicate on all durable goods. In order to control breakage, the breakage slip original travels with the order for replacement and the duplicate goes to the individual responsible for the breakage and what will be done to prevent damage in the future. Requisitions for repair, replacement, or routine maintenance are sent to the central-stores department for action.

Consumables

Items that are consumable and in continual demand should be stocked and stored for accessibility and easy delivery. Art and craft supplies, photographic chemicals, paper, table games, and so forth should be stocked in quantity because they are used regularly. Buying these items in quantity ensures uniform quality and discounts for economy; it also assures the staff that they can plan activities that require such items because adequate supplies can be relied upon.

INSURANCE

Insurance is one way to minimize or cover loss exposure. The treatment of such exposure is called *risk management*. Loss exposure typically has three components: (1) the item subject to reduction or disappearance of value;

(2) the elements that can produce the loss, and (3) the potential economic diminishment or extent of loss.

Items that are subject to loss may be looked upon as assets and income. An awareness of hazards is crucial to effective treatment of loss exposure. Knowing what is subject to loss obviously indicates causation, a problem that must be resolved before the entire range of risk-treatment methods can be focused logically for application in a specific environment.

Hazards can be classified according to their origin as (1) natural, (2) human, or (3) economic. *Natural* hazards include fire, windstorm, flood, earthquake, and epidemic. *Human* hazards include, theft, vandalism, negligence, or failure to satisfy a stated obligation to another. *Economic* hazards may include recessions, changes in consumer habits, competition, and other impacts. These classifications sometimes overlap. Most accidents are the result of human carelessness (see Chapter 7).

There are three possibilities for risk management: avoidance, control, and transfer. Any of these techniques may be appropriate in a given situation, and all may be utilized in some combination. *Avoidance* of loss exposure can be accomplished by never having the exposure or by aborting an existing exposure. Avoidance is sometimes possible, but some exposures are inherent in the operation of a business, and any attempt at avoidance would be tantamount to closing down the business. *Control*, on the other hand, includes all techniques designed to reduce the loss frequency, severity, or unpredictability of loss exposure. The fundamental purpose of control is to change the features of the exposure so that it becomes more acceptable to the operator. Finally, *transfer* occurs when the risk manager decides to transfer the item subject to loss, or the financial outcome of such loss, to someone else. Such transfer can be carried out by noninsurance as well as insurance methods. It is to the latter item that we now turn.

Insurance is a risk-management measure that permits the transfer of financial impacts resulting from accidental losses from the insured business to the supplier of the insurance. Protection is indicated by the terms of the insurance contract. The process of insurance is an arrangement whereby the insured promises to contribute to a fund from which the insurer promises to make particular cash payments to those who suffer losses as indicated by the contract. It is beyond the scope of this book to undertake a comprehensive explanation of the insurance mechanism or of risk management. However, certain aspects of insurance are particularly important to the camp director in determining the kinds of insurance that would be most beneficial to the specific camp, its employees, and its clientele.

Property Insurance

Property insurance covers losses from accidental damage, destruction, or disappearance of property. Most property insurance contracts help the insured to replace or repair the insured property. Some contracts also cover net income losses that are a consequence of property loss. For example, net income may be lost because of extra expenses incurred in continuing operations following an accident, if expenses are continuing despite business interruption. Contracts may be written on a named-hazard or "all-risk" basis. The former specifies the hazards that are covered, whereas the latter covers all hazards that are not specifically excluded.

Liability Insurance

Liability insurance protects the insured against claims arising from common law or statutes that place responsibility for personal injuries or property losses suffered by others. It can be grouped by (1) injury or damage claim, (2) the tortious act from which the liability stems, (3) the property status necessary for the insured's liability to be covered, and (4) the legal principle on which the claim is based.[1]

Those who can claim damages covered by the contract will probably be either employees or those who receive services from the camp (that is, campers). Claims by employees usually arise from job-related accidents or illness. They might be brought under worker's compensation laws, however, and would therefore be covered under worker's compensation insurance. If the compensation law does not apply, the employer's liability insurance will protect the insured. Other liability insurance policies that cover general-public claims exclude claims by employees as employees but not as members of the general public.

The source of liability which originates because of property ownership, operation, and maintenance can be covered by insurance. Comprehensive general liability insurance covers all sources of liability not specifically excluded. It is analogous to the "all-risks" property insurance except that it is complete with respect to activities covered, not hazards. Another significant category of liability insurance is professional liability insurance, which covers against claims based on errors or negligence in the practice of the insured's occupation or profession.

Property damage liability protection may vary according to whether or not it covers legal liability for loss or damage to property in the care or control of the insured. Most liability insurance protecting property damage claims typically excludes claims to damaged property in the care of the insured. Such coverage is available, however. Some contracts for property coverage also cover the insured's legal liability for others' property for which the insured is responsible.

Insurance Coverage

Every camp must carry sufficient insurance coverage. Most camps cannot sustain or absorb the expenditures that can occur as a result of negligence. Insurance protection must be carefully analyzed to be certain that policies will return full value for the loss of supplies, materials, equipment, facilities, or natural resources. Liability protection to cover losses in consequences of injuries or damage sustained by campers, staff, or visitors must also be in effect.[2]

---

[1]G. E. Rejda, *Principles of Insurance*, 2nd ed. (Glenview, Ill.: Scott, Foresman, 1986), pp. 274–95.

[2]E. Schirick, "Buying Insurance Wisely," *Camping Magazine* (January 1986), 14–16.

Most camps are seeking more comprehensive insurance coverage for protection against such hazards as fire, theft, windstorms, damage from falling trees, hurricanes, floods, and other artificial or natural disasters. Certain types of insurance are required by law, and camps must comply with this legal necessity. The operation of motor vehicles for transportation and maintenance should be covered for property damage, personal liability, and injury claims. Health and accident insurance taken in the interest of the camper's as well as the owner's protection is advisable. Worker's compensation insurance is available for all camp employees, but it is most necessary for those staff members whose daily activities require that they work with machinery, heavy equipment, power tools, and the like. Insurance protection to cover the use of animals, boats, firearms, archery equipment, gymnastic equipment, bicycles, and the like is important if these materials are to be used in the activity program.

Transportation

The safe conveyance of campers and staff to and from camp is of great significance to all camp operators. If the camp operates automobiles, trucks, or buses that are used to transport campers and staff, it should adhere to legal restrictions and regulations governing the condition and maintenance of the vehicles. Even if government regulations are absent, the camp should maintain a high standard of vehicular operating efficiency, if only for the economies produced by these procedures.

All staff personnel who are responsible for operating transportation vehicles must be physically capable of such responsibility. They must have the skill, qualifications, and knowledge required for the possession of a state license that certifies that the holder has complied with existing codes for the operation of such equipment. The camp must have some logical plan to follow during the transportation of campers. Adequate supervision—a ratio of one counselor to eight campers—must be provided in order to maintain control and ensure common standards of safety and comfort. Counselors and campers must be instructed in the procedures of vehicle evacuation.

All those being transported should be seated; there is never any reason for standing in a camp vehicle, unless the vehicle is a truck and is used only for emergencies. Generally, only closed trucks are used since the ACA does not permit accredited camps to transport campers in open vehicles. It is much more likely that buses will be employed to transport campers.[3]

UTILITIES

In camp planning and property development, the installation of adequate utilities—that is, power, water supply, sewage system, and roadways—to meet present needs and future expectations is a major consideration. Sanitary engineers from local and state health departments and electrical engineers from public utility commissions can offer valuable advice and

[3]W. A. Becker, "Camp Bus Services," *Camping Magazine* (April 1986), 22–25, 27.

standards for the construction, operation, and maintenance of these systems; there will likely be some legal provision that requires approval of these essential facilities by these same agencies.

Water Supply

If the camp's drinking-water supply is dependent upon a storage tank, the tank should have a capacity of no less than one day's water requirement for the entire camp. The pumping machinery for the system should be capable of producing the day's supply of water in an 8-hour operation. Where flush toilets are installed, there should be a rated use of 50 gallons of water consumption per person each day. Where pit privies are used, water consumption will be somewhat less than 50 gallons a day. Septic tanks or other sewage disposal systems will require up to 60 gallons of water per person per day. Kitchen waste may be disposed of with the septic system, but it will be necessary to construct grease traps as part of the sewer line that serves the kitchen. If a large sewer-line grease trap is not part of the construction, then smaller cast-iron grease traps will be needed under each kitchen sink. The sewer-line grease trap should be able to handle at least 2 gallons of water per day.

Electricity

Most power in camp is supplied by electricity. This power source is basic to the central administrative core of the camp. Primarily, however, electricity will be most vital in the kitchen and in food-storage units. Power to operate the water-supply pump machinery makes electric lines and systems indispensable to the camp. Although there is no need for electric outlets or lights in the campers' living quarters, electricity is essential in the shop, kitchen, infirmary, and central office.

Roadways

A camp road system should provide access from the highway to the administration area (Fig. 3-1). Although there is no need for automobile traffic within the confines of the camp, there are needs for vehicular traffic that must be considered. Access should be opened from the administrative center to the mess hall, kitchen, and infirmary. These areas should be easily traversed by car, truck, or ambulance. The camp entrance should be within easy driving distance of the central administrative units.

The camp itself should not be open to vehicular traffic; natural environment should be preserved to the greatest extent possible. The roadways within the confines of the camp should be barely passable, and then only by camp vehicles designed to negotiate these trails. Road spurs should lead from the parking lot of the administration building to the rear of the mess hall. Another spur should lead to the infirmary. These roads should permit access to food-supply or emergency vehicles. Camp roadways may be of minimal width; they are usually mere trails that will permit the passage of rugged vehicles.

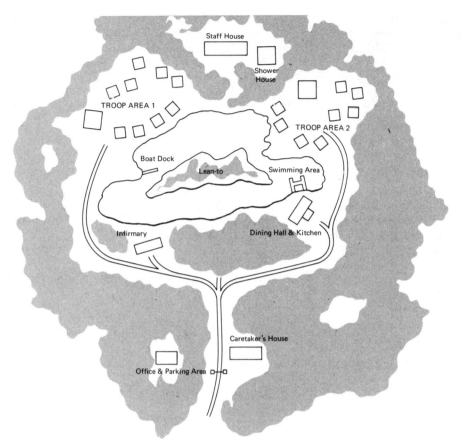

FIGURE 3-1. Roadway system for limited access.

Policy for Visitors

The camp has many responsibilities to the families of campers. The relationship between the parents and the camp is a curious mixture of apprehensiveness and confidence, enthusiasm and anxiety. Some parents attempt to impress counselors with their child's special needs and problems, even when such needs and problems exist only in the parent's mind. Parents' concern and fear may cause them to act in ways troublesome to the camper and the staff. Many camps discourage or restrict parental visiting.

A parental visit can be either a positive or a negative experience for the camper. In the most negative sense, parents tend to transmit their anxiety, hostility, or fear-provoking insecurity to the child. Some emotionally insecure parents fear losing their children's affection and love to the camp counselor, and thus tend to overcompensate when they are with the child. They often smother the youngster in their attempt to regain what has probably been theirs all the time. An otherwise well-adjusted child frequently becomes upset and displays an unwholesome attitude toward the camp, bunk, or counselor after an emotionally charged parental visit. From the positive standpoint, a parental visit can be reassuring to an insecure or anxious child. The child's feeling of rejection may be considerably assuaged by a happy visit.

When camp policy permits regular visits, the counselors, who represent the camp in the minds of parents, become targets or repositories of problems. Parents may criticize the camp administration and leadership to a counselor. Camp policy should forbid the counselor to argue with parents about these matters; rather, the counselor should accept the complaint and assure the parent that it will receive prompt attention. The counselor staff can do much to calm parental fears, allay unjustified criticism, and create confidence in the camp. Parents may attempt to press money on the counselor in the hope that he will show additional favor or attention to their child. Camp policy should firmly discourage any attempt to buy the counselor's affection or attention. The parent who attempts to pressure the counselor into an in-depth discussion about personal problems should be referred to the head counselor or camp director.

Camps that allow frequent weekend visits sometimes find that parents disrupt the routine. For this reason, as well as for the reasons already given, it is best to limit parental visits to one or two each session.

PUBLIC RELATIONS

In any operation in which the good will of clientele, potential contributors, or supporters is necessary, public relations becomes important. The attention of potential clientele must be stimulated, and interest in the program must be aroused and maintained. Private enterprises have long recognized that favorable public relations are vital to their success. The creation and sustainment of goodwill may be consciously planned and propagated. Because the camp's survival depends upon its ability to attract campers, attention must be given to each detail of camp operation that establishes contact with the parent or prospective client.

The interpretive function of public relations concerns the widest possible dissemination of facts about the camp. The general public is informed about the aims and objectives of the camp; the leadership, program, and care of campers; the potential for character development through exposure to outdoor education and values; and other pertinent data that a prospective client should or might want to know. The camp administration is only one source of information. Goodwill is also generated by campers and parents who have found the camp satisfactory in every respect. Paid publicity releases, newsworthy articles, and brochures will also spread information. Interest can be sustained through activities, such as reunions or theatre parties, held during the year for past and prospective clients.

Physical Facilities

First impressions of the camp can be invaluable or disastrous. If the office has a neat, businesslike appearance, if the grounds are well laid out and carefully maintained, if the buildings and structure are attractive and in good repair, the first appraisal of the camp will probably be one of admiration. The cleanliness and attractiveness of the camp can be most important in attracting, retaining, and building interest in the camp.

Employee Contacts

Every camp employee, from the professional staff to the kitchen crew, plays an important role in promoting good will and friendly relations. The counselors will probably have the most frequent contact with clients; thus, their courtesy, neat appearance, obvious competence, and enthusiasm all contribute to clients' impression of the camp.

Advertising

Advertising through newspapers, radio, and television can be done tastefully and with great appeal. Journals that specialize in taking advertisements from established camps are often checked by parents seeking a camp for their youngsters. Newspaper advertising can be fairly effective. If newspapers are being used to generate publicity, then stories as well as paid advertisements should appear about the camp in particular and camping in general. Feature stories about camping that have a human-interest aspect appeal to newspapers, particularly as the summer season draws near.

Printed Materials

Folders, posters, and brochures are invaluable in promoting interest in the camp. They should be attractive and simple, with as many color pictures, as possible.

Motion Pictures

Some large camps have been fortunate enough to develop documentary films that can be shown when recruiting staff members or clients. Frequently, a camp director may be asked to present a slide lecture or to show films of her camp at a civic organization's program. Such opportunities can help build a distinguished image for the camp, as well as attract new campers.

Reunion Activities

Some long-lived camps maintain their relationship with campers and their parents by contacting them throughout the year, as much as three times a year. One contact might be an excursion to a theatre for campers who live in a specific region. A spring banquet to celebrate campers' achievements, or a simple get-together at which old and new campers and their parents meet and discuss their experiences, can be a second meeting. Finally, there can be a precamp entertainment meeting at which slides and films of the camp and its activities are shown. This meeting can be held during the beginning of the camper-enrollment season, and it may even be possible for campers to use this meeting to designate the mates with whom they might like to bunk.

Public Addresses

The camp director should solicit opportunities to appear before potential interest groups. Many groups want to fill their program with interesting and entertaining speakers. Good camp directors are effective speakers. They have many anecdotes and interesting stories to tell about the benefits, adventures, and knowledge that they and others have acquired through camp association.

chapter 4

Camp Health and Sanitation

It is a mistake to think that a camp program should be concerned only with campers' physical well-being. Certainly, many persons continue to think of health as a physical phenomenon. But the holistic nature of humans renders such compartmentalization futile. Concern with physical health should not obscure other factors. The professional camp administrator knows that health comprises social, emotional, and physical well-being. Interaction among bodily organs, physiological functions, and emotions are obvious. Heart rate, for example, may increase rapidly due to anxiety. Emotional problems can contribute to eating difficulties. Poor digestion can affect enjoyment of food. The buildup of fatigue inhibits achievement. Lack of motor coordination can undermine satisfaction in performing physical skills. All these things are factors for concern and are evidence that growth and health involve the entire person.

Social and Psychological Implications for Camp

The relative calm of a home gathering is very different from the organized pressure and give-and-take of a camp bunk. Camp opens up a universe of new personalities, new friends, and new strangers. Campers inhabit a world of designated or chosen tasks, of regulated behavior, and of discipline. Campers have freedom in some areas and restriction in others. Through trial and error, they learn to respect the rights of others.

Camp organization also plays a significant role in molding the situation to which campers will be exposed. It offers the opportunity to join with those of similar background or to bring together those whose social and educational experiences are vastly different. The camp environment demands interaction and socialization, the skills of which must be assimilated.

Camp Environment

The importance of the camp environment in helping campers learn how to live together has never been fully described. It is obvious, however, that the greatest success will be achieved only when administrative and counselor staffs are sensitive and responsive to the potentialities involved. Camp executives must develop policies that recognize the need for campers to adapt to social situations. The administrator must organize the camp in such a way as to contribute to camper growth and development. The counselor staff should lead the program in a manner consonant with helping campers understand the ways in which individuals and groups interact.

The implications of camping as a complete experience cannot be ignored. Whether planners know it or counselors recognize it, living in a natural setting and in a bunk, listening to authority figures, and being criticized or applauded by peers have an impact on the camper's total health and well-being. An attractive, appropriately located, and well-maintained camp with good food service, an exhilarating program, adequate facilities, and modern equipment make an important contribution to the development of all who attend the camp.

Personal Problems

Camp staff should recognize the variety of personal problems that young campers face. Such problems may relate to adaptation to camp routine or discipline, adjustment to sexual maturity, sibling rivalry, peer pressure, and other stresses that affect children and youth. The skilled counselor helps prevent these problems from developing or escalating, helps campers experiencing minor difficulties, and refers those with serious problems to appropriate professionals who have the skill to handle them.

As they go about their daily routines, campers become aware of acceptance or rejection, bias and selfishness, rationalization and projection, envy and hostility. They learn about anxiety and security, failure and achievement. They experience the entire range of human behavior. The social and psychological development of campers should be of as much concern to the counselor as their achievement in various other aspects of the camping program.

Counselor Roles in Camper Health

Counselors play a significant role in the development of campers' social and psychological values. Counselors should be prepared to assist those for whom they are responsible by deliberately inculcating certain generalized social and health principles. No one advocates a rigid or restrictive orientation, but there are some commonly accepted values that are generally viewed as positive for the maturing individual. It is well known that socialization has an important impact upon the child's state of mind. It should be the intention of the counselor to present the desirability of cooperation, democratic participation, honesty, good sportsmanship, equity, and perseverance in social interactions. A camper imbued with these attributes and the opportunity to practice them through the decision-making process has a realistic chance to clarify his position. When faced with alternatives, it is more than likely that the habits of a positive outlook will become the position of choice. This is particularly true if the counselor has offered consistent and fair instruction and is worthy of emulation.

There is no question that psychological state plays a significant part in health. Thus, emotional stability affects one's cooperation, participation, self-confidence, security, and responsibility for one's own behavior. The counselor should provide the support that some campers require in order to make the best possible adjustment to camp. Counselors play a variety of roles for their campers, and the best interests of their campers must be uppermost in their every action. The social atmosphere of the group and the psychological support offered by the counselor can assist individuals to overcome timidity, lack of resolve, and other negative traits. (This relationship will be further explored in Chapters 11 through 14.)

The Physical Environment

Living organisms react to their environment. The environment may produce comfort or discomfort, arouse feelings of pride or shame, delight or revulsion, elation or depression. It can encourage or hinder learning, allow the rapid spread of communicable disease or promote good health, and increase or decrease the possibility of accidents. The provision of a safe, sanitary, and attractive physical environment is a primary objective.

Physical Planning

Attention to the physical environment begins when a camp is being planned and continues as long as the facility is used. Space is provided in living quarters or bunks, and special areas are incorporated to accommodate standard and innovative activities. An ample supply of safe water must be assured, together with adequate plumbing and a sufficient number of sinks, drinking fountains, and toilets. Proper disposal of waste safeguards the health of campers and staff.

Maintenance

Custodial and maintenance services should keep areas clean and facilities in good repair. Camp property, trails, activity areas, and playing fields should show the results of effective maintenance. Camp facilities must include suitable space and equipment for preparing and serving meals. A kitchen, food-storage space, and dining room are now considered integral parts of a residential camp.

Sanitation

Camp life does not encourage good health if campers are unnecessarily exposed to communicable diseases. Good sanitation is a preventive measure, but it must be augmented with specific policies and procedures dealing with such matters as immunization, case-finding, and isolation or transportation to a treatment center if necessary. Practices in these areas should be developed in cooperation with state and local health departments, parents, medical staff, and other personnel who have an interest in these matters.

Safety

The camp environment has direct implications for accident prevention, since campers can never be completely safe unless measures are taken to identify and eliminate environmental hazards and to prevent or plan for disasters. Accidents do occur; only the naive or foolish believe that a camp can be operated without them. However, when parents send their children to camp they do not expect them to be injured while horseback riding, at archery, in a crafts shop, or during a swimming period. They expect that the camp will be a safe place.

Emergencies

Camp personnel have three essential responsibilities in accidents and emergency situations: The first is to prevent accidents if possible, and to reduce risk to a minimum if not; the second is to include safety instruction as part of the camping experience; and the third is to carry out a plan of action when an emergency arises. These responsibilities are frequently neglected because some poorly motivated administrator will assume that an emergency either will not occur or will be handled by common sense. Nothing could be further from the truth. Accidents, fires, floods, explosions, and other emergencies occur at unexpected times and places. The consequences may be exacerbated by panic, forgetfulness, or a lack of skill or knowledge of appropriate procedure. The unexpected must be anticipated. It is better to be prepared and have nothing happen than to be unprepared during an emergency. Policies to account for every contingency must be planned for long before there is a need; and all camp personnel must be familiar with them.

A camp committee designated solely to develop contingency measures for health and safety may consider a variety of safety problems. This group can institute plans for the emergency care of injured campers or staff; for action in the event if fire, flood, tornado, or other calamity; for general safety; for elimination of environmental hazards; and for the prevention of accidents in all parts of the camp. Only after such plans are established can it be said that the camp is satisfying its obligation to provide a safe and healthy environment.

HEALTH SERVICES

Of singular concern to parents is the health of their children. In a well-run camp, every measure is taken to ensure healthful living conditions for the camper. The camp's effectiveness is endangered when the standards of health practices are not high. Any compromise of standard health procedures immediately makes a camp suspect in the eyes of parents and health authorities. Although the camp environment is fundamentally permissive, those aspects of camp life that affect health must be of high quality.

The organization of the camp health service depends upon the resident population, the duration of camp periods or season, the permanence of camp structures, the age group served, and the proximity of the camp to modern medical facilities and competent physicians. Every camp should have a medical consultant; he must be a licensed medical doctor. A general practitioner is quite adequate. The physician must be familiar with public-health practices, specifically contagious-disease control, and emergency medicine. The nature of the clientele of most camps indicates the need for a pediatrician when possible. If the camp caters to the elderly, then a geriatrician is the physician of choice.

Physician-in-Residence

A physician should be in residence at the camp if there are more than 100 campers. If the camp is near enough to a community where there is a medical practitioner who can take care of emergency conditions, some formal contractual agreement may be drawn between the physician and the camp so that the camp receives medical services. These services may consist of weekly visits, first aid, surgery, or the prescription of drugs. All medical supplies and equipment should be stocked before camp begins, on the advice of the physician.

Nurse-in-Residence

An RN should be in residence if more than 50 campers are enrolled at camp. LPNs should supplement the medical staff if the residential camper population requires. The nurse's functions are defined by law, and by the resident or contracted physician. She will probably have standing orders for the administration of prescription drugs.

Health Program

The health program at camp begins with a camper health certificate. This requirement is met when a camper obtains a physical examination from a licensed physician no more than 2 weeks before camp opens. Camp staff are also subject to this rule and must receive a clean bill of health. The health certificate is given to the camp administration, turned over to the resident physician for evaluation, and deposited in the employee's or camper's record. The health certificate gives the medical history, specifying illnesses or accidents, surgery, vaccinations, physical deficiencies, special diets or drugs, and a statement by the examining physician that the child is free from infectious diseases at the time of the examination. Furthermore, there should be a statement that the child is physically capable of participating in normal camping activities. The information contained in the health certificate should be communicated to the appropriate personnel.

Health Concerns

Noncontagious afflictions must receive attention. The dietician must receive a list of campers on special diets. The appropriate staff must be informed of any health problems. Campers with limiting physical conditions must indicate their impairment to the bunk counselor and other staff members who will supervise their activity.

Medical Examinations

The initial physical examination of all campers should be conducted during the first few days of the season, preferably within 24 hours of the camper's arrival.

Counselor Responsibilities

Any visit to the medical office or infirmary, whether by referral of a counselor, by request of the camper, or for a routine check-up, is noted in the camper's medical file. All such records should be retained, particularly if the camper returns for another season. A camper's case history provides important information about the child's health status at the time the record was made. It serves as a reference point for physicians who perform medical examinations. The case history supplies factual support in the event that litigation is initiated after an illness or accident. Proper handling of campers' health problems, duly recorded and attested to, may do much to inhibit false damage claims or suits for tortious actions.

The camp health program involves all personnel and campers. Counselors should cooperate with health personnel to ensure daily assessment of campers for illness or injuries. All campers should have adequate rest, nourishment, and exercise, and must maintain satisfactory personal hygiene at a high level. Counselors must ensure that campers practice a basic health regimen. This means that hot showers must be taken with soap, teeth must be brushed, and faces and hands must be washed before eating and after using toilet facilities.

Sanitation and Food Handling

The handling of food by employees is supervised by the dietician or other qualified food-service director. Proper health and sanitary precautions must be taken in storing and handling food to prevent spoilage, waste, and the transmission of disease-causing contaminants.

SANITATION

Sanitation is an intrinsic part of any healthful environment. To neglect sanitation is to endanger health. Sanitation, the outcome of cleanliness, is concerned with the elevation of hygiene and the prevention of disease. It is achieved by freeing a facility from contamination and removing impurities or pollution. Surely maintenance and good housekeeping are also part of the total health picture at camp; but the functions of washing appropriate fixtures, mopping floors, dusting areas, and disinfecting when necessary will promote good sanitation and health.

Sanitary Codes

State and local health departments publish sanitary codes relating to the operation of summer camps. These codes should be consulted to determine whether the sanitary arrangements of the camp are adequate, efficient, and effective. The procedure elucidated in the codes is particularly necessary to safeguard a pure supply of drinking water. Public health personnel may be asked to inspect the sewage disposal system, garbage handling and refuse disposal, latrines and toilet facilities, the waterfront area, and sources of swimming water. Drinking water, even when certified safe, must be tested at its source each week. Although some administrators feel that this is unnecessary and time-consuming, the health of all connected with the camp depends upon these inspections.

Potable Water

Drinking water, which is usually unavailable in some areas of camp, may have to be piped in from drilled wells or storage tanks. In such cases, additional lines for water fountains may be installed to prevent thirsty campers from drinking from questionable or contaminated water sources usually found on the surface. Sanitary dishwashing requires that all utensils, dishes, pots, and pans used in cooking or serving food be cleaned under live steam process or in hot water (not less than 175°F). Modern dishwashing and drying machines can be installed to ensure sterilized eating and cooking equipment.

Food Protection

Proper sanitation includes protection of food in refrigerator units adequate in size and coolant power to preserve the most perishable foods safely for the longest period of time. The liberal use of frozen foods stored in modern freezer units provides a safe, fresh, and nourishing supply.

Food service and storage brings the problem of insect invasion. Food-storage units, garbage containers, toilet facilities, and living quarters should be as free of insects as possible. The use of covered food containers, insect spray, and chemical toxicants that prevent insect breeding or movement will inhibit the possibility of insect-borne infection or disease.

Pesticide Use

Much has been written and said, especially in recent years, about the ecological imbalance that results from overly enthusiastic, and inconsistent, use of certain pesticides. The cautious use of such chemicals is, of course, preferable to the contagion of harmful insects and vermin. However, the animals that feed off these insects, thereby preserving natural equilibrium, are also harmed by the chemicals. Recognition of this twofold danger of pesticides is apparent in the current search for chemicals that can destroy pests without breaking the ecological chain.

Drinking Fountains

Drinking fountains that are not set at a proper height and thoroughly cleaned at frequent intervals can transmit disease through contact with the mouthpiece. Water pressure should be such that the stream from the tap is sufficient to permit children and others to drink without touching the mouthpiece. Moreover, young children must be taught how to use fountains and how to keep them clean.

Drinking fountains tend to snare atmospheric dust because of their moist surfaces. Therefore, fountains should be inspected several times each day; if warranted, they should be cleaned with brush and soap, and then rinsed with clear water and polished with a dry cloth.

Toilets

Toilet facilities and fixtures are often the source of unappetizing smells. Toilet areas that require washing are walls, floors, partitions, stalls, doors, windows, and sinks. Bathroom facility fixtures that require special attention to maintain sanitary conditions are urinals; toilets; and paper towel, soap, and napkin dispensers. Toilet room walls should be cleaned every 3 weeks. Ceramic tile surfaces should be cleaned daily with soap and water. Painted concrete walls should also be washed with soap and water. Toilet room partitions or stalls are often fabricated from metal, which may be porcelainized, bonderized, enameled, or painted. Stone partitions and compartments are usually constructed from slate or other impervious stone, all of which can be washed with detergent and water.

Doors, and particularly handles or knobs, usually transmit germs from one person to another. All door surfaces should be cleaned on a daily basis. Toilet room windows need to be cleaned once a week on the inside and once a month on the outside. Toilet facilities can be maintained in a sanitary manner if they are composed of impervious material. Floors should be made of impervious material so that any human waste that is dropped upon them may be removed with daily washing.

The toilet seat itself should be kept clean, and those that are cracked or pitted should be replaced before the camping season begins. The entire commode should be washed daily, with special attention to seat hinges, floor bolts, flush handles, and the area under and around the rim of the bowl. The entire toilet bowl must be thoroughly washed daily. If such areas are not treated daily with a stiff brush, they can become the repository of urine salts, which permit foul odors to develop. Urinals also require thorough washing and rinsing each day. Lavatories should be washed with soap and rinsed more often than once each day if they are used frequently.

Dispensers for toilet paper, soap, paper towels, and sanitary napkins must be kept clean. Because parts of these fixtures make hand contact, they should be washed once a day.

Food-Service Areas

All structures that are used for the receiving, storing, preparing, serving and eating food require special cleaning. Auxiliary areas and facilities that are adjacent to or support the major function of food service, such as entrances and exits, windows, toilets for food-service personnel, office areas for the dietician, and refrigeration and storage space for foods and supplies as well as for garbage must also receive specific custodial care. Food-service personnel are responsible for the sanitary condition of all utensils, glassware, dishes, food supplies, and storage areas, as well as all appliances used in the storage and preparation of food.

Floors

Kitchen floors, serving areas, and all entrances should be wet mopped with soap and water and then rinsed after each meal. The dining room floor should be swept and damp mopped after each meal and thoroughly scrubbed each week. Dining room floors should be covered with asphalt, vinyl, linoleum, or some other washable material. Doors and windows should receive particular attention because dust can build up in response to the discharge of moisture into the atmosphere from cooking surfaces.

Doors and Windows

Windows and doors in the food service area should be screened. These screens should be inspected regularly to ensure that they have not been damaged and that they close appropriately. Screens must be secure and must fit properly so that insects cannot gain entrance.

Storage Rooms

Storage and supply rooms are particularly important to food-service sanitation because they serve as the receiving and storage center for food supplies. The bags and boxes in which food is stored offer scant protection against infestation by vermin or contamination by toxic substances. Sanitation standards as published by state public health departments for these functions must be followed at all times. Storage rooms should be properly ventilated in order to avoid moisture condensation. Poor ventilation permits bacterial growth. Proper ventilation permits the displacement of foul odors and reduces the likelihood of heat build-up and concentration of toxic gases.

Garbage Disposal

Garbage and waste that accumulates as the result of food preparation and service must be properly disposed of in order to protect against possible contamination of food supplies, utensils, and equipment. Such disposal minimizes noisome odors and reduces the possibility of attracting the pests that breed in such places.

Pests

Pests are animals and insects detrimental to humans. We are chiefly concerned here with vermin—animal and insect pests that endanger the health and comfort of campers and personnel. Pests such as rodents, flies, ticks, mosquitoes, and cockroaches are the major infiltrators. They are disease carriers, and their presence often indicates filthy conditions.

Rodents in particular are destructive, filthy, and disease-bearing. It was infestation by rats and the fleas carried on their bodies that caused the spread of the notorious bubonic plague that decimated European populations several times during the Middle Ages and thereafter. Rodents, whose bite may carry the threat of rabies, have been known to attack campers. Since rodents need both food and shelter and cannot exist where either is absent, any infestation can be traced to conditions that are favorable to their breeding. Taking steps to remove such conditions is the best solution. Immediate irradication requires extermination.

The initial task in eliminating rodents' food supply is to keep garbage in sealed containers and remove it daily from the camp. The next basic technique is to store all food in rodent-proof rooms or containers. Finally, the premises must be kept clean. Protective cover for rodents can be eliminated be maintaining well-ordered storage spaces; thus they will not have a secure place to hide and multiply. Potential hiding places for rodents (boxes, for example) should be removed or placed at least 1 foot above the floor so that rodents cannot find living space between objects. Structural design should be such that potential nesting places—double walls, space between floors and ceilings, and other dark areas—are omitted. Exterior walls should be sound and should not permit access by uncovered openings. If heavy rodent infestation occurs, a professional exterminating service must be used.

Insects also pose a threat to health. However, insect infestation can usually be controlled with cleanliness, insecticides (where appropriate and permitted), and exclusion from the premises. Maintaining a clean area will do much to eliminate the threat of cockroaches, but flies will be attracted to a clean area by food odors. Screening all likely places of entry is one sure way to exclude flies from food-service areas, and structural design helps control roach invasion. Other insects are not so easily controlled. Mosquitoes and ticks cannot be eradicated unless breeding places, such as swamps or woodlands, are extensively sprayed which might not be ecologically beneficial. Campers will have to tolerate such insects as mosquitoes, but counselors and health officers must be concerned about ticks because they may carry the pathogen for spotted fever. For the most part, insects that are attracted to food-service areas can be controlled by specific insecticides as well as by other sanitation techniques. Local and state health departments are the best source of information about insecticides as well as about basic sanitation and health requirements.

WATER SUPPLY, PLUMBING, AND SEWERAGE

Essential to safeguarding the health of all those residing at the camp is a sufficient supply of potable water, delivered under sufficient pressure to adequate plumbing fixtures. The plumbing fixtures must be linked to a sewage system capable of rapid and clean transmission of wastes to proper disposal sites. Any deficiency in this system will expose the camp population to water-borne contaminants that might produce gastroenteritis, typhoid fever, and dysentery.

The primitive camp standbys of hand-pumped wells and sanitary privies as appropriate for water supply and waste disposal have long since been outmoded. Both public health laws and common sense indicate that camps require safe water supplies and waste disposal. It is fine to "rough it" while out on the trail and make do with whatever potable water and sanitary facilities can be expediently found, but in residential camps, modern sanitary facilities are a necessity.

Safe Water Supplies

Water is essential for maintaining life, for personal cleanliness, and for the removal of wastes. Both quality and adequacy are significant. Camp administrators should understand what constitutes a safe water supply. All water obtained from surface sources requires some treatment to render it safe for consumption and other uses. Although it might appear that water supplied from deeply drilled wells is safe for drinking without treatment, this is not always true; even deep wells can be contaminated by toxic wastes that seep into subterranean aquifers. Therefore, the routine examination and laboratory analysis of the camp water source is vital. Camps that are served by public water systems are guaranteed that the water supply will be safe. When a public water supply is not available, the camp administration must assume responsibility for the construction and maintenance of a water supply.

Ground-water characteristics.   All water in the ground originates from surface water, just as all water is part of the hydrologic cycle and thus is used over and over again. However, the filtering process through which ground water goes may purify it to the extent that it becomes potable without treatment. The process by which surface water travels through the soil and then through underlying substrata provides the chemical and bacteriological content of the water. The water is filtered as it percolates through soil, subsoil, and rock formation. This process removes much bacteria and organic material. Unfortunately, effective purification of water does not occur where the water percolates through creviced limestone or rock; substrata bacteria may not be filtered out. In all but a few parts of the United States, a bacteriologically safe ground water supply is likely if properly constructed and situated wells are developed. Nevertheless, all water supplied from sources of this type should be subjected to laboratory analysis.

Chemical components of non-public water supplies. A number of chemicals find their way into camp water supplies. These chemicals must be analyzed so that the campers' health will not be jeopardized. In some places, high quantities of carbonates and sulfates of calcium and magnesium may be found. These compounds usually produce what is called "hard" water. Water can be softened by exchanging sodium ions for calcium and magnesium ions. Commercial softeners can be used to remove the substances that cause this condition. Other chemicals, such as concentration of sulfates, can produce diarrhea in those who drink water containing them. In many instances the drinker soon adapts to the water without apparent effects.

Among the most dangerous chemical compounds now found in water are those that arise from close proximity to mining, lumbering, and other manufacturing industries which may allow toxic wastes or trace metals to percolate into water sources. Thus, in today's environment, it is not unusual to find traces of arsenic, lead, mercury, diethyl sulfate (DES), polychlorinated dithenyl (PCB), ethylene dibromide (EDB), acids, or even radioactive materials in camp water supplies. Where the natural filtration process is unable to prevent water from being contaminated by these chemical compounds, the water source must either be treated until it is potable, or it must be abandoned. All water sources must be scrupulously inspected and subjected to stringent analysis.

Fluorides occur naturally in some ground-water supplies. A fluoride content of approximately 1.0 part per million will reduce the incidence of dental decay among young campers. Some laboratory studies indicate that optimal quantities of fluoride may benefit the skeletel structure of adults, particularly older adults. If a water supply does not contain fluoride, it may be added. Of course, this requires continual analysis and monitoring.

Water that has a clouded or colored appearance or a strong taste may be bacterially contaminated, have a high incidence of iron compounds, or be objectionable from an aesthetic standpoint. No one wants to drink water that is turbid or odorous, or that has a brackish taste. Although none of these characteristics may be important from a health point of view, their presence will render the water unsatisfactory to campers. Either such water must be filtered, or another water source must be found.

Bacteriologic quality. The bacteriologic quality of water is extremely important to health. If the water source is satisfactory and the procedure used to access it concurs with public health practices, the water should be bacteriologically suitable. This ideal situation does not always coincide with reality, however. It is therefore necessary to analyze the water source regularly for bacteria. Coliform bacteria are the usual source of contamination. In almost every case, the presence of coliform bacteria in a water sample indicates pollution by sewage.

Technical guidance concerning the bacteriologic quality of water is available from state and local public health departments. Public authorities will examine the water source and the distributing process. These data are added to the bacteriologic analysis of water samples. The results of the tests are immediately communicated to the camp administration so that alternative supplies can be provided while contaminated water sources are chemically purified.

Required volume of water.   Each camp must have an ample supply of potable water under pressure to supply its plumbing fixtures. The quantity of water available to a camp with water-supplied fixtures should be no less than 80 gallons per person per day (see also Chapter 7).

Surface water is almost never recommended as a source for a camp water supply. Surface water invariably must undergo sedimentation, filtration, and chlorination to ensure a constant, adequate, safe water supply. A water treatment plant would be ideal for these purposes, but economic considerations would surely preclude such an installation. If subsurface water is unavailable, however, then surface supplies must be relied upon. In such circumstances, a water treatment plant engineered by a specialist might be the only alternative.

When public health–approved water supplies are not available, a deep-drilled well is the most satisfactory source of water. The major concern in the development of a water-supply source is the choice of site. Siting the well requires knowledge about the geologic, hydrologic, and bacteriologic elements that affect water quality and quantity. If natural features are considered, the potential for contamination can be drastically reduced or eliminated. Thus, the well should be located at a higher elevation than are the possible sources of contamination. Surface drainage should be away from the well. Moreover, the site should not be subject to flooding. All sources of contamination, such as sewers, septic tanks, seepage pits, cesspools, and surface water should be over 100 feet from the site, although health department ordinances may require only a 50-foot minimum.

Well construction and pumps.   The water-bearing stratum should be at least 10 feet, and preferably 20 feet, below the ground surface. The well must be constructed with an outside, watertight casing. The annular opening between the casing and the earth should be grouted. The well should have a cap which completely seals the casing or pipe sleeves.

Pumps must be constructed and installed so as to prevent contaminants from entering the water supply. The pump should be of the submersible type so that well pits and their attendant dangers are eliminated.

The well and distribution system should be disinfected after construction or repair in order to eliminate contamination. Assistance in such disinfection should be obtained from the local or state department of health.

Water supply lines.   The water service line from the public main or the well to the camp should be in a trench separate from the sewer line and at the distance specified in state and local health codes. The service line should be of the correct size so that adequate pressure and flow rates at all fixtures will be maintained at a minimum pressure of 8 pounds per square inch for water taps. Toilets should be supplied through flush-meter valves, for which the minimum pressure is 15 pounds per square inch.

Plumbing Systems and Fixtures

The plumbing system includes all the lines, materials, and equipment involved in water supply, distribution pipes, plumbing fixtures, traps, soil, waste, and vent pipes, and all the devices necessary for their operation. The purpose of the system is to supply uncontaminated water to the various outlets (fixtures) and to transport waste to a suitable disposal point for treatment or into a public sewage system.

Plumbing codes must be rigidly followed in the design and installation of the system. Codes are not recommendations, but are regulations to be enforced by health authorities since they directly reflect upon protection of water supplies and ensurance of proper waste removal. All plumbing must be installed as specified by applicable state or local codes. Proper venting of fixtures to maintain seal traps prevents sewer gas from entering occupied structures and also excludes pests.

Back-siphonage. Back-siphonage, a significant cause of water contamination, is the result of polluted water flowing back from a plumbing fixture into a water supply pipe. This occurs because of negative pressure (a vacuum) in that pipe. Vacuums in camp distributing systems are common, and may be produced by shutting off a system and draining it for repair work, or as a result of the use of fire-fighting equipment, which may reduce pressures to a point below normal.

During such periods of vacuum, contaminated material may be drawn into the water supply system. Toilets and urinals operated by flush-meter valves can also be a source of contamination. The valve requires water pressure for closure. If a vacuum occurs, fecal matter may be drawn into the system through the opening at the base of the trap. Air, which would normally be drawn through the rim openings, would not be a sufficient force to protect against this condition.

The camp administrator can do a number of things to prevent back-siphonage. Primarily, the water distribution system should be designed so that it will always have the capacity to supply all the fixtures of the system. Proper hydraulic engineering will ensure that pressure in the water main or service line will be maintained at 8 to 20 pounds per square inch. It will also take into consideration water demand for various fixtures, pressure losses resulting from friction losses in the system, and differences in elevation between the service line and the highest fixture.

Proper hydraulic design guards against any vacuum in the water supply system during normal operations, but it does not protect in situations in which water pressure is lost because of shut-downs for repairs or other emergencies. Consequently, each fixture must be secured by supplying water through an air gap or by a vacuum breaker—a less desirable method. Water supply engineers will be able to offer advice for installation, but the vacuum breaker is subject to mechanical failure unless properly maintained.

Sanitary fixtures.　The condition and number of fixtures affect campers' health practices, and ultimately their health status as well. Personal hygiene is important in the modern camp. Without suitable facilities, counselors and other health-service personnel are hindered in carrying out their responsibilities to campers. The minimum ratio of toilets to campers is 1 fixture to 37 campers, for urinals 1 to 30, for drinking fountains 1 to 100, and for wash basins 1 to 40.

Drainage

Most state and local governments have code requirements controlling the design and installation of the plumbing drainage system. Almost invariably, the basic criteria for such systems call for them to be constructed of durable materials capable of lasting as long as the structure that it contains lasts; piping should be large enough to remove wastes at a rate that will not interfere with the proper use of fixtures; installation of adequate cleanouts should be installed to permit proper maintenance; and all fixtures should be adequately trapped to prohibit entrance of odors or pests. Finally, care must be taken to avoid constructing sewer lines over areas where food is prepared, handled, or stored.

WASTE DISPOSAL

The disposal of sewage from camps may be relatively simple. Connection to the public sewer system provides a convenient and safe method. The responsibility for treatment is thereby transferred to the department responsible for the sewage system. Where no public or community system is available, however, the camp administration assumes the responsibility for safe disposal of sewage.

Elements for Consideration

The type and size of the disposal facility for a camp will vary with its location, population, soil conditions, and available area. Disposal methods should be designed to prevent environmental pollution. Thus, procedures must be undertaken that will (1) prevent pollution of drinking water; (2) prevent water pollution to sources used for recreational purposes; (3) avoid noisome odors and unpleasant sights; and (4) prevent access of flies to sewage.

Primary treatment.　Primary treatment is obtained through the use of a septic system and tank. The tank retains the sewage until solids collect and settle while the clarified sewage is filtered through the system. After disease-producing organisms in the sewage are stabilized and destroyed, the remaining solids must be removed in a manner that will be neither offensive nor hazardous to health. The simplest method is by contract with a commercial firm specializing in the removal of septic wastes. The responsibility for waste disposal transfers to the commercial firm, which must then comply with state and local health codes in the final disposition of the sludge removed from the septic tanks. In some remote camps, secondary treatment of sewage will be encountered. Standard procedures for engineering, analysis of soil absorption of the subsoil, and percolation tests will best determine whether soil absorption and trickling filtration are suitable. All such plans for secondary sewage disposal must be approved by the departments of health that have jurisdiction.

Refuse Disposal

Refuse consists of all wastes other than sewage. Handling of refuse requires some form of temporary storage prior to collection for final disposal. Refuse must be handled carefully so that it does not become a breeding place for animal and insect pests. The quantity of garbage and the frequency of collection will determine the number of garbage cans to be used. If there are large quantities of garbage, it is beneficial to have a separate refrigerated garbage storage room.

Garbage cans should be cleaned after use. This requires the installation of some sort of washing facility where jets of water and live steam can be used to flush out the cans. Cans should be washed in an area reserved for this activity and equipped with adequate drainage.

If a commercial garbage collection firm is not available for refuse disposal and if the local community does not have a garbage collection system, state and local health codes will probably indicate the procedure to be used. Refuse may be incinerated, buried in a sanitary landfill, or deposited in the sewage system by means of a garbage grinder. Local sanitary codes will have to be checked to determine whether these methods are applicable and permitted.

Proper disposal of sewage and refuse and the methods and technology necessary to ensure a safe water supply are vital if the environment is to be conducive to healthful camp living. All the previously cited factors are components of a health service. Attention to all of them will make the camp a secure and salubrious place where the essential conditions for a healthy life can be promoted.

chapter 5

Camp Food Service

Some believe that food is more important to campers than almost any other aspect of the camping experience. This may be true for older campers, but it is seldom true for the youngest. The young camper is generally quite indifferent to the food served at camp. However, food service is important to even the youngest camper because of the feelings evoked by inadequate or poorly prepared and tasteless food. A young camper may not care about the food's appearance, nutritional value, or quality of preparation, but campers eventually realize that bad food makes for an unpleasant dining room atmosphere, and emotional outbursts and negative attitudes are likely to result.

The older camper is immediately concerned about food and all its ramifications. The quantity, taste, appearance, and quality of food is significant to the older camper as well as to the staff. The camp administrator is also concerned with food service because of its effect on camp morale, because it is a camp activity that takes up at least 3 hours a day, and because budgetary regulations require that no less than one-third of yearly operating funds be devoted to it. These interrelated factors play an important role in the operation of any residential camp. Every person at camp is in touch with the food-service program every day. Meal times invest camp life with much of its vigor and enthusiasm. Poor food service is a wholly negative blunder from which most camps do not recuperate.

Food service is now generally accepted as an essential part of both residential camps and day camps. The aims of the camp food service are to offer meals that meet campers' nutritional needs, to develop an enjoyable meal-time atmosphere, and to serve good-tasting food. Properly organized and directed, the camp food service plays an important role in healthful camp living. Good nutrition promotes health, and health has a direct bearing on the individual's ability to participate in the camping experience. After hungry campers have enjoyed a nutritious meal, they are more alert, are prepared to learn camping skills more rapidly, and can sustain more vigorous activity with less fatigue.

A discussion of the aims and characteristics of various types of camp food services will offer a guide to the development of constructive experiences for campers. Other matters to be considered in this chapter are management personnel, and financing practices; standards for nutrition and for facilities; sanitary procedures in food handling; and the programmatic benefits of camp food service. (See also Chapter 7.)

Three complete meals are served at camp each day. Day camps may offer a variety of foods on an a la carte basis, beverages, a full lunch, or simple cold storage of food brought from home, supplemented by milk or juice. Food service at a residential camp requires substantial meals based upon the recommendations of the National Research Council.

The practical aspects of food procurement, storage, preparation, and service for mass feeding involve a series of steps that are determined by the camp's location. Thus, every camp will have its own inherent problems. There are general procedures that can be applied to almost any camp, however. The kitchen staff needs modern equipment and must have proper working conditions. A fair wage often ensures employment of competent staff. Furthermore, meritorious work must be acknowledged. The camp director who remembers to include the kitchen staff and dining-hall workers in the camp program will increase the loyalty and effort of these workers. Good food service requires the employment of an expert dietician who can hire kitchen staff, formulate their duties, and supervise their functions. In order to contribute to the success of the camp, the food-service director or dietician must perform all the duties outlined for that position in Chapter 2.

Dieticians have expert knowledge of nutrition and health needs. These specialists are cognizant of nutrient and calorie values of foods and of the need for vitamins, minerals, and water in a daily dietary regimen. In preparing menus, the dietician should select food using one of three practical plans. The Basic Seven outline, the Right Foods list, and the Four Broad Foods Group, compiled by the U.S. Department of Agriculture, Bureau of Home Economics, are listed in Appendix D.

A balanced diet should also be palatable and satisfying. Dieticians should plan meals that are nutritious and adequate, and that comprise commonly favorite foods. Meal planning necessitates advance preparation to avoid monotonous tastes and type of foods. The food-service director must take pains to ensure that the food will be well cooked, attractive, tasteful, and appetizing. Meals must be prepared so that food retains its appeal, color, and flavor.

Supervision of Food Service Personnel

All personnel, regardless of function, should be healthy and should be knowledgeable about food sanitation practices. The following applications should be part of every food-service operation in camp:

1. The food-service director must be certain that each food-service employee is free of symptoms of any communicable disease or skin conditions that might contaminate food. The prevention of food-borne infection or poisoning demands daily attention to the health of workers. Food handlers should be able to recognize personal danger signals and be responsible for protecting the health of others. This should be part of the in-service training program for all food-handling staff. Should any kitchen worker be ill, provision should be made for a substitute.

2. Pre-employment medical examinations are required of all food-service employees. Periodic medical checkups should be initiated to ensure that employees are free of any disease that might be transmitted by food.

3. Clean personal habits are mandatory. Employees must wear clean uniforms, hairnets as necessary, and appropriate protective clothing, including disposable polyethylene gloves to prevent food contamination. Good sanitary habits on the part of food-service employees must be instilled as employees are shown how to do their work. Written rules governing food handling should be posted and strictly enforced. The following are among these rules:
   a. Do not report for duty when ill.
   b. Wear a clean uniform while on duty.
   c. Wear appropriate head covering while on duty.
   d. Keep fingernails short and clean.
   e. Wash hands thoroughly and often—always after using the toilet or touching the face, nose, or hair.
   f. Keep work surfaces clean.
   g. Use a separate spoon for each taste testing.
   h. Handle silverware by the handles.
   i. Handle dishes by the rims.
   j. Make sure that all equipment is kept clean.

The best method for instructing workers in the skills and techniques of sanitary and safe food handling practices is through group on-the-job training. This may take the form of staff meetings, where problems are discussed and ideas can be generated. Such meetings promote morale and motivate employees to improve their work performance. Audiovisual aids are also valuable. More important, in-service training encourages workers to ask questions and makes them feel that they are contributing a worthwhile and appreciated service that is beneficial to every person associated with the camp. Stimulating employee morale in this manner is an excellent way of guaranteeing good food-service performance.

Sanitary Practices

Careful application of food-sanitation practices is vital for health protection. Adequate space is required for preparing and serving food, as well as for eating. Kitchens require appropriate equipment, including suitable provision for dishwashing. It is essential that contamination be avoided in all food-handling procedures.

Maintenance of hygienic conditions requires close cooperation among the food-service director, the resident medical specialist, and the camp director. In most states, the health department publishes standards for food sanitation. The camp medical advisor and the food-service director must apply the standards adopted by the health department. Facilities and procedures should be periodically inspected. This is part of the food-service director's responsibility.

Space Requirements

Adequate camp dining facilities include a well-ventilated, clean eating area large enough to ensure comfortable, uncongested conditions (Fig. 5-1). Kitchen space for the preparation of food, storage facilities, a serving area, and a dishwashing area are also necessary. The eating area should be completely separate from the kitchen area.

The dining hall should be large enough to accommodate the total population of the camp in one seating and to provide a minimum of 10 to 12 square feet per person seated at one time. Some very large camps may use a cafeteria style of service in order to accommodate a camper population that is too large to be seated all at once. Under such circumstances, it should not take more than 3 seatings to provide for everyone. The 40-inch square table is probably best for promotion of each food service, table conversation that does not rise to a roar, and a noninstitutional appearance. A table height of 29 inches is satisfactory for most uses.

Construction materials used for walls and floors should be selected in consideration of ease of cleaning as well as decor and aesthetic effect. Table tops, draperies, and wall hangings should be chosen with harmony and a pleasing appearance in mind. Acoustical ceilings, adequate lighting, and proper ventilation will greatly enhance the dining environment.

FIGURE 5-1. Dining hall—clean, well ventilated, and well illuminated.

The Kitchen

An overall allowance of 3 square feet for every complete meal served will offer adequate space. Two square feet per meal will be sufficient for kitchen operations, and ½ square foot of space per meal should be allowed for food storage and service areas. Organization of the various work spaces should accommodate the systematic flow of materials, from the receipt of supplies to their storage, either dry or refrigerated, then to preliminary preparation, final preparation, serving, dishwashing, and, ultimately, garbage disposal.

Specific attention should be given to the construction features of the kitchen. Significant conditions are noise-diminishing acoustical treatment of ceilings; illumination of no less than 30 footcandles at all work stations; hooded equipment with grease filters and exhaust fans over stoves; and separate hoods for dishwashing machines. Walls should be covered with a sanitary finish of glazed structural tile, glazed brick, or waterproof hard plaster. Quarry tile is preferred for flooring. Good control of room temperature is needed, especially for those areas that become hot or humid. Attention to such conditions does much to prevent heat exhaustion from occurring among kitchen workers, who are often exposed to high heat and humidity. All doors and windows must be screened. Construction specifications should eliminate seams in equipment wherever possible. Wall-hung fixtures demand less cleaning time and effort than do floor-mounted fixtures.

At least ¼ cubic foot of refrigeration is required for each complete meal served and an equal capacity of 0°F freezer storage, not including refrigerated storage for half-pints of milk. A walk-in refrigerator is necessary when the meal load is 350, although the meal load could be less, augmented by a reach-in refrigerator. A level passageway connecting the kitchen and the walk-in refrigerator permits dollies and other mobile equipment to be moved in and out.

Dry storage space is best situated on an outside wall so as to obtain fresh-air ventilation through a 2- or 3-foot louvered opening near the ceiling. Metal shelves are preferred to wooden shelves because they are easier to maintain and therefore more sanitary. The elimination of uninsulated pipes and other heat-producing conduits or equipment is necessary if a room temperature between 40°F and 70°F is to be maintained for dry storage of food.

Garbage disposal still requires the use of garbage cans with tightly fitted lids. These waste containers should be emptied and cleaned daily. The kitchen should be equipped with a separate sink for handwashing. Its location should be convenient enough to encourage frequent use. Safety practices require careful consideration. Employees should be instructed to immediately mop floors on which water or food has been spilled. Fire precautions must be taken. Approved fire extinguishers and other emergency equipment must be provided along with instruction in their use.

Food Preparation and Service

Of primary importance to food handling and service is the need for healthy workers. Also essential to the sanitary handling of food are good working practices and clean equipment and utensils. Associated with personal hygiene is the condition of food-processing equipment. A clean environment is ensured by effective housekeeping. The kitchen area should be subjected to a schedule of cleaning with all employees knowing the item, piece of equipment, or area for which they are responsible. If the camp has a custodial staff, it is likely that the janitors will be responsible for cleaning the floors, walls, and other parts of the kitchen. However, the food service workers' responsibilities include such daily jobs as cleaning all power machinery after use, cleaning the stove and refrigeration units at least once a week, and cleaning the storeroom as required.

The food-service director is responsible for ensuring that food is never contaminated before or during preparation. All processed food must be in undamaged containers; staple food items must be uncontaminated; and the produce must be fresh. These conditions are best maintained when food is promptly and adequately refrigerated. Prepared food should be held on steam tables for the shortest time possible. If the camp can seat all of its campers and staff at one time, food can be served piping hot, directly from the stove or oven. If a camp uses a cafeteria method for dispensing food, then steam or hot-food tables can be used.

Dishwashing Practices

Dishes, silverware, and cooking utensils must be thoroughly washed and sanitized either with hot water or with a chemical sanitizing agent. Although some camps may wash equipment by hand, a dishwashing machine is preferable in all situations, and is particularly desirable when the meal load is in excess of 150 meals per day. Two-tank dishwashing machines enable more effective washing and sanitizing than one-tank machines. All machines must have attached metal tables of a size sufficient for loading the dirty dish racks and draining the clean dishes. A prerinse sink or built-in prerinse section to the machine is quite effective. Water temperatures should never be less than 140°F during the washing period, nor less than 180°F during the rinse phase. Typical machines provides 45 seconds for washing and 15 to 20 seconds for rinsing.

Alternative Food Service Methods

The all-paper service now being used in many public institutions is an excellent substitute for washable dishes and utensils. If investments have not already been made in dishwashing machine equipment, the use of paper provides an economical and sanitary system that eliminates dishwashing problems. Before a paper service is initiated, however, the means of disposing of increased amounts of waste paper should be considered.

Purchasing Food Supplies

The need to establish a sound business association with wholesale food suppliers is obvious. Guided by the dietician's knowledge of essential foods and the quantity that will probably be consumed at each meal, a basic amount of food can be ordered. Naturally, the quantity of various foods to be maintained will be regulated by the availability and quality of storage and refrigerator units.

The camp should secure bids from several wholesale firms for the supply of food, including canned foods, produce, and meat. Investing in frozen-food lockers to hold perishable items, especially meat, is logical: Foods purchased in large quantities are less expensive, and greater variety in cuts is available when meat is purchased in quantity. In fact, when frozen foods are used, a wide variety of nourishing and tasty meals can be supplied to the camp on a routine basis.

Food Packaging Plans

New food service systems have been tested and found efficient and economical. Many institutions and private firms provide frozen meals to employees. These nourishing, tasty meals are cooked almost instantly in microwave ovens. The precooked frozen foods are subject to intense heat for a short period and then served. As many as 400 or more meals can be served in a very short time by few staff, depending only upon the number and capaciousness of the microwave ovens. The container in which the food is cooked serves as both plate and tray, plastic cutlery is used, and everything is completely disposed of after the meal is finished. In some institutions, almost total automation has replaced the need for food handlers, dishwashers, and dining hall staff. Food is prepared and frozen. Infrared-ray units or microwave ovens cook the food, which is distributed cafeteria fashion. The eaters simply drop the tray down a chute, where choppers reduce the leavings to a fine powder; there is no garbage disposal problem. Any remains can either be used for fertilizer or burned in an incinerator. Food costs for this program are remarkably small because a great deal of labor is eliminated in this process. As more efficient food-packaging processes and cooking systems enter the market, modern camps will be able to adapt them to meet their individual needs.

Food Inventory

The management of all food supplies is the responsibility of the dietician. Food for immediate preparation should be issued for cooking; other supplies should remain locked up. A perpetual inventory system should be implemented. This will accurately show what is on hand at any given time and is also useful for computing per capita food costs each day. Food costs can be determined by adding the weekly food bill and the value of inventory at the beginning of the week. The value of the end-of-the-week food inventory is subtracted from the sum. To determine the per capita cost of meals, the foregoing figure is divided by the number of meals served in one week. In order to find the per capita cost each day, the per capita cost of each meal is multiplied by three.

Supplies delivered to camp must be itemized and accurately recorded, this is best done by comparing the delivered order against the purchase order. Duplicates of delivery invoices, signed by authorized personnel, should be on file in the central office for later checking.

Dining-Hall Operation

The camp dining hall should be an intrinsic part of the program facilities. Time spent in the dining hall can be filled with fun, satisfaction, and good food. Camps should attempt to create a pleasant, leisurely atmosphere of good companionship at mealtimes. Mealtimes should not seem like a gap in program activities, but must blend imperceptibly into the overall program. There should not be any rush or excitement however; overstimulating events are better postponed for after meals. A table comprises each bunk and its counselor. Food dispensation to each table should be routine, orderly, and quick. Hot foods must be served hot, and cold foods, cold. As usual, the counselor plays an important role in maintaining good conduct and a happy atmosphere at table (see Chapter 14). Announcements, songs, stunts, or entertainment can wait until the conclusion of the meal or can be started during dessert. No campers are excused from the table individually, the entire bunk is dismissed at a signal from the counselor when all have finished eating. In some camps, counselors indicate to the supervisor when their tables have finished eating, and then each table is dismissed in order.

Cookouts

Food supplies, preparation, and service are still important when the schedule includes such activities as trips, hikes, picnics, or outings. The same attention to detail and coordination with responsible personnel are required whether meals are served in the mess hall or on the trail. The dietician will be invaluable in helping to plan outside meals. She can show counselors quick, easy methods of cooking and baking using the natural resources of flora and fauna found in the region. The dietician can also pack food supplies for trips. Certain dietary staples must be included in the food pack, but if the trip is extended, then supplementary food gathered from streams and fields will be needed. (More about this aspect of camp life will be discussed in Chapter 17.)

chapter 6

Camp Maintenance

Maintenance of camp property, facilities, and equipment ensures a clean, attractive, safe environment for those who reside at or visit camp. A sound maintenance program is an essential factor in preventing or reducing the number of accidental injuries incurred by campers and camp personnel. The essence of good maintenance is the encouragement of a climate favorable to sanitary, wholesome, agreeable living, with effective and economical use of the needed and available resources. Although a variety of functions must be performed, good housekeeping cannot be looked upon as a special service added only at certain times. Maintenance is integral to daily living at camp.

The task of keeping camp living spaces, sanitary facilities, and activity areas in a usable condition is a complex responsibility affecting the health, safety, comfort, and well-being of all those who use the camp. Duties related to maintenance of all physical property are discussed in this chapter. *Housekeeping* comprises the care and management of the interior environment of camp property and the provision of equipment and services at this property; *physical maintenance* is the sum of all external conditions and influences at a camp site that affect the life and development of those who reside at or use the facility. Under these definitions, the chief elements of plant maintenance can be characterized as (1) sanitation, (2) safety, (3) prevention, and (4) care.

Good housekeeping greatly reduces the incidence of infection brought about by contaminated drinking fountains or sanitary facilities. We have already discussed the need to restrict or eliminate pest infestations, which are inimical to the health of all those living at camp. For the most part, housekeeping involves the washing, sweeping, dusting, and mopping of walls, floors, sills, and fixtures, which can become germ breeding grounds. The thorough scrubbing of toilets, drinking fountains, shower stalls, and living quarters will promote better health conditions and reduce the likelihood of communicable diseases.

Maintenance Objectives

The chief objectives of maintenance are as follows:

1. To extend the useful life of property. This includes all premises, tools, facilities, structures, paraphernalia, equipment, or materials.
2. To maximize the availability and accessibility of all premises and whatever contents are to be used for participation or observation.
3. To ensure the carrying capacity of all facilities.
4. To make available and ready for use all equipment that contributes to the safe enjoyment of activity.
5. To ensure that all emergency equipment is operational and available for use.
6. To ensure the safety of all users of the premises.

In order to carry out these objectives, every camp must routinely perform certain maintenance practices, keep records that deal with such practices, and then regularly monitor all units of the camp, both formally and informally. A number of methods can be used to determine whether or not facilities are well maintained and ready for participants. Among these are formal inspections and informal, or nonstandardized, observations. Both aspects are significant to everyone's safety if they are developed with the cooperation and support of the workers involved.

Formal Inspections

Formal inspections are performed routinely by supervisory personnel. Schedules and suspense files are kept at a central administrative office for easy reference so that all elements of the physical plant are checked regularly. When a safety deficit is noted, it is either corrected immediately or brought to the attention of those who can authorize the necessary repairs or replacements. Such inspections also prevent deterioration of structures and facilities by eliminating minor problems before they escalate.

Informal Inspections

Informal, or nonroutine, maintenance inspections are performed by all personnel. This means that all employees are responsible for observing those aspects of the physical plant with which they come in contact. Because safety is a primary concern, all employees should recognize potential hazards in sections where they work and report any deficiencies in structures, equipment, or other assets.

Maintenance report forms can serve both to facilitate accurate reporting and to officially notify supervisors of safety problems. Maintenance records are also an excellent method for documenting the extent to which the camp makes an effort to ensure safe premises. Maintenance inspection records can show that all facilities are regularly monitored, that deficiencies are noted, and that corrective actions are taken in a timely manner.

Preventive Maintenance

The prevention or inhibition of deterioration of the physical plant and its contents should be part of every maintenance program. Maintenance personnel must be employed on a continuous basis to forestall excessive wear and expensive repairs. The objective of preventive maintenance is to obtain the longest possible life from the camp's premises and assets. Work must be attentively planned and scheduled so that minor repairs and replacement can be made before further damage or deterioration occurs.

Preventive maintenance can do much to offset the failure rates of tools, machines, and equipment that might prove dangerous to users. Outside preventive maintenance can prevent roads, bridges, paths, and other facilities from being eroded, broken up, or washed away. Steps can be taken to shore up, fill in, or channel water (where necessary) so that the accessory facilities do not become the source of accidents. In buildings and other structures, care must be taken of mechanical parts, roofs, floors, accessways, hallways, and surfaces that receive heavy use. It is just as important to make sure that a roof on a cabin is well maintained as it is to resurface outdoor court and game areas. Filling in potholes in an athletic field may prevent a camper from twisting an ankle or breaking a leg. Stopping leaks before they occur may prevent a camper from slipping, falling, and experiencing a traumatic injury that could result in litigation. Preventive maintenance is part of sound managerial policy. Preventing physical plant deficiencies will do much to reduce the risk inherent in nearly every feature of camp activity.

Safety Maintenance

Camps are responsible for providing safe premises. The capacity of a building or other structure to support hundreds of persons assembled to participate in or observe an activity requires facilities that are designed and maintained for safety. Activity areas and facilities can be inspected daily by maintenance personnel and counselors who are assigned to instruct or supervise specific activities or areas. Supervisors can perform more formal, regular, and standard inspections. No inspection should be superficial.

Accidents should be recorded and analyzed, along with information about their cause, so that steps can be taken to eliminate the source, especially if the injury was produced by the physical failure of property. Employees may be oblivious to the existence of hazards, despite their exposure to inservice training and despite administrators' continual requests for awareness. When this happens, an accident will eventually occur because of an unfortunate coincidence of time, place, behavior, and the uncorrected danger. In many instances, maintenance personnel performing a routine job may be the only ones in contact with an existing or potential hazard. If they simply leave the hazard and fail to take corrective action, a camper is almost certain to blunder into it, with disastrous results.

GENERAL MAINTENANCE PROGRAMS

Camp maintenance is vital to the health and safety of all who use the camp. When a structure is built, an accessway constructed, or a lakefront property developed, the camp administration is obliged to maintain it. The fundamental presumption is that the camp's facilities are properly maintained for their expected use. Perhaps campers do not think about whether or not camp authorities have taken steps to ensure the safety of the premises, but it is probable that parents will have taken such ideas into consideration when selecting the camp. Counselors and other camp employees must assume some responsibility for the camp's maintenance, although for the most part this function is delegated to the maintenance staff.

Maintenance Fundamentals for Fire Prevention

Good housekeeping is one of the soundest precautions against fires at camp. It is usually performed by maintenance personnel under the direction of the supervisor. The importance of this precaution can best be understood if one considers some maintenance functions that affect fire hazard; these include, but are not restricted to, cleaning, waste and rubbish removal, incineration, storage, care of supplies, and proper handling of flammable liquids.

Housekeeping. Fire is less likely to begin in a clean structure than in a dirty one. All waste accumulations such as paper, discarded bags, cardboard, wood shavings, and other combustible litter must be removed from the premises every day. If these waste materials are burned, precautions should be taken to prevent the fire from getting out of control. (See also Chapter 7.)

Storage. Storage areas should be routinely emptied of items that are no longer usable such as equipment that is in need of repair or is in such deteriorated condition that it is beyond salvage. Operating supplies that have become useless should also be collected and discarded. Housekeeping in areas that house the dramatic arts activities is particularly effective as a fire-prevention method. Many materials are stored in these rooms, including flats or set decorations, objects made of flimsy fabric, drapes and curtains, and decorations used for camp crafts, art, festivals, or other activities. These items should be flameproofed before they are installed, used, or stored.

Combustibles. Flammable liquids and other substances should meet minimum requirements for maintenance, demonstration, or treatment. These products should be stored in Underwriter's Laboratory (UL)–approved containers that hold no more than one quart each and then placed in metal cabinets.

Fire-control equipment. Adequate maintenance of fire-protection equipment adds immeasurably to the safety of camp property. To be effective, all fire-protection equipment must be functional when needed. This requires thorough inspection and adequate upkeep so that all mechanisms are guaranteed operational.

Facility Inspection Reports

For ease of administration as well as to clearly delineate areas and items to be evaluated, camps may provide standard forms which can be used when the premises are checked. Each item has a space where the inspector can put a mark to denote satisfactory or unsatisfactory conditions. Reasons must be specified when unsatisfactory ratings are given. A copy of the completed inspection report is given to the individual responsible for the area or facility, and a second copy is forwarded to the administrator supervising the division. Items that affect safety require immediate correction.

The typical facility inspection report will probably contain the following items:

1. Physical Condition of Exterior Premises
    a. *Approach roadway.* Litter free, in good repair.
    b. *Approach walkway.* Litter free in good repair.
    c. *Parking spaces.* Litter free, properly lined. Traffic and parking control.
    d. *Signs.* Conspicuous, legible, good condition.
    e. *Illumination.* Sufficient for purpose at walkways, steps, parking lot. In good repair.
    f. *Structural condition.* Evidence of good maintenance practices. Walls and steps in good repair. Gutters and drains operable. Roof sound.
    g. *Grounds.* Litter free, grass mowed, debris removed, pot holes filled.
    h. *Fencing.* In good repair.
2. Physical Condition of Interior of Building or Structure
    a. *Structural adequacy.* Walls, partitions, ceilings, stairs, floors, windows sound and in good repair. Ventilation good. Corridors, passageways clear and free of obstructions.
    b. *Signs.* Conspicuously posted, information clear.
    c. *Bulletin boards.* Informative, neat, attractive.
3. Safety, Security, and Control
    a. *Emergency equipment.* Fire extinguisher servicing current. First aid case equipped and accessible. Security and fire alarm in working order and test schedule followed. Personnel aware of emergency procedures. Drills scheduled and run.
    b. *Control barriers.* Interior ropes, gate locks, and doors in good condition and properly operating. Keys appropriately distributed and accounted for. Proper visitor control. Personnel coverage adequate for the responsibility.
    c. *Hazard prevention.* Electrical distribution systems, fuses, switch charts, and controls accessible. Fire doors closed. Smoking regulations defined, posted, and enforced. Dangerous substances properly protected and stored. No accumulation of rubbish or other debris. Electrical cables in proper condition. Outlets not overloaded. Proper maintenance practices for floors and walkways. Emergency exits properly illuminated and prepared for use. Supplies, tools, and equipment stored in a neat, orderly, and protected manner. All machines in proper working order, guards in

correct positions, machines serviced as scheduled. Machines locked when not in use.
d. *Visitor control.* Interior traffic directions and control. Proper crowd and group control.
e. *Accessibility.* Ramps and other barrier free accessways available for disabled persons. Guard rails and other assistance available, uncluttered, and in good condition.

The facility inspection chart is simply one tool that can be used for recording routine inspections. It can, with variations, be applied to any element of the physical plant operated by any camp. The more extensive the buildings and grounds, the greater the necessity for maintenance management and regular inspection to eliminate environmental risks.

In-Service Training for Maintenance Staff

Just as there is the need to orient and educate maintenance personnel about their functions and responsibilities for the upkeep, cleanliness, and repair of the physical facilities that compose the camp's property, so too is there a need for periodic retraining for job and camper safety. Maintenance is primarily concerned with preserving the outdoor environment in as close to its original state as is possible. It is also concerned with prolonging the life of physical assets, such as buildings, structures, equipment, and tools, whose durability can be enhanced by regular repair, refurbishment, or replacement of worn or used parts.

Maintenance is responsible for the appearance of property. Thus, public relations becomes one of the functions of maintenance operations. An environment that is attractive, clean, and inviting promotes good will and stimulates participation and support. Safety is another essential aspect of maintenance management, as well as an integral part of public relations. This function requires reiteration until safety habits become instilled within all personnel. Safety training may be divided into two components: job-related risks and environmental hazards.

As general policy, each maintenance worker should receive approximately 1 hour of safety training each month. This training can be delivered in the form of group instruction, visual aids, informal supervisory conferences, or any practical method of communicating safety information. The camp maintenance division should establish a written schedule for the program, listing instructors, locations, and the amount of time allotted to inservice safety training. Among the topics to be included are the following:

1. Vehicle operation and safety
2. Equipment and machinery operation and safety
3. Chemical safety
4. Explosive handling and safety (where applicable)
5. Lifting and reaching, hoists and cranes
6. Use of ladders, scaffolds, and staging
7. Storage areas

8. Flammable and combustible liquids
9. Gas cylinders
10. Protective clothing and equipment
11. Fire prevention
12. Electricity
13. Traffic control, warning signs and devices
14. First aid
15. Camper safety
16. Safety consciousness

In-service training should be offered by qualified instructors who, when appropriate, have certificates or licenses that attest to their expertise for instructing such classes.

In-service safety training should do much to promote appropriate attitudes and awareness among maintenance workers. Maintenance workers should become aware of actual or potential hazards that they might observe in the course of their daily functions. Maintenance workers have an obvious responsibility for checking on the condition of indoor and outdoor equipment and field surfaces, as do counselors. However, maintenance workers can perform an invaluable service to the camp by noticing potential dangers that, if not corrected in time, might lead to serious accidents and injuries. Thus, in-service training on the subject of camper safety should make maintenance personnel aware of the following:

Recreational Facilities

1. Storage areas should be uncluttered. Equipment should be replaced following use. Although this is a primary responsibility for counselors, maintenance personnel can be of assistance as well.
2. Fire extinguishers should be prominently displayed and first aid kits checked regularly to see that they are filled. Areas around facilities need to be monitored for litter, broken glass, and other debris. Maintenance crews will clear such hazards whenever necessary.
3. Regular observations of playgrounds, game fields, and other areas should be made by maintenance workers, and reports of unsafe conditions should be delivered immediately to appropriate supervisors for required action.
4. Illumination should be checked to see that it is adequate.
5. Nonskid material on flooring in heavily used areas should be checked for wear and replacement.
6. All maintenance personnel should be conscious of actual or potential dangers at the various sites operated by the camp. Any defects that can be corrected on the spot should be. Reports of corrections and of dangers that require further remediation should be recorded and transmitted for action.

Recreational Areas

1. Keeping grounds in proper condition is a significant function of the maintenance division. This is necessary not only for attractiveness, but for safety. Turfed areas should be well maintained, with surface unevenness reduced to a minimum. Nonturfed game areas should be even and free of obstructions.

2. Maintenance personnel who are responsible for outlying places should be thoroughly familiar with the areas and aware of natural or manmade hazards such as abandoned wells, sink holes, and ravines. Such areas should be posted and prohibited from access.

3. Routine maintenance operations, such as grass cutting, should be performed when campers are not using the area.

4. Maintenance equipment or machinery should never be left where campers are playing. If heavy machinery such as earth-moving equipment or trucks must be used, the schedule should restrict camper usage until the work is completed.

5. No tool or ladder should ever be left where employees may trip on it or where adventurous campers may take the opportunity to experiment.

6. Trash and other debris should be removed in order to prevent injuries from protruding nails, glass, or other obstructions.

7. Equipment that is rented or leased should be regularly checked for defects, and repairs should be made when necessary. Thus, rowboats, canoes, oarlocks, and paddles may require sanding, varnishing, caulking, or other conditioning to remedy worn or weakened spots.

8. Beach groins, jetties, piers, or docks should be regularly inspected for signs of erosion, corrosion, damage, or other natural or man-made wear. Replacement, refurbishment, or repair should be made as necessary.

chapter 7

Camping Safety

In attempting to provide the safest possible environment for campers, the director must act in a most professional manner. By undertaking a comprehensive survey of the areas, facilities, equipment, and resources that the camp owns, operates, or employs, the director can initiate and develop a safety plan.

The purpose of a safety plan is to provide direction for the implementation of a safety program that produces specific action to alleviate or mitigate both environmental and inherent dangers. Moreover, the plan includes the development of practices and procedures determined to be in keeping with the professional standards of the camping field.

The comprehensive safety plan is designed to ensure that every reasonable and prudent action has been taken to administer the camp for the betterment of the campers and to protect them from injuries that might occur in the course of their residence and recreational participation. To this end, the camp management commits itself to perform whatever functions are necessary to prevent campers from assuming unnecessary or unacceptable risk.

Although the ACA has become the mainstay for advancing the camping movement and, in the process, has become the chief advocate for improving health, safety, and personnel standards throughout the field, there are still substandard operators at work. They function on such a low level that campers are endangered just by being at their facilities. Even in camps that are very well run, accidents can and do happen. For the most part, these accidents are spontaneous, unforeseen occurrences for which no one can be prepared. There are occasions however, when even the best-intentioned camp administrators or staff members permit themselves a momentary lapse, sometimes with disastrous results. In the most notorious instances, campers have been killed because those in charge failed to act in a reasonable and prudent manner. Camping accidents run the gamut from mild poisonings by noxious weeds to death by drowning. Some camps operate in remote areas, not within easy traveling distance to treatment centers, or have programs that send campers out on high-risk trips. All these factors promote the possibility of serious injury.

SAFETY POLICY

The formulation of safety policy for the camp is based upon an understanding of the need to protect the life and welfare of campers. Therefore, the camp is *committed* to the idea that a primary professional obligation of the organization is to reduce or eliminte the prospect of serious accidental injury to campers and employees. The camp administration adheres to the concept that safety is the prevention of accidents as well as the avoidance of excessive personal injury and/or property damage that might result from accidents. Camp administrators perform all necessary actions to interrupt accident-producing sequences of events or to modify such events. Plans and procedures must be drawn up and followed so that all camp employees recognize and promptly deal with any hazards encountered as part of their job responsibilities.

Camp administrators should expect all employees to exert every effort in carrying out their responsibilities as outlined by the safety program and activated by the policy. Safety is vital to campers' well-being; it is therefore important to express all safety concerns in a positive manner. Thus, the camp must assess the risks inherent in the activities it operates and the areas and facilities it uses in order to minimize the probability of an accident. The camp can reduce risks without diminishing the excitement and adventure of most camp activities. A comprehensive program of camping opportunities should be maintained while minimizing or eliminating the causes of accidental injuries and potential damage to property.

CAMPING SAFETY CONCERNS

Since camps are situated in the outdoors, there are likely to be natural hazards, which must be recognized by camp administrators. Electrical storms, hidden ravines, dead standing trees, various poisonous plants, stinging and biting insects, venomous reptiles, and dangerous animals all contribute to the attraction and risk of the outdoors. There are also artificially contrived dangers from carelessly thrown matches, artificially created wells, sharp tools, and a number of activities in which injuries may occur.

Typical Hazards

Many camp accidents could easily be avoided if proper care were taken. Camp records and regulatory-agency books are full of reports of camper-related injuries that need not have happened. Risk factors can easily be eliminated if the camp administrator requires conformity to safety policies. The physical plant should be free of attractive nuisances. Broken glass, rusty nails, tools, equipment, and other potentially hazardous objects that tend to attract children should be removed. Machinery must be properly stored. Dangerous substances, such as lead-based paint, insecticides, or toxic chemicals, must be stored in secure places.

Safety Instruction

Instruction of campers and staff in routine safety precautions may be the best possible solution to the safety problem. It is vital that all campers, staff, and visitors know standard safety measures and act accordingly. Because camps deal, for the most part, with immature children, such safety lessons must be reiterated at every opportunity.

As in all things at camp, the counselor is the chief functionary to whose supervision the camper's safety is entrusted. The counselor's reasonable and prudent actions are the camp's most important line of defense against accidents, injuries, and camper infractions of safe conduct. The counselor stands in the same relationship to the camp as the teacher does to the school. The two functions are similar in almost all ways, and the liability is the same.

Among the areas that particularly influence camper safety are such activities as crafts, waterfront sports, riflery or archery, horseback riding, off-site trips, and other sports. In addition, concern for the safe handling of food, a potable and protected water supply, sanitary facilities, medical assistance, transportation, shelter, and maintenance operations requires close attention so that risks are reduced or eliminated. It is the camp director's responsibility to institute sensible safety practices, thereby ensuring that avoidable incidents leading to injury or fatality are controlled.[1]

Camp Crafts and Workshop

The workshop may have tools, chemicals, and power equipment that should be used only with adequate instruction and under the immediate supervision of a specialist competent to handle them. Rules and regulations governing the shop will deal with tool use, equipment and materials storage, fire safety, and proper behavior.

Campers who participate in camp craft activities must receive instruction in the proper use of axes, knives, and fire. Axes must never be left lying around. They should be either stored in a locked container or secured with the rest of the tools in the shop. Knives are handled in the same manner. Campers must practice the proper stance, swing, and cut of axes or hatchets. The safe use of knives must be taught. The use of fire for protection or food preparation should be preceded by instruction in how to start, maintain, and put out fires, and about which type of fire is most effective for cooking, baking, heating, or drying. Above all, campers must be shown how to extinguish fires.

[1]J. R. Udall, "Thinking About Safety," *Camping Magazine* (January 1984), 38–41.

Aquatic Areas

Aquatic safety standards have been devised by the American Red Cross for the operation of various water activity facilities. Long and practical experience has determined their water safety programs. Water safety personnel play the major part in minimizing or eliminating aquatic area hazards. Competent personnel assigned to direct and control swimming and boating activities are the surest means for preventing avoidable accidents. When well-trained personnel are given resonsibility and authority to set up rules and conduct for the use of aquatic facilities, the dangers to campers almost disappear. Whether the camp has access to a lake, river, ocean, or private swimming pool makes little difference. Camper monitoring systems and safety rules must be initiated and enforced. Of course, waterfront personnel must also check the aquatic facility. They must investigate water-source bottoms for weeds, muck, dropoffs, and pot holes. They must protect campers against strong currents or tides. They must be alert for rocky outcroppings and pier pilings. In fact, it is their resposibility to bring such dangerous conditions to the attention of the camp director and to recommend discontinuing use of the area until the hazards are eliminated. If the dangers cannot be eliminated, then other facilities will have to be used.

The waterfront staff should be supplemented by counselors who are skilled in diving, swimming, and water safety instruction. Necessary equipment to prevent drownings may include buoys, rings, tow ropes, long aluminum poles, inhalator devices, and a lifeboat, surfboard, or catamaran for water rescues. However, the best preparation for preventing water accidents will be highly competent staff. Aquatic facility regulations apply to all those who use the area. These rules range from restrictions on night swimming, except under certain supervised circumstances, to limitations on the length of time a camper is allowed to be continuously in the water during a given swimming period.

All forms of boating—whether rowing, sculling, canoeing, or sailing—should be subject to strict rules and regulations governing the use of small craft, the wearing of personal flotation devices, the skill of users, and previous instruction received by the camper. Only those campers who have been instructed in the care and handling of small craft should be permitted to use boating equipment. Boating safety rules as promulgated by the American Red Cross or the U.S. Coast Guard must be adhered to without exception.

More specific rules are as follows:

1. All activities, including but not limited to swimming, boating, canoeing, sailing, scuba diving, and water skiing, will be under the direction of a qualified waterfront director.
2. A ratio of one waterfront counselor to eight campers will be maintained at all times.
3. A method for supervising persons in the water will be established and enforced.

4.   A buddy system or other checking method will be established and enforced, and will be conducted not less than every ten minutes.

5.   While on duty, the waterfront staff will not engage in any activity that diverts their attention from campers.

6.   A written plan will be published so that all staff know what to do in case of an emergency at the waterfront.

7.   Watercraft activities will be conducted during daylight hours only. A vest-type coastguard-approved life preserver will be provided and worn at all times by each occupant of a watercraft.

8.   No nonswimmer will be permitted in a boat, canoe, or sailboat, nor will they be allowed to water ski. Campers will wear vest-type coastguard-approved life preservers while water skiing.

9.   Swimming after sundown is prohibited in lakes, rivers, or ocean and will be permitted in pools only if adequate lighting is provided.

10.   During a boating period, a lifeguard will patrol the watercraft area in a life-boat. The boat docking area or activity area will be separate from the swimming area. The swimming area will not be used for launching or stopping of water skiers.

11.   Life-saving equipment shall be provided for all waterfront activity and be immediately available in case of emergency. The equipment will be kept in good repair and will include, but not be limited to, a buoy, a reach pole, ropes, and a rescue boat. This equipment will be available at all times for boating or swimming activities on a lake, pond, river, or ocean.

12.   Any swimming facility or natural bathing place will be approved by the appropriate state agency and will be operated and used in accordance with any special conditions that may be specified in writing by the agency.

13.   No camp will maintain a natural swimming or bathing area unless careful soundings of water depth and location of eddies and pools and determinations of the presence of dangerous currents, sunken logs, rocks, and obstructions in the stream or river have been made.

14.   The camp operator will post signs indicating the water depth, the location of eddies, and the presence and direction of currents or tides. These signs will be placed and maintained in the water during swimming season.

The Rifle Range

Range safety procedures are determined by the specialist in charge of this activity. Specific rules for the instruction of campers must be strictly observed. No individual should participate in shooting activities unless a qualified and authorized specialist is present. All weapons should remain under lock and key until an organized range activity is scheduled. No one should be permitted to bring a personal pistol or rifle to camp. All bullets should be accounted for and each expended shell should be counted and deleted from the inventory of rounds.

When campers are on the range, National Rifle Association safety regulations should be in effect. Rifles should be pointed up into the air and down range when not actually being fired. A loaded weapon should never be pointed anywhere except at the target. An assistant instructor should be assigned to each shooter to ensure that this rule is carried out. Orders by the range instructor should be complied with instantly. Before firing is allowed, participants must be thoroughly indoctrinated in safety precautions and given detailed instruction on aiming, positioning, and firing. Range safety signals should be well known and recognized by all range users.

The situation which follows need not have occurred. Issuance of poorly conditioned equipment is one of the prime reasons for actions based on negligence.

One incident concerned a 12-year-old boy who attended a camp located at Peach Lake in New York. The camp offered riflery as one of its activities. A rifle range was constructed away from the normal flow of traffic. Riflery consisted of a single-shot 22-caliber rifle with bolt action. Rifles were placed on firing-line mats with the chambers clear and bolts open and in an upright position.

The campers were instructed to take a prone position. Each camper was issued five rounds. Target shooting then commenced. Rifles were loaded on command of the counselor-in-charge. When the campers were ready, they were given permission to fire.

One of the campers was issued an old Winchester whose bolt continually jammed. A counselor-in-training (CIT) went over to assist the camper. The CIT picked up the rifle and in doing so turned it slightly so as to obtain a better look. The rifle fired and wounded the camper in the leg. A major artery was severed, and the boy's leg was subsequently amputated.

The case was settled for $95,000, on the basis that the camp's insurance was for $100,000 coverage. The insurance company's attorney settled the case with the claimant's attorney; the former knew that the monetary settlement would have been far larger had the case actually gone to trial. The responsibility for issuing an old, poorly conditioned rifle clearly rested with the camp. The camp discontinued riflery as an activity in the aftermath of the incident.

The Archery Range

Archery ranges should be relatively isolated, well marked, and protected so that stray arrows will do no damage. The shooting range should be banked at the area of the archery butts; this prevents loss of arrows and eliminates the possibility of injury to a person inadvertently walking behind the targets. All archers must be cautioned that stepping over the shooting line while others are shooting is not only a courtesy lapse, but is also very dangerous. The archery-range supervisor must make this rule clear and enforce it.

Overdrawing can be dangerous because the arrow might be shot into the hand. This can be avoided by making sure that arrows are of a length suitable for the individual archer's draw. Archers must be instructed to keep their arrows toward the target butts when shooting. The commands of the range supervisor must be obeyed instantly. If a cease-fire is ordered, archers should immediately relax the draw and unnock the arrow. The wearing of protective gear, including a forearm guard and finger or hand guards, should be mandatory.

Bows, bowstrings, and arrows should be examined for signs of wear before any shooting occurs. Injuries from snapped bows can be avoided if tackle is appropriately inspected. Arrows that have unaligned feathers or warped shafts can cause potentially dangerous shooting inaccuracies. In most cases, care of equipment will prevent damage or injury and permit better shooting performance. Although there is no one organization that sets nationally recognized instructor standards or certification, a number of associations publish archery standards which may be used as guides; the National Field Archery Association is one such organization.

Sports and Games

Minor injuries such as bumps, bruises, and small cuts may occur from time to time during the course of the numerous physical activities conducted at camp. Such injuries simply cannot be prevented; they are part of the normal course of activity and are to be anticipated. It is the uncommon or major injury that is to be avoided if it is foreseeable. Numerous major accidents result from carelessness, inattention, or other lapses of judgment. Camp records, insurance claims, and lawyers' files are replete with the incidents that have tainted the camping season. Some injuries have been severe enough to permanently disable the victim; others have been fatal. That is why it is so important for counselors to be especially vigilant and to be chosen for competence and intelligence.

The following two incidents are atypical of the kinds of accidents one sees at camp. However, the extraordinary sets of circumstances in these two cases illustrate the need to check campers' fitness for participation and emphasize some of the details that may have to be examined.

A 14-year-old boy from Texas attended a baseball camp at Park State Teacher's College in New Jersey. The youth attended batting practice while wearing eyeglasses, which were prescribed for his poor eyesight. The counselor, a college graduate and certified physical education teacher, was pitching to the boy at a speed that he thought appropriate for this camper to hit.

The camper did hit several balls and felt that he could hit pitches at this speed. On the final pitch, the camper hit a foul tip, causing the ball to rebound from the bat and strike him in the face, shattering his eyeglasses. He sustained severe eye injuries and was subsequently evaluated as being legally blind in the eye. In Texas, eyeglasses that are not shatter-proof can be sold and dispensed. If the eyeglasses had been shatter-proof, it is unlikely that the injury would have occurred.

This kind of accident is foreseeable. If a baseball is pitched at a camper who is wearing glasses, there is every reason to believe that a foul tip could result in the glasses being knocked off or broken. However, it is not possible to have foreseen that this camper was wearing glasses that were not shatter-proof.

The attorney for the defendant felt that the liability was somewhat questionable but thought that it favored the camper in this instance. If the case had gone to a jury, the camper would have gotten a decision in his favor. Under these circumstances, the defendants settled the case out of court for a sum of $10,000.

Another incident involved an 11-year-old boy at a camp located in Gilford, New York. During a game of football, the ball was thrown to the camper and may have hit him in the chest, although this was not ascertained. The child died almost immediately. It was subsequently learned that this boy had had a weak heart since birth. The heart was ruptured at the time of the accident. Whether the football caused any injury is unclear, although that is thought not to have been the case. Rather, the attorney for the company that insured the camp believed that the boy's heart "simply ruptured and he died."

No action was brought against the camp as a result of this incident. The insurance company's files were closed. The insurance company's attorney made the point that if in fact the child did have some heart defect, it should have been brought out prior to his admission to camp so that proper precautions could have been taken.

In both of these cases it was taken for granted that the unexpected could not happen. After all, who can foresee that a child's glasses will not be shatter-proof? In this instance, a routine check to determine whether or not eyeglass-wearing campers had been fitted with shatter-proof glasses would have prevented both injury and loss. In the latter case, a confidential report to the appropriate camp authority might have averted a tragedy. Good intentions are simply insufficient. Sound safety practices must be applied universally.

Horseback Riding

Qualified instructors must be responsible for supervising and directing horseback riding in camp. Basic instruction for beginners, as well as advanced instruction, requires a capable person in charge. An enclosed ring can be used for novice riders. Trails and open fields may serve the more experienced riders. All campers must be able to demonstrate sufficient control of the mount before being allowed to proceed to the next stage of advancement. The careful instructor will attempt to match available horses to the rider's capacity and level of skill.

The stabling of horses is also important if this program is to be successful. Where camps maintain horses on their own property, stables must be located far enough away from campers' eating and sleeping facilities that noisome odors and potential health problems will be avoided. Stable areas must be well drained and cleaned regularly, and the animal's food supply must be protected from vermin or insect infestations. All riding equipment must be maintained in good condition and inspected daily.

Although there is no nationally recognized organization for the certification of horseback-riding instructors, a number of riding schools do exist and some are associated with institutions of higher education. The latter agencies offer courses in horseback riding.

Routinely, the following practices should apply to horse use in a camp activity:

1. All activities, including but not limited to trail riding, jumping, and packing, will be under the direction of a qualified riding director.
2. Whenever horses are being ridden, saddled, loaded, or groomed, there will

be at least one wrangler present to instruct and supervise. The required counselor-to-camper ratio will be maintained at all times.

3. Horses will be appropriate to the campers' abilities.

4. No camper will be allowed in the area unless a staff member is present.

5. There will be no more than one rider per horse. Horses will not be allowed to run, or be driven, freely in or through the camp.

6. A hard hat or helmet must be worn when jumping and when on trail rides; such head gear is recommended at all other times.

7. Minimum first-aid supplies will be carried by all groups riding a mile or more from the center of the camp.

Water Supply

A dependable supply of potable water sufficient to supply 50 gallons of water per person per day should be available. Where pit or chemical toilets are used, this figure can be reduced to 30 gallons per person per day. Primitive camps may not have a water supply. The water-supply system should then be restricted to the following water sources:

Whenever water is obtained from other than an approved public water system, the following will be in order:

1. Wells

a. *Location.* All ground water sources will be located at safe distances from sources of contamination as follows:

Pit privies—25 feet
Sewer or septic tanks—50 feet
Subsurface sewage disposal field or seepage pit—100 feet
Cesspools—150 feet.

Wells will not be dug in areas subject to flooding, unless the casing protrudes substantially above known flood levels or an adequately sealed submersible-type pump installation is used.

b. *Construction.* All wells will be provided with an impervious casing that can exclude subsurface and ground waters that are contaminated or potentially contaminated. If dug wells are constructed, there will be no construction joint within 10 feet of the surface. Dug wells may not draw water from strata into which sewage is being discharged.

All pumps located over wells will be mounted on the well casing, a pump foundation, or a pump stand, so that the top of the well is effectively sealed. Where the pump unit is not located over the well, the casing will be finished above floor level, and a watertight seal will be provided between the well casing and discharge piping.

Openings into the casing for air-pressure relief, sounding, introduction of gravel, or other purposes necessary for operation of the well may be permitted but must terminate above floor and high-water levels. These openings will be protected against intrusion by caps, screens, or downturned "U" bends as suitable.

All new wells will be properly disinfected, and the water produced will evidence satisfactory bacterial quality prior to service. A sample tap will be made on the discharge line close to the pump for purposes of collecting water samples for analysis.

2. Springs

a. *Location.* A spring will not be used if sources of contamination are situated where they would be above the spring or in the path of the ground water flow toward the spring. At no time should a spring be situated nearer then 200 feet to an up-stream source of potential contamination.

b. *Construction.* Springs will be developed with a tight box or an enclosure with a sealed cover having no openings that will permit entrance of contaminating elements.

3. Streams or Rivers: No stream or river sources will be used without treatment

a. *Storage.* Stored water will be kept in impervious tanks protected against surface drainage. No storage tanks will have any connection with a sewer. All tanks will have watertight covers, and all openings will be covered with corrosion-resistant screens capable of excluding pests.

b. *Distribution System.* The water supply lines will not have any pipe connection with questionable water supplies. All plumbing fixtures and other equipment connected to the water supply will be constructed and installed so as to safeguard the water supply from contamination through cross-connections or back-siphonage.

Food Service

In organizing a camp food program, attention must be given to state and local health regulations for food preparation areas and for food handlers. In nearly all states, a food handler's license is required. These licenses certify the health of the food handler, including freedom from tuberculosis, venereal disease, skin infections, and other communicable diseases. Camps themselves should make health examinations compulsory for all food handlers.

Dishes and utensils should be sanitized so as to absolutely eliminate the possibility of food poisoning. All dishes, pots, pans, and utensils must be vigorously washed with sufficient detergent and scalding water. If the camp does not have an automatic dishwasher, it is necessary to ensure that all dishes and utensils are scraped clean of food particles, immersed in water with a temperature of at least 125°F, scrubbed with detergent, dipped into water of at least 150°F, and then stacked on a carrier and immersed in scalding or boiling water. After air drying, the dishes and utensils may be stored in cupboards, chests, or other protected places free from potential infestation by insects, rodents, or mildew. The following rules should apply to food preparation, storage, and service:

1. Food Sources

a. Ingredients used in the preparation of food or beverages will be free from adulteration and spoilage, and will be completely fit for human consumption.

b. All food or beverages to be served at camp will be prepared in the camp kitchen. (Individual lunches for day campers are exempt.)

2. Food Protection

a. All food or beverages are to be prepared, stored, and served so as to be protected from contamination.

b. No beverage or article of food that has been previously served or that has returned from a table will be served to another person or used in the preparation of other foods.

c. Except for dogs being used by the blind, no live animal or bird will be kept or allowed in any room where food or beverages are prepared, stored, kept, or served.

d. Soiled linens will be kept in containers provided for this purpose. No linen that has been used for any other purpose will be used for wiping utensils, counters, tables, or food preparation equipment.

e. Food storage, preparation, and service facilities will be kept clean and free of litter and rubbish by all reasonable and appropriate means.

f. All food waste kept indoors prior to disposal will be kept in tight, nonabsorbent containers covered with close-fitting lids.

g. Waste containers used for storing garbage will be maintained in a clean, sanitary condition.

h. No insecticide or other poisonous substance will be kept in any food-service preparation room. All poisonous substances will be specifically labeled as to contents and hazards. No insecticide or rodenticide will be used in a manner that would cause contamination of food or utensils.

3. Food Storage

a. Food will be stored at least 6 inches above the floor.

b. Cold food or beverages capable of supporting rapid and progressive growth of illness-causing microorganisms will be maintained at or below a temperature of 40°F.

c. Food stored in refrigerators will be protected from contamination. Accurate, readily visible thermometers will be installed in all refrigerators.

d. Frozen food will remain frozen until ready for processing.

e. All perishable hot food or beverages capable of supporting rapid and progressive growth of illness-causing microorganisms will be kept in devices that maintain all portions of the food or beverage at a temperature above 140°F. An accurate thermometer will be readily available.

4. Food Service

a. Self-service of displayed unpacked foods will remove any direct line between the camper's mouth and the food.

b. Personnel serving food shall use tongs or other implements rather than their hands. The use of tobacco in any form by any person while handling or serving food, beverage or utensils is prohibited.

5. Sanitation of Utensils and Equipment

a. All equipment, including counters, shelves, tables, cutting boards, meat blocks, refrigerators, stoves, hoods, sinks, and dishwashing machines will be kept clean and free from contamination.

b.   Multiuse eating and drinking utensils will be thoroughly cleaned and subjected to an approved bactericidal process after each use.

c.   Multiuse utensils used in the preparation and serving of food will be thoroughly cleaned and subjected to an approved bactericidal process immediately following the day's operation.

d.   Drying cloths will not be used.

e.   Single-service containers and utensils will be used only once.

f.   No polish or other substance containing any poisonous chemical will be used
for the cleaning and polishing of utensils.

6. Food Service Personnel

a.   All food-service personnel who prepare, serve, or handle food will wear clean,
washable outer garmets. Food handlers will wear hairnets, caps, headbands,
or other suitable coverings to confine their hair.

b.   All food handlers will keep their hands clean at all times while handling food,
beverages, or utensils.

c.   No person shall work in the food-service operation who is affected with or is
carrying any disease likely to be communicable.

Garbage Disposal

Garbage and refuse from all parts of the camp should be collected
each day and dumped so that sanitary conditions prevail. Kitchen garbage
may be disposed of by having it hauled to dump or burning sites away from
the camp. Commercial haulers can be used, or the camp may have to have
its own dump truck. In any case, garbage from the kitchen and dining rooms
should be disposed of after every meal. A sufficient number of garbage cans
must be available so that whatever waste is generated can be easily removed.
Garbage-can cleaning and storage sites and waste-water disposal areas must
be effectively screened, cleaned, and maintained so that odors, insects, vermin, and potential health hazards can be eliminated.

The camp's sewer system will be used to get rid of waste water. When
the camp's location does not permit the installation of a sewage system,
the camp must find other methods that conform to existing state and local
regulations.

Transportation

Campers and staff must be safely conveyed to and from camp. If the
camp uses automobiles, trucks, or buses to transport campers and staff, it
should adhere to legal restrictions or regulations concerning the operating
conditions and maintenance of the vehicles. Even if government regulations are absent, the camp should maintain a high standard of vehicular
operating efficiency.

All staff who are responsible for operating camp transportation vehicles must be capable of such responsibility. They must have the skill, qualifications, and knowledge required for the possession of a state license that
certifies that the holder has complied with existing codes for the operation
of such equipment. The camp must have some logical plan to follow during

the transportation of campers and staff. Adequate supervision—a ratio of one counselor to eight campers—is needed to maintain control and ensure common standards of safety. Counselors and campers must be instructed in the procedures of evacuating vehicles in the event of accident or necessity. The following transportation safety rules should be observed:

1. When the camp provides transportation for campers, it will assume responsibility between the place of pick-up and the camp, and from departure until the camper is met by parents or by a person designated by the parents.
2. All camp vehicles will be maintained in a condition that meets the state vehicle inspection requirements.
      A seat for each passenger, plus adequate space for luggage and other equipment, is required. Standing is prohibited. No one shall sit on the floors or in aisles. No more than three persons, including the driver, will be permitted to occupy the front seat of a vehicle.
3. If trucks are used, seats or benches must be securely fastened to the truck floor. The sides or tailgate must not be lower than 36 inches and will be closed at all times when the vehicle is in use. A counselor will ride with the campers in the back of the truck.
4. Campers will not be transported on a public highway in a trailer or other slow-moving vehicle.
5. There will be at least one counselor, in addition to the driver, riding with campers being transported in a truck or bus on a public highway.
6. All camp vehicles are to be equipped with a first-aid kit.
7. The camp will operate a continued program of transportation safety education for its campers and staff.
8. Speed limits will be posted on the camp grounds and observed by all vehicle operators.
9. Camps operating vehicles holding under 10 passengers will carry minimum limits of $25,000 for injury to any one person and $100,000 in any one accident. For vehicles holding 10 to 25 passengers, minimum limits will be $50,000 and $300,000.

Accidents of the type detailed in the following summary are caused by negligence and lack of common sense in potentially hazardous situations.

A transportation accident occurred when a newly employed counselor was given the responsibility of transporting campers from one activity area to another. A van-type vehicle was used. The counselor overloaded the van with campers and then proceeded to drive down a secondary road away from the campsite. The counselor evidently lost control of the van when he steered the vehicle off the road. One of the tires hit a soft shoulder, causing the van to overturn. A number of severe injuries were sustained by the campers, including several fractured skulls, broken bones, and serious laceration and bruising of faces and backs.

In commenting on the accident, the insurance company's attorney stated that the driver of the van was a young person who did not use good judgment in transporting all the campers in one van. It wasn't the inappropriate behavior of the campers that caused this accident, but the improper driving of the counselor.

Because of the severity of the injuries and the facts surrounding them the camp was sued for negligence as well as for punitive damages. The insurance policy did not cover punitive damages.

Under the circumstances just described, it is a wonder that the camp was not sued for an amount that would have resulted in bankruptcy. Whenever campers are being transported, driver safety practices must be scrupulously followed. Any recklessness is harmful and cannot be tolerated. Only those who are responsible, mature, and competent should be permitted to transport campers.

Camp Maintenance

The physical plant of a modern camp represents considerable financial investment. For this and obvious safety reasons, the structures and equipment used by campers and counselors should be given the best possible care so as to retain sound condition and long life. Effective maintenance eliminates potential hazards caused by equipment or facilities in disrepair.

Vehicular Access

A camp road system should provide access from the highway to the administration area. Although there is really no need for automobile traffic within the confines of the camp, there are vehicular needs that must be considered. Access should be opened from the administrative center to the mess hall, kitchen, and infirmary. These areas should be easily traversed by car, truck, or ambulance. The camp itself should not be open to vehicular traffic. Road spurs should lead from the camp parking lot near the administrative center to the rear of the mess hall and kitchen. Another spur should lead to the infirmary. These roads should permit access by emergency and food-supply vehicles.

Fire Prevention and Control

The camp administrator must take every possible precaution to prevent fires both in the camp or during off-site activities. When proximity permits, the camp administrator should contact the nearest local fire department to ensure that fire-fighting equipment will be available on call. All camp staff should undergo fire-fighting drills.

Every facility should have wall-bracketed soda-acid fire extinguishers; they can be supplemented by smaller, hand-held foam extinguishers. Where water pressure is sufficiently high, hoses can be supplied at the most critical points. A fire extinguisher should be placed in the kitchen, craft shop, infirmary, maintenance facility, or wherever combustibles are stored. Extinguishers should be a type designed to combat the particular kind of fire that might occur; oil, gasoline, or grease fires require foam, whereas wood responds better to water or sand.

All camp staff should be concerned with fire prevention and control. The fire-safety program should be given detailed consideration and practice during pre-camp staff training. Each counselor should be instructed as to the actions to be taken in order to evacuate campers safely. Fire drills for campers should also be mandatory and should include demonstration of fire signals and alarms. Rules for fire-protection equipment are as follows:

1. The camp will be provided with fire-fighting equipment of a type and quantity approved and recommended by the state fire marshall.
2. All such equipment will be maintained in good operating condition and be readily available at all times.
3. The camp staff will be familiar with the location and use of the fire-fighting equipment available in camp.
4. Containers of gasoline, inflammables, or explosives will be plainly marked and stored in a locker area well away from structures used by campers.
5. Combustible materials, such as paper, rags, wood scraps, and excelsior, will not be permitted to accumulate at the campsite.
6. The camp director will be responsible for the regular inspection of all fire-protection facilities and equipment.

Health Services

Inextricably connected with camper safety are the health services supplied by the camp. In well-managed camps, every possible measure is taken to ensure healthful living conditions. Any compromise of standard health-care procedures immediately subjects a camp to the suspicion of health authorities, especially if contagious infections or serious illness occurs.

Sanitation

State and local health departments publish sanitary codes relating to the operation of summer camps. These codes should be consulted to determine whether the camps sanitary arrangements are adequate, efficient, and effective. This procedure is particularly necessary in order to safeguard a pure supply of drinking water. Public health personnel can be asked to inspect the sewage disposal system, latrines and toilet facilities, waterfront areas, and sources of swimming water. Drinking water that originates at the camp, even when certified safe, must be tested at its source each week. Although some administrators feel this is unnecessary, the health of all who drink the camp's water can depend upon such inspections.

Counselor on Duty

A formal, routine, rotating system whereby at least one and preferably two counselors are responsible for patrolling the camp grounds at night ensures protection against prowlers, fire, or the consequences of unexpected, structure-damaging storms. Counselors can be given compensatory time off on days following their nights on duty.

Whenever there is an accident at camp that could have been prevented, the fault invariably lies with poor human judgment, on the part of either staff or campers. Lack of common sense, failure to adhere to safety regulations, or disregard of campers' infraction of certain basic safety policies are the primary causes of accidents. A basic safety plan should be devised to cover all activities and environmental hazards, as well as the human factor of imprudent behavior or unsound judgment.[2] No contingency should be overlooked in forming the most comprehensive safety program. There is no excuse for negligence in camp; the lives of too many young people depend upon the alertness and responsibility of the staff. If potential dangers are anticipated and a logical safety plan is put into effect, accidents will be reduced to a minimum and life at camp will be safe.

[2]T. A. Reamon, "Accidents Are Preventable," *Camping Magazine* (February 1984), 12–13.

chapter 8

Camp Location and Development

Interest in camps and camping has rapidly expanded since the 1960s. The population has a better understanding of the values afforded by camps in terms of health, education, social welfare, and recreational objectives. There is also more disposable income available. Federal, state, and local governments have become increasingly involved in promoting camping. Municipalities, through the school system and public recreational service department, have acquired property, developed it, and instituted both day and residential camps. County, state, and federal agencies have performed the same function, thus leading the way to greatly expanded outdoor education opportunities. Camping, whether by trailer, automobile, bicycle, or on foot, has become very popular. Private camps have traded on this accelerated interest.

With competition from many public and private agencies in acquiring land for a variety of purposes, there has been an almost indecent scramble for campsites. Open land is fast disappearing, with the proliferation of highways, housing projects, shopping centers, schools, hospitals, and military reservations, and with all the encroachments of the megalopolis. The rush for land has driven prices up sharply and eaten into the limited supply of land appropriate for campsites. In addition, floods, fires, erosion, air and water pollution, and other factors have been working to destroy ecological ˜ce, thereby further restricting suitable sites for camps. Not surpris-
˜ns are finding it difficult to obtain well-situated, attractive, topo-
˜able land. Standards for selecting and planning day and resi-
˜ becoming increasingly significant.

SITE SELECTION

Eight principal factors should be considered in selecting a campsite. These factors, each of which will be explained in detail, are size, accessibility, topographical features, soil and drainage, water supply, aquatic areas, natural and artificial hazards, and functional suitability. Although fiscal resources will differ, techniques for the selection of campsites apply equally to all camps.

Size

Sufficient space, combining as it does many of the significant elements of physical planning, may well be the chief factor. Adequate acreage is determined by the expected number of campers to be served by the camp. No valid scientific study has been done to determine the actual carrying capacity of a given camp facility for a given number of campers, but a basic ratio of one acre per camper appears sound. Some planners indicate that half an acre is permissible, while others feel that one acre per camper is the minimum. Generally, the camp site should have sufficient acreage to provide adequate open space for the development of necessary facilities. There must also be space for exploratory activities, nature study, forest travels, and solitude. A reserve that acts as a buffer against any possible encroachments is also necessary. With these needs in mind, then, it can be said that 50 campers will be comfortable on 50 acres. The acquisition of additional land on a ratio of 1/2 acre per camper beyond 50 might be worthwhile. Thus, a camp with 100 campers would be satisfactory if it had 75 acres. There should be enough space to prevent crowding and unnecessary confinement of activities and to encourage a feeling of adventure in the woods. The activities that can be offered on 20-acre sites are so restricted that their acquisition for resident camps is futile. Most will concede that a site that appears too large for present needs is more desirable than a small site that will limit present use and rule out future expansion.

Camping concepts and activities are dynamic; they need space to develop. Within the confines of the camp, space is required, depending upon the design concept, to segregate the various activity areas, bunks, and administrative offices. A centralized administration facility will probably require no less than 5 acres. Individual units should be allocated 2 or 3 acres each. It may even be best to separate the units widely, so that isolation from sight and sound can be maintained. Roadways, outbuildings, activity areas, and other necessary structures take up space. They must not be crowded.

The perimeter of the camp should be designated as an impenetrable buffer zone, this requires additional space. Although many resident camps plan activities that will take campers off the grounds, at least for their older campers, it is desirable to have plenty of land for hikes, primitive camping, and an atmosphere of wilderness for younger campers.

The configuration of the campsite is a prime consideration. For safety and supervisory purposes, camps should not be divided by highways. Land for the camp should be self-contained and not broken up by parcels that do not belong to the camp. Strips of land are unsuitable; narrow areas do not lend themselves to many activities, and are apt to foster crowding. It is vital that a camp have privacy. Camps should, by all means, seek to isolate themselves from heavily traveled routes, railroads, resort areas, public camp grounds, picnic facilities, or other publicly controlled developments. The noise, dirt, and interference of industry, community, or traffic should be scrupulously avoided.

One exception to these standards should be noted. A camp that is situated in a region of magnificent, permanently available natural resources may have acreage that is sufficient only to house the campers and allow them to perform activities that do not require much space. The camp may abut a state forest, federal preserve, or other natural area that precludes the purchase and development of land by the camp. Such a camp is fortunate, although the standards of selection still hold true. If the camp, even with limited holdings, can profitably make use of natural resources that do not belong to it, the site has been selected according to the indicated guidelines.

Accessibility

The geographical site of the camp should be decided by the activities to be programmed; by whether the camp is for temporary or permanent (or both) resident camping; and by the origin and distance from population centers from which the majority of campers will be drawn. Agency camps will, of necessity, be required to maintain proximate distances from populations to be served. Fig. 8-1 is typical of the facilities available at a public

FIGURE 8-1.   Layout of public camp facility.

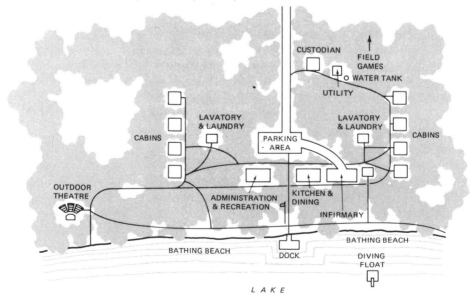

camp. A public agency camp will generally be close to the community and population served. Public agency camps may have various seasons and work in conjunction with different organizations. Therefore, the camp facility may be in use over a longer period of time, for short durations, or for outdoor education and school camping. It should be within 1 to 2 hours' travel time from the community it serves. Some camps are situated at even greater distances, but they are rare. In some cases in which the city still preserves vast tracts of wilderness, a camp may be located within city limits and still satisfy established guides for site selection. Public and institutional camps must be within easy reach of the clientele that they were established to serve. In effect, the amount of use that a camp facility will obtain is directly related to its accessibility.

The private commercial camp, on the other hand, need not use the element of proximity to population density as a criterion for site selection. Private camps may be situated at an extreme distance from any population center and still cater to client needs. Many private camps draw their clientele from all parts of the country, and 3 to 8 hours of travel time, depending upon the mode of transportation, may be needed to reach the camp. However, the camp should be located on secondary or tertiary public roads that are maintained and open during the operational season of the camp. The approach to the site should be by first-class highways. The roads leading directly to the camp itself and giving access to the camp need be passable only for camp needs.

When the campsite is isolated from nearby towns, costs of operation are higher than if communities are close at hand. It is advantageous to have a small community within several miles of the camp for several reasons. The town can provide medical assistance and police and fire-fighting agencies. There will be utility lines. If bulk buying is not the policy of the camp, supplies can be purchased in town. These features do not have to be within sight or sound, but they are helpful to have within a few minutes' fast driving time from the camp. It is also desirable to have one or more points of interest not far from the camp. Historic sites, scientific facilities, or cultural centers provide interesting excursions.

Topographical Features

The best campsites have a varied topography. Terrain features should include meadows, woods, hills, gorges, waterways, and other natural phenomena that make the land adventurous and attractive. There must be areas suitable for program, residential, and administrative activities. The contour of the land, the amount of relatively flat, open space, the percentage of dense woods, and the percentage of land in rocky outcroppings, ravines, or promontories will have a direct relationship to the type of program that can be arranged.

Safety factors must be considered in terms of topography. The site must be selected for its escape features as well as for living adaptability. Where the danger of forest fires or floods is present, routes to immediate safety must be planned. Attractive terrain features may be dangerous features. Precipices, bogs, waterfalls, or other tempting hazards will be beneficial only if their size, location, and distance from the residential areas of the camp limit their potential as attractive nuisances.

Natural scenic beauty is of inestimable importance in selecting a campsite. The camp's desirability is enhanced when there are scenic vistas to enjoy. Trees also make a camp more interesting and attractive. The best woodland sites arc those with varied and mature tree cover. Trees will best serve the camp's purposes if they are at least 25 years old, and thus able to provide both beauty and maximum shade. Trees act as a windbreak, provide a cooling effect on a hot day, help purify the air, and tend to prevent erosion. Open spaces are as desirable and necessary as forested spaces. Heavily wooded lands should alternate with meadow or open space. Many camping experiences require fairly level, cleared space. The importance of a varied topography should not be underestimated.

Soil and Drainage

Soil conditions inevitably decide drainage. Safe and economical septic disposition depends on good soil conditions. Porous or gravelly subsoil provides a better drainage bed than does loamy soil. Sites on which ground water approaches the surface are to be avoided. In order to determine developmental potential, a competent authority should test the soil on sites being considered for acquisition. A camp site is made less desirable when poor soil conditions prevent quick absorption of liquid matter. Because good drainage is a prerequisite to a safe, healthy campsite, the terrain should have high ground with gentle contours. It is advantageous if slopes are such that they permit easy drainage from latrines, septic tanks, and septic fields away from aquatic areas and water supply. Natural waterways should be unimpeded so that heavy rainfall accumulation can dissipate without flooding. Gullies, washes, and other natural indications of heavy water impact giving rise to erosion should be looked at with suspicion and avoided if possible.

A campsite that is always damp or where there are swamps, bogs, marshes, or low-lying wet areas possesses great potential for trouble—and interesting activity. Program possibilities may be generously enhanced by wetlands, because of insect, bird, fish, and game habitation. Such areas are also dangerous to the health and comfort of the camper. Damp grounds combined with sudden chill can lower resistance and give rise to upper respiratory tract infections. Stagnant pools are breeding grounds of mosquitoes.

Water Supply

The need for a safe and adequate supply of water for drinking, cooking, and washing is so obvious that it is one of the preconditions for the develoment of a campsite. In arid sections of the country, water supply is a constant source of worry, expense, and difficulty. In those regions where abundant water is available, the supply must be tested for potability and adequacy. Whether the water is derived from a mountain stream, drilled through rock strata, or comes from a dug well is immaterial. Insofar as camper health is concerned, water must be absolutely safe to drink. An exemplary campsite is useless unless there is a safe water supply. If neither surface nor ground water supplies prove adequate, the site will have to be abandoned. It is possible, of course, to purify whatever water is found or even to pipe it to the campsite, but these are extremely expensive operations.

The average per capita consumption of water in resident camps varies widely. In some instances, it may be as low as 20 gallons per person per day. On the other hand, water consumption may reach a level of 75 gallons per person per day. The more water-consuming equipment the camp uses, the greater the supply will have to be. Flush toilets, showers, drinking fountains, and the like must be taken into account when estimating water consumption. As noted in Chapter 3, it has been estimated that an average of 50 gallons per capita per day will meet the water needs of most, though not all, resident camps. When the prevailing philosophy of the camp inclines toward primitive living, less water will be needed. Day camps require approximately 20 gallons per person per day.

Aquatic Areas

In sections of the country that are providentially furnished with water resources, swimming and other aquatic activities are a must. Where water resources are plentiful, the variety of waterfront areas may serve as one guide for the selection of a campsite. Any water resource—an ocean, gulf, bay, estuary, lake, river, pond, or stream—can be adjacent to or actually located on the camp property. Extremely dry regions of the United States may still offer resident camping; if the campsite meets all other criteria, this basic lack can be surmounted by constructing a swimming pool.

Water resources that can reasonably serve as aquatic activity areas must be surveyed for health or safety hazards. Natural water areas used for swimming should contain safe water. A scrupulous examination of inflow must therefore be made to determine possible sources of pollution. An otherwise perfect site may be rendered useless if the aquatic facility is contaminated. Composition of the bottom, rocky outcroppings, currents, tides, undertow, sudden dropoffs, and movement of sandbars should be charted where possible, in order to avoid dangerous conditions. Water hazards can make the job of camper supervision that much more difficult.

Natural and Artificial Hazards

Certain natural conditions that present some danger to the camper prevail in all parts of the country. To the extent that such natural conditions can be identified and cleared, the site may be useful. When humans have invaded an otherwise choice site and created hazardous conditions, the site may have to be eliminated or the condition removed.

Natural hazards include poisonous flora and fauna, ravines, waterfalls, dead trees, precipitous slopes, or other phenomena that abound in most wild places. Animals disturbed in their natural habitat may cause injury, but they are more likely to avoid entanglement and run. It is usually only when threatened that an animal will turn and attack. Although insects, snakes, and some birds can cause injury, they can be avoided by a sound educational campaign. Teaching the camper how to get along in the outdoors will spare him much discomfort and major or minor injury. If the camper readily identifies poison oak, sumac, and ivy; recognizes poisonous reptiles; and learns how to control his enthusiasm for daring displays of foolish bravado, he will be happier and safer.

Artificial hazards—mine tunnels, excavations, abandoned wells, quarries—should exclude the selection of the site marred by them. If the site contains many valuable features, and conditions prevent any other site from being selected, all such man-made hazards must be explored, identified, and clearly marked. Because many of these dangerous areas are attractive nuisances, they must be off limits for all personnel and campers.

Functional Suitability

A campsite must be appropriate to the objectives of the camp. Wilderness camping must be conducted in the wilderness. A camp that plans to offer trips must have access to regions that are conducive to trips. One that expects to specialize in aquatics should have a waterfront capable of providing opportunities for swimming, canoeing, sailing, and scuba diving. An equestrian camp needs enough riding trails. A camp that is to be used for winter as well as summer camping needs areas for sleighing, skating, and skiing. While camp design and program are significant factors in choosing a campsite, some of the natural phenomena of a site may actually determine a good deal of the program.

SITE DEVELOPMENT

Once a campsite has been selected, a comprehensive master plan is required to guide the logical development of the camp. A topographic map of the tract is used to prepare the plan. The plan is necessary whether the development involves a simple site layout or the comprehensive growth of a large area. A master plan considers the environmental factors that were significant in choosing the site, the camp's functional objectives, immediate and future needs and capacity, seasonal or year-round use, and the relationship between areas of the site that can be used in planning the program. The master plan is a graphic illustration of the eventual design and construction of the camp, indicating how it will look, where structures will be placed, and how the program spaces will be arranged. Planning prevents waste and fruitless effort. It can eliminate poor or inadequate construction sites. Because the master plan more than pays for itself by reducing the potential for costly errors, and because it allows advantageous use of all physical phenomena at the site, it may be worthwhile to employ a professional camp planner.

Part of the master plan is mapping the area in question. The charts will be accompanied by written recommendations describing the site, explaining the available natural resources, outlining the advantages and disadvantages to be considered, and establishing developmental priorities. Designing and constructing the camp may require several years, with the most important elements receiving priority. One must be able to get to the site before it can be developed. An access roadway must therefore be constructed first. As previously indicated, the campsite is only as good as its water supply. Ensuring the source of an adequate supply of water must be the second priority. Electricity for heat, light, power, and waste disposal are relatively early needs. Although deep woods camping may prohibit the installation of utilities, even the most primitive camp must be constructed on a priority schedule. When the initial items are completed, the site is ready for some use. Permanent structures can be added. Where indicated, special construction can be developed for flood, fire, and erosion control; dam building, reforestation, and landscaping may also be considered.

Surveying

In master planning the campsite, natural resources should be maintained and the character of the land should be recognized and appreciated. The advantages of the site should be exploited. The site's aesthetic features should be left untouched, insofar as possible. Humans have a bad habit of trying to improve upon nature, with disastrous results. A site that is especially adapted to any program possibility should be recognized and capitalized upon. The basic standards of campsite development include aesthetics, relations between space needs and program, and unaffectedness. Each necessitates awareness and concern, yet all must be coordinated into a unified entity.

Topographic Mapping

A fundamental step in planning any campsite is the use of a topographic map of the tract to be developed. This tool will show the limits of the site and its chief terrain features and contours. For the areas of the site that appear to have potential for development, vertical contours should be demarcated in 5-foot intervals, while the horizontal scale should not be more than 100 feet to the inch. Although a thorough physical familiarity with the campsite is an absolute necessity, only careful study of topographic and general charts of the area will permit complete knowledge of the tract. The aphorism of not being able to see the forest for the trees holds in cases such as these. It is one thing to hike over any property and become acquainted with what lies within the boundaries; it is quite another to accurately relate distances with time elapsed in going from one point to another. The relationship of one area to another is more clearly seen and measured when reference is made to maps.

Surveys

Whether a survey is necessary for a specific site will be determined in part by the size of the area. Extensive land holdings on which permanent facilities will be developed require a survey. The survey will account for a minute portion of the total capital expenditure for the property and its development. A very small campsite, on the other hand, probably will not require a topographical survey, although the land must be surveyed on the ground to determine exact boundaries of space owned and for other legal reasons.

The detailed inspection of the tract, together with pertinent notations on the drawing, will be decided by the planner. However, the following factors are usually included in any site analysis: areas to be developed for structures, sports fields, trails, service roads, and utility lines; places that are highly adapted for unique functions; and places that should be avoided in any contemplated development.

SITE LAYOUT

The physical design of any camp should be reduced to the lowest common denominator without simplifying to the extent that there is no development at all. It is relatively easy to make a dude ranch or resort hotel out of a good campsite. When the creature comforts are so completely developed, as in the case of luxury spas, the essential nature of camping is lost. Camp development should be kept to simple functional facilities. Surely there may be added refinements, but not enough to overwhelm and destroy the fundamental purpose of camping.

Camp Spaces

Determinants that shape a logical plan include estimated immediate and future capacity, camp objectives, and the type of program that will be available. Thus, the bare outline of the proposed camp comes into being. Priorities in setting aside land are spaces for camper living quarters, access roadways, utilities, sanitary facilities, administration structures, service areas, recreational fields, and activity areas. Detailed development of these places and items is not a problem at this point.

Administrative Area

The administrative structure, which includes the camp office, storage areas for supplies, materials, and equipment, the maintenance facility (if there is one), and the parking area should be situated as close as possible to the camp's main entrance. They should be the first permanent structures visible upon entering the camp. The infirmary or isolation tent or unit should be situated relatively near the office and parking lot, but removed from the living quarters of campers and counselors. The camp dining facility and kitchen should be centrally located, if possible, to all sections of the camp. If there is a centralized hot-shower facility, it too should be conveniently placed, although not near the dining hall. Residential units may be scattered throughout the camp tract, wherever appropriate ground conditions for construction prevail together with pleasing long views.

Decentralized Areas

The concept of decentralized camping has led to the development of segregated living units or bunks as separate enclaves containing a variety of facilities that almost make the bunks self-contained (Fig. 8-2). The unit system requires a layout that is quite different from the old regimentally arranged camp. Thus, a decentralized system provides for small groups of several bunks. Each unit or enclave will consist of from 5 to 8 bunks constructed in circular formation. Each enclave is a camp within a camp, having its own sanitary facilities, camp fire circle, perhaps an outdoor grill or kitchen fly, and even a unit shelter in which a variety of recreational activities may be held, particularly on rainy days. The layout of the unit dictates that living quarters be constructed first and then utilities laid out with respect to the tents or cabins. Sanitary facilities should be no closer than 100 feet from the living quarters or kitchen, but not more than 100 yards away. If there is an outdoor kitchen or grill, it should be situated so that prevailing wind conditions will always blow the smoke and odors of cooking away from the tents or cabins. All access trails and roadways should serve the units. These service utilities will be developed after the unit layout has been constructed. Trails must never cut through a unit. A minimum of interconnecting trails may be cut between units.

FIGURE 8-2. Layout of a decentralized camp containing small-unit living.

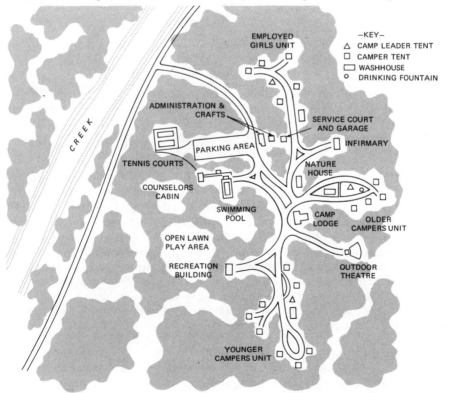

Service Roads

In a camp covering extensive ground, a service road to the administrative area, the centralized dining hall and kitchen, and the infirmary is imperative to hastening the delivery of goods or for facilitating emergency transportation. The service road should not wander throughout the camp but be restricted to these central places. Emergency needs sometimes arise, however. For this reason, it may be necessary to cut minimal or brush trails to unit sites. Such trails are wide enough to let a jeep-type vehicle through, but otherwise forbid passage to vehicles equipped for highway conditions. This prevents automobile use at camp and preserves the natural setting.

Camp Structures

All camp structures should be functional and plain. They should be appropriate for the activity and the situation for which they are designed. As much as possible, camp structures should be fabricated of native materials to blend into the natural setting. Camp architecture should carefully harmonize with its surroundings, becoming an integral part of the environment. Even extraordinary facilities such as the camp council ring, swimming pool, and outdoor grills can be arranged, constructed, and appointed so that they fit into the site.

Camp Design

The design of the campsite will depend upon the physical contours and terrain features of the tract. In general, however, any camp layout will be in the form of a circle, centered around facilities that are important to the entire camp. Unit groups may be removed from the central facility and relatively isolated from each other, as far as the campsite will allow, but each unit, regardless of distance from the central point, will establish a roughly circular formation when diagrammed on a map. No living unit should be more than one-quarter of a mile away from the central program areas or all-camp facilities. It may be that the tract will afford the development of the camp dining and kitchen facility as the centrally situated structure. If so, all other facilities will be planned around it, radiating from this center like spokes from a wheel. Other centralized structures may be the camp hot-shower house or the recreational hall. A variety of open fields for sports and games should also be planned nearby.

In some instances, the development of the camp will permit only a semicircular arrangement, with the waterfront facility as the pivot. In such circumstances, all living units and necessary structures will be placed at appropriate distances from the waterfront.

Another layout for efficient and effective development, the wineglass form, is a variation on the semicircular arrangement. A camp that is essentially two camps in one, such as a coeducational camp, may be best served by this formation. When the configuration of the tract and physical resources are so disposed that neither the circular nor semicircular formations are feasible, it may be that the wineglass formation will be most useful.

In this design, the administrative units are grouped at the entrance. The camp service road is constructed so that it bifurcates at a suitable point and proceeds right and left to the living units for males and females respectively. The camp may be developed around a lake, centered on a main facility (the dining hall), or built so that the waterfront divides the camp naturally. The cluster of structures comprising the administrative units is the base, the service road is the stem, and the two sides of the camp, outlined by the road, become the bowl of the wineglass. Figure 8-3 represents a site layout for which the wineglass design was chosen to best exploit the given tract.

The Master Plan

Many public agencies, particularly recreational service departments, have failed to understand the necessity of the master plan. This oversight

FIGURE 8-3.   The wineglass camp layout.

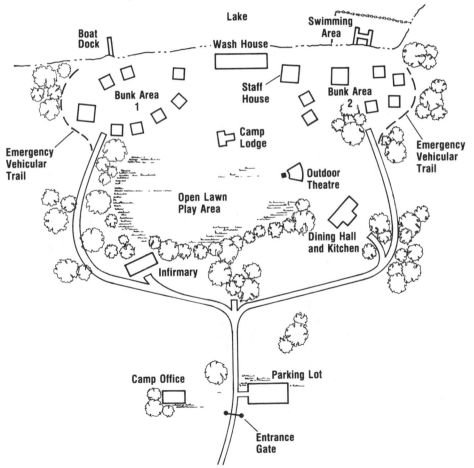

has usually been due to expediency, lack of sufficient funds for proper priority construction, an inability to suitably arrange campsite accommodations, lack of adequate space for appropriate development, poor planning on the part of the maintenance staff, failure to obtain technical assistance from qualified consultants, or any combination of these factors. Public camp grounds are notable for their inadequacies. Whether for short-term residents or for family camping, the public campsite, in some areas, is woefully short on the features that normally enhance the camping experience. One extenuating circumstance may be the result of having to cope with great numbers of people on relatively restricted sites. Where space is at a premium, the public campsite does not hesitate to construct tent spaces or cabins quite close to one another, privacy is therefore almost nonexistent. In such situations, the solitude that contributes so much to the camping experience is lost.

The public campsite is often not designed to exploit the best features of the terrain, but is arranged to facilitate the management of the area. Most public campsites are laid out in a grid or regimental pattern and are highly centralized. Advantage is not taken of land contours, and shelters are usually scattered about as though planning were a waste of time. It is not surprising that many public camp operations must be reconstructed, overhauled, and rearranged for maximum use at additional cost. There are public departments whose planning and administration of camps are outstanding. Such facilities are quite attractive, provide great satisfaction for campers, and adhere to sound planning and developmental practices. Such agencies are unique and recent, however.

This is not an indictment of public-agency camp operations. It must be understood from the outset that the public camp is not program oriented, except for day camps and children's resident camps. Only when children are sent to the public camp as residents does the camp have a counselor staff and a program. In other instances, such as family or transient camping, the public camp merely provides the site and program facilities. Campers are completely on their own. Thus, the camp is designed to accommodate large numbers of people, rather than around nature-oriented resources and activity areas.

DEVELOPMENT OF STRUCTURES

Most resident camps, in setting up living quarters for campers and staff, attempt to arrange accommodations on a decentralized plan. Each camper is thus treated as an individual and is not lost in a mass package. The value of bunks' maintaining their identity within the larger camp has proven itself. Camp administrators have repeatedly discovered that small groups have better morale, derive greater satisfaction from participating in camping experiences, have increased opportunities for self-expression and skill development, and have easier access to individual counselors. Decentralization of living quarters also has an immediate health benefit: Contagious illnesses can easily be controlled and confined to one small group if the group is segregated from the other units.

Almost any shelter constructed of any material can be used in the permanent, temporary, or combined resident camp. This is also valid for day camps. All structures of a permanent nature must be constructed to ensure against rodent infestation. Shelter construction can best be accomplished during the initial building stage by placing rodent deterrent material between the structure and potential entry ways. In the following pages, only those structures or quarters that are most effective and appropriate will be discussed.

The Tent

A variety of tents can be used in most camp situations. One example is the umbrella-type tent, which has an external frame and single-unit construction, including a floor piece. Such a tent does not have to be set on a frame or platform; it is staked to the ground. One disadvantage is that during heavy rainfall, the flooring of the tent may become soaked through unless the earth around the bottom of the tent has been ditched to drain off or channel the water flow away from the tent.

Most resident-camp tents are constructed of heavy duck, have split corners, and may be opened or closed at both ends as desired. Tents must have sides high enough to permit comfortable standing. Optimum space for use and for ventilation is accomplished if the height of the tent is sufficient. Such tents are designed to be erected on wooden platforms. These platforms should be set into or on concrete or other nonwooden piers for permanent foundation. All tents should be reinforced at stress points with brass grommets. The rope rigging must be manufactured with slides so that slack or tension can be introduced as daily weather conditions necessitate. All tents should be mildew-resistant, and water- and fireproof. Some of the newest tents are manufactured with these treatments built in and come equipped with slides and grommets as needed.

Standard tent sizes should be large enough to accommodate at least four campers or two staff members. A 12-by-14-foot tent provides an interior space of 168 square feet and permits sufficient head space for each camper. A minimum of 40 square feet per camper is considered desirable. Tent frames should always be constructed of wood, preferably with hardwood floors, pitched slightly to permit water runoff. The piers on which the platforms are set should be raised not less than 18 inches from the ground in order to permit air circulation beneath the tent, allow groundskeepers to remove any accumulated trash or refuse, and prevent damage to wooden parts by destructive insects. There are other forms of this type of tent, some requiring frames on which to rest, others containing interior poles. They may take almost any geometric shape.

The Indian tepee is the most glamorous of tents, lending an atmosphere of adventure and authenticity to the camp environment (Fig. 8-4). It sets the stage for reciting Indian and nature lore and local legends, provides

FIGURE 8-4.   The tepee—glamour tent of camps. (S. I. U.
Photo Ser.)

sleeping quarters, and serves for camp council meetings during inclement
weather. It is the only tent, besides the canvas cooking pavilion or kitchen
fly, that permits an inside camp fire. The tepee does require long, straight
poles for erection, which may sometimes prove to be a disadvantage. The
tepee is structurally sound and can withstand high winds, cold, and dampness.

One other form, the two-person pup tent, must be mentioned here.
This tent and variations of it are best used as temporary sleeping quarters
when "packing-in" or going on overnight hikes. Assembled from halves that
can be quickly buttoned or clasped together, they accommodate two
campers in sleeping bags. Although such tents, when properly treated, can
be permanent sleeping shelters, they should not be so used. They lend a
change to life in permanent installations; used continuously, however, they
restrict camper movement, do not provide adequate space, and lack sufficient space for storage.

Tents for Short-term Encampments

Tents that are used for shifting from site to site on a trip out of the
main camp must be light, compact when disassembled, and easily assembled

by one or two individuals. As with tents designed for permanent residence, the shift tent should be waterproof and mildew and fire resistant. It should withstand heavy gusts of wind, and be designed to reflect the warmth of an open camp fire, without smoking out the inhabitants. Among the variety of light tents that can be used with relatively little instruction are the wall, cone, pyramid, modified pyramid, wedge, shelter halves, modified shelter halves with fly, and lean-tos (Fig. 8-5). If the material is already cut when

FIGURE 8-5. Eight ways to pitch a tarp. (*Source: The TentCamper,* copyright 1957 by Walter E. Stern, tentmaker, New York, NY 10034.)

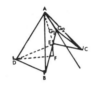

Tepee
A tent 6½ ft. high with a 5 x 7 base—peg down B, C, D, E into an oblong. Raise A as high as possible, connect G-1 and G-2 and attach guy lines. Fold triangle E, D, F, inside of tent.

Winter Tent
A completely closed tent for winter use, not too roomy. Raise C and B with 2 2½ ft. poles, have 5 ft. at A, peg down D and E with same peg.

Adirondack
Attach 5 ft. poles at E and F, pull out back to form 5 x 7 oblong, fold under triangular flap.

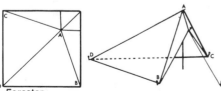

Forester
One of the most common shapes of tarp pitching, but rarely done well. Use low pole in winter, higher in summer, by varying the distance between D and A. When pitching from tree, support D-A with extra rope to prevent sagging and pulling tent out of shape.

Dining Fly
The 6-pole way of pitching a tarp—guy lines should line up with diagonals—large unencumbered space for dining table underneath.

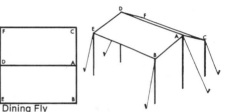

Kitchen Fly
Five pole way. Pull out center with bent sapling or push out with properly shielded pole (use tin can or crutch tip).

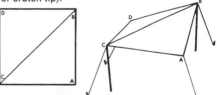

Quick Shelter
Two pole way. To put a tarp up between 2 trees or 2 poles for a quick shelter, use rope to support tarp and pull out side guy lines well.

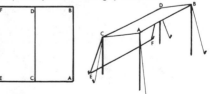

Wind Shed
To protect camp fire, to provide shelter for supplies or wood, and many other uses, you can pitch this 4 pole way.

purchased, some brief instructions will suffice to enable campers to pitch their tents with little difficulty.

Tents of this type may be suspended or held in assembled form by ropes attached to poles, guyed to trees, or held by any handy sturdy object to which ropes may be tied. Each tent serves a specific purpose, and each has distinct advantages and disadvantages. These tents are available, relatively inexpensive, and easily set up.

Lean-tos.   The lean-to is best as an expedient or overnight shelter and should not be used for permanent residences in the established camp. As indicated by its description, the lean-to may be built of logs, boards, or branches and brush. It has three sides, gives a low, sloping appearance, and can easily be heated with a well-laid reflector fire. The lean-to has several drawbacks. It is cramped, cannot easily be kept insect free, is expensive to screen, and may not be entirely closed against wet or cold weather conditions. If a canvas flap or hinged wooden cover is used to close the lean-to completely, proper ventilation is reduced, as is the ability to see out. There are no windows or other apertures in the typical lean-to. The diagram of an Adirondack shelter (Fig. 8-6) shows the lean-to construction.

The Cabin

Cabins have generally become the main residential structure of most established camps (Fig. 8-7). They are of wood frame or log construction and should be kept as simple in concept as possible. Cabins may be used exclusively for summer or, with additional expense, be winterized for year-round use. Cabins should be large enough to accommodate 4 to 8 campers. There should be sufficient interior and storage space to permit at least 4 cots on the floor or 4 double-decker frames. Wall heights should be maintained just above the beds. In the case of double-decker bunks, wall height may be raised to the level of the second tier. As much of the cabin wall

FIGURE 8-6.   Lean-to or Adirondack shelter, with reflector fire.

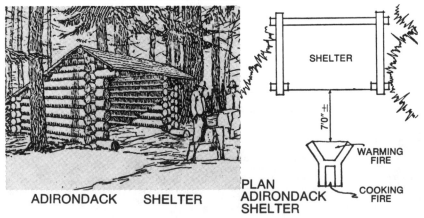

ADIRONDACK   SHELTER

PLAN
ADIRONDACK
SHELTER

SHELTER

7'0" ±

WARMING
FIRE

COOKING
FIRE

FIGURE 8-7.   Typical camper cabin—for summer use only.

space as possible should be open and screened. Roof overhangs should be wide so that the cabin may remain open even during rain storms. Cabins should be able to tolerate winds of up to hurricane force.

Cabins should include built-in storage to accommodate campers' clothing and equipment. Cabins need not be wired for electricity for illumination. Wall sconces for covered candles or kerosene lamps are most effective and contribute to the rustic atmosphere. Those residential camps operated by public agencies in state or federal preserves, forests, or parks must abide by fire regulations. It may be that the only light that can be used is a protected lantern variety, completely encased in a glass container and fed with a mixture of air and liquid petroleum gas that is pumped in to provide a brighter flame.

When cabin openings have to be covered, a light plastic material, operated by ropes through pulleys, can be used. Such plastic covers are not windows, but may be translucent. These coverings do not require any great pressure or strength to position them, so even the smallest camper may close a cabin equipped with such shutters.

In some instances, as in a health camp or when campers are very young, a counselor may also reside in the cabin. Normally, however, counselors and other staff are housed in their own cabins or other structures within the unit enclaves, or in a more centralized location.

The Unit Lodge

Each living unit made up from 6 to 8 bunks, with their attendant coun-selors and supervisor, may have a shelter or pavilion that can be used for a variety of activities and functions depending upon need (Fig. 8-8). Different camps have different names for these shelters; here it will be called the unit lodge. The lodge may be constructed of the same materials as the cabins. In a few instances the lodge is more strongly built or more exotic in appear-ance. It may function as a recreational center for the unit during rainy weather, may be used for interunit parties or social affairs, may be a storage facility for unit supplies and equipment, or may double as a kitchen and mess hall if the camp does not have a central dining facility. The lodge may also be used as a guest house and can be designed for year-round use.

Another possibility is a pavilion-like structure—merely a roof sup-ported by columns or posts, or enclosed on one, two, three, or four sides. It may also have a wide deck or terrace on one or more sides. The terrace may be a colonnade or it may be open to the sky. Since the lodge will be a multipurpose structure, serving many functions concurrently or separately, it should be suitably arranged. Fundamentally, the lodge will have a kitchen, a storage room, and a large multipurpose area; it may also have toilet and washing facilities. The latter convenience depends upon the camp's objec-tives and the reasons for the construction of the lodge. If the lodge is for summer camping only, toilet facilities and even the source of water may be

FIGURE 8-8.   A unit lodge.

outside. The kitchen must be commodious and adequately equipped to permit several campers and a counselor to cook or clean up after a meal. Kitchen equipment should include a wash stand or sink, an electric or gas cooking range, sufficient shelf and cabinet space, and a refrigerator. An essential item in any lodge is a fireplace that can serve for both heating and cooking. The fireplace should be designed to reflect a great deal of heat and deny any percentage of heat loss by escape up the chimney. Fitted with cranes and hooks, it can be an efficient cooking hearth as well.

Outdoor Unit Utilities

When there is no central dining or kitchen facility, or even if one does exist, it may be feasible to provide each unit with a mess tent or outdoor kitchen (Fig. 8-9). These structures add much to camper enjoyment and offer opportunities for developing individual responsibility and judgment. Allowing campers to be on their own, relatively speaking, to plan, prepare, and serve meals provides a good exercise in self-reliance and personal growth.

The outdoor kitchen may be nothing more than a brick or stone fireplace to which a tent fly is attached. A more elaborate form is a pavilion with the fireplace and grill at one end and all other sides open, or three or four sides closed. If the structure has closed sides, equipment and storage space may also be contained within the facility.

Each unit will have its own sanitary facility consisting of pit privies, wash shelters, a shower house, or, if water supply and soil drainage permit, flush toilets. When pit privies are used, all washing structures must be maintained separately. If flush toilets and good plumbing are available, then all sanitary facilities can be housed in a single structure.

Administration Structures

Every camp should have one designated administration area (Fig. 8-10). On this site will be situated the main office for the camp director, office space for central office staff, commissary or camp store, supply depot, maintenance shop, camp garage, parking lot, custodian's house, and miscellaneous structures of this kind. Also designated as administrative structures, but not necessarily at this site, are the camp infirmary, cook's quarters, centralized kitchen and dining hall, hot-shower facility, camp director's cabin, pump house, and water storage tank (if required).

The administration site is generally, although not always, the very first area that visitors see. Since first impressions are long lasting, it is vital that campers and parents be positively influenced by their first view. The site should be well maintained, attractive, comfortable, and pleasantly landscaped. It need not be elaborate or luxurious.

The administration site should be within one-quarter mile of the unit enclaves. It probably should not be located in the center of the camp, unless the center is of no use for any other site. The administration site should be chosen for its supervisory advantage, fairly level ground, and adequacy of space for whatever structures are required.

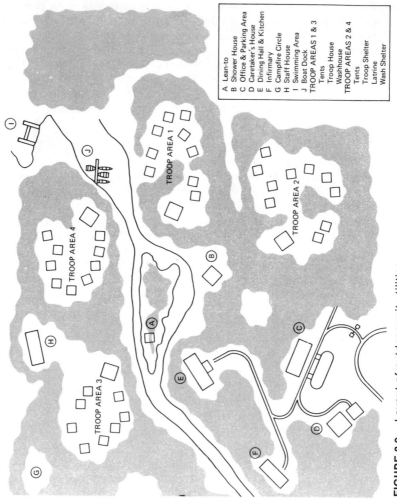

A Lean-to
B Shower House
C Office & Parking Area
D Caretaker's House
E Dining Hall & Kitchen
F Infirmary
G Campfire Circle
H Staff House
I Swimming Area
J Boat Dock
TROOP AREAS 1 & 3
   Tents
   Troop House
   Washhouse
TROOP AREAS 2 & 4
   Tents
   Troop Shelter
   Latrine
   Wash Shelter

FIGURE 8-9. Layout of outdoor unit utilities.

FIGURE 8-10. Camp administration building.

The Camp Office

The camp director must have office space. Whether it is in a separate building or in a combined structure containing the commissary and central-supply depot is immaterial. It may be a tent set up for that purpose. The office should be just beyond the camp entrance, as near to the road as possible. A road barrier, which may be used to prevent traffic access to any part of the camp, should be set up at the office as a control point. The visitor and camp parking lot can also be directly behind or at the side of the office.

In large camps, the central office structure should provide adequate space to transact the camp business, house the commissary, and contain sufficient office space for the work force and for files, business machines, and other equipment. The camp library, laundry facility, visitor's lounge, and mail room may also be a part of this facility.

The Infirmary or Health Center

The infirmary is a temporary receiving station and is not meant to take the place of a hospital. It is best to make the infirmary an unpretentious structure, highly functional and simple, well ventilated and cool. It may be a two-wing tent or a permanent building. It must be easily accessible by road for emergency vehicles, but relatively isolated from the rest of the camp. It should be easy to find, however, on a quiet site within easy walking distance from any unit, but preferably not within 200 feet of a central dining facility.

The infirmary should contain space for cots, a nurse's station or office, and supplies and required equipment; there should also be room for food preparation. In a large residential camp, the structure may be expanded for a resident physician and an emergency treatment room. A good rule of thumb is to have one cot for each 25 campers. When the camp is located far from a hospital, a more elaborate installation is required; isolation rooms and even an emergency surgery unit should be planned. If an injury or illness warrants isolation or surgery, however, the camper should be removed from camp and placed in the hands of competent medical authorities as soon as possible.

Maintenance Structures

If the camp owns motor vehicles, some type of garage should be considered. The garage may include a maintenance shop, with adequate work space for repairs and preventive maintenance. The shop area will contain work benches, tables, tools, and supplies so that repair jobs can be performed throughout the year.

The garage and shop facility should be unobtrusive and undistinguished. It should be a completely functional structure, as concealed from view as possible. The building material should be fireproof or fire resistant. The building itself should be tightly constructed and designed to prevent rodent infestation or damage.

Noncounselor Personnel Quarters

Living quarters are generally furnished to all personnel employed by the camp. Some camps are so isolated from any community that camp personnel cannot live offgrounds. Living quarters for kitchen, custodial, and office personnel should be entirely separate from campers' and counselors' quarters. Employees who begin their workday at a very early hour, such as cooks and kitchen help, will probably retire early. For this reason the quarters should be segregated. These structures may be part of the administration complex. Space requirements are the same as for any other camp resident. Cabins should be equipped with lavatory facilities. If these are not available, the quarters should be close to a central wash house and toilet facility. No kitchen staff member should have living quarters in the kitchen or mess hall.

The Dining Hall and Kitchen

The single largest structure of any camp is the central dining hall. While it can serve as a recreational center on occasion, the dining hall should not be designed with other functions in mind. It serves the camp poorly to combine the primary function of the dining hall with living quarters, offices, infirmary, or other facilities. Such combinations rarely result in greater economy. The dining hall must be large enough to accommodate the total number of residents the camp will eventually have. Some camps have such a large enrollment that two or more dining halls are required. In some instances, the dining facility serves residents in shifts.

The dining hall may be a tent, a pavilion, or an enclosed building. In any case, it must be well lighted, well ventilated, and satisfactory for activities associated with mealtimes. Because camp songs, cheers, and even skits or stunts may occur during meals, the structure should have some acoustic control.

The dining hall should be accessible to all living units by a short walk. It should not be so far into the camp that access roads and vehicular traffic cut across activity or unit areas. The dining hall is shaped for the land on which it stands as well as for functional efficiency. Since the kitchen, refrigeration, and storage areas will be integral parts of the building, they must be taken into account in any design. The dining hall may be T-shaped, I-shaped, L-shaped, or rectangular. Other modifications are possible, depending upon terrain features and contours. Of necessity, as well as to comply with health department regulations, all kitchen and dining areas should be well screened against insects and should be rodent proof.

A soundly designed and fully equipped kitchen is significant to the entire camp. A well-planned kitchen is efficient and economical, allowing tasty, well-balanced meals to be prepared and served with a minimum of wasted time, effort, and supplies. Kitchen equipment should be of the finest institutional type. The heavy initial investment will more than pay for itself in both the short and the long run. Food-service planners or consultants should be hired so that adequate specifications will be incorporated into the structure.

It is obvious that food preparation will require supplies on hand. Refrigeration equipment able to handle the amount of food supplies necessary to feed the camp for a short time—at least one or two days—is mandatory. Health department regulations dealing with food handling and preservation must be rigidly observed. If there is one structure of the camp that absolutely requires electrical power, it is the kitchen and refrigeration units. Although ice may be an acceptable substitute for mechanical refrigeration, the latter is the most efficient and desirable. This is particularly true as more camps begin to rely upon frozen foods and prepackaged meals.

The Staff Lodge

The staff house or lodge, which may or may not be considered a valid part of the administration structure, is necessary at any camp that is relatively isolated from nearby communities. It is a place where off-duty counselors may relax and participate in a variety of social activities. In some camps, a unit lodge may be designated as a staff center after certain hours. Even though the two structures may contain identical features and equipment, the staff center should not be close to campers' quarters.

STRUCTURES FOR PROGRAM ACTIVITIES

No camp development is complete without a variety of structures designed primarily to enhance the programmatic aspect of the resident camping experience. These facilities are differentiated by function, although in
some instances one structure can be used for several different activities.
Among the facilities of universal importance are the main camp fire or
council ring; the aquatic facilities, which may include swimming pool or
waterfront area, marina or dock; a central recreational center or lodge;
stables; rifle range; and other facilities necessitated by the objectives of the
camp. The matter of game fields will not be considered here because the
dimensions and construction of these are well known. The subsequent development of sports and game fields are completely subject to the aims of
the individual camp. Obviously, camps organized primarily for sports training will concentrate on the development of such spaces. Camps concerned
with nature-oriented activities will not lean toward such development.

The Council Ring

Nothing so typifies camp as the camp fire (Fig. 8-11). In most decentralized camps, each unit enclave has its own council ring and camp-fire
circle. They are best placed within the circle of living units, although it may
be appropriate to locate the camp-fire circle close to the unit lodge or outdoor kitchen. Even when each enclave has its own camp-fire circle, it is still
necessary to have an all-camp council ring, particularly for formal investi-
ture and Indian ritual ceremonies. The atmosphere of camaraderie that em-
anates from the council ring lends enchantment to the camp setting.

The council ring should be located in a sheltered area, not necessarily
in the center of the camp, preferably away from scenic views. It is best located in the woods on fairly even ground. Any natural amphitheatre formed
by a depression ample for seating the entire camp population will serve
admirably. If such a bowl is unavailable, the level ground at the foot of a

FIGURE 8-11.   The camp-fire circle.

COMMUNITY CAMP FIRE CIRCLE

slope is a good substitute. Some natural object, such as an oddly shaped tree or a great rock that provides a focal point, can be part of the circle. The ring should not exceed 30 feet in diameter. Its floor will be used for dancing, skits, stunts, games, and rites, so it should be level and hard. Seats around the ring can be of split logs. Campers will invariably come to the ring with blankets to cushion the seats. No artificial lighting should be used anywhere around the council ring. Flambeaux may be placed here and there, but the light from the camp fire is really all that is needed or desirable.

The Recreational Hall

A central hall used for all-camp gatherings, particularly during inclement weather, is often advantageous. This structure may be a large barn or shed-like building near the central dining hall, quite simple in design, with nothing to distinguish it except its size. The dining hall may sometimes be used for recreational purposes as well as for dining. If the dining hall cannot be used as a recreational center, the adminstration may consider constructing a central recreational hall.

The recreational center will have a large rectangular floor that can be used for a variety of indoor court games. Dances may be held there. A slightly raised stage and proscenium arch at one end of the hall will be useful when presenting plays or holding formal presentations, orientation sessions, staff conferences, and other activities of a social, competitive, or passive nature. Because camping is primarily oriented to outdoor experiences, the recreational center may be justified on the basis of camper control through activities on rainy days.

Aquatic Facilities

If a natural waterfront is not available, some constructed swimming facility—a pool, an artificial lake, or a pond developed by damming a stream—will have to be provided. When the camp property includes a waterfront, the dock is its main facility. The dock can be temporary or permanent, depending upon water conditions, climate, and other variables. The dock has one function: It serves as an enclosed swimming or mooring area that maximizes instruction and supervision. It should be of letter form—A, E, F, H, I, J, L, or T—modified or combined as needed. The shape and size of the dock will be influenced by the number of campers using the facility, the campers' water skills, the topography, the proximity of deep water to the shoreline, the use (or not) of boats, and the preference for permanent or temporary structures.

The distance from the camp center to the waterfront, unless the camp is constructed along or around it, should be at least 300 yards, to discourage solitary swimmers. When the swimming facility is a pool or a pond, it should be readily accessible to living units and sanitary facilities, including the hot-shower house.

Examples of various docks and moorings are shown in Figure 8-12. The actual construction should be arranged by competent, experienced

FIGURE 8-12.   Camp structures and waterfront with I, T, and L docks.

dock builders. The technical aspects of construction and equipment are better left to manuals that focus on these structures and are therefore not explained in this volume.

The dock, regardless of the shape chosen, is necessary to provide safe
instructional and recreational swimming areas for the campers. Floating
docks are recommended where there are tidal changes or where the danger
of ice floes is great during winter months. Cribs are best where bottoms
slope steeply or are treacherous. This last safety area is for nonswimmers
only. Boating facilities such as moorings, boat houses, and canoe racks
should also be part of any waterfront planning.

chapter 9

Selecting
and Orienting
Counselors

Camp administrators recognize that the degree to which the aims of a camp are realized depends heavily on the quality of its counselors. Counselors bring more to camp than teaching skill in nature study, aquatics, or crafts; they also bring leadership for the campers. Because counselors must be effective leaders, camp administrators give much thought and effort to pre-camp season staffing efforts. In this chapter, recruitment, selection, and orientation of counselors will be discussed.

RECRUITMENT

The most difficult problem confronting the camp director is that of recruiting the counselor staff. There is little question that the competence, leadership, and character of the counselors determines success or failure of the camping season. So important is the counselor to the camp that all other aspects—facility construction and maintenance, business records, even food service—become insignificant by comparison. The camp succeeds only if it recruits mature, skilled counselors.

Where does recruitment begin? The director of an established camp who has the nucleus of a competent staff even before she begins to recruit for a new season is in an enviable position. Counselors from past seasons, and former campers who have reached the proper age and wish to return to the camp as counselors, constitute her first draft. But if the camp has just been founded, the search for qualified personnel is time consuming and sometimes frustrating. Camp directors maintain a file of colleges and universities that offer courses in recreational service education, outdoor education, camp counseling, elementary and secondary education, physical education, or other skills required of the camp counselor. Letters written to the department heads or professors responsible for these courses often elicit names of potential candidates. Letters to college placement bureaus may also produce a list of interested persons. The camp director might invest some time in speaking with high school guidance counselors, giving them information about her camp and about camping in general. Nonstudent candidates include some teachers who seek camp employment during the summer, and early retirees of military services. Advertisements in metropolitan-area newspapers may produce some results. Placing notices in journals read by those qualified and interested is even more effective. Notices in the Journal of Health, Physical Education, Recreation and Dance (JOHPERD); *Parks and Recreation; Camping Magazine;* state health, physical education, and recreation publications; and home economics, social work, and education journals may supply the camp director with a surplus of qualified candidates from which to select her staff.

Aggressive recruitment has been made absolutely necessary by the competition among camps to find the best possible personnel. When potential candidates reply to an advertisement or an announcement by a placement bureau or professor, the camp should respond by sending them an application, along with the camp staff brochure. The brochure, an inexpensive device, should be readable, first of all, and have some color and pictures. It should include information about the camp, including its history and setting, job descriptions, and salary and benefits. The number of campers and their ages should be stated, along with information about the camp's facilities, structures, program of activities, and health requirements. If it is effective and truthful, the brochure may be the most helpful means of convincing a competent potential counselor to apply for a position.

Other useful techniques are presenting addresses at career days in secondary schools and colleges; enlisting the cooperation of former counselors, campers, and other staff in interesting promising persons in counselor assignments; and distributing pamphlets, leaflets, and posters to social, civic, and service organizations.

Locating possible candidates and having them fill out applications is merely the first step in hiring qualified staff. The next procedure is selection.

SELECTION

After counselors are recruited, examinations are given to test their ability and merit. Some abilities are readily tested; other can be judged only on the basis of previous performance. Examinations reveal whether the candidate actually possesses a particular talent, skill, or attribute, and to what degree. Of course, tests are also used to eliminate undesirable candidates. Examinations may be written, oral, practical, or a combination of the three. Tests of general aptitude, intelligence, achievement, motor skill, and even health may be included. Written tests should cover, as far as possible, the entire range of knowledge pertaining to counselor positions. Oral tests, although sometimes administered, are almost completely subjective and exceedingly difficult to rate equitably. Since they are also time consuming, they may be profitably eliminated. Practical tests require candidates to demonstrate their skill in a given area. They are often given not so much to determine the degree of skill possessed as to rate the candidate's familiarity with the materials employed within the program and his ability to use them creatively. The effectiveness of the examinations depends totally upon the validity of the tests themselves. The results give the camp director an objective basis on which to grade applicants.

The personal interview is the method preferred by most camp directors for assessing personality and appearance. It gives some indication of how the candidate acts and expresses himself, of his level of poise and maturity. The interview, which is not the same as an oral examination, is also useful in obtaining background information and a brief personal history of the candidate. Adroit interviewing—but not prying—will usually evoke voluntarily contributed information that reveals the candidate's character and intelligence. Carefully worded questions designed to bring out latent hostility, bias, or fleeting loyalties can indicate more about counselor potential than most written or practical examinations. However, only an experienced interviewer can elicit this type of information.

After the tests and interviews, the next stage is induction or employment by the camp. Interested applicants must first be advised of all duties, responsibilities, remuneration, benefits, and privileges that will be part of employment. This information, which is vital to reinforce the original recruitment information that gained the candidate's interest, is best provided in the camp contract. The contract itself is legally binding on both the camp and the candidate. It states all functions and obligations of each party to the other, all financial arrangements, and any other pertinent facts that will ensure compliance by both parties. A typical contract is provided in Appendix B.

If the candidate signs the contract, a new phase in the relationship between the counselor and the camp begins. Since most camp directors begin to seek staff at least 6 months before the opening of the camp season, contact with the newly appointed counselor should be maintained from the time of hiring until the precamp counselor orientation program. Contact can be maintained by providing a counselor's manual pertaining to the details of camp operation and the counselor's place and function within the overall organization. The counselor will then be able to read and assimilate information that will enable him to participate fully in the camp's success.

ORIENTATION

Some time prior to the campers' arrival, counselors should be oriented to the camp's philosophy, policies, rules and regulations, and standards and expectations. Camps usually organize a preseason staff development workshop that operates from 3 days to 2 weeks—rarely longer. Many camps prefer a 1-week staff orientation in order that peer relations may be firmly founded, skills and talent discovered, responsibilities scrupulously defined, and routine functions habitualized.

When a large percentage of counselors are new to the camp, or even to camping itself, the job of transforming experienced and inexperienced counselors into a smoothly functioning and efficient group of prepared leaders may make the difference between a great camp season and a mediocre one.[1] Coincident with this operation is the requirement that the camp be ready for effective performance at the end of the preparatory session. The average camp season is from 8 to 10 weeks, with extremes ranging from 6 to 12, depending upon the section of the country represented and the closing of school. Dealing with camp orientation for counselors requires careful attention to detail and much effort on the part of the camp director. As a good administrator, the camp director will probably consult with some or all of her head staff concerning the content of the orientation. She will be interested but should not play a dominant role during the preparatory period. Particular phases of the orientation may be profitably delegated to program and division heads, or to others whose knowledge and skills may be best used in developing the most highly skilled and competent counselors possible.

Theory and Practice

The precamp orientation workshop should be balanced between talking and performance, between philosophy and activity, between rules, regulations, policy, and practical application. There should be time for work and time for recreational experiences. New staff members will be excited when they arrive. Almost any trip to camp is long and tiring, even for mature persons. It is wise, therefore, to initiate the orientation program in a leisurely manner, accelerating and getting into the working sessions that require attention and effort after the first day.

Camp Philosophy

The specific topics and discussions included in nearly all precamp orientations will concern the history and organization of the camp. The philosophy of the particular camp will be discussed in relation to camping in general. All workshops of this type offer some discussion of counseling and leadership, including the development of professional attitudes toward campers and peers. Health, safety, and emergency procedures used in cases of illness, accident, or injury will be given attention. The development and promotion of routine, recurrent, and special events making up the comprehensive and well-balanced camp program are vital. Pertinent discussions on camper behavior, common problems and how to deal with them, camp schedules, and counselor assignments are some of the topics that may be included. The camp director's experience as well as her reliance upon key personnel and their previous experiences may well determine the topics most significant and pertinent to the camp and to the counselors.

[1]R. Kane, "Here Comes the Kid," *Camping Magazine* (March 1985), 16, 19.

Activities

Among the activities suitable for practical application in the precamp orientation will be familiarization with the camp's physical property and its adjacent natural resources that may profitably be used in camping activities; natural science explorations; nature lore expeditions and exposure; and knowledge and performance of various camp skills. Department and division heads will be expert in one or more of these activities. They will be the resource personnel and serve as general instructors to the counselors. If the camp has employed specialists in any program activity, then the specialists will teach their skills to others. Every camp has a designated supervisor of waterfront activities. It will be this person's function to explain all rules, regulations, and requirements to the camp staff, assign certain waterfront responsibilities to his immediate assistants, and set up standard operating functions for all counselors. The camp medical staff will offer instruction in first aid, ask that specific data be gathered from campers, and make known other needs for the preservation of the health and safety of the campers and the entire camp force. The camp director or her deputy will discuss, among other items, camp policies, administrative procedures, and staff regulations. It may be that in the process of discussion, new policies will be formulated, with the camp staff taking part in developing them.

Interpersonal Relations

Fundamentally, the precamp orientation is concerned with developing sound methods for conducting camp activities and reducing areas of potential conflict. It is an excellent time for forming new acquaintances, ironing out difficulties, gaining understanding of others, and becoming familiar with established procedures that have been successful. It is a time to prepare for good personal relations, to develop counselor skills, and to consider the intangible but vital ingredient for camping objectives to be met: a sensitivity to democratic practice through small-group living experiences. Concomitant with democracy in action at the bunk level is the rapport established between counselors and the relationships between counselors and their immediate supervisors and peers. A feeling for the camp and its success, and a dedication to contributing to a satisfying camp life must permeate the orientation sessions.

Counselor Proficiencies

Certain modes of living preferred in the camp environment should be reiterated until they are habitual. The counselor must be concerned with good grooming, cleanliness, and orderliness, all of which are part of ensuring pleasant group living. Only those efforts that will make counselors proficient, ensure appreciation for camp life, and prepare them to be a constant guide and influence to a group of children should be covered in the orientation program. Of necessity, orientation activities should encourage alertness and the physical and mental preparation to resolve whatever problems may arise when working with the intangibles of human nature.

One valuable instrument for preparing the counselor is the record of other camp seasons. This may take the form of a cumulative record of all problems that have been confronted and their resolution. An end-of-season counselor report that is maintained at the discretion of the camp director can be valuable for informing new counselors of past conditions and situations. However the information is compiled, it may prove a ready asset in ensuring counselor knowledge of specific job requirements. Such reports are generally written by the counselors themselves. They are narrative for the most part, but may be written and rendered formally on a prepared form for easy reading. Such reports relate specifically the various aspects of the counselor situation and any recommendations or modification of actions, responsibilities, or functions that were suggested. In this way, the novice counselor may be able to gain an accurate picture of his position without delay. Any techniques that have proven successful may be retained and reused as needed. There is no wasted time in trial and error; the end result will be greater efficiency and effectiveness.

As previously indicated, the counselor should have a reasonably accuate concept of his duties and responsibilities prior to signing his contract. To further his comprehension of his assignment, he should discuss the details of his position with the camp director, if possible, but certainly with his immediate supervisor. When counselors' questions cannot be answered by the supervisor, referral to the assistant administrator or to the director herself is preferred. When the counselor understands his job and all the reasonable auxiliary tasks that he may be asked to perform, he will feel composed and ready. Secure in the knowledge that he has the skill and the capacity to act surely and well, he will work effectively and with self-confidence.

Rationale for Orientation

The precamp orientation or training period is extremely important for new counselors as well as for those who are returning. The precamp orientation provides the opportunity for all staff to become acquainted with one another as well as to learn or review the camp's operational policies. Furthermore, precamp training permits the staff to become familiar with the campsite itself, as well as the various activities that may be programmed during the camping season. Orientation offers a chance for individual counselors to initiate some program-planning ideas that can then be examined by peers prior to their application with the campers.

Counselors should meet with those who make up their designated units and the supervisors of those units. The entire procedure of precamp orientation and training is designed to prepare staff for effective performance. With this in mind, it is vital that the camp director and her assistants plan a program that will at once welcome the staff to the camp, provide learning experiences that will hone camping skills, and permit staff to demonstrate specific skills and to participate in the general experiences that will be a part of the camp's program of activities.

Precamp orientation sessions should make use of a variety of interesting and dynamically presented instructional methods. Sessions should be planned to give practical experience in a wide variety of nature-oriented and other essential camp skills. Guest speakers, demonstrations, audiovisual aids, discussion groups, and brain-storming sessions can all be used to great advantage. A balanced program should be worked out so that each person has some contribution to make, and so that physical activity alternates with sitting, listening, or discussion sessions.

The camp's philosophy and administrative guidelines can be promulgated from the first moment of the orientation. Whatever the frame of reference, the precamp training program will enable it to be carried out. The quality of the orientation period will surely affect continued in-service staff development while the camp is operating. If the camp administration wants its counselors to be creative, use ingenuity, and become a group of cooperative and willing workers, then the precamp preparatory program needs no further justification.

Among the concepts to be presented during the precamp orientation period are the following:

1. The camp's traditions and value system
2. Operational policies and procedures
3. Camper clientele
4. Personnel policies
5. Counselor duties, responsibilities, and behavior
6. Camper behavior, problems, and discipline; camper guidance
7. Principles of ecology, conservation, and natural preservation
8. Health and safety practices
9. Emergency procedures
10. Activity skills
11. Familiarization with the camp's physical property
12. Cooperative relationships with other staff
13. Program planning and development
14. Supervisory techniques and problem resolution

These are just a few of the topics that can be encountered in any well-conceived precamp orientation program. Greater emphasis may be given to one area of concern over another, but counselors and other personnel will certainly be prepared to lead campers and to function in a manner that should enable the camping season to be successful.

The following outlines some of the activities that can be included in a camp orientation workshop. Of course, the workshop should be structured on the basis of the individual camp's needs.

Typical Orientation Workshop Activities
Monday

11:00 AM	Counselors and other staff arrive at camp
11:30 AM	Preliminary greetings from camp director
12:00 PM	First camp meal (breakfast or lunch)

1:00 PM   Assignment to bunks

1:15 PM   Unpack belongings, stow away gear

2:00 PM   First general staff meeting
        Introduction of department heads and division supervisors
        Assignment of counselors to unit supervisors
        Distribution of staff manual
        Announcement of orientation schedule and future staff meetings

3:00 PM   Recreational period (swimming, informal group meetings, and so on)

5:00 PM   Second meal (lunch or supper)

6:00 PM   Staff meeting to familiarize personnel with campsite

7:00 PM   Recreational period to relax, write letters, and so on

8:00 PM   Camp-fire activity
        Presentation by camp director about camp history
        Prepared skit or stunt by head staff
        Camp songs

10:00 PM   End-of-day ceremonies, lights out

Tuesday

7:00 AM   Reveille

7:45 AM   Breakfast

8:30 AM   Clean up living quarters

9:00 AM   Meeting
        Camp organization
        Familiarization with camp facility
        Possible camp program
        Assignment to groups for instruction and practice

10:00 AM   Formation of groups
        Water safety
        Boating and small-craft handling
        Swimming instruction
        Crafts
        Nature study, Indian lore
        First aid and health procedures
        Sports skills and physical activity
        Special events (camp-fire, trips, program possibilities)
        Camp cookery
        Camp crafts

11:30 AM   Recreational period

12:00 PM   Lunch

1:00 PM   Relaxation period

2:00 PM   Meeting
        Camp policies on counselor behavior
        Camp routines
        Assignment to new groups for instruction and practice

3:00 PM   Formation of groups (as assigned)

4:30 PM   Brief break (shower or bath)

5:00 PM   Supper

6:00 PM   Recreational period (planned or spontaneous)

7:00 PM   Camp-fire activity
          Presentation by camp director about past camp seasons
          Head staff camp-fire activity
          Discussion of camp-fire program
          Camp songs
10:00 PM End-of-day ceremonies, lights out

Wednesday

7:00 AM   Reveille
7:45 AM   Breakfast
8:30 AM   Clean up living quarters
9:00 AM   Meeting
          Camper–counselor relationships
          Supervisory problems
          Assignment to new groups for instruction and practice
10:00 AM Formation of groups for continued instruction and practice
11:30 AM Recreational period
12:00 PM Lunch
1:00 PM   Relaxation period
2:00 PM   Meeting
          Camper problems
          Parental visitation
          Sick call and health practices
          Assignment to new groups for instruction and practice
3:00 PM   Formation of groups
4:30 PM   Brief break
5:00 PM   Supper
6:00 PM   Recreational period (planned or spontaneous)
7:00 PM   Camp-fire activity
          Demonstrations of camp-fire activities
          Camp songs
10:00 PM End-of-day ceremonies, lights out

Thursday

7:00 AM   Reveille
7:45 AM   Breakfast
8:30 AM   Clean up living quarters
9:00 AM   Meeting
          Leadership of small groups
          Camper problems
          Counselor responsibilities
          Assignment to new groups for instruction and practice
10:00 AM Formation of groups for continued instruction and practice
11:30 AM Recreational period
12:00 PM Lunch
1:00 PM   Relaxation period
2:00 PM   Overnight trip (hike, canoe, or bicycle)

Determine campsite
Pitch camp
Cook supper

5:30 PM   Supper

6:30 PM   Camp-fire activity (trip procedure and evaluation)
Inspect all sites and examine shelters
Camp songs

9:30 PM   End-of-day ceremonies, lights out

Friday

7:00 AM   Reveille

7:45 AM   Breakfast cookout

8:30 AM   Strike camp

9:00 AM   Return to camp (hike, canoe, bicycle, or camp vehicle)

11:30 AM   Relaxation period

12:00 PM   Lunch

1:00 PM   Meeting
Discussion of overnight trip
Evaluation, suggestions, recommendations
Camper age groups and their developmental characteristics

2:00 PM   Formation of groups for continued instruction and practice

4:30 PM   Recreational period

5:00 PM   Supper

6:00 PM   Relaxation period

7:00 PM   Camp-fire activity
Counselor skit
Camp songs

10:00 PM   End-of-day ceremonies, lights out

Saturday

7:00 AM   Reveille

7:45 AM   Breakfast

8:30 AM   Clean up living quarters

9:00 AM   Inspection of living quarters by unit supervisors

10:00 AM   Meeting
Small-group activities
Rainy-day activities
Religious services and training at camp (problems and practices)
Assignment to new groups for instruction and practice

11:00 AM   Formation of groups for continued instruction and practice

12:00 PM   Lunch

1:00 PM   Relaxation period

2:00 PM   Meeting
Critique of counselor quarters inspection
Mealtime activities (songs, announcements and so on)
Assignment to new groups for instruction and practice

3:00 PM   Formation of groups for continued instruction and practice

4:45 PM   Brief break

5:00 PM   Supper

6:00 PM   Recreational period

7:00 PM   Camp-fire activity
           Camp rituals and societies
           Demonstrations, exhibits, stunts
           Camp songs

10:00 PM   End-of-day ceremonies, lights out

Sunday

7:00 AM   Reveille

7:45 AM   Breakfast

8:30 AM   Clean up living quarters

9:00 AM   Meeting
           Sunday camp activities
           Entertainment (movies, excursions, concerts, and so on)
           Evaluation of instructional groups

11:00 AM   Recreational period

12:00 PM   Lunch

1:00 PM   Relaxation period

2:00 PM   Meeting
           First day of the season
           Settling campers into bunks
           Critique of orientation program
           Additional announcements, notices, schedules
           Assignment of campers to bunk counselors

4:00 PM   Recreational period

5:00 PM   Supper

6:30 PM   Free evening (trip to nearby town in camp vehicle if possible)

11:00 PM   Return to camp for lights out

Monday

7:00 AM   Reveille

7:45 AM   Breakfast

8:30 AM   Clean up living quarters

9:00 AM   Camp inspection prior to opening

10:00 AM   Prepare to meet campers

10:30 AM   Meet campers

chapter 10

Building Counselor Effectiveness

While the precamp orientation is most effective for counselor preparation, it is not the only available forum for staff development. Orientation deals in theory and the practice of skills; it does not include actual experience with campers, and thus cannot foresee all the problems to be encountered or provide answers to all the situations that arise during the camp season. For these reasons, an in-service staff educational program must be conducted throughout the camp season. The program can be performed through supervision, staff conferences, individual critiques, and observation. The assistant camp director, unit supervisors, division heads, and specialists may assist the camp director in these tasks.

All too frequently left to chance, in-service education must be planned as carefully as the orientation program. Counselors work 24 hours a day; their responsibilities are extensive. Lack of time often leads to discontinuance of instruction and diminished performance quality. It is often difficult to bring the entire staff together for specific instruction. Staff meetings called to dispose of routine problems, to disseminate notices or changes in camp policy, and for the continual development of the camp program may therefore be the best times for in-service instruction.

The camp director and the head staff must make every minute of these meetings valuable.[1] Scrupulous attention to the daily activities of camp life, conditions of the camp, counselor morale, camper attitudes, and any other problems that confront counselors should be examined in developmental sessions. Staff meetings should be scheduled weekly as part of the counselors' functions; they must never conflict with time-off allotments arranged

---

[1]D. Freeman, "Power of Positive Modeling," *Camping Magazine* (April 1984), 16–17, 28.

by contract. When required, individual conferences should supplement the staff meetings.

PERSONNEL MANAGEMENT

Continuous in-service education is an essential part of personnel management, especially in camping agencies. Although many of the camp's employees have qualified backgrounds, there are just as many with little or no prior experiences directly associated with their functions. Many camps are dependent upon personnel who have had comparatively little, or even no, academic preparation for their work. Those lacking the academic background may offer skills valuable to the camp program. There is little question that in-service education affects the quality of work produced. It facilitates the job of the camp director, qualifies staff to perform more valuable work, promotes leadership ability, and affords a greater opportunity for examining applied techniques in resolving problems. High standards of counselor performance are effected in response to this procedure.[2]

In-service education specifically attempts to enhance professional competence by consistent examination of factors such as personality, work conditions, personal judgment and intelligence, morale problems, skills, and environmental conflicts. In-service education starts with obstacles and seeks to discover the underlying causes of the problem. This process encourages innovation and logical study of facts for the determination of possible solutions.

Among the particular learning experiences the camp director can provide to promote counselor skills are demonstrations, individual conferences, group or staff conferences, and recommendations for professional reading.

Demonstrations

Demonstrations involve a carefully arranged performance of one or more activities that allow the observer to learn basic movements, sequential efforts, and instructional techniques. It provides a controlled series of events so that new skills can be assimilated or familiar skills can be improved. Usually, specialists employed by the camp organize demonstrations.

Individual Conferences

Individual conferences are usually scheduled when problems are confronted during employment. They establish supervisor–counselor rapport so that conflicts, disagreements, or meritorious service can be appraised and discussed without interference. The private talk is one of the best methods for encouraging counselor performance. It must be assumed, however, that a good working relationship has been established between supervisor

[2]C. E. Knapp, "Staff Education: Balancing People and Activity Skills," *Camping Magazine* (April 1984), 22–24.

and counselor, and that the supervisor refrains from any threatening or coercive measures. Utter frankness and objectivity are essential. What is well done deserves praise; what is poorly performed requires assistance. The individual conference can be scheduled by supervisory request or counselor initiative. It can be useful in ascertaining needs, in resolving personal problems, or for providing confidential information about campers.

Staff Conferences

The group or staff conference can be formal or informal, depending upon the maturity of the counselors and the relationship between the supervisor and those attending. Initially, the staff conference may have a rather formal agenda. Once the camp season is in progress and worker relationships have been established, however, the staff conference can become less structured. Of necessity, the supervisor will nominally control the conference, but emphasis should be placed upon free and open discussion without fear of retaliation. Counselors should have the chance to express themselves on any number of issues concerning the operation of their bunks, the division, or the camp in general.[3] The staff conference must not degenerate into clique meetings, harangues against personalities, or boredom. Gripe sessions are tolerable, but staff conferences should not be devoted to this practice. Whenever camp conditions reach a point at which staff complaints are valid, every effort must be made to resolve such conditions. It is not unusual to learn of counselor conflicts with peers, petty jealousies, minor irritations, and other issues that are unavoidable when individuals work in close quarters. If such behavior becomes generalized, however, it will be most apparent at staff meetings. The cause of such problems must be determined and eliminated before it threatens the entire camp.

Professional Reading

Every camp should have a shelf of published materials dealing with the organization, administration, and supervision of camps. Books, pamphlets, magazines, and other items can be placed at some central location for the staff's convenience. Pertinent materials can also include posters, films, filmstrips, an idea file, and records. Subjects to be covered include camp operation, child development, outdoor education and nature-oriented activities, behavioral problems, health, safety, and camper welfare. The administration can stimulate appreciation and use of these materials. If staff selection has been effective, it is likely that the counselors will want to learn as much as they can. Maturity and sound judgment will motivate counselors to look upon professional reading as an opportunity to become more highly qualified in carrying out their responsibilities to the camp, the campers, and themselves.

---

[3]J. Glick and C. P. Brand, "Shared Responsibility," *Camping Magazine* (April 1984), 18–20.

SUPERVISION

Supervision at camp is primarily concerned with achieving and uniting excellent environment, qualified personnel, and camper satisfaction and welfare through organized programming. Camp supervision is chiefly oriented toward enhancing counselor performance so that maximum benefits to all campers will be achieved. To better understand supervision, one must realize that it is inextricably bound to leadership. Leadership is the ability to influence other people in the achievement of common aims or ideals. Supervision uses leadership along with specialized knowledge, skills, or techniques to foster cooperative relationships and to ensure effective services.

The Supervisory Process

Effective supervision almost always requires innovation. Working with people demands an understanding of ego needs, insight into human behavior, and most important, the realization that each human being is unique. Each person brings his background, education, skills, talents, and beliefs to his current situation. Therefore, supervision obligates the supervisor to listen rather than command, to assist rather than criticize. Valid supervision encourages the worker's talent, develops a democratic atmosphere, and enhances sound personal relationships for maximum cooperation. Good supervision is directly aimed at providing valuable experiences to those who participate in the camping program. It engenders creative ideas and activities so as to benefit the ultimate consumer: the camper.

Increasing awareness of the need for favorable responses to supervision in the camp operation requires leadership, not mere authority, in assisting and coordinating the work of staff personnel. Leadership in the supervisory process will stress personal involvement and dedicated effort for the mutual benefit of the camp, the camper, and counselor.[4] Only in this way will staff realize a sense of satisfaction from having accomplished the objective for which they were employed. Integrity, initiative, and a desire to cooperate are obtained through leadership. Individual characteristics are appraised and effectively blended for optimum program strength, group energies are maximized, and the personal growth of individual counselors is encouraged. If the supervisor imposes arbitrary control or autocratic methods, counselors' initiative and potential will be stifled. Supervisory leadership should generate the desire to emulate, offering a guide to the counselor rather than demanding conformity to someone's notion of what is required.

Efficacious supervision uses educational techniques. Counselors will perform better when they become aware of certain facts about the camp, the camper, the program, and all other pertinent aspects of camp administration.[5] An effective supervisor provides information about functional op-

---

[4]J. S. Davis, "Crisis Management," *Camping Magazine* (May 1984), 27–29.
[5]D. Beck, "Effective Staff Supervision," *Camping Magazine* (February 1986), 17–19.

erations, supplies truthful replies to questions, and gives assistance when requested or needed. Problems are more easily resolved and areas of conflict more readily handled when there is a working relationship and an atmosphere of mutual confidence and support on the part of the counselor and the unit supervisor or camp administrator.[6] The staffs' tendency to seek out supervisory assistance in overcoming weaknesses or difficulties is directly proportional to the degree of trust and confidence engendered by the supervisor.

> Supervision must embrace people and things for this is the nature of the work. It is sometimes assumed that these two factors may be treated separately, but this is not valid. There is a pressing need for people who have both technical competence and an understanding of the needs of individuals and the eccentricities of human behavior ... Supervisory leadership, which relies upon objectivity as well as cooperative understanding when dealing with the human factor, is required.[7]

The following are among the functions of the supervisor:

1. Interpretation of camp policy to the staff
2. Analysis and development of techniques leading to the improvement of all camp activities
3. Appraisal and enhancement of instructional skills used by counselors
4. In-service education
5. Provision of technical assistance for improved competence
6. Evaluation of camp staff, with recommendations for improvement
7. Evaluation of the camp program, with recommendations for necessary modifications
8. Evaluation of supervisory methods for better performance

Supervision occurs whenever assistance is rendered through personal contact. Contact is made and maintained by scheduled meetings, staff conferences, or informal interaction in the course of normal daily events. Appointments must be scrupulously kept. Camp tasks should be well thought out and assigned on an impartial basis. The supervisor's behavior must be responsible and dependable, and must indicate a mature understanding of both personal and professional problems. Above all, the supervisor must be objective in his judgments.

The supervisor can best perform his counseling function when his subordinates feel that he is readily accessible and sincerely interested in them as individuals. The supervisor should be sensitive to his subordinate's feelings so that they will discuss their problems without feeling that someone

---

[6]H. D. Sessons and J. L. Stevenson, *Leadership and Group Dynamics in Recreational Services* (Boston: Allyn & Bacon, 1981), pp. 229–30.
[7]J. S. Shivers, *Principles and Practices of Recreational Service* (New York: Macmillan, 1967), p. 336.

is prying into their personal affairs. The supervisor must give all such problems, whether trivial or complicated, the careful consideration, sympathetic understanding, and attention necessary to alleviate them.[8]

For supervision to be effective, it may be that irritating environmental causes must be removed. Interpersonal conflicts sometimes retard counselor efforts. When this occurs, the underlying factors that appear to promote conflict should be examined and practical steps taken to eliminate them. Where there are personality conflicts, experiential dissonances, or other problems arising from varying backgrounds and personal characteristics, measures must be taken to regain cooperation. Transfer to different camp assignments may resolve the problem. In serious situations, it may be that only separation from the camp can accomplish what reassignment cannot. It must be noted that discharge from employment is a reflection not only on the former counselor, but also on the camp's method of selection. This is another reason that the screening of candidates is of utmost importance to the camp's well-being. If living or working conditions—poor food, poor facilities, excessive strain due to understaffing—are responsible for poor counselor performance, these irritants must be erased quickly.

Counselor Achievement

The best supervision promotes a climate in which the inventive, creative counselor is not only permitted but also encouraged to contribute to the camp program. Attempts at creating new ideas and activities, together with questions about traditional methods, are sought. Through democratic practices of questioning the accepted and being recognized as an individual with valuable and stimulating contributions, the counselor is motivated to perform at higher levels of skill and confidence. As the counselor achieves self-mastery and self-realization through handling campers' problems and camp activities, she obtains a sense of security, satisfaction, and leadership capability. Consequently, the counselor becomes devoted to the camp that has provided an opportunity for growth and development. This appreciation is demonstrated in the counselor's loyalty to the camp, dedication to the welfare of the campers, and ego involvement with the success of the camp season.[9]

Professional attitudes toward the camp and its clients can be promoted even when the counselor is not a trained professional. Such personal attributes as loyalty, dedication, tact, reliability, initiative, and enthusiasm must be stimulated in the counselor. Better counselor–supervisor relationships and added counselor motivation for innovation and effectiveness will result. Supervision as a leadership process not only elicits counselor receptivity to advice and assistance; it also inspires self-evaluation of personal efforts. It is essential that the supervisor encourage self-evaluation in the counselor. Unless the counselor is prepared to accept criticism and to try

[8]J. S. Shivers, *Recreational Leadership, Group Dynamics and Interpersonal Behavior,* 2nd ed. (Princeton: Princeton Book Company, 1986), pp. 277–82.
[9]W. A. Becker, "The Key to Staff Motivation," *Camping Magazine* (May 1984), 32–35.

to improve her work habits and skills, little will be accomplished. Despite direct command or proffered advice, the counselor will not display enhanced work performance until she herself recognizes the need for it. In the last analysis, it is the counselor who must believe that she has a need to improve before any improvement will occur. Supervision—objectively given, scientifically based, democratically oriented, and inventively practiced—will nearly always foster counselor esprit de corps, and the results of such efforts will be enjoyed by the camper. The success of supervision can be evaluated in terms of counselor effectiveness, program satisfaction, camper happiness, and the final success of the camp.[10]

MAINTAINING COUNSELOR MORALE

If counselors are the common denominator of the successful camp season, then the camp's effectiveness is necessarily dependent upon good morale among counselors. The director and the head staff are the keys to good staff morale. The director's ability to recruit and employ good personnel and to develop a democratic atmosphere in administering the camp plays a considerable role in promoting positive attitudes among staff. The director's willingness to receive and accept ideas, recommendations, and advice from the staff goes a long way towards establishing relationships that are vital for staff cohesion, efficiency, and loyalty.

A definite enumeration of functions and responsibilities, a sharply defined connection between administration and staff, and a willingness on the part of each employee to do whatever is necessary to enable the camp to achieve its objectives are factors to be considered in advancing positive morale. The camp director must therefore avoid getting too deeply embroiled in the technical details of administration; she must share her attention with head staff, counselors, and campers. The director must employ enough assistants for managing camp business and clerical detail so that she has time and energy for guiding personnel. The director sets the philosophical and ideological tone of the camp. Her understanding of democratic practice will eventually pervade the entire camp. If she expresses confidence in the staff's abilities and indicates high performance expectations, it is likely that her staff will adopt her standards.

A counselor committee may be inaugurated, or, if counselors have established genuine rapport with their supervisors, the supervisors may act as a mediating force between the counselors and the administration. Liaison between the counselors and the director should be proposed. In addition, direct suggestions or recommendations may be made for the operating efficiency of the camp. The director is wise to listen to such advice unless, in her best judgment and experience, she is sure that the proposals thus generated are divisive.

[10]H. Dimock, "The Art of Camp Supervision," *Camping Magazine* (February 1985), 26–28.

Preventing Undesirable Counselor Behavior

The effective counselor is mature and attempts to cooperate with his peers. He avoids cliques. Small groups of staff members who gather together to the exclusion of others frequently form the nucleus of a disaffected minority that may destroy staff morale. The clique can be formed as a result of certain individual maladjustments to the camp environment, because of previous acquaintances, or because of an avowed common dislike for someone or something. Subgroups of this negative type may be thwarted by staff meetings, in-service education, supervisory leadership, and common sense. Staff or camp policy must never be criticized in front of campers; to be equally shunned is the ridicule of other counselors, activities, and campers.

Personal Entanglements

Counselors who involve themselves in the social life of communities close to the camp can cause problems for the camp. Although no modern camp can dictate what counselors may or may not do in their time away from camp, the camp has an obligation to see that staff morale remains high. Entanglements in local problems or with local citizens can lead to deterioration of staff behavior. Occasionally, encounters with members of the opposite sex in nearby towns result in inappropriate consequences. This is particularly true when two counselors compete for the favors of the same individual. The resulting tension is not only difficult for the counselors themselves, but it also tends to disrupt their fulfillment of their responsibilities. Whenever social distractions seem to be playing havoc with the counselor's job performance, a personal conference with his immediate supervisor is in order. Counselors should be warned against such distractions prior to employment.

Time Off

All camps allow counselors to have time off away from camp, and it is usually written into the contract. No counselor, no matter how well qualified and devoted, can be expected to maintain high-caliber performance unless he has some respite from his responsibilities. For this reason, 1 or 2 days off each week are required, with a counselor's preference for a specific day given due consideration. However, time away from camp should be so used that the counselor is refreshed and ready to resume his responsibilities. Thus, the counselor should avoid overextending himself on his day off by traveling such long distances that he will need a recovery period upon his return. Hiking, driving, bicycling, or other methods of travel away from camp are excellent when done in moderation.

Sound Health

The counselors' responsibilities demand that he be in reasonably good mental and physical condition. Activities that devitalize the counselor, making him physically and mentally sluggish, must be avoided. All counselors need sufficient rest, nourishing food, and exercise if they are to respond to the stimulation around them. They cannot afford to be irritable, impatient, or just plain tired. The remedy for reduced counselor efficiency may be a better health regimen. Nervousness as a result of fatigue does not enhance the counselor in the eyes of the campers. The counselor who cannot maintain the pace at camp finds himself with more behavior problems as campers determine his inability to keep ahead of them. It may not be from maliciousness that campers sometimes bedevil a counselor, but from a sense of mischievousness that all children possess. Sufficient sleep and physical activity should shake the cobwebs out and enable the counselor to assume his rightful role as guide, friend, and leader.

Hygiene and Habits

Despite the most careful selection and orientation, a few counselors will no doubt be employed whose personal hygiene habits are questionable. Such individuals somehow slip through the selection process, and it is only after their deplorable habits are known that measures can be taken.

Rarely do counselors have drinking problems. Alcoholics seldom become counselors, partly because the supply of liquor is limited. There are always means of obtaining alcoholic beverages, however. When a counselor drinks to excess, the entire camp is hurt. Only one solution is sensible: instant discharge. No parent wants his child around an alcoholic. The possibility of injury, either mental or physical, is too great. The trustworthiness of the drinker is also suspect; the welfare of the camper is secondary to his own selfish interests, and such conduct can never be tolerated.

Gossip

Camps are frequently situated near small towns—and small towns are notorious for provincialism, gossip, and intolerance of outsiders. Counselors would be well cautioned to respect the prevailing traditions and local mores. Such behavior as frequenting local taverns and conducting oneself boisterously, regardless of its innocence, becomes distorted in the mind of the gossip monger. The counselor must conduct himself in a manner that is reserved, decorous, and unobtrusive in the community that supplies the camp. It is unfortunate that good spirits, a loud laugh, or other honest behavior can be misconstrued and turned to slander, but it does happen. The best defense against narrowmindedness is strict adherence to socially acceptable behavior.

Leadership

Leadership ability is learned, and few people have the patience to become leaders. Nevertheless, the counselor must be a leader. The leader is able to initiate action and serve as a stimulator to her followers. No counselor should ever resort to arbitrary practices, show favoritism, or attempt to fix behavior by imposing rigid regulations. Arbitrariness leads to suspicion and mistrust. Favoritism indicates emotional bias and a closed mind.

Rigidity relies upon coercion, and threats negate the objective of camping and create conflict among campers. Reasonable explanations for rules or regulations, guidance toward desired goals, and objectivity with campers will result in better attitudes and habits, and more enjoyment.

Coercion

Coercive behaviors among counselors are not to be tolerated. Physical punishment and violent scenes bring out unmitigated rebellion and animosity among campers. The counselor who uses these methods to achieve his objectives fails to understand the reason for the camp's existence. Counselors who brutalize campers are incapable of good guidance practices.[11] They lack the ability to lead or motivate. A counselor who inflicts punishment has failed to relate to and recognize the camper's need. Certainly campers sometimes exhibit behavior that appears to require strict disciplinary action, but it should be referred to the unit supervisor or to the administrator. Extreme behavior may indicate the need for psychological assistance.

Camper Behavior

Because campers are human and young, there is bound to be a certain amount of rule infraction. Children, wittingly or not, invariably break, bend, or test restrictions, regulations, or policies designed to protect them. If the intent of the infraction is malicious, the action must be carefully analyzed to determine the cause. Punishment meted out harshly will not resolve the problem; the unacceptable conduct will continue unabated. It may be that the camp environment cannot offer the proper means for combating excessive behavior. In such a case, referral or recommendations to the camper's parent or guardian is the best course. When minor infringements or even serious breaches in rules are made by campers however, the counselor should attempt to determine the reasons for such disturbances. If the behavior warrants, specific limits can be set.

Punishment, such as withholding certain privileges or prohibiting attendance at particular activities, may be indicated. The punishment must be equal to the questionable behavior. Punishment is easily contrived. Campers who are boisterous during rest period, who engage in dangerous activity at the waterfront, or who violate decorum while eating can be disciplined in proportion to the event. Preventing the camper from leaving his bunk after rest period ends, immediately restricting the camper from the waterfront, or requiring the camper to leave the table may have a more salutary effect than indiscriminate or harsh measures.

Counselor Relationships

Relationships among staff members are the most significant factor in determining camp cohesion and morale. Where there are sound interpersonal relationships, there is willingness to pull together, to be part of a team

---

[11]R. Ditter, "Protecting Our Campers," *Camping Magazine* (January 1986), 20–23.

effort, and to assist, without reservation, in every aspect of camp life. If counselors feel thwarted, insecure, or resentful, there is bound to be a behavioral manifestation. Hostility toward other counselors for real or imagined slights and a vague sense of tension can combine to produce an explosive atmosphere which is rapidly discerned by campers. When counselors do not get along with one another, they cannot perform effectively. Campers who become embroiled in such problems may report vague apprehensiveness. The campers become aware of staff proclivities and sense the tenor of the situation. When campers begin to discuss staff dissension and line up in factions, camp morale is just short of collapse.

Hearsay or rumor may ignite the fuel of petty jealousy and vanity. Unfair or partial treatment of one counselor or one group can expose the camp to an unpleasant condition. Careless gossip, a hastily expressed criticism, or an exasperated statement in consequence of long-smoldering frustration can be the initial rupture that develops into overt disaster for the camp. Any number of foolish acts can damage staff morale and result in hard feelings and poor counselor relationships. Inability to countenance disagreement, contrary arguments, or different points of view indicates a closed mind, immaturity, or both.

If counselors are incapable of relating their individual skills and status to the overall picture of camp life, the scene may be set for deterioration of camp morale. Unable or unwilling to appear lessened in his own eyes, the egocentric counselor may provoke anger, irritability, or other negative reactions from staff members. In attempting to build up his own image, such a counselor may undercut other employees, be overly permissive with campers, disregard camp policy, or somehow provoke retaliation. The final reaction to negative counselor behavior is discharge, for if the behavior is not stopped in time, the camp itself may fail.

Counselor Responsibilities

The duties and responsibilities of counselors pervade every minute of the day. Even when campers are safely abed for the night, the counselor is still at work. The conscientious counselor is vitally concerned with each camper in her charge, with all campers in general, and with the smooth operation of the camp. Thus the counselor must be accorded some periods of total rest or change from the daily round of her camp duties. She needs time to relax and to seek privacy from her campers at least once each day. Supervisors, together with the program director, should enable each counselor to have no less than one free period from camp responsibility every day. Such a time can be arranged when there are scheduled activities that do not require the entire counselor force for guidance or supervision, such as during a general camp swim, a tournament, or a field-day exercise, or when the bunk is under the instructional supervision of a specialist. Although it is likely that some long-range personnel plan for free periods can be arranged, it is still a part of daily scheduling. The vagaries of weather, if nothing else, makes necessary a daily appraisal of free periods.

There are certain onerous jobs that have to be done. Malingerers find excuses to avoid these less-than-ideal tasks. The best counselors, while not overjoyed at the prospect, realize that assignments like these are necessary if the camp is to flourish. They do them. No one wants to move heavy equipment into place, particularly if the day is hot. No one happily accepts night duty when others have time off. For the good of the camp, counselors cooperate in all of these endeavors. The outcome of good counselor morale is a successful camping season. The counselor will have played an active role in the development of other humans. He will have gained respect and affection. And when the camp season is over, he will be remembered and missed.

chapter 11

Counselors and
Their Responsibilities

The counselor should be at least 18 years old, and a high school graduate. Many are college students or graduates, with major studies in recreational service education or related fields. Previous camp employment, while not necessary, is helpful. Like anyone who works with children, the counselor must have good character, intelligence, and skill. Counselors must have qualities that are related to the camp's objectives. They must be genuinely interested in young people. With this comes an even greater intangible: having the kind of personality that makes children interested in them.

In the better camps, those that realize that the counselor is a motivational influence for the good of the camper and the camp, applicants clearly unfit for the job are rejected. Standards for counselor acceptance are slowly and steadily being upgraded.[1] The would-be counselor should view counseling as an art and a science.

COUNSELING FUNCTIONS

Counseling in camp is not—as it is usually perceived by the uninitiated— the task of babysitting, keeping children out of trouble, or drilling campers in a variety of nature-oriented skills. Counseling is a fundamental force through which the camper may realize his potential. A poor counselor can be a real tragedy for the child who comes to camp and for the camp itself. To be a counselor, with the lives of a number of children possibly depending upon one, is a complicated role if carried out effectively. It is true, however, that an excessive number of uneducated, uninformed, indifferent, and

[1]T. Strueli, "Searching for a Star-Studded Staff," *Camping Magazine* (March 1985), 41–45.

in some cases lazy, slovenly, dishonest, or immoral individuals hold counselor positions. Their work is decidedly poor. They sneer at preparation,
are interested only in their own personal pleasures, and reject the subtleties
of counseling skills.

Such counselors are found in camps for a variety of reasons. They are
nearly always found in camps operated by public agencies when patronage
influences employment practices. In camps operated by organizations, and
in which religious affiliation is considered more important than skills and
knowledge, the same situation can obtain. While it is dangerous to the field
of camping (and to the particular camp indulging in such practices) to employ incompetent or dishonest individuals, some are hired every summer.
The immediate effect is frustration, both of idealistic young novices and of
conscientious counselors. Low salaries and profit-motivated operators also
explain the ease with which wholly incompetent individuals continue to be
employed in the field, despite standards established by nationally recognized agencies. Counselor certification may be one possible solution.[2]

THE COUNSELOR'S CHARACTER

Above all, the good counselor must be emotionally stable. Emotional stability is important because the counselor must be consistent in her treatment
of all campers in her bunk; the campers must be able to count on a counselor who will not vacillate or pick favorites. The counselor is the solid
friend upon whom campers can lean. Consistency does not mean rigidity
or parochialism, rather it means being a steadying influence. The counselor
remains the same for each youngster—sharing her attention, being fair,
friendly, and composed.[3]

A counselor should be mature, self-reliant, and able to deal with positive and negative situations calmly and with equanimity. She should be secure in her place among her peers. She should know where she is going,
why she is headed in that particular direction, and how she will achieve her
objectives. She should have the ability to understand, accept, and handle
hostility, indifference, and opposition in her group. Other character traits
important in a good counselor are discussed in the following sections.

Sensitivity

Counselors should have a sympathetic understanding of children's
needs and actions. They must respond to the emotional and behavioral
needs of the campers in their bunk without sentimentality. They are therefore sensitive to each camper's need for affection, attention, mastery, fun,
security, and adventure, and can satisfy those needs because they perceive
them. Their sensitivity to others generally, and to their own campers partic-

[2]A. Evert and W. Johnson, "Outdoor Adventure Leadership: A Study of Current Issues
Facing the Profession," *Proceedings: Intermountain Leisure Symposium* (Provo, Utah: Brigham
Young University, 1983), 53–56.
[3]T. M. Shea, *Camping for Special Children* (St. Louis: C. V. Mosby, 1977), pp. 170–72.

ularly, is reciprocated as the campers learn to trust and relate to them. One cannot play at being affectionate and considerate, for children know when adults have genuine affection and interest in them. If the camper recognizes a valid attempt on the part of the counselor to guide, help, and anticipate his needs, he will respond in kind. The counselor then can exert profound influence upon the camper. Both gain from the relationship: The camper learns, enjoys, and achieves, and the counselor has satisfaction from a job well done.

The counselor must learn to discern children's covert requests for help. The very young child will be quite open about asking for assistance. The more mature camper will masks his needs or erect a façade of unconcern. The counselor must be able to pierce the camper's camouflage and give assistance in a manner that will enable the camper to take advantage of the assistance without impinging upon his feelings.

The counselor must be able to empathize with her campers. If she is aware of the campers' aspirations and is prepared for their behavior, she can answer their needs. Since the camp bunk is democratically oriented— or should be—the counselor who is sensitive to others can influence and assist each camper as well as stimulate mutually beneficial relationships among bunk members. In this way, individual and group aims are attained.

Concern

The counselor's genuine concern for the welfare and happiness of his campers motivates his actions and is quickly recognized. The counselor is considerate of his campers, and has the skill to assist them in practical ways. He makes the campers feel that he is a friend. He is ready to explain activities, offer instruction, and make each camper more comfortable within the bunk environment. Although he is not emotionally involved with the conflicts and frustrations of his campers' lives, he does care about their emotional and physical well-being. The counselor is a warm, sympathetic figure who knows what to do in any situation. He is the person to whom the camper can come with a grievance, hurt, fear, or problem, and reasonably expect skilled and immediate help; he resolves what seems insurmountable to the camper. Concern is giving a smile, an encouraging word at the right time, a plan for action, or a suggestion for a better method of performance.

Concern is indicated by the counselor's efforts to learn something about each of his campers before they arrive at camp. It is illustrated by his willingness to study carefully all pertinent information about the child provided by the camp. When the child arrives at camp, it means a cheerful hello, assistance in getting settled, and introductions to bunkmates. He then shows that he can teach, help, guide, supervise, and lead (Fig. 11-1). He facilitates activities so that members of the bunk can have a better time.

Enthusiasm

Enthusiasm is essential for the would-be counselor. The counselor must be an initiator, one who promotes ideas and activities, enters wholeheartedly into the scheme of things, likes being with people, and enjoys

FIGURE 11-1. The counselor has many skills and can assist campers in his charge.

them and herself in the process. The counselor can chat easily with the members of her bunk. She has the ability to interest campers in unfamiliar ventures as well as to make the routine of everyday life seem worthwhile. She makes a game out of onerous duties. She is fun to be with, and she charges the atmosphere in which the campers live with her own brand of congeniality. She sees something good in the worst situations without being a Pollyanna. She has a cheerful outlook even when it is raining or when the group has been frustrated by a temporary setback. From her advantage of maturity and experience, she knows that everything can turn out well if one has common sense and patience. She also realizes that children are immature and lack patience. She therefore anticipates the grumbles and frowns, and channels interest into some purposeful activity.

Communication

The counselor expresses his idea simply and effectively. He is easily understood by all members of the group, there are no deep messages or hidden meanings in his speech. He is intelligent, intelligible, and alert to clues and changes of mood. His friendliness and approachability are contagious, and the campers in his charge respond to him for these very qualities. His optimism and unfailing good humor put conditions in their proper perspective. He can explain to a young boy that a booted ball is not the worst catastrophe that ever befell a baseball player, convince another camper that she will learn to tie a running bowline knot, or console a for-lorn child whose parents did not write to him again. He has an apparently endless supply of exciting stories, snappy songs, funny skits, daring stunts, and a high degree of skill in various camping activities. He likes what he is doing, and he likes those with whom he shares camp life. He innovates and proposes imaginative ideas on which campers can build worthwhile ambi-tions or valued activities. Above all, he is a stimulator. He is fun to be with, and everyone feels a little more secure, friendly, and happy in his presence (Fig. 11-2).

Intelligence

Perhaps more than anything else, in terms of personal attributes, the counselor must be intelligent. Without intelligence, nothing is accom-plished at camp. Unless the counselor has the ability to understand, she will be incapable of good performance or of meeting the needs of her campers. Intelligence is the power to know. The intelligent individual is creative and seeks answers to puzzling questions. Intelligent people are more likely to

FIGURE 11-2. A shared moment promotes security. (Courtesy: Donna Richardson.)

be independent, and they tend to dominate people and situations, rather than conform or follow. They are more inclined toward movement and activity. Socially, they appear to be more gregarious, cooperative, and understanding of others.

Competence

The counselor must have some skill in the various activities in which her group engages. In order for her to assist each camper in achieving success or satisfaction, she must herself possess competence. As well as competence in activity, the counselor also must be skilled in human relations and understanding. If she is to facilitate group interaction and solve individual camper problems, she must be competent in the dynamics of socialization as well as recreational and camping activities.[4]

Counseling demands comprehensive knowledge, subtle insights, intricate competencies, and a dynamic personality. This is a large order, and is assuredly greater than administrators are currently willing to pay for. Counseling is not a simple process. The work of guiding, leading, and being responsible for the health, safety, and well-being of children cannot be done successfully by uninformed, apathetic, incapable individuals of drab personality and limited life experience. Experience, know-how, and desirable personality are absolutely essential. Skill in counseling is impossible unless there is a zealous desire to develop and progress both personally and professionally. The counselor must accept the hard work and study necessary to learn better methods and to become more knowledgeable.[5]

But is all this really important and necessary? Who appreciates the prepared counselor who has these qualities and capabilities? Is not the job of the counselor really much more simple than has been indicated here? It has long been performed by many lesser personalities, by those endowed with less intelligence, fewer skills, and absolutely no preparation. That is the great weakness of the camping movement. The single most important factor, after survival, is sound leadership. To provide that leadership, the counselor must be equipped with education and personality, with experience and intelligence, with physical fitness and sound mental health. It is impossible to be a successful camp counselor without first understanding the nature of children in terms of personality and development; the relationship between the camp and the camper; the association of individual children within the bunk to the enclave of which they are a part; and the relationship of camping experiences to the development of the camper. It is unrealistic to think that anyone will be able to fulfill the counselorship adequately without first understanding the skills necessary for guiding and counseling children in democratic groups in an outdoor environment.

---

[4]R. G. Kraus and M. M. Scanlin, *Introduction to Camp Counseling* (Englewood Cliffs, N.J.: Prentice-Hall, 1983), pp. 63–64.

[5]R. E. Wilkerson, *Camps: Their Planning and Management* (St. Louis: C. V. Mosby, 1981), pp. 74–81.

Physical Fitness

The counselor must have the physical fitness and endurance to keep up with, or ahead of, campers. Working with young people, particuarly in the outdoors, the counselor is constantly called upon to exhibit physical capacity and stamina. Whether it is in lifesaving, hiking, climbing, constructing temporary shelters, instructing in motor skills, or participating in other strenuous but expected activities, the counselor must be fit to perform. The counselor must be in optimum condition for effectiveness.

Personality

Personality, regardless of its various definitions, has sometimes been confused with intelligence. In a few instances the substitution has been successful—for example, in a field in which human relations factors are paramount. When the field is concerned both with the dynamics of social relations and technical proficiency, however, personality alone is inadequate. Counselors who lack sufficient technical preparation and understanding of camping ideology and practices are destined to mediocrity and are sometimes unable to perform satisfactorily. Nevertheless, personality does play a key role when coupled with intelligence, and the effective counselor has a poised, integrated personality. The counselor who is secure in his knowledge of people, places, and things is not fearful about his status. He will not resort to authoritarianism. He will accept each child's uniqueness and guide him accordingly.

The Successful Counselor

A counselor must have sharp, accurate understanding of the camper. Just what is taking place within the minds of the children under her jurisdiction? Counselors will have little success without the ability to see what understandings, attitudes, and habits the camper is acquiring. What happens when a child is first exposed to resident or day camp? What happens when he sees a long view of a serene lake, participates in outings and council-ring activities, is bullied in the bunk, must make his own bed, listens to arguments about social inequality or religious preference, is reprimanded or given a pat on the back, becomes part of a small group of both aggressive and submissive children? The adult too often interprets the child's feelings in terms of his own desired result or his own adult responses. Some counselors' unawareness of what campers actually experience is astounding to those who have never observed it. The artful and sensitive appreciation of the minds and emotions of campers displayed by superior counselors is also as incredible. The counselor who understands how different kinds of activities, surroundings, and facets of the natural environment affect the camper can use the camp environment to the camper's benefit without usurping his choices.

The following characteristics describe the successful counselor:

1. Has a good sense of humor.
2. Is optimistic, cheerful, and outgoing.
3. Is friendly, sympathetic, and understanding.
4. Is fair, objective, and does not play favorites.
5. Is never sarcastic or threatening.
6. Is considerate of campers' needs and feelings; puts the camper at ease.
7. Is courteous; has good manners.
8. Makes the camper feel secure; helps with personal problems.
9. Is reasonable and flexible.
10. Is enthusiastic about camp, campers, and activities.
11. Is honest, sincere, and consistent.
12. Uses common sense and is intelligent.

The following behaviors are expected of a successful counselor:

1. Offers practical help.
2. Explains clearly any ideas, activities, or rules that are difficult to understand.
3. Makes activities interesting; camouflages routine tasks to make them more attractive than they are.
4. Maintains control of the bunk and has the campers' respect.
5. Practices democracy; gives campers a voice in making decisions affecting bunk life.
6. Requires that campers fulfill their obligations quickly, properly, and efficiently, whether it is cleaning living quarters, brushing teeth, writing letters, or making beds.
7. Is skilled in many activities, but is not a know-it-all.
8. Knows what to do or whom to ask when help is required.
9. Is not afraid to request assistance.
10. Is always appropriately dressed for camp life and activities; is neat and clean.
11. Plans activities in advance.
12. Recognizes and accommodates campers' individual differences.

Counselor Preparations

Counseling cannot be adequately performed on the basis of experience and common sense only. It also includes meticulous study of pertinent and reliable information, and a period of experience under competent supervision. Counselors are not born; they are developed by sound preparatory methods and guidance. Obviously, experience and evaluation will play a large part in improving skills, but this experience is assisted by the educational effort of basic preparation. In addition, the counselor must be able to make bold innovations and modifications of known techniques when unexpected or unusual conditions arise. When dealing with humans, established procedures may have to be adapted to meet human needs. Information on these subjects is available, but the best preparation after this information has been assimilated is flexibility.

Can these skills and knowledge be developed by an interested person? Yes! To develop them, the counselor must engage in a tenacious, incisive evaluation of his own experiences and act to strengthen the weaknesses he finds. This can be done only when the individual recognizes that counseling is not an amateur's game.

THE COUNSELOR ON THE JOB

The counselor's primary responsibility is the care and well-being of a bunk of campers. The number of campers in any living unit, whether tent or cabin, ranges from 4 to 8 children. These youngsters are the counselor's personal charges, and the quarters are their home away from home. Acting almost *in loco parentis*, the counselor is in direct contact with his campers nearly 24 hours each day for the entire camp season. It is therefore important that the counselor familiarize himself with each camper's background, interests, skills, talents, fears, weaknesses, and so on. The counselor should know which of his campers have camped prior to the current season, which have been to this particular camp, and which are new to camping.

The aims of the camp should be directly related to the counselor's objectives for each camper and the bunk as a whole. Aims are derived from the campers' ages, capabilities, experiences, expectations, and the level at which they are presently functioning. Naturally, aims are also associated with the counselor's desire to have campers learn new skills and activities, and to improve those skills that they possess. The hope is that, with the counselor's assistance, the children in the bunk will quickly become a group. They will learn to work, play, and carry out plans and projects together. It is the counselor's responsibility to assist each camper in finding ways to express himself positively and contribute to the overall success of the bunk. Each camper will learn to offer ideas and actions as well as to appreciate others' contributions to the group's goals.

THE CAMPER'S FIRST DAY

The counselor first meets her new campers in either of two situations. She may be one of the staff members assigned to travel to the camp with a party of children after meeting them at some predetermined place. This initial contact can serve to make a lasting positive impression of the counselor. The counselor should greet each camper, especially those who are alone or who do not appear to have made previous acquaintances. The counselor should introduce herself to individual campers and try to engage any solitary child in brief exploratory conversations, gradually widening the circle of campers until several are engaged. This technique should be repeated as often as necessary. Those campers who do not easily converse with their peers may have to be given individual attention. The point of departure is an excellent time to help campers overcome feelings of loneliness and insecurity by having some of the campers assist with chores, such as shifting luggage or keeping an eye on small suitcases until they are loaded aboard the train, bus, or automobile.

Meeting Campers

The counselor may meet his entire bunk of campers for the first time at the camp. This situation is more than likely if the camp has had a preseason orientation program for staff. With all the camp's pertinent policies, rules, regulations, and layout of facilities in mind, answering campers' questions should present little difficulty. The counselor has more to do than disseminate information, however. He must know why such policies, rules, and regulations exist, and should explain them clearly.

No matter how many seasons a counselor has been employed at camp, the first day always triggers anticipation and anxiety. The counselor wonders what the children will be like, how the season will progress, whether the campers will respond to suggestions, and so on. The counselor is anxious because on the first day he will make either a good or bad impression on his campers. Sometimes the counselor's lack of confidence or experience manifests itself in snappishess and a brusque approach.

The first day is the best time to set the pace and atmosphere for a friendly, enjoyable, and adventurous summer. The wise counselor puts his best foot forward, smiles reassuringly, and forgets his personal problems and feelings. By studying the small pictures and personal data sheets that the camp has supplied, the counselor will have information about each camper that will help allay fears and doubts. By the first day, the counselor knows each child's first name or nickname. He is there to help each child settle into the bunk. Campers are looking for a summer filled with excitement and new experiences. They have had a busy day getting to camp. The full impact of being away from home will hit them just as the excitement of arriving and meeting new people dissipates.

The counselor should be calm, efficient, and knowledgeable. She is the anchor to which each camper can grab onto during the first hours of stress. She stands out in a situation filled with strangers, and she should capitalize on this fact. She should answer questions, show the way, and generally make each child welcome. The first few hours at camp can mean the difference between a homesick child and one who eagerly awaits tomorrow's activities. This is the time for the counselor to develop rapport. She must firmly establish the first friendly impression that she gave.[6]

Forming Groups

The bunk may contain campers who are old friends, total strangers, or a mixture of both. The counselor is the agent who turns strangers into friends; his objective is to form a wholesome group. The first step in developing a cohesion among a number of campers who have been grouped

[6]C. Knapp, "Survey Reveals Camper's Perception of Staff," *Camping Magazine* (March 1985), 48–49.

together without formality is to focus attention on the immediate common task. Since they will be living together in the bunk, they must learn to share in its maintenance, this requires effort, but combined energy makes the workload lighter and creates a positive experience. When the campers recognize the need for cooperative effort, there is a better opportunity for establishing close relationships. Getting to understand another's reactions requires a little time. Each camper must learn to cope with and accommodate himself to other children's idiosyncrasies. Discovering new approaches to teamwork is the stimulus for beginning group life in the bunk.

Living Arrangements

The arrangement of living quarters is usually standard because of space requirements. Cots, beds, or bunk beds are placed for maximum use of open space without isolation. Typically, there are lockers in which to store clothing and valuables, footlockers, trunks, or suitcases can also serve as repositories. The presence of familiar articles gives the camper a feeling of having a bit of home in the new place. The counselor's success in helping campers to feel at ease, stow away their gear, and make themselves comfortable depends upon several factors. The weather can retard or enhance opening day at camp, inclement weather can modify the best-laid plans. Therefore, the counselor must have an alternate plan for helping campers settle in during a rainy or cold day.

Developing Cohesiveness

The counselor can use several techniques to develop a feeling of group unity in his campers. One is to have common assignments that can be completed only with all bunk members assisting. Another effective way of involving all campers and enhancing group development is to turn the campers' attention to some enjoyable activity that they have had a hand in planning. The activity can be undertaken almost as soon as the campers have put away their belongings. The campers should suggest several interesting activities and then, after a consensus has been reached, prepare for the event. It might be a combination exploratory hike, cookout, and bunk camp fire. It might be a spontaneous fishing party at a nearby lake. It could be the creation of a bunk insignia or totem (Fig. 11-3). Whatever the activity, it should be determined, planned, and participated in by everyone in the bunk. The activity is something that sets the bunk apart from all other bunks—something that only the campers of this bunk can share. The activity starts with comparative strangers and turns them into a high-morale group within a relatively short time.[7]

The Need for Success

All camp activities must have a high probability of success. It is even more important for the first experiences to be absolutely successful. The

---

[7]G. C. Oswald, "The Group Experience," *Camping Magazine* (Sept.–Oct. 1983), 16–20.

FIGURE 11-3.   Crafts fun fosters cohesiveness. (Courtesy: Donna Richardson.)

counselor can leave nothing to chance. Once a project has been determined, the counselor's meticulous attention to detail, with the campers contributing ideas, is mandatory. *Nothing succeeds like success*—this cliché is especially significant for children's groups. If the first few activities are fun and satisfying for the campers, they will come to realize that their cooperative efforts, as much as anything else, helped them to have fun. Naturally, the counselor should emphasize camper contributions to the objective. Should anything cause failure or dissatisfaction, however, the counselor must shoulder full responsibility, he will then suffer the embarrassment of failure and a concomitant loss of face and influence with the campers. In order to ensure success, projects must be undertaken with complete confidence and know-how. A project should be short enough to maintain interest and leave the campers asking for more, but of sufficient duration to allow participation.

The counselor is largely responsible for campers' leisure. He should have an inexhaustible supply of possible activities; he must also elicit ideas from bunk members in order to give them a share in making decisions. All activities should serve some purpose. Certain chores and individual responsibilities, such as bunk cleaning, personal hygiene, or letter writing, profitably engage campers' attention.

Whatever the experience, the counselor has certain expectations. He should keep his objectives in mind and attempt to channel camper interest and enthusiasm so that camper goals coincide with his own. Campers want to enjoy themselves, they want to learn new skills, strengthen old skills, and complete projects successfully. In planning and arranging these experiences, the counselor should try to strike a balance between individual and group needs. Individual development proceeds hand in hand with the development of the group.

Individual Needs

Counselors do not always work with the bunk as a whole. The bunk is made up of individuals who have personal requirements that may not be appropriately resolved through the medium of the group process. In these instances, the counselor should turn her attention to the camper's problems and interests, listening sympathetically to the child and noting what he does *not* say, as well as his manner and tone. On occasion, a discussion of any number of ideas or opinions can open new vistas for the child. Imparting factual information about a subject on which the camper has erroneous, negative, or fearful ideas will help build confidence, security, or a brighter outlook.

Some campers need more personal attention than others. Some children are self-reliant and capable of getting along anywhere; others are hesitant or shy. The counselor can provide the support necessary to help the child find himself. It may take time to instill confidence or teach a skill in which the youngster can take pride and gain self-respect, but this is the real meaning of counseling (Fig. 11-4). The sooner the camper is freed of dependence upon others for sympathy and for protection from nameless anxiety or the desire to withdraw without a good cause, the more successful will be the counselor's efforts. While it is physically impossible for the counselor to give undivided attention to all campers in equal degree, it is necessary to recognize individual differences and needs among campers, and those that require additional attention should receive it. Those campers who are able to adjust and cope with situations should be encouraged to do so.

The Counselor's Daily Responsibilities

The counselor is responsible for everything that happens to the camper during the camping season. Camper behavior generally takes its cue from the counselor, and it is essential for the counselor's conduct to be worthy of emulation. The counselor sets an example every moment of the day, and her every action should be exemplary.

Being a camp counselor is a great educational opportunity. It is a test of physical, emotional, intellectual, and moral stamina. It requires participation in a variety of interesting activities and the acquisition of stimulating knowledge and new skills. Intelligence combined with diligent effort will result in a summer of counselor growth and development.

Hygiene

If the counselor resides in the bunk with campers, it is especially important that he be an exemplar of good hygiene habits. He should be the

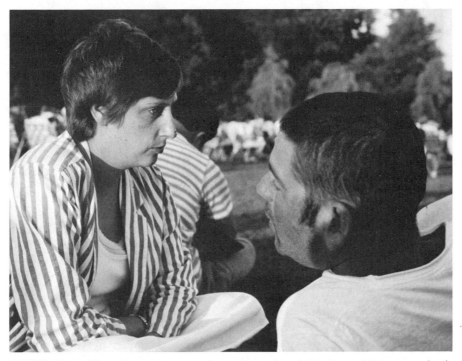

FIGURE 11-4.   The older camper needs someone to confide in, and the counselor is there. (Courtesy: Camp Kennedy for the Disabled, Manchester, Connecticut.)

first to arise in the morning and be appropriately dressed for a strenuous round of activities. Counselors must make sure that their campers are dressed suitably to avoid chills and dampness from dew-soaked grass on the way to the mess hall for breakfast. Campers must be checked daily for signs of illness. Rashes, boils, headaches, nausea, or other symptoms require examination by the camp medical staff. Morning routines such as brushing teeth, washing, and combing hair can be made into a competitive drill or game that the younger campers will enjoy.

Even well-meaning children occasionally slip up when it comes to fastidiousness, due simply to immaturity or haste. Campers are constantly on the go, and they either forget or do not take the time to attend to personal hygiene habits. They will wear the same underwear and socks until the garments have become stiff with dirt and perspiration. The counselor cannot simply assume that campers will comply with her request that they wash properly and change soiled clothing, she must unobtrusively check her campers to determine that all have attended to their hygiene needs. Hot showers with soap should be standard procedure several times each week, despite cries that swimming sessions get one clean enough. In order to separate soiled from clean clothes, dirty laundry should be placed in a convenient and appropriate receptacle, such as a laundry bag. Wet swimsuits or damp clothes should be hung to dry. Campers should not lend their personal items to others. The counselor must never borrow anything from campers, and should discourage this practice among campers.

Mealtimes

The bunk always goes to activities together. After reveille, campers prepare themselves for first call. This is a preparatory summons by bugle or bell that signifies the flag-raising ceremony each day. All campers are present, and each bunk in turn is designated as the flag honor guard. Directly after the raising of the flag, all bunks eat breakfast. Good table manners are required. Because there is always sufficient, well-prepared, good food for all campers, campers do not need to rush to get seconds. The counselor serves each camper before he serves himself. This method ensures that every child receives adequate servings of all foods available for any given meal.

Table manners necessarily hinge upon the demeanor and expectation of the counselor and the standards he sets and keeps. Meals should be quiet, leisurely, and enjoyable. The counselor must quickly and firmly discourage all negative conduct; there should be no yelling, grabbing, using hands instead of utensils, or bizarre behavior. Initially, campers will test the counselor's permissiveness at meals as they do in other situations. A pleasant, courteous approach and high expectations for good manners will set the tone and atmosphere for the season. Some campers may come from environments where food is a luxury rather than a necessity; they must be discouraged from eating too quickly or sitting in ways that appear to be protective of their plates. Campers should be given instructions on how to sit, what to do with their hands, and how to use utensils. For the record, it is wise to enforce the rule that second helpings will not be served until all have finished their first portion. This will tend to slow the pace of eating, particularly if the counselor eats slowly.

Food must not be taken from the mess hall. Extra portions can be shared equally among those campers who want them. Children lose a great deal of salt and water through perspiration during hot summer activities, and dehydration is a risk unless such nutrients are replaced at mealtimes.

Meals should be anticipated with enjoyment—not viewed with distaste, as a chore or a punishment. Quiet conversation and attention to eating are the counselor's primary concern. Some singing or even table activities can be permitted after the meal is finished. On rare occasions, bunk cheers may be allowed during the course of the meal. When announcements must be made, counselors should see that conversation ceases.

Positive Behavior

The counselor should be positive in her role of exemplar. She should call attention to good habits, postures, eating skills, and so on. Grimaces or grunts from campers when certain foods are brought to the table must be discouraged. The counselor must never criticize any food, by word or gesture, in front of campers, if something is definitely wrong with the food, a word to the immediate supervisor or head counselor is sufficient.

The nagging counselor is a poor counselor. Counselors who resort to sarcasm or ridicule may actually cause deterioration in camper conduct and relationships. It is better to speak privately with a misbehaving camper than to embarrass him by scolding in front of his peers. At meals, those who sometimes cause problems should be seated close to the counselor, so that their actions can be better supervised. Counselors must never withhold food from campers as punishment, nor force children to eat. There are a variety of reasons that children have eating problems (see Chapter 14), and these emotional problems require special attention. In cases of physical illness, the camp medical authority will take proper action.

Maintenance of Living Quarters

The cleanliness of the cabin or tent is the responsibility of those who inhabit it. Quarters cleanup can be either a chore or a game. The morning cleaning assignment, performed as a team effort, takes little time. Beds must be made correctly; clothing should be folded or hung as required and all personal belongings neatly put away. A rotating monitoring system, whereby each camper takes the inspector's role, may be effective. Cabin or tent maintenance can be a time for healthy cooperation. The counselor should take the lead by making his bed neatly, tightly, and quickly. He must show the campers how hospital corners are made and how to draw the sheet and blankets so that they are tight, with the top sheet folded over the top blanket. By assisting where necessary and supervising discreetly, the counselor can be reasonably sure that the cabin will be neat and clean.

The counselor should inspect cabin shelves and footlockers daily. This prevents ants or other insects from finding contraband sweets that youngsters may have hidden and forgotten. Once each week, all dirty linen and laundry is gathered, and clean laundry is returned. This is an excellent time for a real shakedown and cleaning session in the bunk. The floors should be mopped; sills, shelves, and lockers should be dusted. Beds should be stripped and mattresses turned. A head counselor's inspection will probably occur soon after the morning cleanup period.

Rest Periods

Most camps have a rest hour between 1:00 and 3:00 PM. The hottest part of the afternoon can be debilitating for campers if strenuous activities occur during these hours. Campers need to rest or relax for the next round of activities, which may continue until bedtime. Rest hours are best supervised by counselors. While it is not necessary for campers to sleep at this time, sufficient quiet and an absence of vigorous physical activity are required so that those who wish to sleep can do so. Conversation should be kept to a minimum. Reading, letter writing, quiet games, soft music, or just sitting and observing cloud formations can be enjoyable and restful. The rest period after lunch can also be used to buy candy from the camp store. Prior to the rest hour, each bunk can make out a requisition form on which each camper lists a candy selection. The candy provides campers with quick energy and assuages the desire for additional sweet foods.

Mail

Letter writing and receiving are very important. Campers want to receive mail from home, and parents want to know how their children are doing. At least once a week, or more often depending upon inclination, the child should write home. The camper will probably ask the counselor what to include in the letter. Without dictating, the counselor should indicate bits of information that the child can elaborate on—skills acquired, honors gathered, friends made, trips taken, experiences undergone. The counselor should place himself in the parents' position and suggest answers that parents would like to receive if they could ask questions directly of their children. Envelopes should be checked for correct and legible addresses.

Censorship is unthinkable; no letter should ever be opened by any camp staff person after the child has sealed it. Under no circumstances should the counselor read letters unless the child specifically requests it.

When campers do not receive mail from home for more than 7 days, official inquiries are indicated. The counselor should notify her immediate supervisor and a check should be instituted. Efforts to reach the camper's parents are made, with the object of having the camper receive a letter. Sometimes the home situation is so poor that the child never receives mail. A good substitute is for the child's own counselor, on her day off, to post a card to the camper. It is a bit beyond the call of duty, but it may work wonders for an otherwise neglected child. Other bunk members may feel that their counselor is playing favorites, but mailing cards to all the bunk members will circumvent that possibility.

Evening Routine

Getting campers ready for bed is as important as getting them up in the morning. When the campers return to the bunk after evening activities, it is time for the nightly routine of washing up and preparing for bed. There must be no snacking prior to bedtime. Camp fire activities occasionally include wiener, potato, or marshmallow roasts, but these are the only times food is available after supper.

The counselor must be sure that his campers are wearing suitable sleeping garments and not wearing dirty socks or underwear. Every camper must have sufficient blankets since summer nights can be rather chilly. Campers must never share the same bed, blankets, or sleeping bag. Each child must have his own bedding.

The counselor may finish the day's activities with a short story-telling session or by reading to the campers. Such activities are valuable for campers from 4 to 12 years old. In some instances, depending upon the sophistication of the story or camper, groups may include teenagers. Children will get ready for bed faster if they know that they will be told or read a story once they are in bed. Stories can be on almost any topic of interest. A brief discussion about the day's events can ensue, with the counselor taking note of particular activities in which each camper participated successfully. The nightly story or discussion should never be so exciting or horror-filled that it will keep the camper in a state of anxiety or wakefulness; this defeats the purpose of the activity. Sometimes it is valuable for the counselor to give some extra attention to a camper with a problem. Sitting on the bed and tying up a loose or frayed emotional experience may be just the right way to complete the child's day.

THE COUNSELOR AND THE PROGRAM

The counselor is essentially concerned with the campers in her bunk. For a successful camping season, the counselor may be assigned to a number of different program areas designed for the health, happiness, and welfare of the campers. The counselor must be an integral part of the total camping program, as well as being responsible for the well-being of her charges. For these reasons, vital associations will develop between the counselor and other staff as the counselor is requested to contribute her skills and knowledge to program-administration aspects of the camp. She must possess a genuine interest in her campers, as well as a positive outlook concerning her responsibilities for leadership in the general operation of the camp program.

Cooperation with the Medical Staff

The counselor must be alert to camper health needs and be able to determine whether a camper requires medical attention. As previously noted, the counselor must inspect each camper daily for any symptoms of illness or infection. All symptoms, regardless of their apparent insignificance, should be reported to the medical staff person. Reciprocally, any directions for medication, activity restrictions, or other medical advice must be carefully followed.

Generally, the counselor's objectives are to maintain the camper's vitality and prevent injuries. Therefore, she complies with all health rules and regulations published or advised by the camp medical staff. To ensure optimal physical health, the counselor must insist that campers receive proper rest, diet, and activity. She must check sanitary habits, clothing, and general bunk cleanliness. She should see that appropriate protective gear and clothing are worn to prevent undue exposure to heat or cold, or insect, floral, or faunal poisoning. She should encourage good mental health practices, such as emotional stability, integrity, or fair dealings and be firm in her demand for compliance with all rules and regulations for healthful living. In addition, the counselor will minimize environmental hazards. She will develop campers' skills in the use of axes, saws, knives, sharp tools, and fire. She will maintain the area in the immediate vicinity of the bunk. Knowledge of first aid and as well as of the physical features of the area will do much to avoid injuries from accidents or more serious impairment due to careless handling of those who have been injured.

Cooperation with the Aquatic Staff

General counselors are usually designated as lifeguards during all-camp swimming activities. When the bunk has a scheduled swim, the counselor will probably be asked to give instruction. All campers must be instructed in stroking and breathing. Counselors must be familiar with all regulations relating to aquatic facilities, and teach them to their charges. As always, the good example set by the counselor will discourage infractions of safety rules and help prevent water accidents. It is absolutely vital that each counselor cooperate in the operation of the aquatic program.

Another area of counselor involvement concerns health practices that might affect swimming activities. No camper should be permitted to swim when he has running sores, an upper respiratory tract infection, or an infected wound. Counselors should watch carefully to see that campers do not become chilled while swimming; the most obvious sign is blue or purple lips, which indicate extreme chill. Campers must leave the water and dry off when they show signs of fatigue or chill. Proper footgear should be worn to and from the waterfront to prevent injury, and precautions against athlete's foot must be taken.

Counselors with good swimming skills should volunteer to participate in any of the aquatic activities that require skill. The counselor can help the waterfront staff with water shows and pageants, instructional activities, competitive performances, or lifesaving techniques. The counselor may be the best person to instruct members of his bunk because campers will have more confidence in a known and trusted person than in a comparative stranger. All counselors employed by the camp should therefore have aquatic skills.

Cooperation With the Special-Activities Staff

The success of the summer camp program hinges upon good leadership. The counselor plays a key leadership role in almost every activity. She must be interested enough in all segments of the program to give positive assistance. A counselor does not build herself up at the expense of deriding another. The counselor who is fundamentally a group leader and secondarily an instructor of skills will participate in the dynamics of bunk life, consider herself a member of the group, and encourage her campers to learn and enjoy as many activities as are offered by the camp. She wants her bunk members to take advantage of every program opportunity because she knows that as they succeed in learning new skills, they will develop self-confidence.

The camp program is composed of routine and special activities. Among the specialized staff are those who are highly skilled in crafts, nature experiences, drama, motor skills, and music (Fig. 11-5). While there are other specialities, these five constitute the platform of both regular and unique camping experiences. Regardless of her own personal skills, as long as the counselor is enthusiastic about camper potential in each of the experiences, her influence will be felt. The counselor has an obligation to all staff members to encourage campers to engage in as many activities as possible.

Camping Contributions

Camping is exciting. By its very character, it is filled with adventurous and stimulating events that tantalize the senses and emotions. These natural

FIGURE 11-5. Tips from an expert pay off in fun and satisfaction. (Courtesy: Crane Lake Camp, West Stockbridge, Massachusetts.)

opportunities are further enhanced by planned and scheduled activities designed to teach new skills, expose campers to new learning situations, and assist them in normal growth and development. All camping activities offer some value for the participant. The counselor must be willing to guide the camper's efforts. The counselor realizes that each special event or routine exposure can build one more facet of camper satisfaction. By his acceptance of employment, the counselor pledges cooperation to each part of the camp program. He must recognize that all staff members are striving toward the goal of camper enjoyment and benefit. Each staff person relies upon the support of all counselors to achieve overall success for the camp and the camper.

Counselor Abilities

Camp counselors should have some fundamental skills and special interests. They need, in addition, an ability to transmit their knowledge. Implied here are the abilities to organize, coordinate, initiate, and lead. The counselor must innovate and use whatever resources are at hand. He seeks primarily to do all of those things necessary for the health, safety, and welfare of his campers. Cooperation with other counselors and specialists is essential. A thorough knowledge of the activities to be taught and of the preparation and motivation of the group to be instructed, collection of all materials necessary for the experience, and the skills needed to demonstrate the fine points of the activity are all part of the counselor's competencies. The counselor must enjoy working with youngsters and be aware of their individual and collective needs.

The following are some practical techniques that should be evident in all facets of the counselor's work:

1. Start with campers at their own level.
2. Start with the campers' own questions, problems, activities; help them to produce their own aims.
3. Assist campers in adopting the accepted objectives of their own living unit.
4. Be democratic in planning and selecting activities; make sure that each camper has the opportunity to suggest ideas and contribute in making decisions. (The counselor, as part of the group, also contributes ideas to stimulate camper thinking and offers meaningful choices.)
5. Receive suggestions cordially and give evidence that such ideas merit attention.
6. Develop a unit of purpose and esprit de corps through interdependence.
7. Make the camping experience so vital and so much a part of the campers' lives that the activities will suggest continual exploration and satisfaction.
8. Accept mistakes as routine; do not demand perfection or a high degree of skill from children who cannot perform at such levels.
9. Help each camper recognize his own capabilities and weaknesses in terms of his contributions to bunk life, to grow as a consequence of that recognition, and to achieve fulfillment in accordance with his own level of skill.

chapter 12

The Counselor's Understanding of the Camper

Camping, as an organized activity, should be imbued with the ideal of democracy. Since the bunk is an intensively social group made up of individuals, it is only by democratic means that personal achievement occurs. The best camping experience can be developed from the realization of the need for leadership and the insights and skills required at all levels of any organization or group. Democracy rests upon individual contribution and willingness to serve voluntarily. Does this mean that democracy is antithetical to leadership? Although efforts based on force may be successful, they are seldom satisfying to the individual who is coerced. Leadership is never founded on force, neither innovation, enthusiasm, nor cooperation can be engendered by edict. The joining of many individuals and the harnessing of their respective education, skills, and strengths to reach some objective is a tremendously intricate process demanding much of leaders and followers. Groups efforts are often fruitless. To offset wasted energy and ineffectiveness, particularly in the camp setting, the counselor-leader must have a fundamental understanding of what motivates people to perform and behave as they do.

The counselor wants to learn how to motivate his campers to participate more fully in bunk life. He needs an understanding of the individuals with whom he is dealing. He must be aware of their varied backgrounds and possible reactions to situations that will confront them at camp.[1] To be a more effective counselor, he must recognize individual differences, age group characteristics, and the personal problems that campers bring to, or develop, at camp.

---

[1]J. A. Friedrich, "Understanding the Camp Group," *Camping Magazine* (Feb. 1985), 29–31.

Perhaps partly because problems do seem inevitable, there are as many investigators who hold that group camping has negative outcomes as there are those who feel that it can have only beneficial consequences.[2] Some vehemently oppose the concept that positive social, psychological, and physical values are inherent in outdoor group living. Some specialists feel that the values of camping are a myth—that the public has been systematically duped by indoctrination, and that representatives of camping agencies have bombarded the public with brochures and statistics neatly packaging the values and joys of outdoor education and camping, without any real evidence that they exist. These so-called values are being questioned—and the questions should be carefully studied.

THE IMPACT OF CAMPING

Many adults who are personally unable or unwilling to live outside a highly urbanized environment boldly recommend a liberal dose of camping as the remedy for whatever makes the child insecure or unhappy. The natural environment is supposed to contain some ameliorative elixir that magically banishes all cares and maladjustments. But the outcome of camping in terms of changed attitudes, conduct, sociability, leadership, cooperation, security, and other attributes has not been subjected to any widespread, controlled research. Little has been done to evaluate the claims made for the positive effects of camping on the camper.[3] Possibly, an occasional separation of parents and child is valuable to the mental health of all concerned.[4] It is probably valid to generalize that many children do profit from and react favorably to camping.[5] However, some children sent to camp spend insufferable days not merely homesick, but frustrated, rejected, indifferent, and traumatized, having gained nothing positive from the experience.[6] Increased social pressures at camp and the need to conform to certain group behaviors may cause particular neurotic inclinations. The problems and conflicts produced as a result of emotional or physical stress must be recognized.

Camping, like any valued experience, can be overdone. Some individuals simply are not prepared for the experience of close social contact in small groups. Physical, sexual, psychological, and social problems manifest themselves in every human being at one time or another. The camp environment may be precisely the stimulus necessary to introduce emotional trials with which the individual cannot cope. Counselors are the single most important figures in alleviating some of the pain, stress, and frustration. They

[2]"What Is the Role of Camping," *Camping Magazine* (Feb. 1985), 22–24.

[3]W. M. Hammerman and M. F. Chenery, "Research in Action," *Camping Magazine* (May 1985), 37.

[4]H. Loren, "Single Parents, Children and Summer Camps," *Parents Guide* (Bradford Woods, Ind.: American Camping Association, 1981), 10–11.

[5]F. Bavley, "Two-Year Experiment Proves Camps Can Change Camper Attitudes," *Camping Magazine* (Sept. 1972), 18.

[6]S. Welch, "More Kids Want to Be Hugged," *Camping Magazine* (March 1985), 40.

must be prepared to encounter and resist negative aspects of camp life. To perform competently, confidently, and effectively, counselors have to recognize behavioral peculiarities and react wisely to them. Emotional maturity, along with knowledge of what to expect and how to handle problematic situations, must be an integral part of every counselor's preparation.

The camper age categories which follow have been provided to assist in the understanding of the commonalities and differences that can and do occur at each developmental level. No hard and fast generalities apply, however. Within each age group there is a range of skills, interests, strengths, and weaknesses. There can be vast differences between individuals at any age, and this is particularly true between the sexes.

Camper groups can be designated by any label. The use of "freshman" through "senior" is not to be construed as the only, or even the primary, identification of age groups. Almost any name can be chosen to identify camper groups. These may be drawn from Indian tribes, plants, animals, birds, fish, states, teams, or other appropriate subject. In fact, it might be highly beneficial to have the campers themselves choose what they will be called. This action may help to produce cohesiveness and provide a rallying point around which the campers may cluster. Any positive activity that promotes esprit de corps should be encouraged.

AGE GROUPS

This chapter's chief objective is to offer a view of the camper at every age, in order to further a more complete understanding of his wants, capabilities, and specific problems. Through understanding the child at each stage of development, the best possible program can be arranged. The child's readiness to acquire skills will largely determine whether he achieves satisfaction from camp. For our purposes, campers will be categorized in the following age groups: elementary (4–6), freshmen (7–9), sophomores (10–12), juniors (13–15), and seniors (16–18).

Any age group will comprise children of many types. Different body developments; height and weight variations; keen intellects and slow, pedestrian ones; those who are quick, agile, and strong, and those who are clumsy, weak, and incapable all appear in every age group. In short, there is no general picture that provides for all of the variables. It is improbable that all children of a given age will exhibit all the characteristics of that age. It is likely, however, that some children will show some traits at each age. Each child is an individual and develops at his own rate.

The Elementary Group (Ages 4–6)

Many children have their first camp experience at 4 years of age. It is often traumatic. The initial impact of the first night alone can have a decided effect upon the child's future. Emotionally, this age is most significant in terms of the child's expectations. It is an age of establishing and developing family relationships. The child has developed a self-concept. There is a definite awareness of right and wrong. Children of this age ask a great many

questions about sex and sexual matters. They use words and phrases calcu-
lated to shock adults. Often, children of this age use foul language without
knowing what the words mean. This is a time for testing. It is an age at
which independence from the home and from parental control begins to
manifest itself.

Most children of this age feel relatively insecure. They need constant
reassurance that they are loved and wanted. Jealousy is easily aroused at
this stage. Hostile feelings and resentment can build up against any person
who appears to stand between the child and his parents. Whatever friendships are made are usually quickly broken. Children of this age generally
enjoy small-group activities, although parallel play is much more to their
liking. Heterosexual groups are acceptable, and there is no differentiation
in activities for boys or girls.

Physically, children of this age experience rapid growth in both height
and the large skeletal muscle groups. They are very flexible. Children of
this age do not perform physical activity smoothly. Any evidence of better
coordination is quite noticeable. Because they are small, they fantasize considerably. They often talk to themselves, have imaginary playmates, and
place a great deal of faith in their ability to command magical powers. Many
children at this age are superstitious, make wishes on stars or incantations
concerning the cracks in sidewalks, and resort to hocus-pocus in an effort
to compensate for their helplessness.

Children of this age are capable of profound thought. They are aware
of life and death. They require attention and regularity. Nonetheless, they
are able to exhibit extreme forms of behavior that seem to indicate a desire
for irregularity. They have a relatively short attention span. Activity is the
hallmark of this age, and it is difficult for the child to sit still for any length
of time. The child of this age has begun to learn to read and enjoys drama-
tizing activities. He is familiar with activities of daily living, knows right
from left, can dress himself and feed himself, but is in no hurry to accomplish tasks that are set for him. Spontaneity, rather than highly organized
activities, is necessary at this age. There can be scheduled and regularly
planned experiences for them, but intricate and detailed rules, regulations,
and drawn-out explanations will be lost. Running, jumping, swinging, and
chasing are very appealing to them. There must also be a time for passive
activities, keeping in mind the short attention span. Of course, there are
exceptions and some children will have relatively long attention spans.

Freshmen (Ages 7–9)

Chronological age may have a considerable relationship to general
characteristics exhibited by children of this age group. As has previously
been stated, however, merely because a camper has reached age 8 and is
classed as a freshman is no reason to assume that she is socially, physically,
or emotionally 8 years old. There is the distinct possibility that emotional
development greatly lags behind physical attainment.

The child in this age group suffers from extremes. She is no longer
infantile, but she is not yet independent. There is a great desire and temptation to try unfamiliar and challenging experiences, coupled with a direct

need for attention and the security of parental (adult) control. The child in this stage of development has the intellect to plan ahead. She is able to forego present pleasures for greater benefits at a future time. Nevertheless, while she appreciates the need to wait for future pleasures, she remains impatient with delays. This is indeed an age of frustration and attempted independence.

Campers between the ages of 7 and 9 are more discerning about companions, conformity, and the difference between right and wrong than is the elementary group. They evince an enormous curiosity about everything. There is an increased reliance upon their own capabilities, and less upon the magical world of make-believe. The 7-year-old is particularly difficult to get close to. She resents any kind of control and is most negative in her behavior. On the whole, children in this age bracket are forming opinions and learning how to conduct themselves by emulation. This is the stage of hero worship.

The freshman is capable of accepting responsibility. She can complete simple tasks, can read and write, and is particularly concerned with belonging to some group and having friends. It is an age at which ideals are beginning to gain acceptance and hero figures are necessary supports. There is an inclination to embroider ordinary affairs. Imagination combined with daily experiences reveals certain felt inadequacies as well as desires. The child is self-conscious about fallibilities and is extremely sensitive to slights or sarcastic remarks. Children tend to be cruel to one another. A chance to crush an adversary by pointing out some weakness, foible, or handicap is gleefully exploited. The child takes an almost sadistic pleasure in inflicting pain by verbal abuse, rarely is the abuse physical. Defense mechanisms, such as withdrawal, are prominent at this period.

There is, at this time, a remarkable social development leading to co-operative endeavors and group activities. At 7 and 8, boys and girls can participate in joint activities. At 9 there is often a distinct separation between boys and girls, however. The 7-year-old child appears boisterous, is not well coordinated, and displays a lack of readiness for organized, competitive games. At 8, the child is much more concerned about ownership of objects and selection of companions; she has an increasing awareness of the world around her.

Age nine sees the child as a comparatively able person. She is well coordinated and has command of many motor skills, although she finds it difficult to master fine muscle activity. She is prepared to participate in informal group games but does not appreciate highly competitive team activities. She has an interest in various activities, and her eagerness to learn provides a wide selection of experiences from which to choose. Children of this age may be quite social, but essentially stay with friends of the same sex.

Sophomores (Ages 10 –12)

Precocity may be rather noticeable in this group. There are some very advanced children at this age who could fit very well into the junior category. On the other hand, there are average sophomores who are still freshmen at heart—emotionally, socially, and physically they remain immature. At ages 10 and 11 cooperative activity is easy to initiate. Team play and group effort is much more advanced. Organized competitive activities play a prominent role at this stage. One can reason with a 10-year-old and give fairly complicated explanations for certain cause and effect relationships. The child is capable of objectivity, questioning, and assimilating a surprising store of data. He is much more capable of self-criticism and attempts to adjust to whatever weaknesses he displays in a variety of skills.

This is really the age of the group. Campers enjoy regulating their own behavior and want a hand in planning their own activities. They also need adult supervision and look to adults for guidance in their own decision making. There is an increasing desire to serve and be useful. Concomitantly, there is an increased need for solitude and privacy. The child has secrets, hides personal treasures, is fully aware of ownership rights and privileges, and is interested in pursuing individual activities. The 10- to 12-year-old is better able to handle sexual concepts. Frank explanations, delivered without embarrassment, are needed. It is not unusual for children in this age group to make reference to reproduction and to the sexual organs involved in the process. Language has greater meaning, and children tend to use "loaded" and more sophisticated words to convey meanings. Although there is still little co-ed activity in this group, the more advanced children may have the first stirrings of heterosexual involvement.

One particular characteristic of the sophomore is the variance in physical maturation. The range of body development is wide. Increasing weight may be noted in some girls, along with the onset of menstruation. Boys become physically stronger and have greater stamina. Muscular coordination is better and competitive activities are desired. There is a demand for excitement, along with a willingness to subordinate some interests in favor of acquiring and perfecting motor skills. There is also a buildup of intellectual accomplishments. Games of chance, reading, adventure, quizzes, and other activities that stimulate intellectual participation are required.

Juniors (Ages 13 –15)

The single most discernible characteristic at this age is tremendous physical change. Secondary characteristics develop. Weight and height gains are typical, as is the appearance of pubic and axillary hair. Bodies begin to take on an adult shape. Although females tend to mature more rapidly than do males at this stage, the latter begin to catch up in late adolescence. It is typical for emotional problems stemming from appearance, sexual apprehensiveness, and conduct to become acute during these years.

Along with physical maturation and rapid changes is an increasing recognition of sexual conflicts. Problems arise as a result of self-consciousness, insecurity, inferiority, or fear of the future. Muscular coordination is diminished, which tends to surprise the adolescent. He has been accustomed to competing successfully in various physical activities. Suddenly, he finds that he misses more than he catches, gets tangled up in his own feet, and makes depth-perception errors. Clumsiness and a gangling appearance may be his prevailing condition for a time. In boys, the vocal

FIGURE 12-1. Young teenagers still enjoy ritual and costumes.

cords thicken, and the voice deepens and sometimes breaks at unexpected and embarrassing moments. Girls are much more conscious of their feminine shapes. For them it is a time of whispered confidences, awareness of boys, and lapses in self-confidence.

This age group has personal problems of compelling proportions, many of which stem from a determination to be independent and free of parental control. The early adolescent is ambivalent (Fig. 12-1). On occasion he is immature, dependent, affectionate, and attention-seeking. Sometimes he is aloof, condescending, and dogmatic. He is completely unpredictable from one day, or even one hour, to the next. He is usually motivated toward participation in highly organized team activities. He has good gross motor skills, although he sometimes fumbles. He has developed greater social concern for peer status. Nothing is more important than being with the "in" group. He has the intellectual capacity for abstract reasoning and is able to handle a good deal of responsibility. His powers of concentration are developed to the point where he can remain at one assignment for longer periods. Interest in the opposite sex increases. The spectrum of physical, social, emotional, and intellectual characteristics runs from those of a child to those of an adept adult.

During this emotionally stressful period, both sexes need understanding and support from their immediate families, but even more so from professional personnel who work with them. The anxiety that is produced at this stage of development may not be well understood by the child undergo-

FIGURE 12-2.   Co-recreational activities with counselor guidance encourages ease of adjustment.

ing them. The importance of good peer relationships is therefore essential. One sure method for assisting at this crucial time is by organizing heterosexual groups, which, through recreational activities, can provide satisfactory physical, psychological, and social needs outlets (see Fig. 12-2).[7]

Seniors (Ages 16 –18)

The older children get, the greater is the pressure upon them to behave in socially acceptable and adult ways. The typical adolescent lives up to adult expectations. She responds maturely and intelligently in most instances. Adolescents can be invested with responsibility concerning the health and safety of younger children and can be relied upon to fulfill their obligations. There are those who cannot be given such responsibility, however. They lack the maturity and judgment necessary to carry out such assignments.

The older adolescent continues to demonstrate the need to break loose from parental jurisdiction. Complaints, including major and minor irritations about parental restrictions, outlooks, opinions, attitudes, and val-

[7]T. Kando, *Social Interaction* (St. Louis: C.V. Mosby, 1977), p. 195.

ues often intensify. The potential for rebellion is a constant source of worry to concerned adults. Almost all parents feel that there is a loss of communication between themselves and their children.

The older adolescent begins to restrict herself to fewer activities. Personality traits crystallize. The extrovert becomes even more gregarious; the introvert withdraws even further. Heterosexual activities are popular. Sexual relations, ranging from hand holding to intercourse, are not uncommon.

The older adolescent camper wants to be on her own. She seeks to plan, initiate, and regulate the types of experiences available to her. She may want to be a junior counselor or CIT. She resents being with younger children unless she functions in the capacity of supervisor.

The awkwardness usually associated with young adolescents has vanished. The older child has learned to command skilled responses from large and small muscles. They are strong, coordinated, capable, and willing to perform. While physical strength is a primary factor in the selection of activities for males of this age, just the opposite is true for females. Many males are addicted to highly competitive team sports and gross motor activity; females tend to withdraw from these experiences and seek activities that require grace, poise, and dexterity. To a considerable extent, physical strength and endurance bring prestige to boys at this age,[8] girls are much more concerned with grooming, social conduct, and fashion. But even here there are few rigid rules characterizing the late adolescent. For some time now, strenuous and vigorous team and individual sports have been increasingly popular among girls. These differences and interests must be taken into account within the camp activities program.

At camp, the older adolescents should be far removed from residential units for younger campers. They feel important in their own right, and should be treated differently in many respects. Minimum restrictions in terms of hours, activities, and quarters are necessary. A less formalized regimen should be planned with them. Exploratory trips by foot, bicycle, canoe, or horseback can be exciting. They are mature individuals and must be accepted as such, unless proved otherwise. They are capable of obtaining great value from the camping experience. They are also capable of creating conflicts and problems that competent staff personnel must be able to resolve.

[8]J. Q. Kizziar and J. W. Hagedorn, *Search for Acceptance: The Adolescent and Self-Esteem* (Chicago: Nelson-Hall, 1979).

chapter 13

The Counselor's Influence on Camper Adjustment

The camp environment, a factor that significantly influences both social behavior and skill development, fluctuates daily and even hourly, especially among the youngest campers. Its social and physical forces vary with changes in weather, the counselor's mood, the experiences to which attention is directed, the campers' attitudes and a legion of other factors. The camp environment directly reflects the counselor's understanding of his campers and their needs, his ability to motivate their behavior, and his success in adapting activities to individual needs.

PERSONAL ADJUSTMENT TO CAMPING

Children and youth need to learn skills of getting along with people.[1] Human living is group living, and unless an individual knows how to work and play with others, he cannot live successfully. Camp personnel cannot expect all campers to have satisfactory human relations skills; camp experiences should help campers grow in their ability to know and understand others.

Similarly, campers of all ages are faced with health problems, physical or emotional. They must understand themselves as living organisms, learn how to maintain their health, and become familiar with ways of preventing disease and avoiding accidents as well as to become accomplished in the skills of outdoor living. Camp personnel must continue to design programs that focus attention on the skills and attitudes that enable campers to deal effectively with intragroup living and to assimilate skills that will enable them to find enjoyment in the outdoors.

[1] M. F. Chenery, "The Self-Start Attitude," *Camping Magazine* (March 1985), 20–22.

Some campers live in environments that are not conducive to mental or physical health; their social attitudes and motivations toward others may be adversely affected by their home surroundings. They need to increase their capacity to face problems that have impact on their mental health.

The task of assisting campers to become productive members of the small group is crucially important to all counselors. In order to create and maintain a group environment that encourages sound emotional and physical health, the counselor should turn his attention to the following questions:

1. Is the group living process related to behavioral adjustment?
2. How do growth and development affect democratic involvement?
3. What effect does the organization of the program have on camper achievement and satisfaction?
4. What group procedures and experiences help meet the health needs of campers?

This chapter considers each of these questions, with particular emphasis on the effect of various procedures on enhancing campers' lives. A camper's emotional health is affected by the camp environment, and this environment results in part from the counselor himself and his application of his knowledge of skill learning, camper growth and development, and program organization.

ADJUSTMENT PROCESSES AND BEHAVIORAL CHANGES

Effective application of what is now known about how campers mix and adjust is fundamentally important. When campers thrive, the counselor is pleased, and campers gain satisfaction from their achievements. When camping does not offer satisfying experiences, the counselor is disappointed, and campers may become depressed, disgruntled, uncooperative, and despondent.

Acceptance and Understanding

Learning to cope with new surroundings and unfamiliar situations and people is a personal matter; the learner does his own learning. Children and youth learn continuously from their experiences in the environment with which they interact. Their behavior is the consequence of the interactions of their experiences within the camp. In the microcosm of the bunk, their behavior reveals their unique qualities and their acceptance and understanding of the camp world, both of which are influenced by previous experiences.

To be effective, the counselor cannot simply tell campers what to do. When the camper has difficulty accepting and understanding, it may be not because the camper does not want to adjust, but because the ideas being presented may be interpreted as unimportant or somehow unconnected to the immediate living situation. It is vital that the counselor know how chil-

dren and adolescents perceive what is being said or done. Telling and counseling are not identical. When a counselor tells a camper to do something,
he cannot be sure that the camper will accept and interpret the words as
they were intended.

Physical, Mental, and Social Interrelationships

Camp counseling is a process of relating to children and adolescents
in such a way as to facilitate both their ability to assimilate information and
the actions necessary to promote democratic self-sufficiency within small
groups. It consists of creating the kind of emotional climate in which
campers will feel secure enough to venture and explore; an innervating
climate that provides a range of stimuli broad enough to be significant to
campers with different backgrounds, needs, abilities, and objectives; and a
physical environment that is healthful, attractive, and pleasant. The interre-
lationship of the emotional, social, and physical elements must be recognized as having an important influence on adjustment and personal development.[2]

If a camper is fatigued, or is disturbed by some emotional problem,
her behavior may be quite different from what it was the day before. If
campers are required to sit still for an extended period of time, they may
lose interest and begin to fidget in order to satisfy their urge for physical
activity. If campers are placed in situations that call for a higher order of
social skills than they possess, they may become frustrated and withdraw.
Tasks that are far beyond the campers' intellectual ability may also create
harmful tensions and frustrations. Thoughts, feelings, association with others, and physical well-being are inextricably bound. The effective counselor
studies each camper, helps him adapt to the small-group environment of
the bunk, and facilitates the development of new skills, appreciations, and
learning with patience and kindness.

Individual Differences

In recognition of the changes that accompany campers' growth and
development, the counselor must modify the activity program to conform
to individual differences. It is possible, of course, to characterize campers
at each stage of growth and development and to establish expectations for
every age. However, such information should not cause the counselor to
turn a blind eye to the fact that each camper must be considered an individual, with her own innate talents and abilities, growth rate, level of development, and hand–eye coordination. The rates at which different campers
develop and grow physically, socially, emotionally, and mentally vary
greatly, even within age groups, and this must be taken into consideration
when planning activities for a bunk.

Camping experiences will not be personally meaningful for campers
unless provision is made to accommodate individual differences. A counselor needs to use techniques that facilitate his knowledge of each camper.

[2]P. Pitcher, "Reality Therapy," *Camping Magazine* (May 1985), 30–36.

He guides, advises, and plans recreational experiences that should be satisfying and enjoyable for every camper.

Counselors should be sensitive to individual differences in physical skills, in ability to express ideas verbally, and in emotional and social adjustment. They must constantly facilitate the camper's achievement in all areas of growth and development. They try to adapt planned activities to the needs of each camper.

An important change in counseling methods and procedures occurs when counselors become aware of differences in campers and accept responsibility for satisfying individual needs. Programs can be adapted by regrouping campers, varying activities, modifying materials, providing individual assistance, using particular instructional techniques to sustain interest, changing the amount of time necessary for the completion of tasks, simplifying procedures for the learning of new skills, and offering activities on various levels of difficulty. Effective counseling calls for developing a satisfactory method of caring for individual differences. It promotes healthful living within the bunk as well as within the larger environment of the camp.

Attention to Needs

The counselor is in a strategic position to observe and identify campers who may require special attention. Some campers may have emotional problems as a result of being away from home or because of other previous experiences. Such problems may prevent the camper from interacting constructively with others. Some campers may be exceptionally endowed with talent in graphic arts or may have unusual scientific ability. Regardless of endowment or learned ability, the camp bunk is the best place for youngsters with special needs. These needs can generally be met if the counselor is able to make provisions for them. Special interest groups can occasionally be formed, with the staff specialist assigned to offer individual stimulation or particular activities that can satisfy the demands of eager young minds and especially talented campers.

The camper with special needs is an individual with distinct fears, hopes, and aspirations. His need for affection, peer status, and personal development must be met within the framework of his differences. He, like any other member of the bunk, should be assisted in gaining a sense of being a worthy member of his group (Fig. 13-1). Modern camping practices foster camper growth and development in many ways. They permit campers to explore, to investigate, and to actively engage in a variety of self-understanding and self-accepting behaviors. Campers are helped to acquire the skills necessary for enjoying outdoor living and are simultaneously gaining insight into problem solving and learning to cope within the give and take of a small social group.

Passive and Active Experiences

Camping activities should be scheduled so that periods of concentration and sedentary activity are followed by opportunities for exercise of

FIGURE 13-1. The counselor can offer invaluable support in ensuring the acceptance of each camper. (Courtesy: Crane Lake Camp, West Stockbridge, Massachusetts.)

large-muscle groups. Brief periods of quiet activity interspersed with vigorous physical activity are valuable. Rest and relaxation can be provided through such activities as storytelling, quiet games, reading, art, and letter writing (Fig. 13-2). Campers invariably need guidance in selecting a balanced program, if such selection is part of the camp's offering. If the camp program is preset so that each bunk goes to a particular activity at a certain time of the day or evening, then there is a built-in alternation of activities.

Some campers become heavily involved in extra activities such as the camp newspaper, drama club, or music ensemble. Such activity is desirable because it offers the camper considerable pleasure and satisfaction. However, counselors should assist campers so that their activities are balanced and varied, thereby reducing the likelihood of tension and fatigue from excessive involvement.

Relaxation Needs

The counselor's knowledge of a camper's level of physical and emotional development and of any health problem he might have is valuable in determining the kind of activities that will provide for optimal physical effort and relaxation. The bunk environment should be such that campers obtain adequate rest at night. The counselor may need to monitor her charges to see that all get to sleep without difficulty.

The need for relaxation periods depends partly on the kind of activity program offered and the emotional tone of the bunk and other activity settings to which the camper is exposed. Anxiety, fear, boredom, and frus-

FIGURE 13-2. A reflective moment: time out to write a letter.

tration produce fatigue; interest, enthusiasm, and achievement minimize fatigue. A change in the kind of activity is often as invigorating as a rest period.

Activity Needs

Outcomes of vigorous play and the ordinary experiences of outdoor life at camp go beyond the physical aspects of human development or the acquisition of safety experiences. Emotional development and social skill assimilation are also components. Vigorous physical recreational activities help campers acquire skills that build feelings of adequacy, promote confidence, encourage bunk spirit, and facilitate learning new activities. Sufficient equipment, supplies, and space are basic to the camp's program of activities.

THE COUNSELOR'S GUIDANCE ROLE

The counselor has 24-hour-a-day contact with campers. This is an unparalleled opportunity to provide guidance to enable campers to optimize their potential and become better persons for the association. The counselor's impact upon the camper carries with it a high degree of responsibility. As a parental surrogate and authority figure, the counselor's every gesture, tone of voice, and facial expression influences the camper's behavior, attitude, and ability to adjust to the small group. Many campers emulate and even idolize the counselor.[3] Counselors must live up to the enormous responsibility that this outlook places upon them.

Every contact with campers offers opportunities to become better acquainted with them as individuals. Each encounter encourages a well-timed situation in which campers can be motivated to stretch themselves and seek personal achievement in cooperation with other group members. Such associations can also produce acceptance of behavioral consequences and of the need to take responsibility for one's own actions. In the final analysis, the counselor should be a worthy role model who contributes to the camper's knowledge and experience.

Establishing Rapport

The foundation of the camper–counselor relationship is the counselor's ability to establish and build the camper's confidence in his integrity, fairness, sensitivity, and concern. Trust increases the likelihood of the exchange of confidences which is so necessary if the counselor is to understand each camper. By taking advantage of opportunities to learn more about campers' behavior and helping them to understand themselves, the counselor will better accept them as individuals with unique needs. To the extent that the counselor respects each camper's personality, emotional state, and level of maturity, mutual trust and confidence will develop.

Rapport is built slowly and carefully as the counselor continues to associate with the camper in the bunk, during programmed activities, and in the course of normal daily events. On occasion, however, there is the opportunity for a more personal encounter as the counselor recognizes the camper's need to talk to someone about personal problems or questions, which may be introduced as trivial topics. The counselor must be an able listener, quick to discern the real need that is sometimes masked in light banter. The counselor must create an environment in which campers' willingness to unburden themselves is encouraged. The counselor must develop the camper's confidence in her as a person who is consistently fair and responsible, and who can be counted on to do what she says she will do. The counselor who maintains consistent values and behavior, so that the camper knows how to approach her, has developed an image of constancy upon which the camper can rely. This trait, almost more than any other characteristic, contributes to the development of a secure relationship.

The counselor must be willing to listen attentively to the camper's expressions of concern, bewilderment, and real or imagined woes. Only in this way can the counselor gain insight into the basis for the camper's frustrations. Attention to what the camper is trying to communicate, overtly or covertly, provides invaluable cues, thus placing the counselor in a better position to help campers understand their emotional confusion and recognize the forces that influence her feelings.

[3]D. Freeman, "Power of Positive Modeling," *Camping Magazine* (April 1984), 16–17, 28.

Counselors should encourage campers to communicate by finding aspects of their experiences, behaviors, or skills that can be praised, encouraged, or reinforced. It is wise for the counselor to promote communication by responding positively, in context, and limiting any drawn-out explanations or value judgments that might be difficult for the camper to comprehend. It is fine to offer advice and counsel at a level that the camper can accept. Being overly judgmental or prejudicial against the camper will retard his self-appreciation and may intrude, to the harm of the relationship, into the relatively permissive association that has been developed. The counselor will have many opportunities to demonstrate his attentiveness to the camper and his willingness to offer the necessary assistance.

The informal setting of the bunk offers just the opportunity the camper needs to "open up" and voice opinions, vent feelings, or simply reveal more of herself than would ordinarily be the case in a more formal situation.

Confidence Building

The ability to empathize and to search out cues enables the counselor to obtain valuable knowledge about campers' attitudes, opinions, anxieties, or problems. Encouraging the camper to articulate his concerns may enable him to formulate ideas, arrange his thoughts with greater logic and clarity, and make objective value judgments. The opportunity to talk things out increases the likelihood of finding a solution or an acceptable alternative.

Campers soon discern whether or not a counselor can be trusted. To the extent that rapport has been developed, there will be a shared trust. If this is reinforced, then the camper will confide in the counselor. Nevertheless, the counselor should remind the camper that some topics may have to be revealed to the camp director if the nature of the information requires such action. Only when the camper understands this ethical principle should the counselor continue to elicit such information. If after being apprised of this condition the camper decides to offer the information, it is a mark of profound trust in the counselor. The presumption here is that the counselor has developed rapport and the camper is willing to reveal confidential information that could be significant in preventing or alleviating situations of concern to the entire camp. This is not a plea for spying—far from it. Rather, it is an overriding concern for maintaining the confidentiality of the camper–counselor relationship and respecting the camper's right to privacy.

Grouping

As campers progress through the various age-related associations that characterize a camp, they become part of many different groups, remaining longer in some than in others but nevertheless learning new attitudes and ideas and employing different skills. The groups that are primary for the camper—that is, those that have more meaning and influence on his development and behavior—tend to provide a variety of dynamic interactions. A group is much more than a collection of individuals; it has its own person-

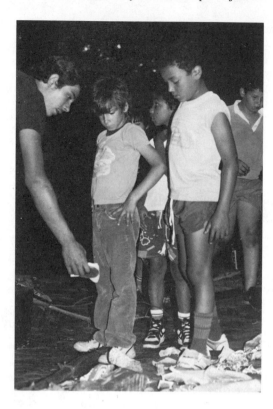

FIGURE 13-3. The counselor makes sure that everyone gets a fair share. (Courtesy: Leona Gwaz, Camp Schade, Connecticut.)

ality. The personality of a group is dynamic because it depends upon the network of interpersonal relationships that form it. The group's personality changes as campers get to know one another better, live together, and find common and stimulating outlets among the varied offerings of the camp program. Fundamental needs for recognition, affection, and a sense of belonging are met in group life.[4]

In the bunk and throughout the camping environment, the counselor makes many decisions about campers' membership in committees and other peer associations. These decisions either enhance a camper's self-respect and confidence, or create feelings of rejection and valuelessness. Counselors recognize that the group powerfully affects each camper's outlook and feelings about himself as a member. The need to be approved by others is an important incentive for acceptance into a preferred group.

Throughout the day and for different kinds of experiences, counselors continually group and regroup campers (Fig. 13-3). Teaching new skills in the same way to all campers results in too slow a pace for the rapid achievers and too fast a pace for those who pick up new skills more slowly. Grouping can be used to encourage the greatest possible achievement according to

[4]R. Kraus and M. M. Scanlin, *Introduction to Camp Counseling* (Englewood Cliffs, N. J.: Prentice-Hall, 1983), pp. 63–67.

each camper's ability. Campers may be able to win status and recognition from their peers when groups are formed to use outstanding abilities or talents. Some campers are able to identify with their bunks or with smaller activity groups, thereby experiencing a sense of contributing with others.

At times campers may be grouped because they have a common need for learning specific skills or information. In swimming, for example, campers may need help learning to float, swim, kick, or breathe before they can enjoy water sports and games in which others are skilled. Some kinds of permanent groupings are not appropriate for all campers because they have grown and developed faster than is usual. As a counselor recognizes the influence of group membership upon a camper's attitudes toward camping in general and individuals in particular, she contributes to the camper's personal development and achievement and enables him to participate more fully and obtain more value from the camping experience. (Fig. 13-4).

Residential Responsibilities in the Bunk

Democracy is a fundamental and lasting ideal of American life. If democratic values are to be inculcated and assimilated by children, they must be "lived" in all phases of the camp experience. Such essential components of democratic relationships as concern for others, acceptance of responsibility, self-direction, cooperative action, meeting individual needs, and im-

FIGURE 13-4. The counselor is responsible for developing group spirit. (Courtesy: Crane Lake Camp, West Stockbridge, Massachusetts.)

proving human welfare significantly promote healthful living within the bunk and in the camp in general, and encourage personal and socioemotional growth.

In camps in which democratic processes are valued, the counselor is a guide and mentor. Adhering to group-formulated standards is important, and each camper should learn to understand, accept, and carry responsibilities appropriate to his level of development. Campers should learn that each member of the group has rights and must be respected.[5] When a counselor provides a broad range of experiences to guide each camper toward maximum development of his capacities, it is easier to identify the unique contributions of each individual. Children develop feelings of belonging and status through their contributions to group activities.

Each camper needs an opportunity to be a leader as well as a follower within the group. For every reward, for every idea, plan of action, or set of standards developed to improve bunk living, there are related responsibilities to be undertaken. Individual development and group welfare require concern for others. Housekeeping practices in the bunk and around the camp offer many opportunities for counselors to involve individuals or groups of campers. Procedures, standards, rules, and good health practices may relate to the various duties that contribute to an orderly and attractive bunk, use of equipment or supplies during camping activities, camp safety practices, and behavior during outings.

Counselors are employed to provide close supervision for children and general supervision for adolescents living at camp. Counselors must have the understanding, maturity, and skills necessary to effectively resolve the ordinary problems that beset all growing children. When extraordinary situations arise that are beyond the counselor's experience or expertise, they should be referred to the staff person best suited by experience and ability to deal with them. Thus, the unit leader, unit supervisor, assistant director, or camp director may be the final arbiter of complex problems that require superior knowledge for solution. Nevertheless, the counselor is the first line of emotional support for campers. The counselor, through close and daily contact with the camper, is the first to discern difficulties with the camper's adjustment to camp life. The counselor must be able to maintain campers' morale and help them fit into the camping environment without losing individual identity.

[5]C. Donckers, "Resolving Conflicts," *Camping Magazine* (May 1985), 14–17.

chapter 14

The Counselor and the Problem Camper

It is not unusual for residential camps to go through an entire season without having to deal with stolen property allegations, serious homosexual activity, assault, extreme insecurity, anorexia, or enuresis. There are typical problems that occur in almost every camp, however.[1] Some are serious enough to require psychiatric care; others are strictly run-of-the-mill, and camp administrators have come to expect them. Although such problems may be routine for the camp, they can be traumatic for the camper. The underlying causes for camper maladjustment should be assiduously determined and, when possible, eliminated or reduced.

GENERAL PROBLEMS

Behavior extremes are symptomatic of deep-seated or fundamental disturbances. Camp counselors are not psychiatrists; they are not prepared to offer remedial assistance for emotional maladies. Counselors should be prepared for a variety of behavioral problems, however, some of which may indicate extreme disturbances. Knowledge of some behavioral manifestations and their likely causes will help the counselor avoid snap judgments or responses that can further traumatize an already hurt child. In nearly all such situations, the counselor will have to refer the problem to the camp administrator for final resolution. In many cases, prompt counselor assistance by gentle guidance, friendliness, calmness, and awareness do more for the camper than anything else. Counselors must recognize that their pri-

---

[1] C. B. Rotman, "The Problem Camper: To Tolerate, Treat, or Terminate," *Camping Magazine* (Sept./Oct. 1973), 16.

mary responsibility is for the camper. The knowledge of possible problem areas and recognition of the fact that sympathy and tact are two of the best techniques for problem resolution will make the camping season more valuable for all concerned. Problems may be expressed in a number of ways, but they are essentially the child's response to previous associations, guilt feelings, insecurity, or fear.

BEHAVIOR PROBLEMS

Behavior problems encountered at camps can be categorized as those of an antisocial nature; those that are manifested as personality problems; and negative habits. Socially unacceptable activities include sexual perversion and acting out, sadism or excessive cruelty, substance abuse, stealing, lying, temper tantrums, fighting, and chronic disobedience. Personality problems include constant showing off, timidity, excessive depression, selfishness, nervousness, stubbornness, and introversion. Negative habits include enuresis, eating difficulties, speech disturbances, sleeping problems, finger sucking, nail biting, masturbation, and soiling. These problems should be looked upon as surface characteristics of unsatisfied psychological needs. They are symptoms of psychological and physiological maladjustment. Each child requires individual attention; when such attention is provided, many of the problems can be alleviated. In many cases, common sense and an understanding of human growth and development are of incalculable value in reversing problems that might eventually need professional attention.

Homesickness

The most common problem for children on their first trip away from home is homesickness. Gone are familiar surroundings and people. The camp is strange; fear of the unexpected arouses discomfort (Fig. 14-1). Homesickness is best dealt with by preventing its onset. The child should be thoroughly familiarized with the camp through brochures containing pictures and, if possible, by meeting some of the staff and his own counselor before the start of camp. The camper needs security, acceptance, and the knowledge that he has some adult to depend on for attention and comfort.

Some homesickness occurs in consequence of child–parent relationship. If the child feels unloved or unwanted at home, his placement in camp seems to reinforce what he fears. This apparent rejection may cause severe reactions. The camper may fear a parental break during his absence, and the fear can become so profound that he may run away from camp to make sure that the family remains intact. In other instances, the child may fear sibling replacement of parental affection during his stay at camp.

Homesickness can often be treated by a sympathetic counselor. In cases of isolation and withdrawal by the camper, it may be determined that his bunkmates reject him or that he cannot, for a variety of reasons, participate in the scheduled activities. Such situations can be handled with comparative ease. A change in bunks or an introduction to new activities may

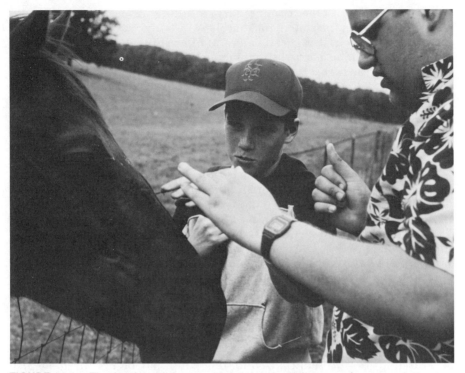

FIGURE 14-1. The fearful child may withdraw and needs counselor support. (Courtesy: Donna Richardson.)

overcome this problem. If the cause is so serious that the camp cannot deal with it, the camper must return home. Under these circumstances, the wise administrator might suggest a competent outside authority to assist in the matter.

Sexual Acting Out

One can envision a cartoon depicting a school teacher addressing her class of young boys and girls with this statement: "The board of education requires me to give you some basic information on sex, reproduction, and other disgusting filth." To some people, any expression of sexual interest or activity is indeed evil and needs eradication. But present educational and psychological practices stress the need for utter frankness and openness in answering questions or instructing about sexual behavior.[2] Sexual conduct at camp can present problems to the staff and the administration. Of chief concern here are the causes of such problems and the best methods for constructively handling them.

[2]N. Tallent and C. I. Spungin, *Psychology: Understanding Ourselves and Others* (New York: American Book, 1977), pp. 154–56.

Masturbation.   One commentary resulting from the now-famous Kinsey reports was the statement that 99% of the population masturbates and the rest lie about it. A certain amount of masturbation occurs in almost all children; it can be learned spontaneously or from others. Excessive masturbation may answer a need that is beyond sexual satisfaction.[3] It often represents a search for love, attention, and satisfaction. When a child is unhappy, alone, or has few interests, he may turn to the one method whereby he achieves self-gratification. To offset masturbatory activity, more attention and care must be directed toward the child. If his attention is turned outward to new, challenging, and enjoyable activities, masturbation may be considerably diminished.

Excessive or compulsive masturbation is abnormal. The causes for this behavior must be brought to light and the child helped professionally. Moralizing and restrictive measures should not be contemplated; they neither assist the child nor rid him of his guilt about the act or the fantasies that accompany it. The best tactic for the counselor is an unemotional response and complete honesty. Compulsive masturbation in the child probably requires extensive psychiatric treatment.

Homosexual activity.   It is quite normal for children to experiment sexually with each other. It is not unusual for members of the same sex to compare genital organs, this may even be considered appropriate activity unless it carries erotic overtones. But homosexual expression is of concern to the camp administrator at any time. By placing a homosexual adult or peer in a position to seduce a child, the camp may be encouraging such activity. In other instances, homosexual activity may result from attempts by maladjusted or physically weaker children to buy favors or ingratiate themselves with older campers who are more popular, stronger, or have influence with others.

When such activity is discerned, it is important to find its causes so that the participants can be helped.[4] Careful handling of the case is absolutely necessary. No threat of punishment or hysteria should accompany the disclosure, experimental sexual activities of this nature need calm, objective treatment. The intent of the participants—experimentation or eroticism—must be determined. Perverted conduct requires treatment by a competent authority. The counselor and camp director must have absolute self-control. The camp must give the child every conceivable opportunity to find satisfaction and pleasure in other ways; the child must be given attention and drawn into the program. All seductive and encouraging influences must be removed. Every case of this type—and they are rare—should be handled in the same way as are all other events.

Heterosexual activity.   Coed camps provide opportunities for mutual attraction and stimulation. Effective supervision will probably deter any un-

[3]R. Roser, R. E. Fox, and I. Gregory, *Abnormal Psychology,* 2nd ed. (Philadelphia: Saunders, 1972).

[4]R. R. Bortzin and J. R. Acocella, *Abnormal Psychology,* 4th ed. (New York: Random House, 1984), pp. 302–3.

desirable sexual activity, however. Especially among adolescent campers, there is a strong and growing interest in members of the opposite sex, and this is normal. The coed camp has the opportunity to develop constructive and wholesome attitudes and practices in campers. Social experiences at dances, mixed sport activities, dramatic productions, camp-fire activities, and parties are ideal situations for acquiring appropriate behavior and poise.[5] Counselors should be worthy of emulation. They must be adult, have good judgment, and conduct themselves in ways that can be used by the campers as an example for the present and future. Under no circumstances should the counselor allow her level of conduct to drop to that of a camper. This is particularly true of the senior campers, whose age might approximate that of the counselor. Counselors should never recount their sexual experiences, and they must never use foul language or vulgarisms to become "one of the boys." Counselors will gain little and lose much with such behavior.

Some heterosexual expression finds outlet in pornographic pictures and literature, erotic fantasies, and stories. In these cases, the counselor is offerd an opportunity to teach. When interest and attention are so clearly indicated, the counselor can clear up erroneous conceptions and present a healthy sexual attitude. Frankness and good sense must be combined; discussion should be open, calm, and routine.

Stealing

Theft of property is a common problem in every camp. Whether the camp is restricted to a wealthy clientele or is an institutionalized or agency camp concerned mainly with the economically deprived, stealing prevails. Stealing is merely one more manifestation of underlying disturbance. Stealing occurs for a number of reasons, not the least of which is the desire for attention. Attention is certainly what the thief receives. For some emotionally deprived children, even negative attention is, unfortunately, equated with love or affection. It is a method of gaining the security of status, or of negating neglect.

While stealing cannot be condoned, it often indicates specific needs that have never been satisfied.[6] The concern is for rehabilitation through assistance. Some children's home background is so alienated that society's values are perverted. Where the environment permits or tacitly approves of theft, theft will be regarded as acceptable behavior; the child has no way of learning that stealing is wrong. This has been particularly true where stealing certain commodities to sustain life prevails. In some subcultures, stealing is looked upon as a way of life. The child is taught at an early age to cheat, lie, and steal from outsiders. It is little wonder, then, that this same conduct occurs at camp.

But why should a child who "has everything" steal? The child may

[5]R. G. Kraus and M. M. Scanlin, *Introduction to Camp Counseling* (Englewood Cliffs, N.J.: Prentice-Hall, 1983), p. 266.
    [6]E. Palter, "How to Help When Stealing Occurs in Camp," *Camping Magazine* (May 1972), 16.

receive all the material possessions in the world without receiving love and attention. If the child's needs for affection and supervision are left to hired hands, if parents cannot or will not spend time with their children, then the child steals to obtain what he lacks. To many children, material giving is synonymous with love and affection. The objects become symbolic of love. It may be that overabundance of possessions leaves the child without any sense of material worth. He simply takes because the object is available rather than because he attaches any value to it. Another child may have no sense of property rights, having been taught to share everything; thus there is a poor understanding of ownership. The child, under these circumstances, could be innocently carrying over his conditioning at home, where everybody shares, to the camp situation. He does not consider this stealing, but sharing. Of course, stealing may also be symptomatic of a desire to own something. Investigation of motivation readily disclose these underlying causes.

Some children steal for the thrill of the chase, to show off. Stealing shows others that the child is not afraid of authority. She may attempt to involve others in stealing. The more forbidden the activity, the greater challenge it is to the ingenuity of the camper who requires satisfaction in this manner. There are also campers who steal in the hope of being caught. Such children have terrible emotional conflicts. They feel ashamed about some supposed reprehensible thought, desire, or wrong of which they believe themselves to be guilty. They subconsciously seek to atone by being caught at a punishable offense. In such cases, the theft is so overt and clumsy that the child is quickly found out. As this is exactly what the child wants, she needs help, not chastisement.

Theft may occur as an act of revenge. When a camper is weaker than his peers, not particularly skilled or able to perform well, and is slighted, ignored, or abused, he may resort to theft of some valued object in retaliation. This is the child's way of inflicting hurt or defeat upon those who have hurt or neglected him. He has come to realize that material possessions are highly valued; to take such articles causes severe hardship for his antagonist. For the timid or fearful, stealing is a method of gaining self-respect. It is an unfortunate method that must be stopped.

Children who have always been materially deprived may find it difficult to abstain from appropriating valuable objects when given the opportunity. Placed in close proximity to those who handle material goods carelessly, or simply being exposed to attractive articles that they have never had, may motivate theft. When one has been denied toys, tools, equipment, and other pleasure-giving materials and is tempted by their availability, the craving to possess them can become overpowering. This is understandable but not, of course, permissible.

The counselor may be able to help such emotionally or economically deprived children. He must bear in mind the motivation for theft. What are the factors that urge a child to steal? In many instances, planned personal attention, channeling of interest and activity, determination of how the camper may achieve peer status in acceptable ways, and refusal to make an issue out of some camper's thrill-seeking behavior can modify or eliminate the problem. The counselor has an opportunity to change unacceptable behavior by working intensively with the camper. Assuming that stealing is a problem without clinical aspects—one whose origins come from neurotic illness—there is much that the counselor can do. He must deal with the underlying causes and not restrict himself to mere punishment of the effects. Compulsive stealing or theft that is pathologically inspired requires medical treatment. Little can be done for the camper unless the camp is oriented to such problem behavior and has competent rehabilitative staff.

Speech Disorders

The etiology of speech disorders arising out of biological or physiological deficiencies does not concern us here. Only those speech disorders that have their origin in severe emotional conflict may come within the province of a camp problem. Stammering, for example, can be a sign of emotional immaturity. In general, most stammerers show a variety of psychological maladjustments, including anxiety, nervousness, insecurity, inferiority, and self-consciousness. Such children also desire to withdraw from social situations in order to escape painful conditions. Social contacts seem to dramatize the speech defect, which heightens the stress placed upon the child in that situation. With additional pressure the speech pattern tends to deteriorate further, and another vicious cycle is begun.

Stuttering can occur as a temporary signal in individual reactions to acute or highly stressful situations.[7] Whatever undermines the child's security may lead to the disruption of the motor coordination involved in speech. Causal factors include injuries suffered during participation in camp activities, a sudden scare, violent arguments with peers, or intense pressures by demanding parents or from within camp. One has heard of people being scared speechless or shocked into silence; the same holds true for anger. An individual who becomes highly agitated as the result of an argument, or who becomes emotional about an idea, may react by stammering.

Fundamentally, the counselor can help ease emotionally caused speech problems. She can best help the camper by eliminating the environmental conflicts that are placing too much pressure on the child. A knowledge of the child's home life and history of speech difficulty, along with a thorough understanding of the child's reactions to the camp situation, may be sufficient information for some help to be given. A casual acceptance of the speech defect, avoidance of telling the child to speak more slowly, and helping the child to adjust to his surroundings can be the best antidotes. Speech problems that are emotionally caused will not be removed through kindness: special treatment is usually required. Nevertheless, kindness and understanding on the counselor's part will help give the child security and a chance for satisfying experiences.

[7]R. R. Bortzin and J. R. Acocella, *Abnormal Psychology,* 4th ed. (New York; Random House, 1984), pp. 396–97.

Substance Abuse

The nonmedical use of drugs is both illegal and dangerous. The issue of substance abuse is so pervasive and serious in society that its recognition as a camp problem demands attention. Camps must maintain an uncompromising attitude toward drug and alcohol abuse. It is inconsistent with the values of camping and is unacceptable at any time. When counselors have a substance abuse problem, the camp administrator can take swift and foreseeable action. The counselor is simply dismissed for nonconformity to the camp's behavioral expectations. Counselors are adults, and their problems cannot be permitted to interfere with the effective and qualitative experiences offered by the camp. The counselor is summarily dismissed and may even be referred to police authorities.

When campers are involved with substance abuse, the consequences are far-reaching and may finally damage the camp's reputation. Of course, the primary responsibility under these circumstances is to help the camper. There must be no flexibility toward the use of drugs or alcohol by campers. There should be clearly understood policies, rules, and regulations prohibiting the use of either substance in the camp. It does not matter that some youngsters may come from home environments where drug and alcohol use is a permissible activity. It cannot matter that some elements of society tolerate or even encourage substance abuse. The highest responsibility of a camp is to the health and well-being of campers and of all personnel working with campers, which precludes substance abuse by anyone. Nothing should be permitted to endanger the well-being of campers. Beyond that, camp administrators have the moral obligation to both campers and their parents to guard those in their care against the hazards associated with such use.

Protecting campers against substance abuse must be explicit in all literature sent by the camp and during subsequent interviews of the parents of potential campers. When a youngster is actually in camp, counselors must be alert to any behavioral changes that might presage the use of impermissible substances. Naturally, counselors should be cautioned during their orientation, and later during inservice education, about the necessity for being absolutely certain that substance abuse is occurring before they confront or accuse a camper. Once drug or alcohol use has been detected, the counselor should work with the camper and try to discover why he is using these substances. More significantly, the counselor must immediately end such substance abuse. Infraction of camp policy in this matter cannot be tolerated. Some arrangement must be worked out whereby the camper signifies a willingness to live within the established policies of the camp. If this cannot be accomplished, then the counselor has no alternative but to turn the case over to the camp administrator for further action.

Camp administrators will be under extreme pressure to prevent further substance abuse by the camper. Either the camper will be advised, counseled, and prevented from using harmful substances, or he will be dismissed from camp and returned to his parents. To the extent possible, the camp administrator, working with the counselor, should do everything that can be done to stop substance abuse. If the camper is recalcitrant or incorrigible, however, there is nothing left but to remove that individual from camp. Surely, administrators and counselors want to help campers to be healthy and happy; that is their major professional responsibility. When youngsters refuse to be helped or when they refuse to deviate from unconscionable behaviors, there is little that the camp can do. Unless the camp is set up to treat substance abuse cases, separation seems to be the only alternative.

Nail Biting

Although nail biting occurs most frequently during adolescence, it is also common among children. The incidence is particularly high among children who have been raised in institutions. Some behavioral theorists indicate that nail biting is a technique used to reduce tension under stressful situations. It is highly probable that nail biters are more anxious than other individuals. The camper's nail biting may be physically painful to him, the cuticle is eaten through and bleeds, or else the nail is torn off the finger. When the camper shows this symptom, it is likely that the child is punishing himself for some real or imagined guilt.

Typical reactions to nail biting are punitive threats, application of vile-tasting liquids to the nails, ridicule, and other poorly motivated actions. Such treatment is a waste of time and is of dubious value. The counselor can help nail-biting campers to discharge tension more suitably if she has patience and understands that stress or hostility on the camper's part is responsible for this behavior (Fig. 14-2). The cause must be determined before the effect can be reduced or eliminated.

Enuresis

Enuresis is defined as the habitual involuntary discharge of urine after the child reaches 3 years of age. It most commonly occurs at night (bedwetting). Enuresis usually occurs in association with a dream in which the sleeper fancies that he is urinating in a latrine, he awakens to discover that he has wet the bed. Sometimes enuresis occurs during dreams of a sexual nature. The frequency of enuresis varies from nightly to as seldom as two times a week.

Enuresis can be caused by various factors, including anxiety, fear, need for attention, hostility, immaturity, abnormal family relations, or pleasurable sensations from urination. Parental indifference and insecurity may arouse hostility in the child toward the parents, against whom bedwetting is used as revenge. In a few cases, being cold may produce enuresis; the child wants to urinate, but refuses to leave a warm bed to do so. Often, the child is completely oblivious to the wetness and the smell.

Camps can easily handle the symptom of enuresis. The liquid intake of these campers can be reduced or omitted prior to bedtime, although this questionable practice makes the enuretic feel rejected, singled out, or embarrassed, and can lead to prolonged enuresis. A night patrol can be organized whereby the camper is awakened and taken to the latrine. As for sanitary conditions, a rubber sheet over the mattress and good laundry service eliminate odors.

FIGURE 14-2.   Individual attention sometimes eliminates anxieties that produce negative behaviors. (Courtesy: Camp Kennedy, Manchester, Connecticut.)

The underlying cause of enuresis may be biological, but is often emotional and may stem from the home. An attempt should be made to determine whether the camper had been enuretic at home. If the enuresis has
been a long-term problem, the counselor can do little unless the home environment changes, although he can still attempt to reduce the camper's fears
and anxieties while at camp.

Eating Difficulties

Perhaps the most common problem affecting camps is eating habits
and difficulties. For the camper, good food, rather than just food, is absolutely necessary. The camper may not have the best guidance, companions,
housing, or activities, but good food, well served, makes negative aspects of
the camp bearable. The best leadership, program, housing, and friends
mean little if the food is of poor quality, tasteless, or unappetizing. Meals
should be an integral part of the camp program, eagerly awaited and enjoyed. But even when the food is excellent and meets every nutritive standard, there is always at least one problem eater.

Each person is different in terms of food tastes and needs. Not all
campers require or can metabolize the same amount of food. Campers who

eat a normal amount, unless their table manners are impolite or disgusting, offer no problems. But the counselor invariably will be confronted with campers who are finicky, who refuse to eat anything, who are gluttons, who vomit after each meal, or who have eating habits nothing short of appalling. The counselor must learn to deal firmly, wisely, and equitably with each case. The main problems center around those campers who, as a consequence of emotional or neurotic involvement, reject, regurgitate, or gluttonize food.

Food rejection, when initiated by fad dieting, is usually a response to emotional conflicts arising from parental indifference or overprotectiveness. It can be a means of punishing an authority figure (usually a parent) for any number of reasons. The child's hostility to the parent is expressed through the rejection of food. Food is not only a staple of life; it also signifies warmth, care, love, and attention. From infancy on, oral gratification and satisfaction comes through food and feeding. Reinforcing this concept is the body contact between the infant and mother as a result of being held while feeding, and later while being helped to eat. As the child develops, she is given less attention and must learn to eat without help. Some food rejectors behave this way in order to punish the parent by causing anxiety; thus, attention is regained. Other children, particularly those who have younger siblings who now require primary attention, try to recapture their infant status by regression; they will not eat unless they are force-fed, the parent is reduced to an anxious state and the child receives his attention. As far as the child is concerned, the score is even. But this is an abnormal pattern and one that must be broken. Extreme forms should be referred to psychiatric care.

However, there are cases in which a well-established pattern of food rejection can be changed while the child is at camp. Barring suicidal tendencies or other pathological influences that preclude modification at camp, the simplest solution is unconcern, or apparent unconcern. Children are endowed by nature with the ability to detect hypocrisy. (If you want the truth about anything, ask any child under 10 years of age.) This sensitivity enables the child to see through false unconcern on the part of the counselor. The counselor must be well-equipped to handle such situations. She must understand the reasons behind food rejection and be confident that the child will not allow himself to starve. Furthermore, she must show no alarm if the child rejects many meals. This is the camper's way of testing authority. Should the counselor forget herself and show concern or anxiety, the camper will merely repeat the same pattern carried on at home. Wholesome unconcern about whether or not the camper eats will soon convince him that he is not going to arouse attention by not eating. Assuredly, the counselor will make all the supportive efforts that she would ordinarily make. She will assure the food rejector, as she does for each camper in her bunk, that she is a friend, confidant, leader, and guide. She will not, under any circumstances, force-feed, no matter how long or in what pattern the food rejection continues. When the camper realizes that he cannot command the attention that food rejection usually obtains for him, he will cease rejecting, particularly as hunger forces him to eat. The child may eat intermittently at first, in order to test whether the counselor will react to his eating. If the counselor refuses to rise to this bait and remains stable and unconcerned, the camper will finally drop this attention-getting device.

The opposite of food rejection is gluttony. Overeating, when it does not have origins in physiological deficiency, is generally viewed as a psychological problem. The etiology of gluttony lies in emotional conflicts within the family. Perhaps one of the parents has ambivalent feelings about the child. Since food is the symbol of the love, security, and satisfaction the child requires, then overeating is a way to obtain physically what is actually lacking in the parent–child relationship. When parents latently reject the child, food becomes the vehicle through which the parents repress the awful acknowledgment that they reject their own child. The child, responding to the rejection, tests his parents' love in the same manner. Food is excessively demanded in place of the withheld love. Compulsive overeating also provides compensatory satisfaction for frustrating situations and offers relief from unendurable tension.

Overeating leads to obesity when the metabolic rate cannot keep pace with the intake. The fat child is often taunted about his appearance and may be the butt of jokes and sarcasm. The child attempts to ameliorate his frustration and inarticulate rage by overeating still more. Thus the cycle continues. The glutton's behavior also differs from that of normal children. The obese child desperately avoids physical activity of any kind and leans toward sedentary experiences. He is unable to compete in motor skills and docs not want to. He is more timid, demonstrates greater dissatisfaction, and is less socially and emotionally mature.

The counselor can attempt to control gluttony by initially giving small portions to all campers and then providing seconds for those who want more. She must not allow the overeater to indulge himself. Since food is a symbol of love, security, and satisfaction, the counselor must substitute group activities and her own attention in order to deflect this behavior. Working with the child, patiently instructing him in physical skills, building his self-confidence, preventing heckling by others—all may have positive effects in reducing food intake.

Other eating problems include atrocious table manners or poor eating skills, which may be overcome by adequate and intensified instruction. The chronic complainer poses other difficulties. Complaining about the food served at camp is an attention-getting device. This attempt to gain recognition for rebelling against authority is particuarly common among junior and senior campers. If complaints are justified, food preparation and service must be upgraded. If the protest is unjustified, however, the counselor may confront the protestor privately and ask for specific items of inadequacy. Typically, chronic complainers have nothing factual at which to point. Generally, if the food is good, the protesting camper will make little headway with his peers. Unfounded complaints about any aspect of camp, particularly food, should stimulate investigation because they may be clues to certain personality defects. It may be a case of the child requesting help in the only manner he can. There may be some personal maladjustment that is emotionally disturbing to him, but which he cannot bring himself to identify or recognize; the complainer represses his defect by railing against a safe object. It may also be a way of expressing hostility and releasing aggression. The camper can vent antagonism against an impersonal arrangement—the preparation or serving of food—without fear of retribution. The counselor must try to understand the motive for such behavior and treat the cause rather than the conduct.

Timidity

The excessively fearful child generally offers a serious problem in a bunk. Her inability to join her peers may arouse hostility toward her in others, who always detect this fearfulness. The timid child is most frequently beset by homesickness. Her home life has often been one of zealous overprotection, and limitation; she has been sheltered and denied access to normal outlets and activities because her parents have been anxious about real or imagined potential injuries. She has probably been taught that passivity and acceptance is the better part of discretion. Because she is used to being dominated at home, she is easily influenced by the demands of others, especially if the threat of force or violence underlies the demand. Timid children are not usually distressing to others; as they are not competitors, their underlying maladjustments frequently go unnoticed. The timid child is often the camper who is most cooperative—the goody-goody, or the quiet one. This is unfortunate, because too often her submission is not looked upon as a problem symptom. Her tendency to submit finds favor with the short-sighted counselor, but she may later become a problem to the psychiatrist. The behavior of the timid child is one of retreat from participation whenever possible. She is fearful, lacks confidence, and is unprepared to meet life situations adequately. The withdrawing mechanism can reach maladjustment proportions when its use begins to block social intercourse. The shy child is frustrated in her normal development by lack of activity. She is too anxious and is incapable of sharing her problem with another person because she lacks the courage to express her conflicts to anyone.

The timid camper requires acceptance, recognition for any accomplishment, and help with developing self-confidence. This can be achieved if she is placed in situations in which she will be undistinguishable from all other participants, but in which her success is ensured. For fear of failure, she does not want to hold the limelight. She needs to have her confidence in performance develop slowly and surely. If she can gain a sense of peer approval and acceptance, she will be helped considerably.

Realizing that the submissive camper is conforming out of fear and an inability to relate to and respond to authority figures, the counselor must encourage nonconformity. He must become permissive in association with the camper. The counselor must show the camper that it is valuable to disagree—not for the sake of disagreement, but if there is a valid doubt about a statement or situation. The counselor helps the child by indicating the social acceptability of the enjoyment of making noise, of being disheveled, or even of becoming angry in appropriate situations. He helps the camper to get less satisfaction out of conforming and more gratification out of being herself, with full awareness of her own feelings toward any given condition or person. The counselor, knowing each of his campers, can help the timid one by stopping other members of the bunk from exploiting or taunting her.

Hostility and Temper Tantrums

Hostility is expressed through varying forms of behavior, depending upon the age and previous experiences of the individual. It is expressed in generally aggressive activity that rejects thwarting or irritating stimuli. Frustration produces hostility, which is manifested in screaming, kicking, striking, sulking, or crying. In older persons it may be expressed by cursing, sarcasm, or withdrawal.

The temper tantrum is an overt manifestation of hostility, used to gain some desired objective. By having temper tantrums, the child discovers that he can gain attention, and that others will reward him in order to pacify him. He therefore builds upon these early experiences. When he has been thwarted, he will manifest his hostility through the tantrum. The best approach to this behavior is to remove the camper from the group so that he cannot injure anyone and to protect him from prying eyes. The camper should be allowed to scream, stamp, fall on the ground, and beat his fists on the ground, but he should not be pacified by rewards. The counselor should remain with the camper, although doing so may be hard on the ears, to be sure that the child does not injure himself. When the temper tantrum finally subsides, and the counselor shows no anxiety or response, the child will begin to understand that his conduct will not secure the desired end. It may take some time for this idea to sink in, but in time the tantrum will disappear and a socially approved method of obtaining goals will be substituted.

Occasionally there are campers whose hostility is so intense that they are unable to discharge their aggression, except at the peril of the whole group. The counselor must protect her charges from the camper's aggression, if that aggression threatens injury or disruption of the group. Children can also be cruel to those who cause difficulties, and the counselor must also be able to protect the maladjusted child. The counselor should be able to handle most of these situations through adroit use of camping activities and through her influence upon the group.

Bullying

Hostility may be expressed in a tendency to bully. Bullying grows from some emotional deficiency in the child's life. When the child feels unloved or unwanted, he tends to express his feelings by overt hostility against safe objects; he cannot very well fight his parents. He does not understand the lack of affection and expresses himself forcefully in the only way he can. The bully neither shows understanding for the rights and feelings of others nor exhibits common courtesy. In acting out his maladjustment, he conducts himself in a violent manner. There is always a suggestion of force or threat in the activities of a bully.

Bullying may develop in consequence of marked superiority in size and strength. In an environment that stresses the pecking order, it is usual for the biggest and strongest child to take what he wants when he wants it. Might makes right under such circumstances. When, on the other hand, the child is frustrated or threatened without being able to attack directly and release tension, displaced emotion sometimes surfaces later, far removed from the original frustration. The bully may be afraid to attack an antagonist who is stronger than he. He therefore seeks a weaker, safe target to attack. If the bully finds that he can get by with aggression against smaller or weaker children, he is likely to use this outlet to vent his hostility.

Because bullying leads to destructive acts of cruelty against others, it must be prevented. Some children are not used to kindness and react negatively to it. They initially take advantage of the counselor who is kind to them. Nevertheless, they must be given kindness and attention despite any temptation to meet force with force. Continual kindness and firmness eventually overcome force. Superior power should be used only as a last resort to stop physical attacks upon another or in self-defense.

Malicious Lying

Children fantasize and exaggerate without abnormal tendencies; however, the pathological liar has no concept of truth. He neither recognizes the truth nor can distinguish between lie and truth. Such individuals need psychological assistance. When the child expresses untruths of gross exaggeration or distortion, the desire to injure should be quite apparent. The malicious liar does know the difference between lying and telling the truth. The malicious liar may be neurotic, but if so, the malice is generalized against everyone. In some instances, malicious lying is a transparent effort to provoke punishment for some real or imagined guilt. The deliberate lie is told in order to escape punishment or gain some advantage, or as a form of vindictiveness. Ordinarily, the counselor would counteract the motive of the liar to injure another by arousing members of the bunk against the object of attack, or even by using the counselor's superiority to chastize. Lying to avoid punishment will probably have been preceded by the performance of a forbidden activity that merits punishment. To understand the reasons for lying, one must determine the context in which it occurs. While looking for causes, however, the counselor cannot allow the camper to escape responsibility for a malicious lie. When the child knows the difference between right and wrong, he must be held responsible.

When the counselor is sure that a lie has been told, she should talk calmly with the camper, stating that she is not convinced. It is best never to take the obvious conclusions to be drawn from the malicious lying of a camper. It must be recognized that lying is a consequence of either purposeful behavior or a profound neurotic illness that requires skilled help, not punishment. While malicious lying cannot be tolerated or condoned, there are ways of dealing with it that may prove beneficial to the camper. The child must understand that no action will be taken against anyone toward whom the lie is directed. Every attempt must be taken to determine why the lie has been told. If lying is based in pathology, then little or nothing can be done in the way of remedial treatment at camp. If the lie is told out of fear of punishment for antisocial acts, however, then positive action may be begun. Campers who innocently or naively transgress regulations should be informed about those rules and the necessity for their enforcement. Campers who behave in unacceptable, punishable ways should have their conduct investigated so that reasons for such behavior can be understood.

Tardiness

Some campers have a psychological block against promptness. No matter how they prepare to meet a schedule, they are inevitably late. Inability to reach a destination on time is closely associated with a desire to resist authority (Fig. 14-3). This occurs whether the obligation is pleasant or distasteful and may, in fact, have absolutely nothing to do with the current experience. It is simply a safe way for the child to express hostility or resentment. Dawdling with food, clothes, or chores, and thus failing to appear on time, the camper usually loses something enjoyable or satisfying, thereby ironically creating his own punishment. This is characteristic of the immature camper, whose hostility is unconscious and whose inability to express

FIGURE 14-3.   Dawdling and tardiness can be a child's hostile response to authority.

anger directly leads to this substituted behavior. Punishment for procrastination solves nothing. The basic reasons for this type of conduct must be analyzed and made clear to the child; only then will he stop creating difficulties for himself and others.

The counselor cannot hope to directly approach such a deeply embedded conflict. Nevertheless, she must have some knowledge of similar situations and appreciate the problem that lateness presents to the camper and the program. Despite the informality and leisure orientation of camp life, there are scheduled activities that must be based on some kind of timetable. Tardiness detracts from the camping experience both for the late camper and for other campers who may be depending upon his presence. It may be helpful to give the child a simple assignment that carries with it a limited amount of authority and responsibility. A modicum of success may be enough of a stimulus to break the cycle of tardiness.

TREATING PROBLEMS

While all the aforementioned problems and situations exist to some degree, one should not assume that all campers have emotional or personality problems that disrupt camp life. On the contrary—these problems are rarely encountered unless the camp is primarily devoted to treating problem children. Camps generally have a cross-section of normally developing boys and girls who come to camp ready to have a wonderful time. This chapter has been included in order to apprise the counselor of potential conflicts. Most problems encountered—such as homesickness or poor eating habits—are commonplace. Nevertheless, the counselor must recognize typical behavior manifestations and understand that they are symptomatic of underlying causes that require careful handling and mature consideration. Counselors are not expected to function as psychologists. However, knowledge of children in terms of age-group characteristics (which are generalized at best), child growth and development, and learning theory, along with the understanding that children seldom act by the book, will make the counselor more competent, skillful, and effective.

chapter 15

Camp Program Organization

The program—a camp's organized attempt to achieve its aims—is raison d'être of every camp. Through the program, various activities become integrated, supporting one another. Various experiences, both active and passive, are presented to stimulate participation. Program comprises anything that happens to the child at camp; it is a dynamic interplay of events in the ordinary course of daily living and involves peer relationships, spontaneous behavior, modified behavior, adherence to prearranged schedules, conformity to specific codes, and individual adjustment to changing conditions.

CAMP PROGRAM FUNDAMENTALS

In planning a program of activities, factors such as the owner's or sponsor's objectives for the camp, the campers' desires, the parents' requests, and the camp's resources, must be considered. These demands are neither so great nor so complicated as they first appear; the camp generally has the resources to provide tremendously varied activities. The campers' quest for fun and excitement usually coincides with parental concern for skill development and learning, and with the camp's aim of outdoor education. In the best educational sense, the most logical camp program not only uses the campers as a point of departure, but also takes their advice for initiating the program. Campers should help choose what will be offered; this participation will evoke the most valid statements of campers' views. If they share in program planning, the campers will feel greater responsibility for the success of the activities and will take a more proprietary interest in the camp itself. Self-expression, self-confidence, and independence are fostered through camper involvement. From the campers' point of view, camp is for them; it is designed to please them. Not all campers have the intelligence, skill, or experience to assist in program planning; nevertheless, to the extent that each bunk can have activities separate from those of large units or of the whole camp, even those campers can be asked for suggestions or given several alternatives from which to choose.

Planning consists of collecting, defining, and relating all possible activities into a smoothly coordinated and functional schedule. By selectively adapting those activities most appropriate to the environment, integrating them so as to provide reinforcement, and adding to or subtracting from the viable program, a broad, varied, and flexible continuation of activities is available to meet the needs of all campers.

Although it is important to plan for camper participation in many outdoor experiences, a too highly organized and routinized program denies spontaneity. It is desirable to include unplanned periods in the daily schedule, so that campers have time to think, sit on a log, write a letter, read a book, hunt for frogs, or gaze at the clouds. As more campers are enrolled, the necessity for detailed planning becomes essential. In order to reduce any rigidity that might be a consequence of early and systematic program development by the administration, however, counselors and campers must be given an opportunity to share in planning. Many successful programs are initially organized in barest outline form only and are fleshed out later. The details of the daily schedule and some special events are introduced into the program after discussions during general sessions with counselors and mature campers. Although democratically derived programs are difficult to achieve, it is also true that such programs have a greater chance of fulfilling their aims. The staff should not attempt to manipulate campers in an attempt to hurry this process.

The democratic concept promoted in todays' camps necessitates the full participation of all those who receive value from camping activities. Campers' interests and needs are determined by questionnaires, precamp personal interviews, and bunk discussions after camp has begun. These findings are used as one basis for program arrangement. The production of program is increasingly based upon sound educational, social, psychological, and recreational standards and principles. To be effective, camping must be guided by realistic objectives. The interests, needs, capabilities, and limitations of the campers must be considered along with the environment and resources of the camp; the camp's philosophy; the duration of the camping period; the supplies, materials, and equipment at hand; and counselors' and specialists' competence to guide or instruct activities.

Even the decentralized camp requires some all-camp or centralized activity. However, small-group planning for decentralized living facilities and program structures identifies the bunk within an enclave as the unit from which a daily schedule of activities originates. Unfortunately, the dynamics of daily interrelationships may also deprive the less articulate, passive, introverted camper from doing what he wants to do some of the time. The minority must be protected from the whims, overzealousness, and control of the majority. For this reason, a variety of program-planning units— the bunk or basic living unit, clubs or interest groups, instructional groups, all-camp activities groups—may be initiated. These give each camper the opportunity to belong to many groups in which his own needs, talents, and skills find satisfactory outlets.

Modern camps and associated agencies generally recognize that certain facilities, equipment, and supplies should be available for free play or unscheduled activities for individuals and self-organized, self-directed groups. Camps are also aware of the need for a certain amount of promotion and organization, which can multiply the number of activities and participants in the program, and make for greater efficiency and usefulness of the available facilities. The need for supervision of activities and the provision of positive leadership by counselors must also be recognized, so that educational, social, and cultural outcomes can be realized.

THE BALANCED PROGRAM

Innumerable activities can be conducted by camps. They can be grouped into categories for ease of understanding; each major category contains many subgroupings that suggest a continuing series of interesting and challenging experiences. The normal recreational life of children and adults includes selected activities from all of the following categories. These activities can be graded from simple, elementary forms to complex, expert forms. Regardless of individual interests and skills, there should be some activity in which each camper can participate. That is why it is so important for the camp to offer a total program. The tendency to stress one activity to the exclusion of other categories is to be avoided.

General Categories

Arts and crafts.   This category enables individuals to express themselves freely (Fig. 15-1). That self-expressive act allows ego-centered involvement to be translated into a healthy process of self-realization. Through woodworking, leathercrafts, plastic arts, and the like, the camper is apt to lose himself and thereby answer a need for nonconformity in a situation in which he is normally restricted by social custom.

Dance.   Dance satisfies the basic need for movement. It is a process of symbolic communication, expressing many sentiments as well as fulfilling feelings. Dance has satisfied many ambivalent desires, including hostile urges. Activities normally associated with this form of expression are social, interpretive, square, round, folk, modern, tap, ballet, and clog dances.

Drama.   In drama, the human voice and body are used in a communicative process that provides satisfaction through the expression of ideas and emotions. Drama provides self-expression, either directly or vicariously. Catharsis and empathy are closely related to dramatic productions. The many forms of this activity include charades, blackouts, shadow plays, shows, skits, stunts, tableaux, storytelling, and impersonations.

FIGURE 15-1. Capturing the moment—the young artist gains self-expression.

Education.   All experiences are educational, whether or not one is conscious of learning. Some learning takes place in a formal setting, such as the schoolroom, while other learning is informal. Although it is true that nearly all camping experiences teach campers something, there is a specific educational aspect of camp. A formal class in mineralogy, social dance, or swimming closely approximates a classroom experience. Classes offered as part of the program can be recreational as well as educational. Many individuals consider formal courses, taken during their leisure, to be highly rewarding. Included in this category are classes in typing, photography, geography, mapmaking, and foreign languages.

Hobbies.   Hobbies offer an engrossing, stimulating form of activity usually not connected with the vocational experience. Hobbies, which may include almost any human activity, provide outlets for creative self-expression, self-determination, and self-realization. They also fill the need for companionship since hobbyists often meet to explore the manifestations of their particular interests. Activities of a collecting or learning nature are usually considered hobbies.

Motor activities.   This category encompasses sports, games, and exercises. The enhancement of physical vigor, the improvement of physiological functioning, and the release of hostility through competitive experiences or individual acts in a social setting—all are effected through motor activi-

ties. These activities also enable individuals to satisfy their need to participate and to learn how to behave toward others. The category includes individual sports and games, such as swimming, archery, climbing, rowing, and
fishing; team sports, such as capture the flag, tennis, and field events; and
exercise, such as calisthenics and weight training.

Music.   The value of music to individuals varies, but it almost always
has some attraction for both performer and listener. Nearly everyone appreciates some sort of music. Activities in this category include general singing,
choral groups, instrumental groups, opera workshops, solo performances,
operettas, and musicals.

Nature lore.   Camp crafts are among the most requested and necessary outdoor activities (Fig. 15-2). Many skills and much satisfaction are combined in performing camp crafts. Wilderness camping particularly provides
opportunities to use these skills. The great open and wilderness areas are
part of the heritage of every camper. Americans have a traditional love for
the soil, and seek natural sites to relieve themselves from the stresses of
urban life. Outdoor experiences should include conservation education, nature science, trips, and other stimulating contacts with the outdoor world.

Service.   Activities associated with altruistic or humanitarian programs are included in this category. Service activities have long been used
to productively fill leisure and to satisfy the human urge to extend sympathy

FIGURE 15-2.   Learning survival skills at camp. (Courtesy: Crane Lake Camp, West Stockbridge,
Massachusetts).

and give aid. The release obtained from wholeheartedly giving service to others, the exchange of too much self-concern for self-giving, results in satisfaction for the giver as well as the receiver. Because no other experience provides this sense of personal extension, it is essential that any all-inclusive camp program include service activities, which might include teaching a skill to a slow companion, cleaning up quarters, and volunteering to visit campers in the infirmary.

Social activities. Social needs must be satisfied throughout life. Bunk living is an intensely social situation where campers have to mix, get along, and adjust. Socially approved behavior and good mental health are fostered by a wide scope of social activities, including special-interest clubs, parties, mixers, and cookouts.

Special projects. Participation in extraordinary activities is usually exciting. The camper who takes part in a once-a-summer celebration gains from her experience and contributes to the delight of others, be they performers or spectators. The range of special projects is fully discussed in Chapter 22.

The Special-Interest Camp

Program organization and promotion must be approached differently by different types of camps. At special-interest camps, the program tends to become largely a routine function. The campers attend the camp in order to pursue their interests with the help of highly skilled instruction. Program administration at these camps consists primarily of setting up facilities for efficient use, issuing schedules that prevent time-consuming arguments or conflicts, promoting activities to ensure maximum benefits to the participants, and establishing regulations for the use of facilities. Programming at such camps is therefore largely paternal; all energies are devoted to the efficient teaching of the activity for which the camp is known.

Relative Worth of Activities

Routine activities are of greatest value in developing the powers and skills of campers because they are repeated daily and their effects are cumulative. Recurrent scheduled activities are developmental in value largely in proportion to the frequency of their repetition. Special events are valuable chiefly because of the preparation and instruction required to make them possible, but indirectly because they are useful in sustaining interest in a program that might otherwise tend to become commonplace and monotonous.

In planning the camp program, care should be taken to observe a balance between routine, scheduled, and special projects. If only routine activities take place, the camping program will be dull. If the program is dominated by repetitious scheduled events to the exclusion of freedom of choice for the campers, the whole program will be too regimented. Staging special events too often and under high pressure frequently removes the joy and spontaneity which should always accompany such events. By careful study of the camp and the interests and needs of its resident campers, a coordinated program involving all types of activities can be implemented.

SCHEDULING ACTIVITIES

All camp activities are scheduled so that campers know when experiences of particular interest to them are available. Even free-play activity times are listed. The activities schedule enumerates the possible activities that may be developed by the camp. Among the possible types of activities are those that can be called informal routine, recurrent, and special events.

Informal Routine Activities

It is the camp administrator or program director's objective to encourage and initiate as many informal routine activities as possible. Ideally, the camp should be physically attractive and well enough equipped to appeal to all campers. The customary equipment and apparatus encourage routine activity. The equipment should include all of those items needed for individual, dual, or team activities and games, hiking, climbing, fishing, cooking, crafts, and other camping activities. The decentralized camp also has enclave structures for indoor activities. Such routine experiences include table games, club meetings, interest groups, and the entire range of social experiences.

Routine activities are not all spontaneous; many of them are planned by the campers and the counselor in charge. Interesting ways to use the equipment must be constantly invented and taught. New nonequipment games and events must be introduced, especially on rainy days; old or familiar games and events should be revived. The most common criticism of camp programs is that they are repetitious and boring. The director should constantly think of program innovations, stunts, emphases, and variations to introduce so that something new and different is going on constantly. The camp should be a place that offers incentives and invitations to do and learn interesting new things.

Recurrent Activities

Recurrent activities are scheduled in advance, and participants are enrolled for a number of sessions or classes. These are usually group activities, such as instructional classes and competitions, in which a certain number of campers take part according to rules. A given time and place must be set aside for them. They are repeated on a daily, weekly, or monthly cycle until the schedule has been completed, the season is concluded, or the program is finished.

Many of the scheduled activities are self-managed. When the equipment, fields, or meeting rooms are not needed for the activities conducted directly by the staff, they are usually made available to self-directed groups of campers who have the maturity and experience to manage themselves.

The camp program staff should organize as many groups of this kind as possible without entirely relinquishing staff control. The development of an extensive program of camper recreational activities requires this technique. Unless self-directed groups are part of the program, the number of campers served is generally limited by the capacity for direct staff leadership. Thus, the total number of activities is restricted. Aside from this, however, the educational value of the activity is often greatly enhanced when the group manages itself and selects its own leadership.

Special Events

The special events at every camp give spice to the program. They attract anew, discover new talent, provide an incentive to practice, give an ever-changing flavor to the program, and create an opportunity to secure some educational outcomes not otherwise possible. Their endless variety is limited only by the imagination of the counselors in charge and the campers who assist in the planning.

It is a common error in planning and staging special events at camps to imitate too closely the standards of professionally produced entertainment, as to both the nature of the entertainment and the skill of the performers. The camp theatre production cannot compete with professional theatre or other forms of commercial entertainment, nor should it attempt to do so. Moreover, the objectives of prefessional entertainment are wholly different from those of the camp program. The former caters to audience approval, while the latter endeavors to provide satisfying experiences for the performers—the entertainment of the audience is secondary.

Special events should provide opportunities for as many to participate as possible; they should not exploit a few individuals. They should be truly representative of the activities learned at camp and should be the incentive for days, if not weeks, of routine, but not arduous, preparation.

Preparing the Schedule

Every camp should have an hourly, daily, weekly, monthly, and seasonal schedule. The camp director may find it helpful to chart the program for the entire season. Events during the season that influence the program, such as opening and closing days, thematic projects, historical events, local traditions, and certain emphases that will characterize the program, should be placed on the chart as a guide. The program for each week or session can be worked out in more detail as the season progresses.

The program for the week should be posted in a conspicuous place so that all can see it, become interested, and make suggestions for other stimulating experiences. The daily program is the counselor's plan of work for the day. The director and the counselors should think through each day's work in advance, always planning something new or interesting for the campers. Naturally, campers are available for additional help in formulating the program.

In a decentralized camp, it is inadvisable to prescribe the same program for all units. All enclaves usually have a coordinated series of events.

Special all-camp activities are set forth in the master program announced for the entire season. The program of each enclave should be designed for and adapted to (1) the needs, interests, and experiences of the campers, (2) the resources offered by the facility itself, (3) available professional leadership, and (4) the skills, talents, and resourcefulness of the campers. These factors vary greatly between any two units. The supervisor of each enclave should be given freedom to establish the program for his units with only the necessary prescription from the central office of the camp to ensure a well-balanced, varied program. Failure to allow this freedom results in an ordinary, commonplace program.

The program is only a plan; adhering to it too strictly is often inadvisable. Numerous unforeseen situations arise that dictate changes in the program. To adhere at all costs to prescribed or preconceived programs devitalizes the camp and its activities. Catching the interest of campers, whose focus of attention is transitory and changeable, and involving them in newly programmed events is a real test of the counselor's discernment, leadership, and skill.

No counselor or specialist can know everything necessary to conduct a successful program. The individual supervisor will find it helpful to build up a library containing materials on all phases of the activities that he schedules and conducts. The supervisor who refers again and again to such material will generally have the most diversified program.

ASPECTS OF PROGRAM CONTROL

Every camp is faced with the problem of determining what policies afford the most comprehensive program for the satisfaction of campers' needs. Certain rules and regulations must be established and enforced if the most effective service is to be provided. Two areas that require particular attention will be discussed next.

Intracamp Versus Intercamp Activities

All camps must decide whether their own controlled program of activities will be conducted on an intracamp or an intercamp basis. This problem usually arises in connection with the athletic program. Some early private camps subscribed to the theory that each camp could have a representative team in one or more standard sports. These teams would compete in leagues and tournaments with teams from other camps. To encourage wider participation, teams were organized according to classifications based on age, weight, sex, or other factors tending to equalize competition.

One of the results of this procedure was that camp directors often gave most of their attention to the campers who were most likely to qualify for places on the representative teams. Directors became coaches who were more interested in producing winning teams than in providing varied services to large numbers of campers, many of whom had no opportunity to become members of representative teams. The early days of the camping movement were characterized by an oversupply of physical education graduates whose preparation had encouraged a coaching attitude. The inherent weaknesses in the intercamp plan led to its complete abandonment in many places and to a reliance upon intracamp activities in which competition was toned down and emphasis was confined to skill development and individual performance in various activities. Winners of unit contests were not matched with winners from other units. Stress was then placed upon the organization of as many groups as possible to make the competition interesting.

The present tendency, wherein organized team sports are part of the program, is to combine both plans in order to derive the advantages of both. Intercamp competition is limited to teams whose members are emotionally mature and capable of accepting winning or losing without attaching a great deal of significance to the event. Sports competition at camps should be limited in any circumstances. With the exception of sports camps, the typical team sports are out of place at camp. Various means are employed to tone down the importance of intracamp competition to avoid the evils of overemphasis. In many modern camps, intracamp activity is accentuated during special weeks when specific sport competitions are scheduled. Most intracamp activity is more social than competitive in nature.

Awards

Granting trophies or other awards of considerable extrinsic value to winners of camp competitions is now regarded as inimical to the development of good attitudes on the part of campers. It emphasizes winning rather than participation and develops an attitude of unwillingness to participate unless the prize competed for is of sufficient value. It also discourages those who have little or no chance to win from entering competition. The present practice is to grant no awards or to present only awards of insignificant extrinsic value, such as ribbons or certificates. Group awards, in the form of plaques, cups, and banners, are favored over individual awards, since the former encourage group cooperation rather than individualism. The granting of inexpensive awards with great intrinsic value is justified on the ground that they serve as a permanent record of achievement and as an incentive to participate and improve.

PROGRAM EVALUATION

Efficient administration not only concerns itself with measures that facilitate the formulation and conduct of a satisfactory camp program, but must also constantly evaluate this program qualitatively and quantitatively. Qualitative evaluation is rarely possible in terms of objective measurements; it is dependent upon appreciation of values, sense of fitness, clearly defined purposes, and subjective appraisal of performance and outcomes in terms of these purposes. Except for personal interviews with the campers who participate in the activities, little can be done to measure the program qualitatively. Qualitative programmatic evaluation cannot be made from records; rather, it requires frequent visits to various activities to observe the program in operation. Observation and evaluation by the camp director and program specialists should be the basis for advising counselor staff and for issuing written program material and instructions.

Quantitative evaluation of camp programs can be made from records. A camp's productivity can be evaluated constantly by inaugurating a system of reporting such factors as (1) number of campers enrolled, (2) number of campers who participate in activity offerings, (3) group activities briefly described, (4) special events prepared and conducted, and (5) number of campers who returned after one season. The use of statistics as a means of program control and evaluation has possibilities that have not been fully realized. More effective use of statistics for such purposes requires greater refinement of methods of recording and reporting than has been accomplished by most camps. Several camps, particularly those in the public sector, have been very attentive to the collection and analysis of data; perhaps their legal accountability has something to do with that reporting.

Camp attendance is directly related to the efficiency with which camp staff plan and conduct the activities and other aspects of group life. For this reason, the reporting system should provide for accurate statistics on events that lend themselves to accurate measurement and whose attendance reflects planning, organization, and leadership. Among the camp activities for which fairly accurate statistics can be reported are the recurrent scheduled activities such as classes under leadership, club meetings, dual and individual competitions, musical and dramatic performances, rehearsals, tournaments, excursions, and mass-participation activities. The number of campers in special events can also be reliably reported.

The forms used to report activities should be carefully designed to provide for accurate data. Statistics should be taken from these forms daily, weekly, and monthly. They should be consolidated for purposes of study by the camp administrator and unit supervisors and used as a basis for advising staff during in-service education, program reformulation, and a variety of administrative adjustments. Instructions should be provided so that records are made daily or at the conclusion of each activity. Simultaneously, care must be taken to ensure that superfluous information is not requested, and that the task of recording information does not become such a burden to the staff that other essential duties are neglected.

Programmatic evaluation indicates whether the program has achieved the stated objectives for which it was established. A list of positive objectives would include social acceptability, enjoyment, health, skill development, participation, adventure, and opportunity. The contributions that result from well-planned, well-directed, and inspired outdoor activities may be appraised and demonstrated.

By questioning the program's meaning, some indication of its worth can be ascertained. The following questions may be raised in order to evaluate the program:

1.   Is there carry-over value for the program participants?
2.   Does the camper gain a sense of achievement through participation?

3. Does the camper experience a sense of social acceptability and responsibility through participation?
4. Are individual differences in skill, maturity, aptitude, and intellect taken into consideration in formulating the program?
5. Is there opportunity for creative self-expression?
6. Does the activity uncover and develop leadership qualities?

Although a relatively large number of activities usually associated with the outdoors, and particularly with camping, have been identified and explained in the preceding chapters, no attempt beyond a superficial coverage of experience has been offered. There are several instances in which program information is detailed enough to be applied. To ensure that instructional components and complete information about activities are available, a comprehensive listing of camp program activities and related subjects is found in Chapters 16–21.

chapter 16

Conservation and Nature Sciences

With an active sense of adventure and a common interest in the outdoor world, the counselor and the campers can share the fun of an exploratory trip to a cave, beach, swamp, stream, meadow, or gravel bank. There will be something interesting for all; one does not have to be a naturalist to appreciate the flight of a heron, the flash of a scarlet tanager, the thrill of finding what might be a gemstone, the apprehensiveness and curiosity as the group approaches a huge wasps' nest built into the branches of a small tree. Observing a pair of birds feeding their young is a moving experience that appeals to children of all ages. The summer is a wonderful time to watch for these phenomena. By the end of July, most birds have nested, bred, and flown, but the goldfinches are just starting to brood. Bird nests can go into collections by the middle of August; most birds will be finished with them by that time. Observing insects can fascinate an interested child for hours on end. Fields during the summer, especially if preceded by a wet spring, harbor a fantastic array of crawling, hopping, flying, and slithering insects. An uncut field is often decorated by spider webs. Careful observation may be rewarded by a visit from a praying mantis or from insects that camouflage themselves to resemble twigs. Children's delight in learning about nature is evidenced in many campers' bringing home a container full of swamp life. Collections of water striders, whirligig beetles, small fish, snails, and larvae are often camp souvenirs that parents had not expected.

Even rainy days can be spent outdoors. Campers can dress suitably for a walk in the woods and look for mushrooms and bright-colored fungi. The earth on which the group walks is 6 billion years old and contains an infinite variety of spellbinding information. The rocks can be collected, classified, and arranged by hardness and density.

Observing the variety of trees, ferns, and grasses, looking at a drop of water through a microscope, and appreciating living in harmony with wild things is all part of nature lore and science. While being introduced to nature sciences, campers must learn that it is only through conservation of natural resources that the greatest number of people can have the greatest enjoyment of these resources for the longest time.

THE NATURE PROGRAM

Only the guidelines of a possible nature program are presented in this chapter. The opportunities to learn, explore, and seek new wonders in the everyday world are infinite. In camp, the counselor is a guide who can open new vistas to the young. The nature specialist can introduce an impressive array of things to do, places to go, and items to make and see. The natural sciences, will all their ramifications, are part of the nature program, not isolated classification subjects. The program should be presented so that the camper begins to realize the close relationship and intimate association of all things in nature. The counselor can help campers to recognize a variety of plants, animals, and minerals, and encourage them to collect samples in order to give them a greater understanding of ecology and of the interdependence of natural phenomena. The camp can thereby stimulate the campers' curiosity and excite in them the desire to learn more about things they either have never seen or have simply taken for granted. For the camper, starting a collection of mineral samples can lead to a life's work, a lifetime hobby, or to the study of other sciences. This possibility is one of the reasons for establishing camps.

In the following sections, ideas for making the natural sciences program informative and interesting will be presented, along with projects to foster conservation education.

ASTRONOMY

No sight is more impressive or more beautiful than the night sky filled with stars. On a clear summer night, a luminous cloud appears to stretch across the heavens. The observer is actually looking edgewise through our own galaxy, the *Milky Way*. Our sun is only one of at least 100 billion stars that make up the Milky Way. It is situated on the outer edge of the galaxy in the center of our solar system. To arrive at some idea of how great the distances are that separate the stars and the galaxies themselves, one must figure in terms of light-years. One light-year is the distance that light travels in one year at the speed of about 186,000 miles per second. For example, the sun is 93 million miles from earth, or 8 minutes by light. Alpha Centauri, one of our closest star neighbors, is a mere 4 light-years away, or 26 trillion miles further into space. The brightest star, Sirius, is 8.8 light-years off. The Milky Way is at least 100,000 light-years from one end to the other and measures 10,000 light-years through the center of the galaxy. The sun, with its system of planets, is approximately 30,000 light-years from the center of the galaxy.

Some interesting examples of distances in the universe illustrate the idea of the vastness of space. If the universe were to shrink to microscopic size, the sun would be the size of the period at the end of this sentence. The nearest star would be another period 10 miles away. Other stars even more distant would be reduced to the size of a penny, and would be hundreds and thousands of miles apart.

The Amateur Astronomer

During the summer, night-by-night observation of the stars can be greatly enjoyable to campers. Stargazing requires almost no equipment and very little preparation. Most important is that the campers be comfortable. Looking at stars high above the horizon can cause a stiff neck or an aching back. A blanket spread on the ground can be a comfortable observation point. It is best to dress appropriately, as the ground tends to cool off at night and the air becomes chilly. No equipment is necessary to see the stars; thousands can be observed on any clear night, particularly when there is no moon. Enjoyment can be heightened with field glasses, however, because details of the planets and the moon can be seen. The higher the power of the optical instrument, the more details and stellar objects are seen. Telescopes, bought or made, contribute even more enjoyment because they allow even finer observations.

The study of stars requires merely a little practice in basic identification. For the beginner, the recognition of a dozen constellations and ten of the brightest stars is usually sufficient. A systematic study of stars, the identification of lesser constellations, and the location and study of clusters and nebulae require more serious efforts. Even very young campers can learn to recognize nearly all the constellations, bright stars, and visible planets.

Star Motion

The sun is about average in size and brightness when compared to other stars. It moves at approximately 12 miles per second, along with the solar system, toward the great blue star Vega in the constellation Lyra. The sun, which is similar to all other stars, travels along its path, as do all other stellar objects. In the universe, nothing remains motionless. Some stars travel hundreds of miles per second. Some are traveling in the same general direction as the sun, while others are headed in precisely the opposite direction. Many stars are moving as parts of systems or clusters. Some stars consist of two or more components that revolve around a common core as they travel through space. The stars in a constellation are not necessarily related. They may be of completely different magnitudes, moving in diametrically opposed directions and at varying speeds. Some are growing old, others are being born. Although the constellations present an unvarying picture to the observer, they are constantly changing shape. The stars that make up the outline of the constellations are steadily shifting their positions. In any constellation, some stars may be further away than others and unassociated with them. Because the stars are so far away, no one can possibly see them moving, except over a long period of time. Those who observe the stars are looking into the past; nothing in the night sky is actually there at the moment of observation. For example, if one were to look at the constellation Orion, the light from the brilliant stars that dot his right shoulder and left foot are so distant that it has taken 270 and 650 light-years respectively for eyes on earth to see them. A look at the great nebulae in the constellation Andromeda brings to the observer something that occurred 750,000 earth years ago. The light shining from the great nebulae has taken that many years to travel to earth.

Constellations

The constellations have been extremely useful in assisting with the charting of the sky. Some constellations were identified several thousand years ago; others were identified by the astronomers of the seventeenth century. The boundaries of constellations have been definitely established and are recognized by astronomers everywhere by international convention.

Circumpolar constellations.   The term *circumpolar constellation* suggests that the viewer is somewhere between the equator and the poles. To an observer in the north temperate zone, the stars seem to spin overhead as the earth turns on its axis every 24 hours. Stars near the pole remain in view as they turn around; stars closer to the equator rise and set. At the pole, all constellations are circumpolar (Fig. 16-1). For stars located between the pole and the equator, latitude determines whether they are circumpolar. For example, the bowl of the Big Dipper does not set at latitude 40° north, but in Florida, at latitude 30°, it does set and therefore is not considered circumpolar. When the sun is north of the equator during the summer, it becomes circumpolar north of the Arctic Circle. Among circumpolar constellations of the northern zone are the Big Dipper, the Little Dipper, Cassiopeia, Cepheus, Draco, and Perseus. One of the most thrilling moments for the amateur astronomer occurs when he first sees the Big Dipper and can then identify the other constellations nearby. The intelligent counselor takes advantage of this initial wonder and tells the legends of the great figures whose outlines appear in the heavens.

Circumpolar constellations, with their key stars, can be an effective guide in locating other constellations (Fig. 16-2). Once the Big Dipper is recognized, the pole star, Polaris, in the Little Dipper can be seen. Simply trace a line from the pointer stars in the bowl of the Big Dipper to locate Polaris, the last star in the handle of the Little Dipper. A line drawn through the base of the bowl of the Big Dipper to the east leads to the star Castor in the constellation Gemini. A line through the handle to the bottom of the bowl leads to Regulus in Leo Major. By following the curve in the handle of the Dipper, a continuation of the line directs the viewer to Arcturus in the constellation Boötes. Naturally, the counselor must be sure that the constellations are actually above the horizon at the time the campers are looking for these checkpoints.

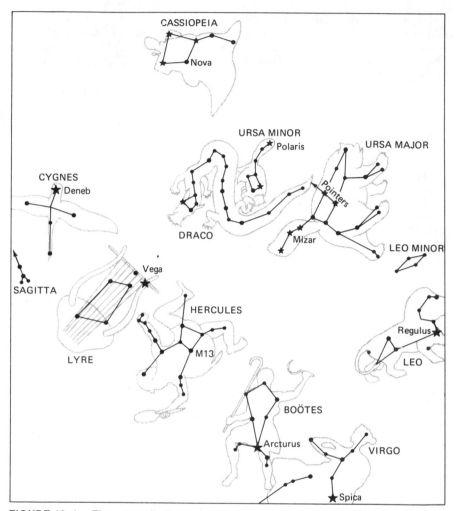

FIGURE 16-1. The constellations of summer at about 9:00 PM in the middle northern latitudes.

Summer constellations.   Although the weather is generally favorable for stargazing in the summer, the sky is not as brilliant as it is in the early spring. There are many constellations on view, however, and the Milky Way is rather impressive. The spring constellation Leo begins to sink into the west, but a number of constellations and bright stars rise in the east to replace it.

The constellation Boötes, although a late spring constellation, is visible for most of the summer. The major star in Boötes, Arcturus, is an excellent point from which to begin exploring the summer sky, using the sky chart in Figure 16-2. To use the chart, face north. Hold this book open overhead so that the top of the page is directed toward Polaris. The approximate

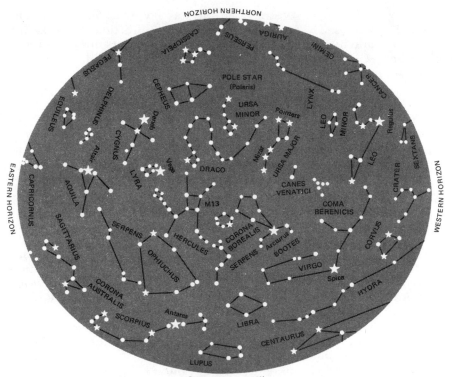

FIGURE 16-2. The circumpolar constellations.

time for which this chart is drawn is 9:00 PM. Rotate the chart clockwise one-eighth of a turn to see the position of the stars and constellations three hours earlier. The Northern Crown, Corona Borealis, may be found just east of Boötes. Directly south of the crown lies the thin outline of Serpens the Snake and Ophiuchus the Snake-bearer. South of these constellations lies the faint outline of Libra. To the southeast, the curved shape of Scorpius the Scorpion can be observed, with its brilliant star Antares to distinguish it. Due north of the Scorpion and immediately past the merging constellations of Serpens and Ophiuchus is the great constellation Hercules.

Landmarks of the late summer sky are the three first-magnitude stars of Cygnus the Swan, Lyra the Lyre, and Aquila the Eagle. South of the Eagle's great star Altair may be found the constellation Sagittarius the Archer. Sagitta the Arrow lies between Altair and the first magnitude star of Cygnus. To the east of Deneb and forming a triangle with Sagitta and Aquila is Delphinus the Dolphin. The Dolphin is composed of four stars in a diamond formation and a fifth tail star. The southern summer sky is enriched by many star clusters and faint stars near the constellation of Sagittarius. Figure 16-2 illustrates some of the constellations, with the stars that distinguish them dotted in for easy reference.

Study of the night sky can open the way for many interesting and entertaining studies. The sciences of optics, light refraction, spectroscopy, meteorology, and hydrology can be introduced to campers through stargazing. Ancient Greek and Roman history, mythology, and literature are touched upon in discussing constellations.

BIOLOGY

Because biology deals with all living organisms, it includes many sciences. Biology can be divided into *botany*, which deal with plants, and *zoology*, which deals with animals. Botany, too, has several branches. One of these is *bacteriology*. Zoology includes *entomology*, the study of insects; *icthyology*, the study of fishes; *ornithology*, the study of birds; and *anthropology*, the study of humans. Biology can also be classified in terms of form and structure. *Morphology* is the study of the form and structure of plants and animals. *Physiology* is the study of the function of organs and parts of organisms of plants and animals. *Paleontology* is the study of fossil plants and animals. *Genetics*, the study of heredity, is also a branch of biology, as are *organic evolution* and *ecology*. These two sciences deal with the succession of plant and animal types and the study of organisms in relation to their inanimate surroundings and to the other organisms that impinge upon and influence their lives. Morphology can be divided into *anatomy*, the study of the gross structures of organisms; *histology*, the study of tissues; and *cytology*, the study of cells. All of these studies are subdivisions of biology. The interdependence of any living organism illustrates the relationship that all sciences have to one another. Thus, the study of astronomy, while dealing with stellar objects and heavenly bodies, is concerned with the sun and the solar system. Without the influence of the sun and other necessary factors such as breathable air and good water, life as it currently exists on the earth would be impossible.

Living Organisms

It is relatively simple to distinguish a living plant or animal from an inanimate object. Nevertheless, attempts to formulate a definition of life in precise terms have been rather unsuccessful. The consideration of some of the distinguishing characteristics that separate living from nonliving things may be more valuable to campers than teaching a disputed definition of life.

Organization for the performance of different but related functions is vital. The structure of organisms reveals that they are made up of viable units called cells. These cells are themselves highly organized. In multicellular organisms the cells are grouped to form tissues, and tissues are grouped to form organs. Inorganic matter has no such organization.

Movement of some type is essential to nearly all living things. However, some kind of movement also occurs in the inorganic world. There is a responsiveness to stimuli. A *stimulus* can be defined as any physical or chemical change that activates modification in the behavior of an organism, but does not in itself provide energy for the response. There is nothing that corresponds to this phenomenon in inorganic matter.

Growth by intussusception is probably the most unique characteristic of living matter. With the exception of crystal formation, which does not meet the specific criterion involved, there are no processes identical to intussusception in the inorganic world. Living matter depends upon chemical balance and adjustment. The intricate chemical process of any living organism is due to molecules that are composed of atoms in an almost infinite variety of combinations. The organic substances, carbohydrates, fats, and proteins occur only in organisms or their products.

Photosynthesis is probably the ultimate source of energy for all living things. The chemical energy stored in food is released when they are oxidized. It is true that photosynthesis can be promoted artificially without the presence of living organisms, but only on a very small scale. Nearly everyone has had experience with the oxidation of materials in inorganic matter.

Water is the essence of life. Without water, life ceases to flourish. The prototypes of all living organisms had their origins in water. These animals later moved onto the land, as is vividly illustrated by plants and animals alive today. Life is continuous, and continuity plays a vital role in evolution. It is unknown for living organisms to arise from nonliving matter. Every living organism is the end product of a continuous series of living organisms extending back to the initiation of life on earth. The chain will continue unbroken so long as nothing interferes with the environment in which the organisms abide. Unless some unforeseen natural disaster or artificially contrived holocaust develops, life will continue.

New living organisms arise from the process of reproduction. In asexual reproduction, the entity develops as a result of cellular division. In sexual reproduction, two cells, termed *gametes,* unite to form a zygote which is, fundamentally, a new living individual. Each species is adapted for the peculiar or unique conditions of its environment. In order to maintain life, a plant or animal must be able to function under the conditions presented by their environment.

With this brief introduction to some of the concepts and groupings of biology, let us ask questions that humans have always wondered about. Why is life so varied? Why are there so many different kinds of birds, fishes, trees, flowers, insects, and animals? The answers to these questions lie in the adaptation of each organism to the peculiar conditions of its environment. Organisms vary in size, shape, color, and internal structure because their environments require it. The converse is also valid; organisms live in different environments because they differ in structure.

Not only are plants and animals different in terms of the roles they play in the living world, but they are different in essential features. Their functions may be complementary as well. Green plants produce organic food materials from inorganic matter in their environment. They are primarily concerned with building up a store of energy in chemical form. Animals are absolutely dependent upon green plants for their food. They are chiefly concerned with using the energy that green plants have manufactured.

Not all plants contain chlorophyll, that remarkable substance which permits the use of light energy. Plants that do not have chlorophyll must obtain food from other plants or animals, whether as *parasites,* while the host is alive, or as *saprophites,* feeding on the excrement or the dead bodies of other organisms. Saprophitic plants are as important to the living world as green plants are, they cause decay and break down organic compounds that are returned to the inorganic world in simple compound form. From these raw materials new life forms can then be generated. One large group of plants, the fungi, are devoid of chlorophyll and live in parasitic or saprophitic form. Although the best known of this species are those bacteria that cause disease, life could not continue on earth without the decay caused by the saprophitic group.

Generally, animals obtain their food by eating other organisms that eat green plants. Ultimately, therefore, all animals are dependent upon green plants for survival. They use the chemical energy that has been stored by the plants. The contrast between plants and animals is most marked by the features of food relations, energy relations, locomotion, cellular structure, organization, and evolution.

LIVING THINGS SEEN AT CAMP

Algae are thallus plants with chlorophyll. Almost all of these plants live in fresh or salt water, the greatest number being found in the sea. Fresh water forms include minute blue-green algae that form the slime on top of water in ditches and the dark film on moist ground. The pond scums and other threadlike algae are found floating in tangled masses near the surface of ponds and lakes (Fig. 16-3). The branched candelabra plants that grow up in the bottom of ponds are also algae. Included in these forms are kelp, sea lettuce, and rockweed.

Fungi are thallus plants without chlorophyll. They include bacteria; various types of mold, which attack bread, preserves, and fruits; mildews, which attack the leaves and other parts of seed plants; yeasts, which produce fermentation; and mushrooms and toadstools.

Mosses are small leafy plants found on trees, rocks, fallen logs, and moist ground. Liverworts resemble mosses, but usually appear as a mass of small green leaves lying on the ground. Both of these plants reproduce sexually and asexually. The production of spores makes possible the wide distribution of this plant on land by wind.

Ferns are commonly found wherever the earth is moist. They have large, much-divided leaves or fronds that develop from an underground stem. By developing a more highly differentiated and independent sporophyte, the ferns have advanced their evolution a step beyond that of the mosses and liverworts toward the seed plants.

By far the greatest part of vegetation on earth consists of *seed plants,* which include all trees, shrubs, and herbs, and are the most highly evolved of all plants. These plants reproduce on land through a seed that contains an embryo plant provided with resistant coverings to defend it while it

FIGURE 16-3. Campers collect aquatic specimens.

awaits optimal conditions for germination. Trees, shrubs, and herbs are sporophytes.

Conifers are cone-bearing seed plants; most of them are either trees or shrubs. The cone replaces the flower. The seeds formed on the scales of the cones are not enclosed as they are in flowering plants. Typical conifers are pine, hemlock, and ginkgo. The true flowering plants have evolved to a point at which their adaptation to dry land takes the form of pollination, protection, and dispersal of the seed. Insect pollination has been evolved in many species. By their bright colors and scent, flowers attract insects that carry pollen from flower to flower. This has led to adaptation between specific species of flowers and most particularly to species of insects. Fruits, for example, are adapted to different methods of dispersion. Fleshy fruits provide food for bird and animals which, in turn, distribute the seeds. Other fruits, such as those of the dandelion, are adapted to wind distribution. These different adaptations to pollination and seed dispersal explain the wide variety of flowers and fruits. Flowering plants are divided into two classes, the dicots and monocots. The *dicot* family seed has two seed-leaves or cotyledons. The plants produced from these are recognized by their net-veined leaves and their flowers, which are never found in threes or multiples of three. Common dicot families are the buttercup, geranium, carnation, primrose, phlox, snapdragon, rose, cactus, maple, parsley, and aster. In *monocot* embryos, the seed has only one leaf or cotyledon. The leaves of these plants are generally parallel-veined, and their flowers are found in threes and multiples of three. Common families of the monocot group are the iris, lily, palm, orchid, and grasses.

In the animal kingdom, a much greater differentiation exists than in plants. Except for those camps situated on or near salt-water bodies, most observable animal life is not found in water. However, some animals abound in any drop of water. For these reasons, the following brief survey of the animal kingdom includes those forms as well as the higher types.

Unicellular animals consist of a single cell whose locomotion is by means of irregular, streaming protoplasm, a small number of flagella, or many hair-like projections moving in unison. These animals live in both fresh and salt water. They may also be observed as parasites in the bodies of other animals. The amoeba and paramecium are examples of this animal form. There are 3,000 species of sponges; these irregularly shaped creatures generally attach themselves to rock or other objects in fresh or salt water. There are countless small openings on the surface of their bodies that allow water to pass through and be forced out again from one of the larger openings in the upper part of the animal. The common bath sponge is really the skeleton of one of these animals. Small fresh water sponges are found in ponds attached to sunken twigs.

Polyps and jellyfish most frequently occur in the sea. Polyps are cylindrically shaped animals that tend to attach themselves to some object in the water. The hydra is a fresh-water variety of the polyp and is found in ponds, often attached to aquatic plants. Other recognizable examples are sea anemones and corals. Jellyfish float in water and are bell-shaped.

Flatworms come in many varieties. Their bodies are elongated and flattened, with one end differentiated into a head. There are four classes of flatworm. *Planarians,* whose locomotion is produced by undulating cilia, live in both fresh and salt water. Most of them are less than 1 inch long. Parasitic worms with suckers are commonly called flukes. Tapeworms are also parasitic and well-known to humans; they do not have a mouth or alimentary tract, as do the flukes. The long-nosed free-living marine worm called the nemertine worm has an extremely flattened body. There are 8,000 species of round worms; they occur in water, on land, and as parasites in a variety of animals.

There are 6,000 species of starfish. They are rather symmetrical animals with a skeleton composed of calcareous plates and spines. They move by means of sucking disks attached to tube feet. They live only in sea water. Sea urchins, sea cucumbers, and sea lilies belong to this family.

Mollusks are commonly called shellfish. They are animals with soft inner bodies generally covered with a calcareous shell. Snails and slugs are examples of this group. They occur in salt and fresh water as well as on land. The cephalopods are marine mollusks with large eyes, a well-developed head, and long prehensile tentacles. The most well-known and common of these are the octopus and squid. Clams, oysters, mussels, and scallops are bivalves, while abalone is a monovalved creature residing in the ocean.

Segmented worms occur in the sea, in fresh water, and on land. The most common and easily recognizable is the earthworm. Campers will get to know him and his fellows after heavy rains or when seeking bait for fishing.

Arthropods account for nearly half of all the species of living things. The term simply means joint-legged. The body is segmented like that of an earthworm, but the components are generally combined to form a head, thorax, and abdomen. Among the groupings that make up the arthropods are the crustaceans. These are animals that breathe by means of gills and spend their lives in fresh water or in the sea. Examples of this type are barnacles, crabs, lobsters, and shrimp. Centipedes, also part of this group, breathe by means of air tubes or tracheae and live on land. Millipedes are sometimes confused with centipedes, but are actually different by virtue of a cylindrical body whose segments each bear two pairs of legs. The centipede has a flattened body whose segments each bear one pair of legs.

Insects are arthropods that breathe air through tracheas. The body of the adult is divided into a head, thorax, and abdomen. The head bears one pair of antennae. The thorax bears three pairs of legs and usually two pairs of wings. The more highly developed insects metamorphize in their life cycle from larva or worm form to the winged, segmented adult. For this change to occur, the animal undergoes a quiescent stage and forms a cocoon. The characteristics ordinarily used in distinguishing insects are the wings, mouth parts, and the type of metamorphosis undergone. Some insects go through life without any metamorphosis. Other insects have gradual or partial change whereby the young develop into adults without undergoing a quiescent period. Still other insects undergo a complete metamorphosis, and the adult is so modified that its structure and life-styles are unidentifiable with the larva stage. An insect normally has two pairs of wings. These are sometimes absent, however, as in the case of worker ants. Flies have only one pair of wings. Wings may be membranous, parchmentlike, form a protective covering, or be completely covered with scales. The mouth may be adapted for piercing, sucking, or chewing, or may be reduced to uselessness. There are more species of insects than of all other animals (Fig. 16-4). Grasshoppers, termites, dragonflies, lice, flies, fleas, bees, wasps, ants, moths, and butterflies are well known insects.

The *arachnoidea,* or spiderlike, animals have a body that is usually divided into an anterior segment composed of head and thorax, to which legs are attached, and a posterior abdomen. Examples of these are spiders, scorpions, daddy-long-legs, mites, and ticks.

Animals that have a vertebral column and breathe by means of gills or lungs, with their nervous system on the upper or dorsal side of the body and with two pairs of appendages, are called *chordates.* Among the marine creatures of this type are sharks and rays. While it is a rare camp that is situated close enough to the sea for these creatures to be spotted, they are common enough so that their structure and class should be reported. The aquatic vertebrates that most campers come to know are termed *true fishes.*

FIGURE 16-4. Catching tiddlers—an age-old pastime for young campers.

These creatures breathe by means of gills in a gill chamber, covered by a bony flap opening to the exterior on either side of the back of the head. Fish have two pairs of lateral fins. The true fish are known for their great variety. Among them are trout, bass, perch, and sun fish.

Amphibians are a species that begins life in water and, when fully adult, lives in air. The young breathe by means of gills, and the adults breathe through lungs. Adults have two pairs of five-toed limbs without claws. The body is without scales except in particular tropical forms. Frogs, toads, salamanders, and newts are typical of these creatures and occur in temperate zones, where most camps are situated. Campers are generally exposed to these animals whenever they hike across fields or investigate swamps, ponds, or bogs.

Reptiles breathe air all their lives. Their scales are horny and formed from the outer layer of the skin. There are generally two pairs of appendages, snakes being a notorious exception. Examples of these creatures are all snakes, tortoises, and lizards (Fig. 16-5). Except for those camps situated in the deep south, it is not likely that campers will come upon other reptiles such as alligators.

Birds are feathered creatures whose forelimbs have been modified for flying. No birds have teeth, but all have horny beaks. Among the most common of all bird forms observed during the summer are swifts, humming-

FIGURE 16-5.   Young campers learn about snakes first hand. (Courtesy: Crane Lake Camp, West Stockbridge, Massachusetts.)

birds, woodpeckers, geese, ducks, eagles (only in high country), hawks, and perching birds. The perching birds include more than half the known species of birds. They nearly always live in trees and bushes, and feed on fruits and insects. Examples are crows, jays, wrens, robins, sparrows, swallows, and thrushes.

Mammals nourish their young with milk from breast glands, or mammae. They are also characterized by having hair. There are several subclasses of mammals. The most primitive are egg layers. Pouched mammals are the second type. Their young are born in an immature condition and are nourished and protected while carried in a pouch on the underside of the mother's body. Typical of these animals is the opossum. Placental animals are the third class; these retain the young inside the mother's body until birth. Nourishment is transmitted by an organ called the placenta. Among the more familiar placental mammals are those that feed on insects, including the mole, shrew, and hedgehog. Bats vary in their eating habits; some eat fruit, others eat insects, and some suck blood. Carnivorous animals are those that eat flesh. Among them are the skunk, wolf, dog, fox, bear, and cat. Other mammals with which campers will come into contact are those that gnaw, including squirrels, beavers, rabbits, mice, and rats.

Life is found on the prairies and in the forests, marshes, streams, ponds, rivers, lakes, and seas. Almost everywhere on the earth's surface and in its waters, plants and animals live out their lives and engage in the constant activity necessary for survival. The wide and varied distribution of living things has an order and logic that is quite consisent. Each species is adapted to the specific conditions of its particular environment. The various species of plants and animals inhabiting any environment are intimately associated and form communities. This plant–animal relationship is formed by the specific conditions of the environment, the abundance of organisms on which others feed, and the amounts of heat, cold, moisture, and light that allow survival. For example, the plants and animals inhabiting a fresh-water pond are associated in a community (Fig. 16-6). The kinds of plants and animals to be found depend on whether or not the pond will exist during the summer, how much or how little lime the water contains, the amount of decomposing matter available, and the amount of oxygen available. Depending upon these interrelated factors, certain species of plants and animals will be abundant. With them, those animals who are dependent upon the plant life will also be found. Just as cells, tissues, and organs of a plant or animal are organized to form its structure and carry on those functions necessary for the maintenance of life, so the various species of plants and animals of a given environment are brought together to form a community in which each has a place and contributes to the conditions for life sustenance.

FIGURE 16-6. Ponds and marshy areas provide the right environment for birds and insects.

ENTOMOLOGY

Insects live everywhere; a few are even found in the seas. Where other forms of life are neither tolerated nor supported, insects can be found. This wide distribution is possible because insects can fly and are highly adaptable. They are tenacious, quick, strong, and aggressive. They can be carried by hosts, air, and water. Their habits and structures are so diverse that no unitary biological adaptation can be applied to them. Biologically, insects are the most successful of all the groups of arthropods. Although they are only one of 50 classes of animals, there are more species of insects than of all the others combined. It has been estimated that between 600,000 and 800,000 species exist.

The influence of insects on other animals is significant. They are humans' primary competitor in the struggle for survival. They eat our food before we can harvest it, lay waste to forests and wood products, carry disease, infest our bodies, destroy our clothes, and can make life unbearable. And yet insects have become so economically necessary and perform so many useful tasks that humans would have many problems without them.

Insects that are beneficial to humans either produce valuable matter for our use or protect our interests. An example of the first is the honeybee. Up to several thousand tons of honey and hundreds of tons of wax are produced annually by honeybees. Silk manufactured by the silkworm and shellac produced from the wax of lac insects have been highly valuable to the clothing and paint industries.

Some insects destroy others that are harmful to humans. Ant lions, aphid lions, praying mantises, wasps, lady beetles, and tiger beetles are among the predacious insects that control destructive insects by parasitizing them, eating them, or breeding on them. Many insects perform valuable services through their eating habits—many beetles and flies live on both plant and animal leavings. Fecal matter, animal cadavers, and other putrefying materials are quickly taken care of by insects or their young. Many fish, birds, and some mammals depend on insects for food. These in turn contribute food or other products to humans.

More insects are destructive of our interests than are helpful. Harmful insects include those that eat and destroy fruits and plants, those that annoy and harm domestic animals, those that transmit disease, and those that destroy wood and wood products, paper, cloth, and food. Among these insects are grasshoppers, chinch bugs, boll weevils, corn borers, lice, mosquitoes, houseflies, fleas, moths, termites, and carpenter ants.

Insects are classified in at least 25 orders on the basis of their metamorphosis, type of mouth parts, and number and type of wings. In some instances, other features are useful in classifying them. The nature specialist at camp should be responsible for providing campers with opportunities to observe and examine many different classifications of insects. The specialists can teach interested youngsters the basics of entomology. Little or no equipment is needed to collect various specimens for observation. Active colonies can be collected with care and stored in a receptacle that permits campers to watch the insects work, feed, and undertake their daily functions. The camper who is well grounded in entomology has the opportunity to spend fascinating hours studying this vast world that generally goes unseen by humans.[1]

COLLECTING SPECIMENS

The type of equipment used for collecting specimens depends upon when and where explorations will be made. Necessary equipment for daytime terrestrial collecting includes a butterfly net, aspirator, umbrella, sifter and oilcloth, forceps, trowel, pocketnife, and killing jars.[2]

The Net

Although excellent hunting nets can be purchased, they are too costly and fragile for the novice. A general-duty net can be constructed easily for less cost. Its handle is made from a broom stick that has been cut down to approximately 3 feet, saving the rounded end. On opposite sides of the stick, drill two $\frac{1}{4}$-inch holes. One hole should be $6\frac{1}{2}$ inches below the sawed end. Grooves extending from the holes to the rough end will prevent the wire hoop from slipping. With $\frac{1}{2}$-inch wire or a clothes hanger, make a circular shape with a diameter of 12 inches. There should be $6\frac{1}{2}$ inches left at one end of the wire and 7 inches at the other. These loose ends will be used to secure the hoop to the handle. Turn the tips in $\frac{1}{2}$ inch on the ends. The depth of the net should be 1 foot longer than the diameter of the wire hoop, and it should not be longer than the arm of the person who will use it. A fine mesh material, such as bobbinet or voile, can be used for the netting; olive green or white are the best colors. Measure the width of the net by adding 2 inches to the circumference of the hoop. Then lay a 10-inch strip of muslin across the top edge of the net and stitch it in such a way as to present a cross-hatched appearance. Make a U-shaped slot at the outer edge of the net and through the two pieces of cloth. Fold the reinforced material in half, lengthwise, with the muslin on the outside. Stitch the rough edges together. Allow one inch of the unstitched material to remain across the folded side so that the wire hoop can be fed into the net in this space. Slip the material around the hoop. Turn the net inside out and sew the outside seam several times for reinforcement. Place the hoop with its attached net on the pole. Place the two turned ends on the hoop into the two holes in the handle. Wrap electrician's tape around the pole and the wire.

The Aspirator

The aspirator is used for collecting small insects by using suction (Fig. 16-7). Tiny insects are easily damaged by the fingers; the aspirator reduces the amount of handling. It also permits the collector to be highly selective

[1]D. W. Stokes, *A Guide to Observing Insect Lives* (Boston: Little, Brown, 1983).
[2]A. B. Klots, *A Field Guide to the Butterflies* (Boston: Houghton Mifflin, 1951), pp. 9–15.

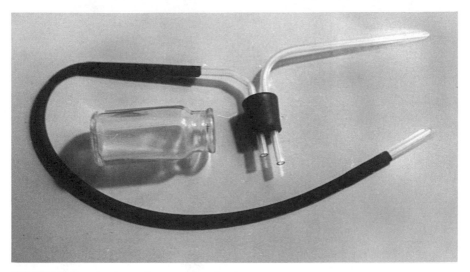

FIGURE 16-7.   Aspirator for catching tiny insects.

in capturing insects. The following materials are used to construct an aspirator:

1. A vial $1\frac{1}{2}$ inches in diameter and 5 inches long
2. A two-hole rubber stopper that fits into the vial
3. Sixteen inches of $\frac{1}{4}$-inch glass tubing about 6 millimeters in diameter, cut into three pieces, one 3 inches, one 5 inches, and one 8 inches, long and curved; all ends should be fire polished
4. Six inches of fire tubing.

Place the 8-inch curved tube through one of the holes in the stopper so that it extends $1\frac{1}{2}$ inches through the stopper. Place the 5-inch glass tube through the stopper so that $\frac{3}{4}$ of its length extends beyond the stopper. Attach the rubber tubing to the 3-inch glass tube that serves as the mouthpiece.

Other Equipment

An old umbrella with a wooden handle is a useful collecting tool. Cut the handle and join the two rough edges by gluing a piece of leather between them. The piece of leather should be long enough to permit the umbrella to swing down when the handle is held horizontally. The umbrella may then be held directly beneath a shrub or branch in order to catch insects that drop off when the branch is vigorously shaken.

The sifter and oilcloth are excellent pieces of equipment for finding insects in cut hay or leaves. The sifter is a wooden frame with a screen attached to the bottom. The screen should have 8 meshes to the inch. The white oilcloth is spread on the ground to catch insects that fall through the screen (Fig. 16-8).

Forceps are essential for handling insects. Insects can be damaged if

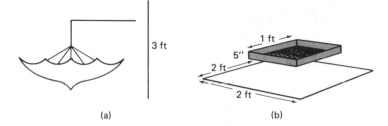

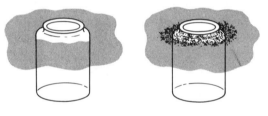

FIGURE 16-8.   (a) Umbrella catcher, (b) sifter and oil cloth, (c) baiting cans or jars.

they are picked up with the fingers because the legs and antennae, in particular, are very delicate. Many insects hide under leaves or topsoil. Use a
trowel to turn over topsoil. Insects also inhabit decayed trees or rotten logs.
A knife is best for finding insects in dead wood.

Any wide-mouthed jar (approximately the size of a peanut butter jar)
may be used as a killing instrument. Place about $\frac{1}{2}$ inch of sawdust on the
bottom of the jar. Cut $\frac{3}{8}$-inch of length of $\frac{1}{2}$-inch glass tubing and place it upright on the sawdust against the side of the jar. Mix plaster of paris and
pour a $\frac{1}{4}$-inch layer over the sawdust, allowing the glass tubing to protrude
at the top. Any of the following can be used as killing agents in this type of
jar: chloroform, benzidine, carbon tetrachloride, or ethyl acetate. Pour the
killing agent into the jar until the sawdust becomes saturated. Pour off excess liquid; too much liquid wets the plaster and damages the specimens.
To recharge the killing jar, open it and place it in a warm, dry area. When
all the moisture has evaporated, put a new supply of killing agent in it.

Baiting is an easy way to attract various insects. A tin can or jar may be used; a large juice can (about 1 quart, 14 ounces) is the best size. Once the top lid has been removed, small holes are punched into the bottom of the can to permit rain to run out. Place four stones around the can and a thin board on top of them so that the rain will be kept out. Set the can into a hole large enough for the top of the can to be flush with the ground. A baiting can is good for wet or dry places, but a wide-mouthed glass jar is best for boggy or swampy areas. A hole is dug, but the top of the jar must be slightly above ground level. Moss or other material is banked up to the top of the jar. These traps may be checked every 3 or 4 hours. They are most productive during the day, but some specimens can be captured at night. Pieces of fish, meat, or sugar are the best, although almost anything can be used. When using sugar in these cans, put it in a paper cup inside the can. Strong-odor baits attract more insects.

When collecting specimens in water during the day, use rakes, seines, strainers, butterfly nets, and a shallow white pan. An iron rake is useful for pulling material from the edge of a stream or pond. The mud can then be put into a shifter. Seines are attached to poles that are about 3 feet long. The screen may be of the plastic window-screening type and at least 2 feet wide. Wind the material around each pole and tack it securely in place. This seine works well in brooks and streams. One camper turns stones and churns up the stream bed, while the camper with the seine is stationed a short distance downstream. The bottom of the net should point upstream, with the handles directed slightly to the rear. In this way the loose debris rides up onto the seine. After enough material has been gathered on the seine, shake it over a white cloth placed on shore. A large kitchen strainer is a good instrument for stream and pond work, although it is helpful to add to the length of the handle. Such insects as water striders and boatmen can easily be caught with this simple tool. A butterfly net with heavy netting is also useful for aquatic collecting. A shallow white enamel tray is fine for sorting out aquatic insects; insects can be seen easily against the white background. Use forceps to pick them up.

For collecting specimens at night, lights and sugaring are the best methods. Suspend a blue or white light from a tree limb or tripod, and place a white sheet on the ground under the light. The insects will land or fall on the sheet and can be easily picked up with forceps. The best time to sugar is about one hour before sunset on a warm, cloudy night when a very light breeze is blowing. Brush the sugar solution on the tree trunks at chest height. Most of the insects can be collected by flicking them into a killing jar. Use a net to catch the very active insects.

GEOLOGY

The study of geology is so broad that only a brief description of some of its aspects can be presented here. Physical geology is concerned with the processes that deal with the rocks of the earth's crust and their composition and structure, and with the forces that have contributed to the shaping of

the landscapes visible on the earth's surface. Among the sciences that contribute to the overall study of geology are *mineralogy*, the study of minerals;
petrology, the study of rocks; *geodesy*, the study of the earth's size, shape, and
other measurements; *paleontology*, the study of fossil plants and animals; and
stratigraphy, the study of the order and sequence of rock layers making up
the earth's crust.

The earth is undergoing constant transformation. We live amid the
ruins of past worlds. Forces that modify the surface landscape are constantly
at work. Some of these changes are extraordinary, sudden, and thrilling, but
it is unlikely that campers will witness them. Nevertheless, the counselor
can introduce the subject of these dramatic changes to her campers by talking about floods, earthquakes, or volcanic eruptions. She can illustrate her
discussion by constructing a small pathway from a stream and showing what
happens to the surrounding dirt when an artifically caused wave overflows
the channel.

All earth movers are not rapid, however. The greatest modifiers take
long periods of time. The development of mountain ranges, the creation of
a desert, the cutting of a valley or gorge by glaciers or rivers require thousands, and even millions, of years. Counselors should teach campers that
mountains are being worn down by frost, wind, running water, and gravity;
that sea bottoms in some areas are rising; that in some regions the sea is
inundating the land; that the coastlines are being eroded by the constant
pounding of the surf against the rocks or sandy beaches of the shore.

The earth on which we walk is really a crust, or thin shell. Below this
lies the earth's mantle, then an outer core, and finally a molten inner core.
The crust is probably not more than 5 miles deep. The mantle, some 1,800
miles thick, is the region of intensely heated matter and pressure. The mantle may very well be the reservoir that feeds volcanoes. The temperature at
this level is approximately 5,000°F. The rocks of the mantle are hard, to
support the enormous pressure that weighs down on them. The pressure is
so great, however, that when there is a disturbance in the mantle, the rocks
bend, twist, and even flow. This is the region where the most severe earthquakes originate. Beneath the mantle is the outer core, which is composed
of liquid iron and probably nickel. It is perhaps 1,300 miles thick, and the
heat is even more intense than in the layers above it. The inner core, or
heart, of the planet is composed of a shrunken ball of nickel and iron under
truly fantastic pressure. It is to the core of the earth that geophysicists look
for answers to questions concerning terrestrial magnetism.

Some think of the earth as a rigid, solid, hard object. It may be solid,
but it is far from rigid. As gravitational force is exerted upon it by the sun
and moon, as the landscape of the earth changes because of erosive and
developmental forces, there are changes in pressure. With these changes
occur internal stresses, which are sometimes felt in terms of earth tremors,
quakes, and volcanic eruptions.

Three basic types of bedrock make up the earth's crust: *igneous rock*,
which was once molten; *sedimentary rock*, formed from crumbled rock mate-

rials, the fossils from living organisms, and minerals precipitated from water; and *metamorphic rock*, which is igneous or sedimentary rock that has been altered as a result of intense pressure, heat, liquid, or gases running through them. Examples of igneous rock are granite and volcanic lava. Shale, sandstone, limestone, and salt are examples of sedimentary rock. Metamorphic rock is seen in marble and gneiss. The crust is fundamentally composed of igneous rock overlaid by sedimentary and metamorphic rock. The surfaces of the continents, for example, are mostly sedimentary formations.

The very forces that seem most destructive to the earth's surface are also those that assist in the birth and development of new matter. The erosive agents cause deterioration in rocks, and these particles are broken off to be carried away and deposited in ever-growing layers. The debris builds up for millions of years and the pressure and heat on sedimentary rocks produces metamorphic rock. Continuous heat and pressure are applied to these rocks and a remelting occurs, which tends to produce igneous rock. The cycle is endless. Sediments, the debris of earth erosion, are washed down into the valleys and sea bottoms. In some places they pile up until the sediments become rock. The process is extremely slow. Of all the sedimentary rocks, conglomerate is the most coarse. It is composed of gravel and pebbles that have been stuck together by some mineral, thus becoming cemented. Such rocks are typically found in river beds, on beaches, and at the foot of highlands.

Sedimentary rocks that form sandstone actually developed from grains of sand. Sandstones are usually made of quartz particles. Water-made sandstone generally forms where rapidly flowing water begins to slow down. A few sandstones originated as sand in piles. These piles were buried beneath debris, turned to stone, and were uncoverd by erosion. Ripples in the rock, caused by wind blowing the sand before it hardened, can be seen clearly. Shales are usually composed of earth and plant matter. They are fine grained and contain clay rather than quartz minerals. Lake beds, deltas, and bays are the most likely places for this form to be found.

Another type of sedimentary rock is limestone. Limestone consists of small particles of calcite, or calcium carbonate. Its color is white, gray, or bluish. The harder formations are quarried for building purposes. Some limestone, such as coral reefs, are made up of skeletons of creatures.

As sea bottoms rose to become dry land or mountain ranges, there were tremendous bending, squeezing, folding, and cracking movements. With the enormous pressures, heat, and other working forces influencing them, a vast array of minerals developed. From prehistoric swamps where giant ferns lived and died, there developed over millions of years deposits that produced peat, coal, and petroleum. From sedimentary rocks a variety of beautiful minerals were created. Magnificently colored, shaped, and structured crystals are constantly being produced in consequence of the shifting nature of the earth's surface and inner strata.

Everywhere the counselor looks he can find evidence of erosion and development. He should relate these phenomena to the campers in ways that will evoke questions and further investigation. Each smooth pebble has a story to tell; the common quartz often found in or near camp sites may begin a lifelong hobby.

FORESTRY

Forestry is an attempt to assist nature in making forests as productive as possible for present and future needs. Well-protected forests provide wood, game, furs, and minerals. They help maintain the supply of pure drinking water. Much of our recreational activity depends on forests. Forestry involves a planned economy for the management and use of forest lands. Included within these lands are areas for mining, hydroelectric power development, irrigation dams, reservoirs for municipal water supplies, and land for the grazing of sheep and cattle. Propagation and maintenance of wildlife, preservation of scenic and historic places and vistas, prevention of erosion, preservation of a regular and constant flow of water, and recreational development are all aspects of forestry.

Most camp sites include forests. A variety of trees, each contributing to the splendor of the setting, will attract campers' interest. Some will want to study the different trees. Collecting leaf specimens, or combining crafts and art by printing leaf designs or producing useful objects from twigs, branches, or other parts of the tree can be interesting parts of their study.

Fundamentally, a *tree* is a plant with a single woody trunk that does not branch for some length between the ground and the first bifurcation. It is composed of roots, trunk, branches, leaves, flowers, fruit, and seed. Tree roots are either *surface* or *tap*, depending upon their shape and penetration. Walnut, hickory, and oak trees are the most notable of the eastern region tap-root species; longleaf and ponderosa pine are distinctive in the southern and western sections of the country. Spruce, birch, elm, lodgepole pine, and hemlock are known for surface-root systems. Other trees develop a combination system of surface and tap, depending upon the environment. Roots serve as an anchor for the tree and supply it with nourishment.

The stem of the tree is composed of inner and outer bark, heartwood, sapwood, and pith. The diameter of the tree is increased by the *cambrium* layer; one layer accumulates each year. When the tree's growth is stunted because of defoliation, drought, or disease, an additional ring may be added, but these rings are much fainter than those of normal growth and are easy to detect. The *heartwood,* located in the core of the trunk, is composed of inert matter whose primary function is to toughen and solidify the trunk. The *sapwood* transmits nutrient solutions from the soil to the leaves. If the cambrium layer or sapwood were cut into and the sap flow were interrupted in any way, the tree would die almost immediately.

The *leaves* are the intricate chemical manufacturing agents of the tree. Thin liquid solutions are carried to the leaves and combined with carbon dioxide to form sugar and starches. The carbon dioxide is divided and combined with water, the extra oxygen and water are exuded, and the process of assimilation occurs in the presence of chlorophyll, which is the energy source for food storage.

In a typical broad-leafed forest, maple, beech, and oak are most numerous, although hickory, chestnut, poplar, birch, and some conifers or soft woods such as pine and hemlock may also be prevalent. These trees grow only where the climate, soil, and other environmental conditions are suitable. There must be moderate rainfall—between 25 and 60 inches a year. The summer must be moderately warm, with an average temperature of approximately 65°F. Trees of this type thrive when the winter temperature falls below freezing. The falling of leaves in the deciduous (hardwood) forest is an adaptation of the tree plants to environmental differences between summer and winter. The broad leaves enable the trees to manufacture starch and carry on their life activities at a maximum rate throughout the summer, when there are prolonged periods of sunlight, warm temperatures, and generally plentiful rainfall. During the shorter days of winter, when there is less sunlight and the air is dry and cold, leaves would be disadvantageous to the tree because of the evaporation of moisture through their broad surfaces. For this reason, leaves are shed and the tree becomes dormant.

Trees, as the dominant plant in any forest, determine in great part what other life forms will survive in the forest community. Like all green plants, trees compete for sunlight. They are more successful than their competitors because they grow high and spread their branches and leaves to catch sunlight. During the summer they keep the forest in deep shade; plants requiring direct sunlight cannot survive. The leaves that reduce the intensity of sunlight entering the forest also maintain a moist atmosphere. Trees provide protection from wind and rainstorms. Their dead leaves, shed bark, and fallen trunks are the source of much of the organic matter in the soil. Trees are not only the largest living organisms in the forest; they are also largely responsible for the existence of all living things in the community they dominate.

Where the trees of a forest are spread out at greater distances and more sun is able to filter through the leaves, smaller trees and shrubs can grow. Sassafras, wild grape, wild cherry, and papaw, all of which produce food for game and birds, flourish. Trailing over the ground or climbing on nearby bushes may be bittersweet, its bright scarlet berries aiding the coloring of autumn. Close to the ground are many small herbaceous plants with soft stems and leaves. These plants grow rapidly during the spring before the trees get their leaves; they have stored up necessary nourishment underground during the winter in fleshy roots, stems, or leaves. These small plants give most of the spring wild flowers of the forest, including hepatica, wild geranium, and jack-in-the-pulpit. There are usually a few ferns scattered about, but they are not abundant in this type of forest. Mosses are abundant on fallen trees and stumps.

Beneath the green foliage, the ground is carpeted with decaying twigs, leaves, barks, and grass, which gradually breaks up to form a mealy brownish matter called humus. The decay that leads to the formation of this material is produced by a variety of fungi as well as bacteria. While the bacteria are invisible, many fungi emit reproductive bodies such as spores. These are the recognizable mushrooms, puffballs, and shelf fungi. These plants, which do not require light, thrive in relative darkness and moisture.

For many of the smaller animals, the observer must look under dead leaves, in tree stumps, or under stones. Investigation of these places will reveal a miniature world. Centipedes run for cover, beetle larvae squirm, and millipedes curl up and play possum. If an ant nest is disturbed, there is an anguished rush as workers scurry off carrying eggs and larvae. Each type of forest has its leaf-eating insect population. Many kinds of beetles, butterflies, moths, bees, wasps, flies, and mosquitoes are abundant. Where there are small flying insects, spiders construct their filmy webs. One can dig under a fallen tree or stump to find a salamander; these creatures are amphibious and require the moisture of the forest floor, and they feed on insects. As the order of life becomes more complex, there is an increasing dependence upon less highly organized creatures for survival. Trees initially produce the environment that permits other plants to grow. These in turn produce nutrients for small animals. The animals are food for insects who, in their turn, supply food for larger predators and carnivores. Birds and mammals of every type are indebted to trees for their existence. By observing these phenomena, the camper will understand the intimate and intricate connections between trees and all other forest life.

HYDROLOGY

The study of water resources and the cyclical movement of water from sea to land and back to sea is an interesting natural phenomenon of which campers should become aware. Water directly and indirectly influences the daily life of all humans in countless ways. In fact, most animated things are composed of large amounts of water. The sea was the origin of life. Humans carry this water inheritance in the saline character of body fluids. Human cells require constant bathing in what, broadly speaking, could be regarded as a seawater solution: blood.

Water is peculiar in its physical appearance. Although it is important in the gaseous state as part of the atmosphere, it is chiefly present on earth as a liquid. This is in consequence, partially, of its heat of vaporization, uniquely higher than that for most liquids with correspondingly simple molecules. Water's solid state, ice, is lighter than the liquid state; for this reason, bodies of water freeze from the top down—a property indispensable to aquatic life.

The water resources of the earth's surface can be divided into two categories: *salt water,* found in the oceans, and *fresh water,* a land resource. Even though humans make greater use of the water found on the continents, salt and fresh water are not completely separable. All water will be salt water at one time or another. Through the action of solar energy and gravity, the earth's water supply moves ceaselessly in a cycle from sea to land and back to sea. Water is carried through the atmosphere, having been evaporated from the ocean's surface, over the land mass of the continents, where it is released by condensation and precipitation. Since water loses its salt content in the process of evaporation and returns to a liquid from a gaseous state during condensation, it is the most desirable and utilitarian form for humans. This endless movement has neither beginning nor end: It is a complete cycle, termed the *hydrologic cycle*. The water cycle plays an important part in weather and annual rainfall in different regions of the world, and influences the type of food supply and living organisms maintained by available fresh water. An understanding of water resources and the water cycle is useful in studying the conservation problems and meteorological factors that affect camp life.

METEOROLOGY

Meteorology, the study of weather, can be a significant program activity at camp. The best procedure for developing interest in meteorology is to encourage campers to study, observe, and perhaps even make predictions about the weather. For centuries, humans have been observing conditions that seem to predict variations in the weather. Many old sayings about weather appear to have a reasonable basis in fact. Consider the saying "Red sky at morning, farmer take warning; red sky at night, farmer's delight." In the morning, with the sun in the east, redness is seen in the west, and showers generally originate in the west. At dusk, when the sun is in the west, redness in the east means that any inclement weather has already passed. This is typical in mid-latitudes, where weather flows from west to east. Another saying tells us, "Rain before seven, shine by eleven." When rain falls in the night and early morning hours, the weather often clears before noon as the sun warms the atmosphere, evaporating the clouds. "If you can see the painter's brush, the winds around you soon will rush." "The painter's brush" refers to high, thin cirrus clouds, which usually mean that foul weather is on the way.

Air Pressure

One may see humans as creatures who live at the bottom of a vast ocean of air. Held in place by gravitational pull, the atmosphere surrounds earth to a height of between 300 and 700 miles. Without the atmosphere, there would be no life. Without air, there would be no sound. The atmosphere is a protective envelope that shields the earth from the direct rays of the sun and keeps it from freezing when the sun sets.

The first and lowest layer of atmosphere, called the *troposphere,* is where all of the earth's weather is initiated. The ocean of air is in constant motion. Many forces acting upon it cause prevailing winds, which blow steadily night and day, and tornadoes, which appear and disappear very quickly. The sun is one of the sources of energy that keeps the atmosphere in constant motion. The sun's rays heat the atmosphere and cause the gases to rise. When the gases have expanded enough, they begin to cool and flow downward again. Since most of this circulatory flow happens at the equator, the motion is pushed north and south to the polar regions. Because the earth is also spinning at the rate of 16 miles per minute, the flow of air is not a straight circle between the equator and the poles. Instead, the earth deflects the flowing mass of air so that it flows at angles to the poles.

Because the earth is slightly tilted on its axis, we have seasons. During the winter, the sun's rays strike the earth obliquely because this part of the globe is tilted away from the sun. The northern hemisphere receives cold weather accompanied by snow. During the summer, the sun's rays strike the same surface at a more nearly straight line; hence this region has warm or hot weather. How hot one gets in summer and how cold in winter depends upon the distance one lives from the sea. The sea is always warmer or cooler than the land. This accounts for the mild winter climate along the seacoast as compared to that of an inland region at the same latitude.

Cloud Formation

Riding on the moving air mass is water vapor. Because of the hydrologic cycle, water is constantly being transmitted through the air. Air temperature, water vapor, and billions of particles of dust form fog; air that is heavily laden with moisture is ideal for producing fog. As the air cools, it is forced to emit some of its water vapor, which condenses on the countless dust particles suspended in the air. Around each grain of dust hangs a droplet of water. These droplets add up to form fog and remain in that state until the air warms sufficiently and the water is transformed to vapor. Clouds are simply high fog. In other cases, when the water vapor is cold enough, a cloud of ice crystals is formed. Clouds are formed in a variety of shapes and sizes. There is common agreement among meteorologists as to the names of particular clouds. Rainy, hot, or cold weather can be predicted with reasonable certainty when clouds are properly analyzed and interpreted in relation to other weather phenomena.

At least once during the summer there will be a thunderstorm. The most reliable warning of these storms is the majestic thunderhead cloud, or cumulonimbus. The afternoon may be clear and hot, but a storm is on the way. The heat which has collected from the sun's rays causes the moist, hot air to rise. When the air reaches cooling heights, water vapor in the air condenses and a cloud is formed. If the rising moist air curents are strong enough, the air will continue to push higher to cirrus levels, where the water vapor is transformed into ice crystals. As the cloud develops, water vapor condenses into rain, and the storm begins. The sharp updrafts, downdrafts, and crosscurrents within a cloud cause the cloud's particles to rub against each other with such activity that electrical charges are set up. If a negatively charged cloud passes over positively charged ground, the cloud releases a bolt of electrons that strike as lightning. Lightning can strike from ground to cloud, from cloud to ground, and within a single cloud. Thunder, which comes directly after a lightning bolt, is created by rapidly heated air that expands at a rapid rate as lightning streaks through it. The distant rumbling is caused by the thunder's sound waves bouncing back and forth within clouds or between mountains.

The Camp Weather Station

A small station for camp should consist of a wind vane, an anemometer for wind speed, a thermometer and shelter, an aneroid barometer, a mercury barometer, wet- and dry-bulb thermometers for humidity, and a rain gauge. The aneroid barometer and thermometer should be purchased because they are difficult to construct, but all other instruments can be made by campers, with the guidance of a counselor.

Instruments. Constructing instruments for meteorological observation is relatively easy. Few items are needed, and most instruments can be built in the crafts shop. To make a hygrometer in order to determine the amount of relative humidity in the air, take two thermometers, a piece of gauze, and a saucer. Mount the thermometers side by side. Wrap the bulb of one in several layers of gauze extending below the thermometer. Fill the saucer with water at room temperature and suspend the wet-bulb thermometer over the saucer so that about 1 inch of gauze is in the water. The water should move up the gauze wick and keep the thermometer bulb moist. After several minutes, read the wet- and dry-bulb thermometers and determine the relative humidity.

To illustrate air pressure, place a heavy book on end on a flattened paper bag. Introducing air into the bag will upset the book.

To make a simple barometer, use a test tube, a one-hole stopper, a curved length of glass tubing 10 to 14 inches long, and some water colored with iodine or methylate (Fig. 16-9). Fill the test tube $\frac{3}{4}$ full of liquid and insert the stopper with the tube extending about 1 inch into the test tube. Invert and then mount the device. The level of the liquid in the glass tube will rise and fall as air pressure rises and falls.

MINERALOGY

Minerals can be studied at almost any camp. Wherever there is an excavation, cut, or eroded area, there will be ample opportunity to discover rocks of all types, sizes, shapes, hardnesses, and colors. *Minerals* are what rocks are made of; they are substances formed by natural processes out of basic

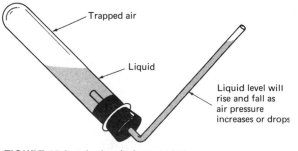

Trapped air

Liquid

Liquid level will rise and fall as air pressure increases or drops

FIGURE 16-9. A simple barometer.

elements such as iron, copper, sulphur, lead, and carbon. Some rock is com-posed almost entirely of one kind of mineral; sandstone, for example, con-sists mostly of quartz. Other rocks, such as gneiss, may contain minerals in varying proportions.

Minerals have several characteristics. They are found in every color of the spectrum. One mineral may appear in different places in different colors. Quartz is a good example. The various colors of quartz are derived from other elements in it. Thus, rose quartz gets its hue from the small percentage of iron oxide contained in it. Each mineral has a specific way of fracturing and splitting. Some split into flat sheets, as does mica. Calcite, on the other hand, divides into blocks. Flint breaks like glass, leaving a curved surface. Light reflection of minerals is another characteristic. Gem-stones are known for their luster. Relative hardness is another feature. Heaviness indicates certain properties of the elements involved in the min-eral.

The camp setting is almost ideal for identifying and collecting mineral specimens. Walks and hikes can be even more stimulating than usual if campers can recognize rocks and minerals. Collecting samples and cutting and polishing them is an exhilarating experience. The most common rock forms—granite, basalt, and shale—are easy to recognize. Some minerals can be rapidly identified as well. Campers can look for specimens wherever bed-rocks are exposed. Steep hillsides, excavations, stream beds, beaches, glacial moraines, and subterranean areas such as caves are likely places to find good samples. Some minerals are very difficult to identify; even experts in laboratories may be hard pressed to recognize them without conducting some tests. But a pocket guidebook to rocks and minerals can assist anyone in learning the identity of many specimens.

A collecting trip should have specific objectives. The area to be visited should be studied in advance to learn how the land lies, and what rock structures and minerals might be found there. Sufficient time must be al-lowed if efforts are to be fruitful. Work should be systematically performed. Too much coverage or unnecessarily expended energy can be disappoint-ing. Equipment needs are few and simple. A knapsack for packing the col-lected samples, a few sheets of newspaper for wrapping specimens, and a notebook and pencil are all that is necessary where the material has already been broken. If the terrain features strata that have been sharply folded or invaded by magma, then other tools are needed; a geologist's pick or ma-son's hammer is vital, along with a cold chisel, a magnifying glass, heavy gloves, and a small knife. Each camper should collect only what he can carry with reasonable comfort.

Specimens should be carefully selected. From the many that are found, very few should be kept. Although hand-sized samples are adequate, some collectors prefer small specimens, which can be studied under a low-power microscope. Specimens should be wrapped in newspaper for safe-keeping. To prevent scratching and chipping, the specimen should be laid on the newspaper and the sheet folded over. This should be repeated until there are at least four layers of paper covering the specimen.

Mineral specimen collecting can lead to other activities, including the collection of gemstones. Lapidary work with semiprecious stones can become a fascinating hobby. The cutting, polishing, and mounting of minerals can prove to be one of the more interesting aspects of specimen collecting.

ORNITHOLOGY

So vast is the subject of *zoology,* the science of animals, that it is impossible to do justice to the field here. The structures, functions, ecology, life habits, classifications, and all the laws and facts that pertain to animal life simply cannot be recounted here. Zoology leans heavily on other sciences. One of these is botany, since the relationship between plant and animal life is so intricate. Knowledge of physics, chemistry, and geology is vital if zoology is to be understood. Here we will discuss ornithology.

Birds are one of the most interesting and widely recognized groups of all animals. They are distributed all over the world. Both urban and rural dwellers come into contact with them. Although most of these creatures are taken for granted, their identification and habits can prove endlessly interesting as a subject for observation and study.

Birds' unique method of movement, flying—which has caused humans to try to imitate them from early historical times—allows them worldwide distribution. There are more than 15,000 species of birds in the world, and they have been thoroughly classified. Because birds appeal to amateur students, the study of birds at camp can be a stimulating part of the program. The habits, ecological relationships, songs, and characteristics for bird identification make tireless enthusiasts of those who appreciate this animal form.

Although birds are more gifted than most animals in the ease and speed by which they can move from one habitat to another, many of them are restricted to particular areas. Commonly, one species will be found in a particular valley or on an island and nowhere else. Many birds have adapted themselves to peculiar climate zones and do not leave them.

Along with mammals, birds are among the most highly developed order of the animal kingdom. It is only in the development of the nervous system that mammals give evidence of a higher progress. In most body parts, birds have a decidedly greater specialization due to their adaptation for flight. Their extreme activity corresponds to a higher metabolic rate and body temperature. The body is usually spindle-shaped with four divisions; head, neck, trunk, and tail. The neck is unusually long to afford balancing and other related activities. The limbs are paired, with the forelimbs adapted for flying. The posterior limbs are variously adapted for perching, walking, or swimming. Fertilization is internal, producing eggs with a yolk surrounded by a hard, calcareous shell. The incubation period is external, and the young are hatched helpless and naked. Birds are the only animals with feathers, which provide insulation, support, protection, and body-heat regulation.

Perhaps no group of animals has more beautiful, striking, and varied coloration than do birds. Although tropical birds have plumage that is unique and magnificent, many temperate zone birds are equally famous for their brilliant colors. The colors are partially due to pigments and to interference colors produced by the reflection and refraction of light. Thus, under some conditions, bird colors appear to vary.

Birds sing because air passes through the syrinx. This vocal organ has a membrane that vibrates to produce sound. In some species the range of sound is phenomenal. In others, sound is rather restricted. Birds also produce characteristic calls when they are frightened, to attract mates, to call their young, or for other purposes. Some birds are voiceless, while others have a special talent for mimicry.

Birds are extremely active and require large amounts of food. Their metabolic rates and body temperatures are the highest of all animals. Their food habits vary among the species. Some birds are strictly vegetarian; others are completely carnivorous. Some live exclusively on insects; others are omnivorous. Some birds, such as the hummingbird, which lives on a diet of nectar from flowers, and the kingfisher, whose eating habits are restricted to fish, are totally dependent upon these items for food. The crow, on the other hand, has an enormous range of diet.

Birds can be identified by their speeds of flight, the territories in which they live, and the way in which they care for their young, as well as by their mating habits, wings, feet, bills, migrations, behavior, and intelligence. There are about 27 birds orders with which they can be identified. Campers interested in ornithology can use an illustrated pocket guidebook to help them identify the birds they see.

chapter 17

Camp Crafts

Camp crafts combine art and skill to make participating in outdoor living safe and satisfying. The skills for easy living in the outdoors are those that urban dwellers never use or think about. Transplanted to the wilderness or the typical camping environment, campers must acquire a set of skills that will keep them comfortable under the most adverse aspects of weather, or permit them to survive extreme environmental conditions. Failure to learn these fundamental arts and crafts could mean the difference between pleasure, contentment, and satisfaction, and distress, despair, and even death. This by no means implies that campers are in any mortal danger at organized or residential camps; it does suggest, however, that one of the functions of the camp program is to teach those activities necessary to maintain the individual, whether on his own in the wilderness or as part of a group on an overnight excursion or long exploratory hike. Once the camper is removed from the boundaries of the camp facility, a new logistical factor applies to the situation. Learning various camp crafts and wood crafts can be one of the most valuable and enjoyable activities of the comprehensive camp program. They appeal to all age groups and can be learned and used by both boys and girls.

AX AND KNIFE WORK

The use of axes and knives at camp has been reduced to a great extent, and even eliminated by many camps. Perhaps this is necessary in camps where wilderness travel and trips away from camp are limited or omitted. Where camp crafts are considered a basic offering for campers, however, the use of axes, knives, and other tools are significant skills to be acquired.

Using Axes

The light, 1-pound ax or hatchet with a 12-inch handle is a valuable tool for almost all the work that has to be performed in the resident camp or even out on the trail. The typical camper will use the hand ax more effectively and safely than the woodsman's long-handled ax. A person who is highly skilled with an ax can do as much with a hand ax as a carpenter can do with a plane. The hatchet can be used for cutting wood for camp fires and cooking fires, for trail blazing, for butchering game, and for splitting kindling. Although it is not recommended, the blunt end of the hatchet can also be used as a hammer.

The hatchet should be made of good steel that will take and hold a sharp edge. Dull hand axes are dangerous. The ax head should either be a continuous part of the handle, if made of steel, or so well wedged that it will not loosen under repeated blows or strokes. Hatchets can weigh from $1\frac{1}{2}$ to 2 pounds, depending upon the weight and strength of the wielder. The hand ax should be sheathed in a leather cover that is tough enough to prevent the ax edge from cutting through it. The hatchet will be carried most comfortably in a rucksack or backpack, but there may be some occasions when it is best kept on the camper's belt.

The hand ax or hatchet, like all tools with an edge, will have to be sharpened periodically. The edge either will become nicked from use or will be dulled when stroked incorrectly. The blade should be filed before it is treated with a whetstone. For safety purposes, the hatchet should be firmly held against some solid object. If available, a vise will suffice for retaining the ax in an upright position with the blade up. The file should be moved from the blade edge to the back of the hatchet. After filing there should be no shoulder on the blade edge. Once the blade as been filed, the whetstone can be rubbed over the edge in a circular motion. A carborundum stone is best for maintaining a sharp edge.

Instructions for the use of the hatchet must concentrate on safety precautions:

1. Always use a hatchet from the kneeling position. A common mistake is for campers to stand up and chop down. The potential to miss the chop and have the hand ax come full circle to glance off the leg or foot is great under such circumstances, depending upon the angle of the stroke.

2. The stroke should be impelled by a full arm swing.

3. When chopping wood, start the stroke so that the hatchet hits at an acute angle to the grain. The blade, hitting the wood directly or at a right angle, will scarcely cut at all, unless the wood is a thin stick. Even then, the wood will be splintered rather than cut.

4. Use a chopping block for halving sticks.

5. When trimming branches from a tree, always stroke on the side of the tree that is away from the body.

6. Splitting wood for the camp cooking fire is probably the use to which most hatchets are put at summer camp. To split wood, hold the piece in one hand against the chopping block. Stand the stick up on end and carefully drive the ax edge into the upper tip of the wood. The handle of the ax can be either parallel to or at right angles to the stick. Since the hatchet blade will be caught

in the wood, lift both the ax and the stick together, bringing them down sharply against the block. This will split the wood in half.

Almost any moderately sized log can be chopped with the hand ax if the strokes are given with knowledge and power. Select a log or branch that is to be cut and used for some purpose, such as fuel or camp furniture (Fig. 17-1). As previously indicated, the hatchet must be used so that it connects with the log at an acute angle to the grain or the wood. The notch for cutting should be as wide as the log itself. Thus, if the log is 10 inches in diameter, the notch for the cut should be 10 inches wide. Chop halfway through the log so that a V-shaped wedge is made on the side opposite from the cutter. Begin another notch on the opposite side from the original cut. When the two Vs meet, the log will be cut through.

If trees must be felled, select the direction in which the tree should fall. Cut a shallow notch with three or four strokes of the ax on the side in the direction which the tree is to fall. On the exact opposite side, cut a notch about one-third of the way through the tree, approximately 3 inches higher than the first notch. Cut into the first notch until the cut appears to be directly under the notch cut into the far side of the tree. Deepen the second notch until the tree begins to lean in the desired direction. Step to the side at a previously chosen position.

FIGURE 17-1. A counselor instructs in the use of a bow saw.
(Courtesy: Donna Richardson).

Using Knives

By age 11, children have the intelligence and motor coordination necessary to use a knife effectively and safely. Younger children can be taught about knives and can learn many forms of camp crafts and wood crafts without having to use knives. When young campers are acquiring any new skill, a controlled situation is mandatory.

The large folding clasp knife is one of the more useful and efficient tools for camp crafts. The knife should be fitted with one large and one small blade. It may also contain a can opener and a ring on one end for easy attachment to a thong or lanyard. A knife with a good steel blade that will take a keen edge, without breaking, is a worthwhile investment.

Counselors who instruct campers in the use of knives should observe and teach the following procedures:

1. Stroke or cut away from the body.
2. Use the cutting blade for woodwork only.
3. Never use the knife as a screwdriver.
4. Never heat the blade.
5. Never leave a blade exposed when the knife is not in use.
6. Keep the blades sharp for use, but not razor sharp.

Knives are invaluable for many tasks: cutting fuzz sticks for making fires, repairing leather goods, carving, whittling, skinning game, cleaning fish, or manufacturing useful artifacts for living out of camp. Every camper who is old enough should learn to whittle; it is an excellent hobby and can be performed with almost all types of wood whenever time hangs heavy. Making fuzz sticks is also a useful skill. Fuzz sticks are small pieces of wood selected for their high burning propensity and prepared so that they ignite rapidly. They should be made of soft wood, preferably pine, hemlock, or spruce, approximately 8 to 10 inches long and up to 1 inch in diameter. The wood should be stripped of bark and without knots on the surface. Place one end of the wooden stick on a wood block or stone rest. With the knife, slice long thin strips, leaving one end of the strips attached to the stick. The knife should always be worked toward the block or stone rest. The slices should be at least 3 inches long and on only one side of the stick. These fuzz sticks are very helpful in starting any kind of fire, particularly if there is little in the way of kindling or tinder available.

Pothooks

Pothooks are by far the most useful item for the outdoor cook. The pothook should be a 6-inch to 1-foot long section of a green sapling, at least 1 inch in diameter. The sapling should have a fork about $\frac{1}{2}$ inch in diameter. With the knife, cut a notch on the section on the same side as the fork. The notch should be cut so that it angles up. This angling prevents an item placed on the notch from slipping out. Any utensil with a metal handle will fit onto a pothook. In order to vary the height of the utensil over the fire, cut several pothooks, making the holding notch at different places.

Like all tools that require sharp edges, knives must be ground periodically. Round carborundum stones are best for sharpening blades. The stones can be held in the hands without being placed on a bench or held in a vise. When sharpening knife blades, hold the handle in the left hand and the stone in the right. Move the stone in a circular motion over the edge of the blade, and hold the blade at an angle from the stone. For the clasp knife, raise the back of the blade about $\frac{1}{4}$ inch off the stone. About 30 seconds of stone work should give the knife a keen edge.

COOKING AND FOOD CARE

Cooking

As with the teaching of all skills, cooking out of camp should start with the simplest aspects and proceed to the more complex. The youngest camper may be overjoyed with toasting a marshmallow, while the highly experienced camper may be satisfied with nothing less than making his own bread and freshly caught trout. Stick cooking is the easiest way to prepare food when on the trail. Although it requires some skill, it is not complicated; and it has the distinct advantage of forcing every person on the trip to do something about getting his own food. The stick-cooking method works well with frankfurters on the end of a sharp green spit, meat kabobs, and wraparound dough from which a crude bread can be made.

Next in complexity is the one-pot meal. The single pot can accommodate almost any concoction. Stews, franks and beans, soups, and boiled foods such as corn on the cob are tasty and nutritious when prepared this way. Skillet cooking is at about the same level as the one-pot meal (Fig. 17-2). Anything that can be fried or toasted can be prepared alone or in combination in the skillet—bacon and eggs, steaks, chops, hamburgers, fish, pancakes, bread, cheese.

With a little assistance and some practice, almost any camper can begin to plan menus for cookouts. A balanced, appealing diet is just as important outdoors as in the dining hall. Vegetables such as carrots and celery can be substituted for lettuce; oranges provide vitamin C. Bacon and eggs together with bread twists made over an open fire, with jam, jelly, or marmalade poured into the hole left by the stick, are filling and nutritious. Thick sandwiches of boiled ham and cheese, cream cheese and jelly, peanut butter and jelly, or thinly sliced meat between two slices of bread, accompanied by water, milk, or juice, are nourishing and should keep campers satisfied until they can cook a hot meal. It is unnecessary to have three hot meals a day when out on the trail; if it is cold and damp, however, hot meals, or at least some foods that can be heated before serving, help ward off chill and fatigue. Canned soup not requiring the addition of water can be opened and heated in the can over an open fire.

Although many comprehensive and simplified cookbooks are available to the counselor, a few highly adaptable recipes follow.[1]

[1]Recipes reprinted with permission of the Campbell Soup Company.

FIGURE 17-2. Using aluminum foil and skillet to prepare a meal.

Quick Chili con Carne

$\frac{1}{2}$ lb. ground beef
1 cup chopped onion
2 cloves garlic, minced
2 to 3 teaspoons chili powder
$\frac{1}{2}$ teaspoon salt
Dash pepper

1 tablespoon shortening
1 can ($10\frac{1}{2}$ oz.) condensed tomato
soup
2 cans (1 lb. each) kidney beans,
undrained
$\frac{1}{2}$ cup water
1 teaspoon vinegar

Cook beef, onion, garlic, and seasonings in shortening until meat is
lightly browned. Add remaining ingredients. Cover; cook over low heat
30 minutes, stirring often. Uncover; cook to desired consistency.
4 servings.

Macaroni and Cheese

$\frac{1}{4}$ cup chopped onion
1 tablespoon butter or margarine
1 can (11 oz.) condensed Cheddar
cheese soup

$\frac{1}{2}$ cup milk
3 cups cooked macaroni

Cook onion in butter until tender. Blend in soup; gradually add milk.
Heat, stirring often. Mix in macaroni. Heat, stirring.
4 to 6 servings.

Yummy Porcupine Meatballs

1 can (10 oz.) condensed tomato soup
1 lb. ground beef
$\frac{1}{4}$ cup uncooked rice
1 egg, slightly beaten
$\frac{1}{4}$ cup minced onion
2 tablespoons minced parsley
1 teaspoon salt
1 small clove garlic, minced
2 tablespoons shortening
1 cup water

Mix $\frac{1}{4}$ cup soup with beef, rice, egg, onion, parsley, and salt. Shape into $1\frac{1}{2}$ inch balls (about 16). Brown meatballs and garlic in shortening in skillet; blend in remaining soup and water. Cover; simmer 40 minutes or until rice is tender; stir often.
4 servings.

Spaghetti Southern Style

2 slices bacon
1 cup diced cooked beef
1 medium green pepper, sliced
1 medium onion, sliced
$\frac{1}{4}$ to $\frac{1}{2}$ teaspoon chili powder
1 clove garlic, minced
1 can ($10\frac{1}{2}$ oz.) condensed tomato soup
$\frac{1}{2}$ soup can water
6 ounces cooked spaghetti

Cook bacon in skillet until crisp; remove and crumble. In drippings, cook beef, pepper, onion, chili powder, and garlic until vegetables are tender. Add soup, water, and bacon. Cover; cook over low heat 30 minutes. Stir often. Serve over hot spaghetti.
3 to 4 servings.

Skillet Chicken Delight

2 lbs. chicken parts
$\frac{1}{4}$ cup flour
$\frac{1}{4}$ cup butter or margarine
1 can ($10\frac{1}{2}$ oz.) condensed chicken gumbo soup
$\frac{1}{2}$ soup can water
2 tablespoons ketchup

Dust chicken with flour; brown in butter. Stir in soup, water, and ketchup. Cover; simmer 45 minutes or until chicken is tender. Stir often.
4 to 6 servings.

Last-Minute Supper

1 can (12 oz.) luncheon meat, cut in strips
1 medium onion, thinly sliced
2 tablespoons butter or margarine
1 can ($10\frac{1}{2}$ oz.) condensed cream of mushroom soup
$\frac{1}{2}$ cup milk
2 cups cubed cooked potatoes (about 4 medium)
2 tablespoons chopped parsley
Dash pepper

Lightly brown meat and onion in butter until onion is tender. Blend in soup and milk. Add remaining ingredients; cook over low heat 10 minutes or until flavors are blended. Stir often.
4 servings.

Smothered Steak Roll-ups

2 lbs. thinly sliced round steak or flank steak
2 cups packaged herb-seasoned stuffing, prepared as directed
2 tablespoons butter or margarine
1 can ($10\frac{1}{2}$ oz.) condensed cream of mushroom soup
$\frac{1}{2}$ cup water
$\frac{1}{2}$ cup sour cream, if desired

(continued)

Pound steak with meat hammer or edge of heavy saucer; cut into 6 pieces long enough to roll. Place $\frac{1}{3}$ cup stuffing near center of each steak; roll pinwheel fashion; fasten with toothpicks or skewers. Brown roll-ups in butter. Add soup and water. Cover; cook over low heat 1 hour or until tender. Spoon sauce over meat often during cooking. Stir in sour cream; heat a few minutes more.
6 servings.

Frankfurter Skillet Barbecue

$\frac{1}{2}$ cup chopped onion
1 lb. frankfurters
2 tablespoons butter or margarine
1 can (10$\frac{3}{4}$ oz.) condensed tomato rice soup
$\frac{1}{2}$ soup can water

1 tablespoon molasses
1 teaspoon prepared mustard
$\frac{1}{2}$ teaspoon vinegar
$\frac{1}{2}$ teaspoon Worcestershire
4 drops Tabasco sauce

Cook onion and frankfurters in butter until onion is cooked and frankfurters browned. Add remaining ingredients. Simmer 15 minutes; stir often. May be served on frankfurter buns.
4 to 5 servings.

Spaghetti Frankfurter Supper

$\frac{1}{2}$ cup chopped celery
$\frac{1}{2}$ cup chopped onion
2 tablespoons shortening
1 lb. frankfurters,
cut in $\frac{1}{2}$-inch slices

1 can (10$\frac{1}{2}$ oz.) condensed tomato soup
$\frac{1}{2}$ cup water
1 teaspoon Worcestershire
6 oz. cooked spaghetti

Cook celery and onions in shortening until tender. Add frankfurters; cook until lightly browned. Stir in soup, water, and Worcestershire. Cook about 15 minutes to blend flavors; stir often. Serve over hot cooked spaghetti.
3 to 4 servings.

Tuna Shortcake

1 can (10$\frac{1}{2}$ oz.) condensed cream of celery or mushroom soup
$\frac{1}{2}$ cup milk
1 can (7 ounces) tuna, drained and flaked

1 cup cooked peas
1 tablespoon chopped pimiento
Hot biscuits or toast

Blend soup and milk; add tuna, peas, and pimiento. Heat; stir often. Serve over biscuits or toast.
4 servings.

Stew 'n Dumplings

1 can (1 lb.) whole onions
1 cup onion liquid and water
2 tablespoons butter or margarine
1 can (10$\frac{3}{4}$ ounces) condensed vegetable soup

1$\frac{1}{2}$ cups diced cooked beef
1 cup prepared biscuit mix
$\frac{1}{3}$ cup milk

Drain onions, reserving liquid; add water to liquid to make 1 cup. Brown onions in butter; stir often. Add soup, onion liquid, and meat; bring to boil. Meanwhile, blend biscuit mix and milk; drop dough, making 8 dumplings, from spoon into simmering stew. Cover; cook 15 minutes more without lifting lid.
4 servings.

Food Care

When packing gear on the trail, the single limiting factor in determining kinds and amount of food necessary will be weight to transport. If campers must transport their own food and other gear, they are restricted in terms of what they can carry. If they can expect to stop at communities and purchase supplies for cookouts during their excursions, more camping gear can be carried without having to worry about food. This seems somewhat unlikely, however, because the usual overnight hike or extended excursion is directed away from points of civilization. Campers can shoulder approximately 20 pounds of gear and food in a backpack; older campers can accommodate 10 to 15 pounds more than younger campers. On a canoe trip, the canoe can be loaded so that supplies will be adequate for the length of the outing. Should there be any portage, however, the canoes may have to be unloaded and several trips made to ferry all the supplies. If a horseback trip is planned, bear in mind that pack horses can be loaded with a little more than 100 pounds of supplies, although burros can carry about twice that weight.

In packing food for trips, dry foods (flour, salt, sugar) and dehydrated products (milk, eggs, potatoes, soups) can be packed in plastic bags and sealed so that they do not spill. Beverages in powdered form should be kept in tightly sealed containers. Plastic containers can hold dried meats, butter, margarine, and a variety of vegetables. If fresh vegetables are to be carried on a prolonged overland trip, it is necessary to arrange for points at which vehicles can meet the campers and transfer one or more days' supplies for campers to pack. Unless the excursion intersects highways or even tertiary roadways, this method of supply is impractical.

Packing-in is the most common method of supplying food to campers on an out-of-camp trip. For this reason, it is best to choose the simplest and most space-saving foods. (Fig. 17-3). Although a broad range of foods is available, particularly as a result of dehydration processes, cookout menus should be kept relatively simple. It is better for campers to try to live off the land (including water resources, of course) and supply themselves with food than it is to transport a complex food supply over many miles on campers' backs. Creating tasty, complete meals from a few simple ingredients is the foundation of the best outdoor cooking. The exertion necessary to maintain the pace of on-the-trail exploration does wonders for campers' appetites. Plenty of fresh air and hard exercise makes every food a gourmet's delight. The only requirement is that the meal be well prepared.

If food supplies are carried in packs, they must be safeguarded against the forays of animals and insects. Airtight plastic or metal containers work best against insects. Water hurdles prevent crawling insects from attacking food supplies that have been opened. A trough filled with water and placed strategically between the insects and the food can prevent a great deal of costly damage. A four-legged bench whose legs are placed in pails or buckets of water prevent crawling insects from getting into the food placed on the bench. Food supplies can be cached between two saplings, high enough from the ground to prevent four-footed animals from jumping up to obtain the food, closed tightly to prevent flying insects from entering the container, and strung in such a manner so that ants and other crawling pests

FIGURE 17-3. Bacon and eggs on an overnight trip.

cannot get to the food. Another food protection method is to attach a double hook to a wooden peg which is threaded with a one-hole rubber stopper, and on top of which rests a pan of water. The top hook is attached to a guy rope and the food is hung under the pan or basin from the second hook on the nether end of the peg.

It is unlikely that food chests will be carried on wilderness trips, so the food cache is probably the best means of defending against marauding animals and insects. Variation of caches can be used, but the anti-ant water barrier, as just described, in combination with a high guy-rope attachment, will do the job. Such perishable items as whole milk, butter, and meat should not be kept for more than 24 hours without some kind of refrigeration. Ice is almost never used when back-packing. If an animal pack or canoe trip is undertaken, however, ice is usually used to keep foods refrigerated. Along the trail, streams or other water courses, which are generally cold, can be used to refrigerate food supplies. Evaporation, a natural method of cooling, is accomplished by placing water-soaked tarpaulin, blanket, or other fabric over food in waterproof containers and allowed to dry; as the fabric dries, it cools the foods packed in the container.

FIRE BUILDING AND CONTROL

There are many methods of making fires. Fires for evening camp activities are quite different from cooking fires made out on the trail. But regardless of the purpose of the fire, the elements for starting and maintaining it remain the same. Every fire is the product of three vital ingredients: oxygen, fuel, and heat (or kindling temperature). Any fire made for camping and cookouts must have combustible fuel, and an initial fire that is hot enough and lasts long enough to ignite the fuel supply.

Starting the Fire

To start any kind of fire anywhere in the outdoors, obtain a few scraps of highly flammable material—a few pieces of birch bark, pine cones, dry leaves, or fuzz sticks. Over these highly combustible shreds, loosely pile a slightly less flammable substance, such as small twigs. Add a tepee of larger dry sticks above this. In the same fashion, lay larger pieces of wood, making sure that air circulation is adequate to reach all parts of the heap. Ignite the interior scraps so that the flame burns in the core of the pile. Long wooden matches are best for lighting fires of this type, but even when matches are not available, wood-crafts methods can be used to ignite a fire. In any wooded region, a camp fire for cooking or for evening activities can be built from wood products on hand. It is always possible to locate a sheltered area; even when it is raining, shavings and kindling can be obtained with a knife or hatchet.

Igniting a fire after a steady rain presents no insurmountable difficulty if the camper packs an ax or knife. Water generally does not seep into the very heart of a log. Select a standing dead tree or windfall, cut a short length of log with the ax, and then cut the piece in half. The center of the split wood will be absolutely dry. Short lengths can be taken from the center for kindling materials. The combustible pieces for igniting the fire can be prepared by making fuzz sticks from the center section of the log and chopping or cutting out additional kindling materials. With wooden matches, ignite the kindling and add more scraps and shavings. To this pile add larger twigs, branches, and gradually larger pieces of wood. As the fire gets underway, wet wood can be added; the fire quickly dries out the wood, and it burns quite well.

Never smother a fire with too much fuel, and do not pack fuel too tightly. Regardless of its purpose—whether for warmth, a quick meal, a ceremonial activity, or a reflector for baking—the fire requires a vast amount of oxygen (Fig. 17-4). A good rule of thumb is to allow space for every stick or piece of combustible material used; the space should be approximately half the width of the wooden pieces. Excessive space between the wood will prevent the fire from taking hold.

A common mistake in fire building is to start a fire and then add material that is too heavy for the fire to handle. The fire usually burns out in the middle section of kindling and fails to eat into the heavier fuel that has been piled over the smaller flammables; the fire dies out because there has been too fast a transition from small combustibles to large pieces of wood.

FIGURE 17-4. A compact altar-reflector combination.

A fire should develop gradually from one size of wood to another until a strong blaze has been built. Once the blaze is strong, it is perfectly fine to add heavy pieces of wood to support it.

Although it seems illogical for those camping on the trail to be without matches, doing without matches is an important skill. When the occasion demands, the competent camper should be able to ignite a fire without using matches. The surest method for getting a flame without matches is still the fire bow, or pump drill (Fig. 17-5). This type of drill consists of a round stick, to which is fastened a wheel with a crossbar fitting loosely on the stick, attached to it by means of a thong or cord. The end of the stick is cut to a rough point so that as it revolves in a small hole in the hearth board, it causes enough friction to produce a spark. The dry fuel is at hand to catch the spark and create a fire.

Making the Pump Drill

1. Take a $\frac{1}{2}$-inch dowel 16 inches long or longer. Roughly sharpen one end and bore a hole of about $\frac{3}{16}$ inch diameter $\frac{1}{2}$ inch from the opposite end.
2. Make a wheel 5 or 6 inches in diameter. Bore a hole in the center of this to fit the dowel.
3. Use a cross bar $\frac{1}{2}$ inch by 2 inches by 11 inches. It is tapered toward the ends until it is about 1 inch wide at the ends. Holes measuring $\frac{3}{16}$ of an inch are

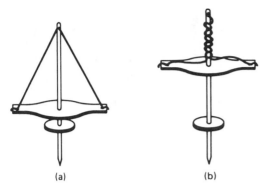

FIGURE 17-5. The pump drill (a) slack and (b) in use.

(a) (b)

bored about an inch from each end, and a $\frac{5}{8}$- or $\frac{3}{4}$-inch hole is bored in the center.

4. Find a piece of soft wood for the hearth, approximately $\frac{1}{2}$ inch by 3 inches by 12 inches. Bore a hole about $\frac{3}{16}$ of an inch almost through the middle of the hearth.

5. Cut a rawhide thong. Glue the wheel to the dowel 3 inches from the pointed end. Tie a knot at the end of a piece of rawhide, thread it up through one end of the crossbar to within 1 inch of the wheel, and tie a knot in the thong below the crossbar.

Using the Pump Drill

Place a thin block of wood under one end of the hearth board to provide for better air circulation. Holding the drill in a perpendicular position, with its sharpened end resting in the hole of the hearth board, twirl the crossbar until it is as high as possible. With both hands on the crossbar, make a quick downward stroke, causing the thong first to unwind, then to rewind. Make another quick downward stroke and continue rhythmically until the drill is revolving smoothly and easily. When the spark comes, let it drop into some very dry shredded cedar bark or other fuel. Gently blow it into a flame.

If the drill is to be used for boring holes, a tiny steel drill can be inserted at the pointed end and fastened in place with ambroid cement.

Cooking and Activity Fires

Novice fire makers invariably construct a conflagration when they first attempt to build a fire for warmth or cooking. Such huge fires are impossible to use effectively. No good meal can be prepared over a pile of smoking fagots, but a tremendous flame blackens utensils and hinders control of the cooking process; the big blaze keeps the cook from the fire and tends to char everything. The excitement of being out on the trail may cause campers to overlook food that has been burned to a crisp, but they will not put up with many meals cooked in this fashion.

Good meals can always be prepared on the trail if one is acquainted with the methods for getting the most out of the fire types and fuels. Efficient fire-building can be economical in terms of effort, time, and avoidance of problems. Of all the variety of fires, there are three basic kinds: (1) a quick, hot, small fire that boils soup or other liquids rapidly and burns down to coals that are not too hot for frying or broiling; (2) a firm bed of hot, glowing coals that maintain a regular, smokeless heat for roasting, baking, or slow boiling; and (3) a large camp fire that can be used in evening ceremonials and activities, or for throwing heat onto those who gather around it for warmth.

Quick Boiling Fire

For the rapid fire, drive a forked stick into the ground. Cut a green stick or pole, lay it through the fork, and weight it with a rock; this allows the regulation of anything put to boil. The bail of the pot should be placed in a notch cut into the green stick so that the kettle is at least 1 foot from the ground. Select dry twigs and sticks, about the size of a pencil in diameter, and make fuzz sticks from them. Place the fuzz sticks in tepee fashion beneath the hanging pot, shaved ends pointing down. Around these tinder pieces build another tepee-shaped pile of slightly larger kindling. The entire pile will be less than 1 foot high. Ignite the tinder. A small, hot fire soon boils the liquid in the pot. As the fire burns, obtain two large sticks, about 6 inches thick; if wood is not available, two flat rocks will do. These are used to support any cooking utensils for frying (Fig. 17-6). The hot fire burns down to embers almost as soon as the pot boils. Remove all of the smoking clinkers, retaining only the glowing coals. With the flat rocks or steady sticks on either side of the embers, a cooking facility is available for quick frying.

Trench Fire

Dig a shallow trench in the ground at the spot on which the fire is desired. The trench can be 2 feet long, 6 inches wide, and 6 inches deep. Make sure that the trench is dug so that it runs lengthwise with the wind.

FIGURE 17-6.   Dingle-stick contraption over a quick boiling fire.

Using the same methods as in building the small, hot fire, wait until the flame has developed and then add larger and heavier pieces of wood. This fire should be made only when the wind is adequate to assist the burning process. On a calm day, it is better to build an on-the-ground fire.

Slow Cooking Fire and Fire Cranes

The camper must lay in a good supply of kindling and wood. Find several flat rocks or bed logs. The logs should be approximately 6 inches in diameter and at least 3 feet long. Place the bed logs or rocks parallel to each other. Across these, rest several small sticks in pairs to serve as supports for cooking utensils. Arrange the shavings and kindling under the utensil rests. The fire will be carried by long pieces of wood placed between the bed logs. Air must be permitted to circulate freely through the fuel. Ignite the kindling. Additional wood may be added as necessary, but if a good supply has been heaped on the tinder and kindling, it produces a good flame that burns the wood down evenly (Fig. 17-7).

Utensils for boiling liquids are easily handled when suspended above the fire. Heating is made more manageable simply by shifting the height of the pot or kettle above the flame or bed of coals. The fire is made in the

FIGURE 17-7. Demonstrating the materials needed for a slow cooking fire.

manner previously described. Bed logs or flat rocks serve as the base within which a fire is built. When the fire has produced a steady flame of not more than 1 foot, or has burned down to a bed of glowing coals, drive two precut poles or sticks of green wood, each with a fork at the top, into the ground on either side of the fire. The sticks can be 2 to 3 inches in diameter and 4 to 5 feet long. Stake them into the ground so that there is at least $3\frac{1}{2}$ to 4 feet of stick above the ground. Cut another green stick that can serve as a cross piece or lug pole. Cut three or more notches into the lug pole from which to hang utensils. Lay the lug pole across the forks of the upright poles so that it crosses directly over the center of the fire. Make pothooks as described on page 254; then hang the pothooks on the notches that have been cut into the lug pole. The heat of the fire can be regulated by hanging various pots on the hooks which have been cut to various lengths. Thus, low-hanging pots will boil quickly; they may then be shifted to shorter hooks in order to cool down enough for simmering.

Baking Fire

Baking and roasting is best done with some sort of device to reflect the fire's heat. Reflector cooking requires a relatively high fire with a backing that can throw or direct heat forward. Wooden sticks at least 3 feet long can be leaned against a rock slab, against a side of poles tied together to form a flat face, or against a big log. Kindle the fire against the backing. The fire itself should be laid on a raised base of green wood so that the fire is higher than the lower edge of the reflector. A high fire can be built by laying down bed sticks, building up a fairly square pile by setting small sticks on top of these at right angles to the bed sticks, and then crossing additional sticks on the ones underneath until the construction is at least 2 feet high. Ignite the fuel, and a high, intense fire will result. The most common reflector is made of aluminum and has a 60-degree reflecting angle. When the fire is burning steadily, place the reflector approximately 10 inches away from the flames. Experience will teach campers the best distance between the fire and the reflector for each kind of food.

Hunter-trapper Fire

This kind of fire serves both to cook a meal quickly and as a camp fire for a chilly night. Two hardwood logs, about 6 feet long, should be cut and laid 6 inches apart on one end and about 18 inches apart at the other. Build a tepee of kindling between the logs, and a log pile around the tepee. Take sticks of 1 inch in diameter and lay them across the bed logs as rests. On these rests, build a square of sticks by laying them down in pairs with the ends crossed. Ignite the tepee. The upper wooden structure should swiftly burn through and drop between the bed logs, causing them to ignite on the inner sides. To maintain or bank the fire for morning use, take two green poles or logs approximately 10 inches thick and lay them across the bed logs. Place additional wood on the support logs for replenishment as necessary. In the morning there should be enough hot coals for cooking breakfast.

Indian Fire

This type of fire is best considered where fuel is hard to obtain, whether because of the scarcity of wood or because of inadequate tools to cut kindling and heavier material. Collect as much wood as possible; this collection will probably yield some tinder materials and twigs or a few larger branches. Cut some saplings, and lay four or five of them on the ground with their butts pointing toward the center. Place tinder and kindling materials at the core and rest the sapling butts on them. The tips of the saplings should radiate outward from the hub like the spokes of a wheel. Ignite the fuel in the center. Place additional sapling butts on the burning pile, with tips arranged as before. As the wood burns away, the poles will be pushed up so that the ends are always in the fire. This saves a great deal of wood chopping, economizes on fuel, and permits the camper to remain close to the fire for warmth.

Altar Fire

The altar, or ceremonial, fire is ignited at the top and burns down. Thus it requires excellent kindling to start a blaze at the lower layers of the pile. The ceremonial fire is constructed with two large bed logs about 10 inches in diameter and at least 4 feet in length. Across these bed logs, place 6 to 10 poles of about 3 inches in diameter and at least 3 feet long. Place as many 2-inch poles on top of the second level. Continue to add layer upon layer with smaller and smaller sticks, until the altar is at least 4 feet high. At the very top, construct a tepee, beginning with good tinder and kindling. Place tinder and kindling between all of the lower layers of the altar. Ignite the wooden tepee. As this tinder and kindling blaze up, a high-intensity flame develops. The fire soon demolishes the tepee, leaving only burning coals that fall through the second layer, igniting the tinder placed there for this purpose. As the fire grows in intensity, it burns down through supporting layers. The fire should burn brightly throughout the ceremonial activities without needing additional fuel.

Self-feeding Fire

This fire is typically laid in a hole in the ground. It is used for preparing of meals, usually stews that take a relatively long time to cook. Dig a pit 1 to 3 feet deep. It should be at least as wide at the top as it is deep, but the pit walls should slant upward from the bottom to the top, thus forming a V cleft at the bottom. The entire pit should be lined with medium-sized, round stones. Flat rocks can also be used if they are not made of shale, which is likely to crack and split when heated. Construct a crane to hold a utensil between 6 and 10 inches above the bottom of the pit. Build a tepee fire in the hole until a large quantity of glowing embers are obtained. By the time the fire has burned down to embers, the stones lining the pit should be quite hot. The stew can then be hung over the pit. Additional fuel can be added about every half hour. The flame does not have to be high, nor will it produce a great deal of heat. It is best for maintaining a slow, even heat over a relatively long period of time.

Fire Prevention and Control

It is necessary to clear the camp ground of combustible materials prior to starting a cooking or sleeping fire. Sweep away or rake to the center any loose flammable stuff, such as dead leaves, pine needles, twigs, sticks, and branches, and there dispose of it by burning. The camp fire or cooking fire may then be built with reasonable security against loose material catching fire and spreading beyond control. Fires should not be built against trees, nor should they be built where there are low overhead branches that can be ignited by high flames or shooting sparks.

Campers must understand that fire prevention is easier than fire control. Although it seems difficult to ignite a fire, a forest fire can occur because of one small spark or piece of glowing ember. One of the basic elements for fire is heat, or kindling temperature; therefore, water, which cools the material below kindling temperature, prevents oxygen from reaching the fuel, and spoils the fuel for ignition, is best for killing fire. But even if the fire is doused with water, there may still be some stubborn sparks; therefore make sure that all possible sources of fire are extinguished before heaping earth or sand over the remains. Live sparks are sometimes capable of remaining lit underground; if there are root systems or humus, the spark may slowly develop into a full-fledged fire that breaks out quite a distance from the original fire. By feeding on flammable materials underground, a raging forest fire may be produced days or weeks after the campers thought that they had extinguished the fire. Always take the time to cool down and completely drown the fire and the potential fuel.

ROPE WORK

Knowing how to use rope for the attaching objects, for hauling materials, for constructing utensils, vessels, and transportation vehicles, and for building shelters and secure living quarters depends upon the camper's skill in using just the right knot for a specific task. In learning to tie knots, use rope or cord at least $\frac{1}{8}$ inch in diameter. The parts of the rope have names, as do all useful objects (Fig. 17-8). The main section of the rope is the *standing part.* Any looped or curved section of rope that is bent back upon the standing part is called a *bight,* whether or not it crosses the rope. The tips of ropes are called the *ends.*

Knots

There are a variety of useful knots, each having some particular strength or value in a specific circumstance. Only those knots that have applications are presented here, along with their major uses and disadvantages.

Plain knot. The simplest knot to tie is the plain knot. It is often used as an integral part of other knots. It consists of passing one end over the standing part to form a bight and tucking the end through the bight. The

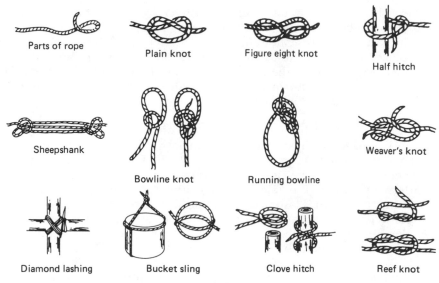

FIGURE 17-8. Various knots, hitches, and slings.

knot is difficult to untie, and it holds fast when placed under any strain. Plain knots are also used to keep a rope from slipping beyond a particular point. The stopper knot is made at any point on the rope to prevent the rope from moving through a ring, hole, bight, or other aperture. Such knots are also used to prevent the unravelling of rope strands when tied at the ends.

Figure-eight knot. This knot is larger and easier to use than a plain knot. It is made by passing the bight under the standing part, recurving the bight over the standing part, and carrying the end through the circle made by the upper bight. The knot takes its name from the appearance that it makes when being tied, which is that of an 8. This is an excellent knot for attaching fish hooks to lines.

Reef knot. This is also known as the true knot. It does not slip when joining ropes of equal thickness. This should not be used when ropes of different thicknesses are to be spliced. It is very easy to loosen. To make the reef, cross the ends of two ropes so that the first, A, slides under the bight of B, over, then under the standing part of B. Bring the two ends up, away from you. Cross A under B, turn B under A, and tighten by pulling on both ends simultaneously.

Weaver's knot. This knot is most effective for joining ropes of unequal diameter. This is the quickest and most secure method for tying together two ropes of greatly differing sizes. To make this knot, cross the ends of two ropes. The right end should be placed underneath the left and held at the point where they cross. With the free hand, bring the standing part of the right rope up over the left and down around its own end, which should be projecting to the left. Bring the right rope back between the two ends on top of the cross, holding it with the left hand. The loop that has been placed around the left hand should be slipped forward over the end of the left rope. Tighten the knot by drawing on both standing parts. The weaver's knot is used for making nets of all sizes, which can be used for fishing and to capture field specimens.

Hitches.   A hitch is simply a twist or combination of twists to bind a rope or line to some object. There are a variety of hitches, of which the half hitch and the clove hitch are best known. The half hitch is made by turning in the end of a rope. The clove hitch has several functions and can be used in different positions. It is able to take a strain while being prepared, cannot slip along whatever it is fastened to, and permits easy loosening when ready. Bring one end around any object to which an attachment is to be made. Pass the end over its own standing part and around the object, and then under its standing part.

Taut-line hitch.   This is one of the more important knots used by any camper who must set up a tent for shelter on the trail. This knot is indispensable for all ropes slung between two objects. The taut-line permits adjustments to be made in the ropes after the tent has been erected. The knot will not slip of its own accord, but it can be worked up or down manually along the tight part of the rope. This offers a ready method for lengthening or shortening the tent ropes which are guyed from tent to stake.

Bowline.   The most widely used of all loop knots, the bowline has practically unlimited uses because it is superbly dependable. It does not slip, cannot jam, and is relatively easy to untie. To make the bowline, form a small bight permitting a long loose end big enough for a loop. Bring the end down through the bight. Pass the end under and around the standing part. Bring the end back over and then under the bight. In order to tighten, pull on the standing part. The bowline can be used to moor any watercraft to a dock, or wherever a loop is necessary.

Running bowline.   Make the running bowline by first making a bowline and then passing the main rope back through the large loop. This forms a slip knot that is superior to any other knot of its kind.

Sheepshank.   If a rope is too long for the purpose to which it is put, the sheepshank is one method to shorten it without cutting. The sheepshank can be used even where both ends are fast. It can be joined together without having to whip the cord. Make a simple running loop and pass a bight through this loop. Tighten the loop.

Bale hitch.   Bend the standing part of the rope over the back of any object that needs to be carried. Bring the ends up over the front of the back and out under the bend. The two long ends can be used to lift or lower. In

FIGURE 17-9. Learning to tie knots at camp. (Courtesy: Donna Richardson.)

portaging, the two ends are brought forward over the packer's shoulders and held within the hands. The pack can be dropped instantly if necessary.

Bucket sling. The bucket sling or hitch comes in handy for suspending any object or container that does not have a handle. Set the container on the rope and bring the two ends up to make a loose plain knot. Draw the two ends down until they come around the upper edge of the container. Tighten the rope, and knot the ends together over the bucket.

Lashing

Lashing is a method whereby rope or cord is used to bind securely together two or more materials made of fiber, wood, or leather. When wooden objects are to be fastened, it is best that they have notches at the points where they are to be joined. The joint thus formed is less liable to slip and makes a more compact fit. Lashing is used when other ways of binding materials are unavailable or when other fasteners would be useless. In making a birchbark canoe, for example, it is more desirable to lash the gunwales to the ribs than it is to staple, nail, or glue the materials together.

In lashing, it is the standing part of the rope, rather than the ends, that is manipulated. Nearly all lashing is begun with a clove hitch around one or more of the objects to be bound together. Another clove hitch finishes off the work.

Diamond lashing.   To join beams, poles, or braces together at right angles, a clove hitch is made around one of the sticks. Wrap the standing part across the joint on an angle and continue wrapping along the joint on the opposite angle until a tightly sealed joint has been made. Finish off the process with a second clove hitch.

Shear lashing.   This method is used to bind sticks or poles together as they lie parallel. When spread, they form a base. Two pairs will serve as a trestle; three poles lashed together will make an excellent tripod. Place the poles side by side and make a clove hitch around one stick near the top. Take 3 to 5 loose turns around the poles. Wind the rope between the poles so that the binding is pulled more tightly together, and complete the shear with another clove hitch. In this manner, the skeleton or framework for a tepee, tripod, windbreak, or clothes dryer can be made.

Pole splice lashing.   To repair a broken mast, flag pole, inside tent pole, or to lengthen a short pole, simply place two poles of about the same diameter end to end. Lay other sticks alongside of the ends so that they extend several feet from the ends in both directions. Make a clove hitch around the top of the splint sticks and the pole, and wrap the standing part tightly around the hitch. Carry the standing part down from the initial winding, make another clove hitch, and wrap the rope tightly around the second hitch. Repeat this process at the point where the pole ends meet and again just below. Finish off with a final clove hitch. The rebuilt pole will be strong.

Malay winding.   This technique is used to fasten reeds, straw, or clumps of grass for matting, roofing materials, flooring, window curtains, or siding for temporary shelters. It is simply a series of figure-8 windings around bunches of fiber or other soft material. The entire construction can easily be shaken apart in short order without leaving any knots in the rope.

Continuous lashing.   This method is used when shorter sticks are needed to join larger or longer poles. Typically, the larger poles are notched to receive the smaller ones. The lashing begins with a clove hitch at one end of a long pole. The hitch is made in the middle of the rope or cord so that the two ends are even. The rope is then brought across the back of the long pole, up and over the first short stick. This process is repeated until all the short sticks have been joined to the long pole. It is as though the short sticks were laced to the longer poles. Complete the lashing with a clove hitch or two half hitches. Tuck the ends in carefully. Continue the procedure with a second piece of rope for the other pole until all the sticks have been joined to it. The result of such work may be a wooden walkway, tabletop, stretcher, ladder, or drying rack.

SURVIVAL TECHNIQUES

It is unlikely that any youngster sent to resident camp will be placed in a situation in which her survival depends on how long she can maintain herself without shelter that has been provided for her, food that she has packed, or camping gear that has been supplied to her. Yet survival techniques should be taught as part of every camp program. Emergencies can arise: a camper could get lost on a trip or separated from her party while mountain climbing or spelunking. To survive, the camper must know how to obtain food, water, and shelter. The experience of learning enhances the camper's feeling of self-mastery and confidence in her ability to survive in rough conditions. A lost camper will rarely be subjected to more than a few hours of solitude. A capable counselor will never leave a child (a youth of 16 or 17 is still a child) to wander lost on any excursion from camp; an organized search is initiated as soon as a camper is reported missing. But it is also true that survival techniques as instructional activity offer additional opportunities for campers to learn new ideas and skills.

Remaining Calm

When the sense of utter aloneness hits a camper who has become separated from his group while hiking or exploring, the worst possible thing he can do is to give way to fear. When the camper first realizes that he is on his own—without, perhaps, food, water, or tools—he can feel depressed and close to panic; he may feel that his situation is desperate. Actually, this is far from true. Even if the camper does not have a supply kit, he can still remain secure in the knowledge that he can improvise and use his intelligence to obtain nourishment, relative comfort, and safety. First, the camper must persuade himself that he will neither starve nor die of exhaustion, no matter how long he remains isolated. As long as the individual retains self-control and can make some attempt to analyze the situation and conditions that gave rise to the predicament, he will not only survive, but may even have an enjoyable experience to retell to all who will listen.

The person who is lost must first sit down and think. At first, perhaps because of fear, nothing comes to mind; sooner or later, however, if he becomes calm, the camper begins to assess the situation rationally. He checks the contents of his pack or pockets to see what he has in the way of food, tools, utensils, containers, clothing, and other items. Once he has established a list of the items available to him, he begins to think about immediate needs.

Depending on the time of day, he may do one of several things. If it is early in the day, he should seek high ground or a tree he can climb; he may then be able to pick up some signs of his party or some idea of which direction he has come from. Food is not terribly important at this time. If it is late in the afternoon, the camper may want to seek shelter. As long as he has the energy, he may wish to construct the simplest trail shelter, a lean-to, against any large fallen tree trunk or outsized boulder. After fashioning the shelter to protect himself from any wind and rain, he should build a fire. For such a situation, the reflector fire is probably best; it is easy to make, and throws enough heat and light to keep the camper comfortable for the night.

The camper now has some time to think about the next few days. He has several alternatives. He can wait for rescue; he can strike out on his own and hope to cut a trail or find some route back to the main party or the previous camp site, if one was made. If the camper is reasonably warm and dry, has shelter, and feels that he can supply himself with food and water, then he should remain where he is. He can best help himself by building a signal fire or smoke signal that can be spotted from the air or by those on foot who are searching for him. If the camper reasons that he cannot remain where he is because of lack of food, shelter, or water, he should try to recall how he became lost. This gives the camper a chance to orient himself. He may be able to reconstruct the path that led him out of his way. The camper can always scratch out a crude map on the ground in an attempt to place himself. Sometimes this method helps the camper think clearly and to extricate himself with little effort from what might be a bad situation.

Making a Plan

Most individuals who become lost in woods, swamp areas, or even on flat plains wander around in circles. For this reason, it is best to have some plan in mind before striking out across territory that is relatively unknown. The camper should consider how long it has been since he last knew where he was. It may be that he can recall the last known landmark he saw and roughly estimate the time he has traveled since seeing it. The camper may also recall other terrain features, such as hills, streams, flat spots, or big rocks. These should be marked on an open patch of ground. The simple map may assist the camper to backtrack with relative ease. From wherever the camper begins, he should leave a clearly blazed sign. If there is a big tree to mark the spot, the trunk should be blazed on four sides. If the camper has neither been found nor picked up his former trail by late afternoon, he should retrace his steps to the blazed tree and prepare to stay the night. He can do this easily if he cut bush marks while trying to find his camp. In all probability, the camper should then sit tight and wait for help to arrive.

A shelter even more primitive than a lean-to can be used. In deep woods, there are always solid fallen trees lying flat on the ground. These can be used either as a backlog for a reflector fire or, if building a shelter is out of the question, as a windbreak. In summer, a bed of leaves or pine boughs can be used for bedding. The camper should choose a spot on which to lie for the night. Naturally, it should be on the lee side of the tree—that is, out of the wind. A fire should be built on that side. The fire can be constructed so that it is as long as the camper's body and at least as wide. This is done to dry out the ground. If the camper has an entrenching tool or can find a flat rock with which to dig, he may scoop out a shallow trench and build his small fire in the trench. He can then line the trench with leaves, boughs, or a tarpaulin, if he is carrying one.

The camper should then collect as much hardwood and other flammable wood as is readily available for the night fire. The night fire can then be built to provide warmth. If matches are not available, manual or friction methods must be applied to ignite the fire. The fire bow is probably best, but if nothing else is available, the primitive rubbing together of two sticks can always be used as a last resort. Sparks can also be struck from a variety of rocks with some steel—the camper's knife, hatchet, or other metal objects.

Preparedness

The remote possibility of becoming detached from an out-of-camp party should not preclude being prepared for such an adventure. Every camper should have an emergency kit, which should help maintain survival confidence and prevent panic. The kit should contain emergency rations, including aluminum-packaged sugar, hard candy, cookies, chocolate, salt, canned meat, dehydrated foods packaged in foil, a canteen full of water, rope, clasp knife, steel hatchet, waterproof container of wooden matches, first aid kit, shelter-half, tarpaulin or rubberized poncho, and a light, self-contained sleeping bag. This gear should weigh no more than 25 pounds and can be carried with ease. If anything must be omitted from the pack, it should be either the sleeping bag, shelter-half, or poncho. The tarpaulin can serve as an effective ground cover, windbreak, or blanket if necessary. Utensils can be made from materials found in the open. Pots and pans are not necessary; they just take up weight and space. With a hand map of the area to be covered, a field compass, and certainly a wrist watch, the emergency gear is complete. Woodcraft knowledge plus the implements included in the kit should permit the reasonably intelligent camper to survive for days and even weeks, if necessary, in relative comfort.

Drinking Water

Without doubt, water or other potable fluids are the most important consideration for survival. One never knows the length of time to be spent living on survival techniques. Most people can survive for many days without food, but few can go for any prolonged period without water. All surface water is suspect of contamination. No matter if it is running or stagnant, any water should automatically be considered polluted. However, if the camper finds herself near a lake, spring, or other source of water, she can safely drink it if she boils it first. To be absolutely sure, water should boil for 5 minutes. Boiled water tastes odd, but it sustains the individual for as long as she must maintain herself. Rainwater provides a safe drinking supply, if it can be caught in a clean container; a dirty container or anything that soaks up water, such as clothes or blankets, can be pressed into service if the rainwater is then boiled.

If no surface water is to be found anywhere in the vicinity and the weather does not indicate rain, other liquids must be found. In an emergency, sap can be obtained from trees. No attempt should be made to milk sap from softwoods, however. Sap from hardwoods such as hickory, maple, and most of the fruitwoods are potable. The camper should try to find fruit trees or berry bushes. Most fruits contain water, and the juice may prove both nourishing and thirst-quenching. Grapevines may yield water if the vine is cut at a high point and held vertically while another cut is made close to the ground. Potable liquid will begin to drip from the lower end.

Food

Suppose that the lost camper is carrying nothing edible. How can he survive? First, every well-nourished person has a good supply of subcutaneous fat or adipose tissue on which to draw. He does not have to eat for several days. There are recorded cases of individuals having absolutely nothing to eat for several days who managed to survive because they had drinking water. In other instances, those without food and water have survived because they did not move around much, and thereby conserved energy and body moisture. Nevertheless, even if caught without food, the camper can live off the land.

The novice often overlooks many recognizable edible plants in his haste to find the familiar fruits, nuts, and berries. Campers should learn to distinguish common edible plants from poisonous plants. Many edible plants can be substituted for green vegetables, meat, and sweets, or can be used to flavor beverages. Although the camper should be able to identify safe plants, even poisonous plants can be eaten in minute quantities without much ill effect. Edible plants include flowering plants, roots, tubers, nuts, berries, and fruits of all kinds, as well as what might normally be considered weeds. Dandelion, sorrel, chinchweed, watercress, wild leeks, onions, garlic, milkweed, cattail, and skunk cabbage, along with many less familiar plants, can be eaten raw or cooked. Preferably, all of these plants should be cut up and boiled. In addition, wild berries such as blueberries, dewberries, blackberries, suckleberries, cranberries, raspberries, and several wild fruits can be used. Tree bark, nuts, and other condiments can be added to these by crushing, grinding, and boiling leaves, stems, or twigs.

In a wooded area, the intelligent person can always find water, food, and some type of shelter. One cannot remain long in a wooded area without hearing or seeing some other living thing. Any living animal can become part of the diet if the stranded person has a weapon; with a little patience and ingenuity, living creatures can be trapped and eaten. When a person has not had any food for several days, normal eating habits will be almost forgotten. Anything that can be eaten, cooked or raw, will most certainly be consumed. Frogs, snakes, minnows, birds, grasshoppers, field mice, and any mammal will be part of the food supply. As Calvin Rutstrum states, "Since you will be converted to a raw meat-eating savage after missing about twenty meals (and this on authority, no matter how nice and fastidious your appetite) don't worry about being able to eat such second-choice items. Your once jaded appetite will now not only tolerate but relish them."[2]

Shelter Building

Even without tools, the camper can construct a comfortable shelter that will keep her warm and dry during the heaviest rainfall. Some features

[2]C. Rutstrum, *The New Way of the Wilderness* (New York: Macmillan, 1958), p. 269.

of building shelters have already been discussed. Many kinds of temporary shelters can be constructed with little effort and some ingenuity. Where tents are unavailable, but wood is obtainable, crude and sturdy protective places can be designed. If the camper has a tarpaulin, less effort is needed. If she has enough rope or heavy cord, quite a handsome edifice can be manufactured. But assuming that all these materials are unavailable, and the camper has only her knowledge to assist her, how can she gain shelter from inclement weather and make herself comfortable?

Stick lean-to. The easiest and crudest shelter can be prepared without any tools. Find an upright boulder or cliff face. A tree, whether fallen or standing, will suffice. Gather as many 6-foot poles or sticks as possible. Lean them against the tree. If the ground is soft enough, drive the poles into the ground at an angle and then lay them against the backing. Cover the sticks with boughs of pine, hemlock, or other softwood branches that can be torn loose from a tree or picked up from the ground. Trees should not be maimed or destroyed, but in an emergency, a human life becomes more important than the health of a tree. One disadvantage to this shelter is that any fire built must be at either end of the lean-to and does not throw much warmth on the individual inside.

Reflector lean-to. The reflector lean-to is constructed in precisely the same manner as any other lean-to, except that its frame is constructed out of poles or saplings that are erected without benefit of a backing. Find poles with crotches intact; the poles should be from 3 to 5 feet long. Find a heavy rock and use it as a hammer to drive the poles into the ground. Set the poles so that the crotches face out to any accessible fallen tree trunk or rock wall. The camper's body length determines the distance between the poles. Obtain two poles, at least 4 feet long, and incline them against the two upright poles at about a 45-degree angle, with their respective tops laid into the crotches. These poles must be driven into the ground or weighted with heavy rocks or a log. Sticks may then be collected and laid across these two inclined poles until the top of the pole is reached. More sticks should then be gathered and leaned against the side so that all three sides are enclosed. Any fire that is constructed in the front of this shelter can be backed against a tree trunk, rock face, or boulder. If these are not available, a backlog can be constructed so that the fire is reflected into the lean-to.

Cut-tree shelter. If the camper has a knife or hatchet, it is relatively easy to construct a shelter. The simplest method is to cut or chop halfway through a pine, spruce, or hemlock tree about 5 feet from the ground. Push the top over until it rests on the ground. Since the trunk has only been cut half through, the top and bottom parts will still be attached. Begin to trim off the branches from the inside and save them for use as thatching or for bedding.

Tripod shelter. A tripod frame can be quickly erected if the camper has a knife or hatchet. Cut three poles of not less than 5 feet long. It is most fortunate if the poles are forked at the top because they can then be interlocked. If this is not possible, and if cord or rope is available, lash the tops together and spread them to make an A-frame with the third pole as the ridgepole. Other sticks or poles can be cut to lean against either the top pole or dug into the ground at an angle and leaned against the A-frame poles; additional branches of pine, hemlock, or fir can be cut and placed along the ridge pole to keep out wind and moisture. If a tarpaulin is available, stretch it over the bare frame and place pine boughs on top.

Tree lean-to.   If two trees are found whose lowest branches form a fork, run a horizontal pole between them and through the crotches. Against this lean poles at an angle so that they slope backward to the ground. Cover the roof with boughs of evergreen and allow longer branches to hang over the sides.

There are many other types of temporary and emergency shelters that the camper can make (Fig. 17-10). Depending upon the tools, gear, and materials available, the innovative camper can construct a variety of shelters—

FIGURE 17-10.   Constructing shelter with whatever is handy. (Courtesy of Crane Lake Camp, West Stockbridge, Mass.)

wooden nooks, tents, frames, woven cords to hold clumps of rushes or grass together, combination logs, sticks, and canvas or rubberized material, te-pees, wickiups, or huts over which are placed evergreen boughs, canvas, or mud and grass. Shelter building will be the result of camper intelligence applied to the situation in which he finds himself, and the instruction he has received in survival techniques.

chapter 18

Exploration and Travel

The modern camp must have an attractive program if it is to maintain its hold on campers. Campers who have spent two or more seasons at the same residential camp may find that it does not offer them the same stimulation it once did. The camp can overcome such boredom by offering opportunities for new and exciting experiences away from camp.

TRIP CAMPING

Trip camping takes advantage of the skills and knowledge of the more mature campers, gives them individual responsibility for maintaining themselves, and provides an experienced guide to assist with the daily needs of food, clothing, and shelter. A trip can be an ideal occasion for getting out into remote wilderness regions, for seeing the country firsthand without modern comforts and conveniences. Camps not fortunate enough to be situated in well-forested and appropriate outdoor settings can look to the trip camping technique as a means by which the program and the outdoor environment can be vastly improved. Camps that are well situated may not require an activity that removes the camper from the confines of the camp; the trip can still be included if only to give campers something new to anticipate, and a reason to gain further skills.

Trip Planning

Trip planning requires the same diligence and coordination as all other scheduled camp activities. Perhaps even more effective planning is necessary because the campers will be away from the camp and exposed to hazards that are more easily controlled at camp. Planning for trips begins as soon as the counselor and campers meet. Preparation requires that campers acquire fundamental skills in wood crafts, camp crafts, nature lore, swimming, canoeing, hiking, and, in some cases, horseback riding. The program director and his assistants in the trips program must take care in scheduling trips to avoid conflicts with special events, visitors' days or other phases of the camp program. Careful consideration must also be given to the regular duties of counselors going on a trip; their absence from camp may temporarily imperil the success of activities that require their support.

Although there are unlimited possibilities for camping in remote and primitive areas, some camps prefer to plan their trips so that campers stop at established camp grounds on privately owned property or at state and national parks and forests. In these cases, a well-coordinated plan is mandatory. If the out-of-camp sites must be shared with other units of the same camp, with different camps, or with the general public, detailed scheduling is essential. When campsites become overcrowded or beaten down as a result of constant traffic in the area, even the most beautiful environment loses its attractiveness. Campers do not want to trek across the land and woods to find that they are going to be crowded by others who may have arrived first and now enjoy the best ground or views. Finally, attention must be paid to matters of food supply, method of travel (hiking, bicycling, horseback, canoe, truck), protective gear (tents, foul-weather clothing, sleeping bags), utensils, and personal gear.

Conduct on Trips

The behavior of campers and counselors when participating on any out-of-camp excursion is very important. Habits and attitudes toward the treatment of private and public property must conform to the highest possible standard. Campers must be thoroughly indoctrinated with the idea that respect for the rights and property of others is one of the most significant features of tripping. The camp's good name, as well as the reputation of individuals participating, make necessary absolute adherence to appropriate conduct. All trippers should recognize the value of courtesy. Good outdoor manners provide the greatest good to all participants without infringing upon their right to learn, and without keeping them from enjoying their trip. The following are minimal rules and regulations that should be part of the standard conduct of all trippers:

1. Observe, collect, and learn about, but do not maliciously hurt, damage, or destroy, wildlife or property.
2. Always observe the common rules of courtesy toward all persons met on the trail, in communities, or at campsites.
3. Always clean up the campsite. Make sure that litter has been placed in proper containers, that additional firewood has been chopped for the next user, and that the campsite is well maintained.
4. Take every precaution to eliminate waste and destruction of wildlife by fire. Confine all fire making to proper areas. Take safeguards to prevent fire damage by constructing fires only when needed and making sure that they are extinguished.

5. Leave all trail signs and markers intact.
6. In wilderness or primitive areas, do not strike out across unknown country. Do not become separated from the party.
7. Always have an emergency kit. This should include a compass, a waterproofed box of matches, rations, and one sharp tool.
8. Never cut across a field or take any produce unless permission has been granted.
9. Follow the directions of counselors explicitly.

Safety Precautions

Camp directors with long experience and those members of the staff charged with programming out-of-camp trips realize that every safety precaution must be taken to prevent danger to campers. Leadership is the single most essential factor in reducing hazards, eliminating risks, and providing the kind of guidance that young people require when they are taken out of a highly structured residential camp situation.[1] The following safety policies apply to tripping and other out-of-camp excursions:

1. Small groups are more appropriate than large ones for extended excursions, particularly orienteering, cross-country saddle, and canoe trips. If possible, the ratio should be no more than four campers to each counselor. On hikes, groups can be divided, but each group should be led by a counselor.
2. Whenever groups or units leave camp on a scheduled hiking activity, one leader or counselor should head up the column, while an assistant or junior counselor brings up the rear.
3. Divide campers according to age, ability, endurance, and maturity. The camper's height may have nothing to do with his hiking capability, although it seems reasonable to group shorter campers together and taller campers together so that each group can keep its own pace. If such groupings cannot be devised, short campers should be assigned to the front of the hiking group.
4. Schedule rest stops for relaxation and recuperation as frequently as the campers require. No forced marches are necessary. The child's welfare is more important than covering any predetermined stretch of ground.
5. When walking along a highway, always walk in single file on the left side of the road, facing traffic.
6. If hiking during the twilight hours, wear white clothing and carry lights.
7. Account for all campers at all times. Establish the rule that each camper, when walking on the trail through brush must be able to see the person ahead. Instruct each hiker to hold any low overhead branches aside and not let them snap back into the face of the person following.
8. Never drink from any water source unless there is a sign indicating that it is a publicly approved water supply. Each camper should carry an emergency kit and canteen of water on any trip, route march, or overnight excursion from camp.
9. In unfamiliar territory, make sure that the group arrives at its campsite for the night long before dark. The campers should complete whatever preparations are necessary for making their bivouac comfortable.

[1] R. Macrae, "Trip Leader Training," *Camping Magazine* (June 1976), 10–11.

10. If the hike does not include an overnight stay, make sure that the return to camp begins early enough so that the hikers reach the established camp in good time for either supper or evening activities.

11. Make sure that every camper who participates in an out-of-camp excursion is capable of looking after himself in an emergency by ensuring that pretrip instructions are given and proper training is offered. Even the youngest campers should be prepared to assume some responsibility for themselves.

Excursions

Excursions are travels undertaken to discover something new. The prospect of seeing new places for the first time, discovering phenomena one has heard about, and actually being a part of nature by living in it is tremendously exciting. The opportunity to combine the investigation of unfamiliar places with all of the preparation needed for being on one's own for a day or more is so compelling and attractive to most campers that it becomes a project for developing the most ideal experiences possible. A variety of excursions, both in and out of camp, can be planned and carried out for the instruction and enjoyment of campers of all ages. Depending upon the camp's location, a variety of field trips can be taken to introduce the camper to natural areas in preparation for exploration and travel of increasingly longer duration. In some camps that serve older adolescent campers, an entire summer camping season may be devoted to out-of-camp travel to wilderness areas where primitive or pioneer camps are set up for living.

Exploring

Most children have the desire to explore. The thrill of discovery and the stimulation of going where one has never been before is intensely exciting. It is very important that the camp administration take advantage of this desire and adapt it to a directed learning situation. Campers are quite interested in further investigation of the historical background, legends, and social meanings of specific land areas. If the camp is situated near an area of local, state, or national historical interest, or has such a place on its property, historical hikes and excursions can be made to these places for the pleasure and satisfaction derived from being in a place where history was made.

One such exploring opportunity offered itself at a camp that was situated in an area that had seen Revolutionary War fighting.

Within the confines of the camp, although at some distance from the central area, was a hill that had a peculiar shape at the summit. The intriguing element of the odd shape at the top of the hill, which was otherwise regularly shaped, was enough to arouse the curiosity of several campers. A walk to the hill turned up some interesting facts. A gravel pit, not visible from camp, and completely overgrown by weeds, indicated where the material for the development of the odd mound originated. Tree stumps at the hill's crest indicated the probable age of the trees and the approximate time the mound was erected. At the top, a stone shaft was discovered. Further exploration proved the existence of an iron ladderway and two vertical slits near the top of the shaft. Library research added that the abandoned stone shaft had been a thriving powder works that was supposed to supply ammunition to colonial forces during the War for Independence in 1777. What happened to the stone tower that was subsequently used as a lookout station could be made part of a literary activity devised by the program director.

On such an exploratory trip, therefore, campers can learn research methods, discover new ideas, and develop a healthy and lifelong interest in subjects to which they may never have been exposed. Exploratory trips in or out of camp may offer opportunities for the study of land use, biology, archeology, and many interrelated subjects enjoyable in their own right.

If the camp is situated in an area where there are nearby wetlands, a field trip can be organized to investigate them. Indeed, the camp should make good use of any unusual terrain or geological features, particularly if such areas have been examined by competent counselors with an eye toward offering the greatest acquisition of information and enjoyment. Any exploratory trip to a swamp, bog, marsh, or other wetland is valuable not only for campers but for counselors as well. Marshy ground invariably produces a phenomenon called a quaking bog. It is a unique experience to realize that one is walking out over water on a closely interwoven mat of spagnum moss and swamp grasses. All the plants observed in the vicinity are also living over the water; this can be demonstrated by having the group jump up and down in unison. Trees, shrubs, and bushes almost 20 yards away are seen to shake. Wild life, plants, and a variety of specimens can be collected and classified, and the ecological significance of each, in terms of its relationship to the habitat, can be discussed endlessly. Such an experience can provide a full day of real and lasting value to campers; it provides an appreciation of living things in relation to one another, and it introduces significant concepts of conservation practices so difficult to attain later in life.

Hiking

The need to know how to walk while on exploratory hikes through woods, fields, or along trails seems to be taken for granted. And yet walking, like other motor skills, requires some adaptation to the terrain features through which the individual is moving. The hiker does not have smooth sidewalks to travel over. She must have her weight evenly distributed along the entire foot, rather than at the heel and then at the toe as does the city pedestrian. The hiker needs to keep her toes, and therefore her foot, pointed straight ahead or slightly inward. She does this to minimize the likelihood of tripping over small projections in the underbrush or on the trail. The hiker must learn to walk with a slight spring to her step. This means that her knees flex at each step. The hiker's stride is probably longer than that of an urban dweller, and there is a slight roll to her gait. Instead of a high, knee-pumping action, the hiker must learn to swing her legs an inch or more to the stepping side. Her feet are placed almost flat with each stride. The center of gravity is not toward the front or back of the foot, but over the entire foot. Thus there is little chance of a twisted ankle or the loss of balance when walking uphill or downhill while carrying a pack.

Foot care.   Nothing is more important to the hiker's comfort than having his feet in good marching condition. While it may not be necessary to toughen the feet, as do mile walkers or soldiers, the camper should be aware that any hiking requires his feet to be able to withstand the stress of a great deal of pressure. Good foot care begins with proper equipment. Heavy woolen socks, preferably cashmere, should be worn for extensive hikes. Stout walking shoes with cut down tops are better than high, laced boots, which do not permit ventilation of the feet. The socks will allow free circulation of air around the feet and will prevent saturation by perspiration.

Preparation.   Counselors responsible for the hiking party should see that campers do whatever is necessary to prepare themselves for long walks. Each morning before starting on the hike, campers should rub talcum powder over their feet and dust some inside their shoes. Powder should be used freely over those parts of the body most likely to become chafed as a result of long walks. Feet should be kept clean and dry, and toenails should be clipped short.

Blisters.   Blisters form on skin that is constantly rubbed. The heat developed as a result of friction between the outer layer of the skin and the material with which it comes in contact causes the rubbed spot to become raised with fluid, separating the outer skin, or epidermis, from the true skin, or dermis. The dermis is quite sensitive and easily infected; it should therefore be kept covered by the blister until the fluid is absorbed, or at least as long as the blister can be kept intact. To maintain the blister, it should be covered with some kind of softening agent (petroleum jelly, for example) and a gauze bandage. If the blister must be opened, it should be perforated with the idea of keeping the area as sterile as is possible. The lancet or needle must be sterilized; the point of the instrument should then be injected at the margin of the blister, and the fluid gently pressed out. Thereafter, the area should be kept covered and dry. If the blister is broken before treatment is available, the edges should be trimmed with sterile scissors, and the area should be treated as a wound.

Building endurance.   Counselors must remember that, although they may be accustomed to a steady pace and experience no fatigue on a short walking trip, young campers find hiking difficult and quite tiring even over relatively short distances. Walking is certainly not enjoyable if the consequences of the walk are fatigue, sore feet, muscle cramps, thirst, and frustration. Counselors should accustom their campers to the rigors of hiking by scheduling nature walks, field walks to nearby places of interest, moderately long walks to historic sights, and finally a full-fledged overnight hike to a reservation within a few miles of the camp. The gradually lengthened walks build the stamina, skill, and degree of tolerance necessary for the camper to feel confident and comfortable on a hike. The counselor should attempt to lighten thoughts of physical effort by suggesting a variety of games, songs, and tactical stops for rest and relaxation.

Although hikes are often organized to cover a particular distance in a given time, there is no reason that hikes cannot take advantage of the scenery and terrain being traversed. The wise counselor knows the limitations of his charges; he is completely aware of their capacity to endure and sustain a steady pace, and he is sensitive to their need for rest stops. Unless the idea of the hike is to develop endurance or is a part of a competitive exercise for speed and distance, there is no reason for pressing campers to do more than they are capable of doing. The fun of the hike comes not only in the walk, but in what is seen and done while walking.

Backpacking

Some hikes are planned for one or more nights to be spent out of camp. These forays demand sound planning, adequate preparation, and previous practice on the camper's part to develop endurance; the camper will also need to have acquired basic camping skills, and will need a compact, fully equipped rig in which comfortable clothing, sleeping gear, foul-weather protection, and basic tools are carried. Packs must be kept as light as possible and still provide whatever supplies are necessary for comfort and protection while living outside. Backpacking must be enjoyable. Campers should not be subjected to experiences that become frustrating because of poor equipment.

The best pack is strong and long-wearing, spacious enough to handle all required supplies and equipment, and easy to put on and take off. It should ride lightly on the lower portion of the back. Perhaps the best pack is made of waterproof canvas with a central pocket, smaller back pockets, and two smaller side pockets. Flaps are provided to close over objects placed inside; the flaps have buckles or snaps that can be closed for security. Loops are also provided for strapping or attaching other articles that cannot be accommodated in the pack pockets. A light metal frame is attached to the sack; leather shoulder straps are slung on the frame. A web of elasticized cloth is stretched across the bottom part of the sack and rests against the lower back or top of the hips.

The pack should be so fixed to the camper's body that it rests below his shoulder blades and on his hips. This will prevent a feeling of topheaviness by lowering the center of gravity. Instability is thus lessened, and the camper can walk with greater ease and comfort. Since the harness actually flares out and away from the back, good air circulation is ensured. This does away with overheating and chafing. The load comes directly down on top of the shoulders and does not pull the walker backward, as there is no compensation needed to counterbalance back strain.

Overnight Hikes

The overnight hike offers the camper a chance to show her mettle. It involves the use of skills, a knowledge of walking, and cooperation among peers, and requires that the camper, once she has begun a trip, follow through and complete the job. Each camper must accept responsibility for a share of the work to be performed. Young campers probably should not be taken on overnights because they do not have the necessary stamina or skills in camp crafts. But they can participate in a modified overnight hike if they indicate a desire and willingness to cooperate with their companions. For a modified overnight hike, supplies can be trucked to the campsite (so campers do not have to carry them), or the campers themselves may be transported to and from the site to eliminate excessive walking.

The overnight hike can be planned for bunks, units, and large groups. The significance of an overnight hike as a method of promoting self-sufficiency cannot be overlooked. The campers, with the counselor's assistance, arrange for their food and plan for shelter, sleeping gear, and adequate clothing. Counselors must be prepared for the work that such a hike entails. Being aware of the importance that the camper attaches to her first trip out of camp, the counselor should extend himself to make it a truly satisfying experience. There is little question that counselor satisfaction is derived from realizing that his efforts have contributed a positive attitude and something of lasting value to the camper.

Overnight hiking gear.   The manufacturers of camping equipment have not lost sight of the fact that "packing in" has become a big business; this has been reflected in the types of material and in the many kinds of gear available to ensure efficiency, comfort, and ease of carrying.

Campers who participate in exploratory trips, overnight hikes, or back-country travel for relatively long periods must be furnished with equipment that is economical in its ability to carry all that is needed. This means that the pack must be strong, lightweight, comfortable to wear, and capable of stowing sleeping bags, eating utensils, food, survival kit, water supply, and shelter. Not all packs must have such capacity. Short trips require fewer supplies and less equipment; therefore, the pack can be smaller. Conversely, longer excursions or expeditions require elaborate packs designed to permit great freedom of movement while enabling the camper to carry a maximum load.

Manufacturers have developed lightweight material, usually made of nylon and webbing, both interior and exterior aluminum tubular frames, and adjustment mechanisms that permit the pack to be shifted according to the hiker's physique and comfort. Most modern packs have jointed frames, which enable the upper and lower sections of the pack to accommodate to the hiker's thigh and shoulder movements.

What is true for packs is also valid for sleeping gear and shelters. Sleeping bags of light weight, but containing filler material that permits body warmth to be maintained and protects the sleeper to a predesignated cold temperature, have long been available. These bags can be tightly rolled and attached to the pack for ease of carrying. Pup tents, shelter halves, domes, and pyramid tents, all made of water-repellent nylon, are exemplary. Of course, new materials are constantly coming on the market. Camp operators should check out such gear by seeing what a reputable consumer's advocate has to report about items that have been tested.

A number of light, strong, safe, efficient backpacking stoves are available. They can be used to supplement the typical camp fire beloved by countless generations of campers, particularly if the weather turns inclement and foraging for fuel becomes difficult. Propane and butane stoves have been popularized by those who travel or live in trailers. Propane or butane cylinders must never be crushed or punctured, however, because of their potential to explode if residual fuel remains. Proper disposal prevents this occurrence. Sterno, the old standby, is an excellent cooking source for small, simple meals.

Finally, the utensils necessary for cooking, water supply, and food supply are available in a variety of materials. Aluminum cooking utensils are the most efficient, while unbreakable plastic plates, cups, and bowls are fine for hot foods and liquids. Again, new materials for every backpacking need continue to appear, and camp operators should examine the newest products to determine costs, effectiveness, efficiency, and other variables to guide their choices.

PATHFINDING

The ability to find one's way through unfamiliar territory or even over known ground under average conditions should be acquired very early by those who participate in outdoor living. Pathfinding is a learned skill that permits an individual to find his way without the use of compass or map. There are times when, in the process of stalking, hunting, or observing, complete attention is absorbed in the activity and the hiker may wander far afield. Under these circumstances, it is relatively easy to lose one's bearings if either compass or map has been left behind. A basic rule for traveling in open or heavily wooded country is to carry a map, a compass, and a waterproof box of matches. The best advice, of course, is not to get lost. By taking reasonable and prudent measures, a camper can avoid a situation in which others will have to organize a search party for him, or in which he finds himself alone and unable to distinguish north from south.

Base Line

When camped for several days in an unfamiliar place, it is best to explore the area immediately to the north and south of the camp. Knowledge of the district above and below the camp, as well as familiarity with some terrain feature that clearly marks the section in which the camp is located will be valuable when returning after a long hike. If the camp is established on a stream, lake, or river, the camper should remember to orient himself in terms of flow. Thus, if the water flows north and south and the hikes are to the east or west, it is impossible to go beyond the base line no matter how far one travels in a given day. If there is no water course along which the camp may be pitched, then other terrain features must be selected. A deep draw that runs the length of a valley, a range of hills against which the camp is nestled, or high ground that cannot be bypassed without instant recognition will do for a base line. In any event, the camper should range above and below the camp for one or two miles in each direction and mark the base line with blazes every half to quarter mile. The arrangement of blazes clearly indicates the direction from camp.

Trail Marking

There is a well-known system of marking by which the hiker or hunter, in unfamiliar surroundings, can guide himself. When the hiker is following a poorly defined trail or establishing a new one through densely forested areas, he should make blaze marks on trees at about chest height. One blaze indicates the direction away from camp; two blazes indicate the direction toward camp. The blazes are cut into the tree on opposite sides. This gives the camper quick reference to his position so he can find his way back to camp.

Bush marks, on the other hand, do not require cuts into the plant. A bush mark is made by bending over the top of a bush in the direction being taken. The shrub can be either snapped or cut, but the attachment should be maintained so that the bush leans in the outward-bound direction. Clumps of grass, tied together and folded in the direction of travel, a mound of stones erected in such a manner as to show direction, or sticks pushed into the ground or placed in combination with stones or other convenient materials can tell the traveler in which direction he must move to reach his base camp.

Divides

In any region of the country there are bound to be rivers, streams, and watersheds. Divides are areas of land that run between streams and rivers as ridges. Instead of following a stream, which may necessitate several fords or even portages, where thick and tangled underbrush may grow to the water's edge, the hiking group should keep to the ridge lines that divide water courses. The dividing ridge generally has limited vegetation, thus making passage easier and allowing scenic vantage points to be reached. Where there are no trails and where dense woods hinder vision as well as progress, the back of the ridge is the most dependable line of march to follow. The ridge divides watersheds and permits access north and south or east and west, depending upon the direction of water flow.

Natural Guides

During the day, when the sun shines, it is comparatively easy to find east and west. When the sun is hidden due to cloud cover, the hiker may still determine east–west direction by slowly rotating any thin, flat reflecting surface, such as a knife blade, and holding it perpendicular to any glossy surface object—the thumbnail, a watch case, or a metal tool. Unless the day is extremely dark, a faint shadow will be seen. The sun is in the opposite direction of the shadow.

At night, a knowledge of the circumpolar stars quickly indicates north. By scanning the skies for the Big Dipper, spotting the two pointer stars at the end of the bowl, and following them to Polaris, north is approximately determined. Cassiopeia or Draco can also be used to determine Polaris.

Moss growth.   Many people feel that the story of moss growing on the north sides of trees is a myth. Nevertheless, this natural sign may indicate a northerly direction to those who are sharply observant. First, moss grows more abundantly on those sides of trees where moisture is retained over the longest period of time. Since moisture evaporates last from the side that has a northerly exposure, it stands to reason that more moss is found on that side of the tree. The tree should be fairly straight, not leaning in any particular direction. The bark must be smooth; no attention is paid to rough knots, forks, or dead fall. Trees with rather straight shafts offer the best evidence since an even distribution of moisture forms all around. Special attention should be paid to trees that have grown in isolated sections, free from competition, so that they receive direct sunlight throughout most of the daylight period. Moss growth almost invariably occurs on the northern surface of the tree.

Conifer tips.   The topmost branch of any tall evergreen appears to incline toward the southeast. In almost five out of seven cases, conifer tips point slightly south of east. One must not look for such signs in deep, narrow valleys or on windswept ridges.

Bark.   The bark of old trees appears to be thicker on the north and east sides of trees, with thickness also being present in a northeastern direction. The predominant direction of bark growth is north.

Plants.   Some plants characteristically follow the sun. The sunflower presents its face to the east and then swings with the sun's orbit. There are plants, such as the rosinweed, that consistently face to the east. Before participating in overland travels through relative wilderness areas, campers can study other plants to determine their heliocentricity or other directional orientation.

Compass Use

One of the important implements in a hiker's kit is the compass. The compass cannot by itself indicate to a lost child the direction in which camp lies, but if prominent landmarks are noted before leaving camp, compass reading brings the individual back to camp. The compass serves a major purpose by indicating an approximate northerly bearing. If the solitary hiker knows in which direction north lies, she will probably reach her destination without undue apprehensiveness.

The compass itself should be strong enough to withstand shocks, but sensitive enough to offer relatively accurate readings. It should have a nonmetallic cover (preferably plastic) and a sight by which readings can be made. A compass should be large enough to be read easily. The needle should be at least 2 inches long, with an arrowhead so distinctive that north is seen even when the lost camper's logical thinking processes are not functioning well. The compass should have a release knob that permits the needle to swing freely when the user desires it.

Magnetism and the compass.　The compass works on the principle of magnetism. The earth has a magnetic field that runs from north to south, with one magnetic pole in northern Canada several degrees west of 90 degrees, and another near Antarctica in the sea; a magnetized compass needle tends to parallel the magnetic field and therefore appears to point in a north–south direction. Because the magnetic field does not lie due north and south, but wanders quite erratically, the northerly direction will vary depending upon the individual's location. Thus, if the camper were in Maine, it is likely that a compass reading of north would actually point 20 degrees west of true north. If the camper were hiking through Idaho, the compass needle would point roughly 22 degrees east of true north. The compass declination or variation from true north can be found from maps of local areas. Government charts show the difference between the compass needle and true north.

The places where the compass needle will point to the geographic north are those that follow a meandering line from north to south where there is no variation. This is called the *agonic line.* It generally runs from the north magnetic pole in a southeasterly direction, and it is not static. It changes by moving westward at a very slow rate. Because of this, all locations to the east of the agonic line actually point west of north. All places west of the agonic line actually point east of north. No matter where the individual is located, as long as he understands compass declination, he can align himself properly with a map and determine precisely where he is and how he must travel to reach a particular destination. The difference in a specific region between true north and where the needle points can be determined from Polaris. To be accurate, the observation should be made when the tail star of the Dipper's handle is nearly in line with Polaris and the two pointer stars are lined up with the North Star. This phenomenon occurs when the handle of the Dipper is either directly above or below the Pole Star. It is at this time that Polaris is almost directly over the North Pole.

Inability to understand compass declination and to adjust for magnetic variation accounts for a great deal of difficulty in the wilderness. The most common error is to assume that the needle always points toward true north, or that the error is slight. Thus a degree of declination error would permit a hiker to miss his target destination by almost a quarter mile if he had to walk 3 miles. In heavily wooded or remote places, this inaccurate reckoning might be disastrous. In compass reading, the degree direction is called the *azimuth.* Thus, if our direction is to the northeast, the azimuth reading will be 45 degrees. Theoretically, it should be relatively easy to retrace one's travels simply by reading the back-azimuth. However, with the probability of changing direction, looping left or right, the back-azimuth might not bring us back to our original starting place.

Perhaps the easiest method for determining the location of a base camp is by first establishing a compass reading of the camp in relation to two or more landmarks. The camp lies at the intersection of these readings. These readings should be indicated on whatever map or chart is available. No matter where the hiker travels, the landmarks are visible, within a reasonable distance. The hiker simply lines up the landmarks until they meet

at the predetermined heading; the camp should be at that point. If landmarks are sighted and the hiker is nowhere near camp, he should follow
the preceding method and take readings of the landmarks, tracing their
headings on his map. He is then at the place of intersection, and his camp,
having already been indicated, is determined in relation to where he is
standing.

Another method to use is the single reading from a landmark. When
in camp, the hiker takes a reading of a distant mountain or other prominent
place and draws a line on the map in terms of the degree heading. The line
should run from the landmark through the campsite. When the traveler
desires to return to camp, he spots the landmark and takes a sight with the
compass. He then draws the degree heading on the map and compares it
with the original reading. The relationship between the two will indicate
where the hiker is presently located. In order to return to the base camp,
he charts a course between the present position and the camp's position.

Timepiece Direction Finder

A wrist or pocket watch may serve in place of a compass, if it is keeping
fairly accurate time. The watch should be turned so that the hour hand
points to the sun. Take a relatively straight and rigid object, such as a nail
or knife blade, and hold it vertically so that it casts its shadow across the
face of the watch. Rotate the watch so that the hour hand is lined up with
the shadow. Halfway between the hour hand and 12 o'clock is the south
point. Naturally, such reckoning is valid only in the northern hemisphere;
it is precisely opposite below the equator.

Map Reading

Map reading is rather simple if the camper maintains the idea that a
map is really a picture of the earth, drawn as if observed from a flying plane
and including only the most prominent terrain features. The relationship
between the size of a feature shown on the map and the corresponding
actual feature on the ground is called the *scale*. Understanding scale is vital
to reading a map. Scale can be explained in a variety of ways. The easiest
is the verbal scale, which simply states that one inch equals so many miles.

The graphic scale is a graduated bar or line that indicates the distance
on the ground of measured distances on the graph. This is usually expressed
in some sort of ratio, such as 1:1,000,000. This means that one unit on the
map corresponds to one million units on the ground. The significance of
large-scale and small-scale maps comes in terms of the areas being por-
trayed. Thus, a large-scale map shows a very small land area, whereas small-
scale maps show very large areas or the entire earth.

Signs and symbols attempt to convey pictorially the feature they represent. Thus, almost anything colored blue is water. A thin wiggly line can be
a stream; a thicker blue line, a river; and an irregularly shaped area in blue
may be a pond, lake, or inland sea. All these terrain features depend upon
the size and area in question. Parallel lines indicate roads; a single line and
cross ties indicate railroads; a crossed pickax and shovel symbolize mines.

Contour lines which indicate vertical differences are drawn in black; vegetation is shown in green; and buildings are sometimes indicated by crosses or flags, or are outlined. Bridges, overpasses, underpasses, conduits, fences, and other features may all be indicated symbolically. A legend at the bottom of the map usually explains any symbols used. Once the symbols are understood, the map is easily read.

Determining Location

Just as a compass can help the individual to locate her position in relation to another known place, a map can help the camper determine her location. When traveling from one place to another, either by vehicle or foot, the camper must find out where she is, both on the ground and on the map. Before she can decide on the best route to take in order to arrive at a particular place, she must orient herself. As campers are usually on foot or on trips with canoes, horses, or bicycles, it is possible to climb the nearest high place and compare or orient the map with the terrain by turning the map until its signs and symbols match the visible terrain features. It is then easy for the camper to locate her position: It is the point where all lines between herself and the features on the ground meet on the map.

Direction

When the map is oriented, usually the top of the map is north, the right edge is east, the left is west, and the bottom south. During the day, the sun may be a guide to determine north and south. At night, the Pole Star is of tremendous assistance in orienting the map. Most maps use reference grids or intersecting lines as an aid in determining points on the map. Such index lines are really vertical and horizontal lines drawn over a map to form a pattern of squares or rectangles. These grids may then be divided into smaller boxes—perhaps ten vertical and ten horizontal lines to each grid square. The map coordinates in terms of the major grid square, and the lesser squares provide a fairly accurate method for locating any point.

Orienteering

Orienteering combines the use of map and compass. The activity can be performed as competition, with one or more persons pitted against other individuals or groups. The idea of orienteering is to traverse an unfamiliar area within a certain time limit. Variations of this activity include traveling over a specified distance and checking in at particular route points along the journey. The checkpoints must be reached at a given time. In route orienteering, the campers are given a predetermined route, which is traveled by reaching various stations. These stations must then be indicated on each hiker's map. The winner has the most station indications correctly designated on his personal map. In sequential orienteering, a given number of routes are designated, with each one being reached in some processional order. The participant must decide which route to use in order to reach these points. The points can all be given initially when the competition is announced, or the points can be revealed as each is reached in turn. Essentially, all map and compass work is orienteering. It can be made into a game, or it can have a decidedly serious, survival-oriented purpose.

HOSTELING

Hosteling is the term given to organized caravans or groups of young people or campers who set out either on foot or by bicycle and tour from place to place (Fig. 18-1). Fundamentally, hosteling is very much like route orienteering in that the camper or group travels from one preselected point to another by a carefully established route. Hosteling for older campers should be organized by a specialist responsible for all out-of-camp trips. The necessity for setting up stops at predetermined points is made with the age and capability of the campers in mind. Hosteling can be designed to provide campers with traveling activities either through unfamiliar regions or through areas with which they are vicariously familiar. Periodic stopovers can be established at homes, farms, or other domiciles by contract between the camp and those who own the property, or the campers can be expected to provide their own bivouacs as they journey.

FIGURE 18-1.   A bike hike—one of the camp's off-facility activities. (Courtesy: Donna Richardson.)

Hosteling can combine aspects of orienteering, survival activity, wood-craft experiences, and exposure to settings that would be denied to the camper who is confined to the residential camp grounds. The campers who participate in this type of activity must be mature, skilled in camp crafts and wood crafts, and have the stamina that it takes to pedal a bicycle for 20 to 40 miles each day. Naturally, there are rest stops or stops to take advantage of a pleasing vista or some other interesting phenomenon. Side trips off the main line of travel can also be encouraged, although some sort of schedule must be honored. One or more counselors should accompany any such group. The counselors must be experienced in hosteling and should be acquainted with the region of travel.

Hosteling campers must be equipped for the tour's duration. They should pack on their bicycles all the gear, except food, necessary to sustain them during their travels. Hosteling campers are likely to be traveling along secondary or first-class highways. They can purchase whatever food supplies they need along the way. However, they should be equipped with sleeping and cooking gear as well as foul-weather clothing. Everything else in the way of supplies is superfluous. Hosteling trips are designed to take campers to remote places, but these natural areas can be approached by roads. Although campers will be out for weeks at a time, they can be scheduled to camp at state and national parks and forests on their way to and from a specific destination. Hosteling campers are unlikely to cut across country and off roadways, simply because bicycles do not travel well under such conditions. For these reasons, food purchases can be made daily, just before the meal is to be cooked, unless the group has reached the interior of a national park or forest. In this case, food should be purchased prior to entering the park, for prices are notoriously high in these enclaves.

The entire hosteling procedure can combine the best of camping. It is a tremendously social activity; the camper is in the company of others for one or more weeks at a time. The camp must secure counselors who can function competently under hosteling conditions. The counselor must have the respect and confidence of those who participate. Aside from knowing what to do and how to do it, the counselor must have complete enthusiasm for the project. He needs physical stamina and mental alertness to carry campers through whatever difficulties arise. He must be able to stimulate additional effort from campers when necessary and gain cooperation when conflict threatens the group's harmony. Close-quarter living for extended periods can try the patience of almost anyone; the counselor must be prepared to calm tensions that arise and ease the campers through what could become an unhappy situation. Hosteling is a great outdoor experience; it can be a highlight of the camping season for those who are capable of participating.

SPELUNKING

The science of cave exploration, *speleology,* fascinates those whose interest is aroused by adventure in unique and unfamiliar places. The activity of cave exploration, or spelunking, requires little or no equipment, unless the group expects to remain in the cave for any length of time. In such cases, food and other supplies for warmth and sleeping are required. The adventure begins as soon as the individual enters the passage or opening that takes him into the cavern or underground excavation.

Caves exist in nearly every part of the United States, particularly in those regions that have great limestone deposits. Evidence of subterranean waterways, such as surface sinkholes, are indications that underground caves exist. Thus, Indiana, Kentucky, Tennessee, Virginia, South Dakota, New York, Missouri, Illinois, Arkansas, New Mexico, and other states have small and large caves that have yet to be explored. Some of these areas are honeycombed with subterranean caverns. The Mammoth Cave of Kentucky is merely one of more than 200 miles of galleries that permit passage. The Howe Caverns of New York, the Luray Caverns of Virginia, and many others offer water-carved grottoes, stalactites, and stalagmites of stupendous proportions. Some of these limestone drippings have been named after figures, faces, or scenes that they seem to depict or portray; their colors and formations are unique and wonderful.

The interior of some caves is gigantic. The domes of the largest rise almost 250 feet high and vary in width from 150 to 400 feet. In some of the caves that permit easy walking, the tour can be performed in approximately 9 hours. When uncharted caves are accessible, the possibility of weeks of exploration is not unusual.

Formation of Caves

Caves are formed by ground water that seeps into cracks and crevices in the limestone. Oxygen and carbon dioxide, accumulated by the water from the air and plants, help the water to dissolve the calcium carbonate out of the limestone. When the water reaches an underlying rock structure that is not easily eroded, it begins to cut horizontally. Although the process is slow, it does admit water in considerable amounts. Carried by underground streams, material such as sand and gravel cuts through the limestone and forms the walls of the cave bed. Over a considerable period of time, great caverns are thus excavated. The vaults of caverns sometimes collapse because of the weight of the overhead rock. When the debris of the dome becomes pulverized and is washed away by natural processes, the result is a funnel-shaped cavity which, when it appears at the surface, is called a *sinkhole*. When the dome remains intact, however, a cave is formed.

The same chemical process that hollows out caverns also causes the same spaces to fill up. Above the water table, stalactites and stalagmites have formed. *Stalactites* occur as the result of dripping water. The water, carrying carbonic acid, that eroded the limestone to form the cave initially continues to drip through crannies. As it falls drop by drop, there is deposited a ring of calcium carbonate, around the point from which the water drips. As additional mineral is deposited layer upon layer, the original ring becomes longer until a tube is formed through which the water maintains its steady flow. The tube hardens in consequence of crystallization and thereafter grows thicker and longer as more mineral is added. It may keep growing for hundreds or thousands of years as the flow of water passes along the tube and other deposits are added on the outside through evaporation.

Stalagmites are formed in almost a reverse process. The water on the ceiling that did not completely evaporate leaves the remains of its lime content at the places where it hits the floor of the cave. Here calcium carbonate builds upward in a series of accretions. In time a stalactite and a stalagmite might meet, forming a pillar. Where the seepage from above flows along some fissure, the dripstone finally joins along this line and makes a solid partition. Thus the same chemical action that cut the cave literally reverses itself and can seal up the excavation by the same process.

Spelunking Methods

Before attempting to explore a discovered cavern, it is best to become familiar with the geography of the area. Topographic features should be learned, and main streams and water courses should be noted for direction and depth. Most caves have an entrance through a hillside. Some are located in high mountains, such as those in the vicinity of Monterey, Mexico. Camping groups can take part in spelunking, but it is inadvisable for campers to attempt cave explorations on their own. A bunk should divide into two groups, unless it is agreed upon beforehand not to talk too much once the expedition gets underway. More than four people tend to make too much noise, and the reverberations may actually cause some confusion. Under any cave exploration conditions, a counselor should be assigned to a small party of three campers. The counselors should be adept at cave exploring and, if possible, be familiar with the particular caves to be explored.

Waterproof flashlights, the most important equipment for spelunking, should be carried by each member of the party. The counselor should also have three or more hard candles and a waterproof box of matches in her pack. The counselor should carry a small lantern that can throw light in all directions, as a supplement to flashlights, which throw a beam in one direction only. All flashlights should have fresh batteries.

Clothing should be of comfortable, close-fitting wool. All campers and counselors should have jackets with many pockets for stowing food supplies, water canteen, and other paraphernalia. Headgear is recommended, particularly as another site for light. It is a good idea to wear a hat that can absorb some of the force if the individual inadvertently strikes his head on a low ledge or overhanging rock. Gloves may be worn to prevent the hands from being gashed by sharp projections.

When entering a cave that has not previously been explored, all must proceed carefully. Each camper and the counselor should carry a large ball of white cord that is unraveled as the exploration progresses. Each camper has a turn at the head of the group and pays out his line until it is unwound. The next camper then takes his place and the procession continues. Either the party will reach the end of the cave, or it will have to retrace its steps and pick up more cord. Some supply houses carry reels that permit paying out the cord so that it does not tangle. Wherever there is the least doubt of the return route, the cord should be used.

The collection of mineral specimens is a valuable part of spelunking. Pure alabaster, shales, parts of stalactites and stalagmites, polished lime-stone, and other minerals can be selected for acquisition. A variety of living things—blind fish, mice, and lizards—can also be collected for later investigation.

SPECIALIZED TRIPS

All outings from camp can be looked upon as special events, since they occur beyond the scope of the camp program's intramural activities. However, there are two very individual tripping activities that require special skills, equipment, and experience above that normally needed for the less complex tripping activities of hiking, cycling, or being transported by motor vehicle. These are canoe tripping and horseback tripping.

Canoe Trips

Canoe trips are especially favored by older campers. They may be of almost any duration because the canoe can be packed with gear and food supplies to last for relatively long periods. Canoe travel requires an expertise in swimming, canoeing, camp crafts, and wood crafts. Because the canoe can travel great distances within a short time, a canoe trip can be planned with the idea of covering vast stretches of territory. The camper who participates in this outdoor experience should have developed stamina by taking short trips. He must pass whatever aquatics, boat-handling, and wood-craft skills criteria are devised for campers. Because canoes can travel at speeds of up to 5 miles an hour on smooth water, and even faster when working with a current, it is probably wise to lay over every third day. The constant pounding of canoe traveling can become tiresome after several days. It is best to spend some time ashore in the typical camping activities that one associates with wilderness travel.

Canoe trips are generally planned in regions where lakes, streams, or rivers abound and where there are connecting waterways or short portages from one lake to another. In some areas of the United States, such as the vast wilderness area of the upper Superior region, there are more than 2,000 square miles of canoe-traveling waterways. The northeast is also well known for its hundreds of miles of rivers and lakes capable of being portaged.

Equipment.   The traditional canoe is made of birchbark, but other wood products have also been applied. Modern canoes made of aluminum and fiberglass are available. Even though it is a rattletrap in rough water, the aluminum canoe is far superior in construction and toughness. Styro-foam built into the canoe beneath the bow and stern decks keeps the canoe afloat when overturned. An additional safety feature of this canoe is its ability to right itself after being upset. If supplies are carefully packed and waterproofed, but particularly packed to float, complete recovery of all materials is possible regardless of water depth. Canoes for wilderness and heavy travel should be approximately 17 feet long and 14 inches deep. The deeper draft allows for smoother sailing and greater stability in rough water or in troughs experienced on lakes during any weather where wind-lashed waves may threaten a shallow-draft canoe. Furthermore, deep-draft canoes are capable of carrying far greater loads than shallow-draft canoes (Fig. 18-2).

The beam should be at least 36 inches, and the bottom should be relatively flat. Canoes with flatter bottoms ride higher and are therefore easier to handle and maneuver in shallow water, riffles, and rapids. The canoe is made more completely stable and offers a better ride if the load is trimmed—that is, if it is equally balanced from side to side. It is more efficient to stow gear and supplies toward the rear of the canoe so that the bow rides slightly higher than the stern. The load should be distributed throughout the canoe, to the rear if feasible, but not packed into the ends. In a canoe with adequate depth, packs can be tied in place beneath the thwarts. Figure 18-3 diagrams the parts of a canoe.

Portaging. When there is no connection between bodies of water, the canoe must be carried. The traverse is made around dangerous rapids and waterfalls, and where the watercourse ends. Portaging is usually welcome after incessant paddling. It offers diversion from the sometimes monotonous regularity of sweeping the water. The easiest method for portaging canoes where there is only one paddler is to use the paddles as a yoke or shoulder rail. The paddles should be spaced so that the blades rest on the shoulders while the canoe is carried inverted over the head. Cushioning for the paddles can be made of any soft material. Woolen or cotton shirts, jackets, or spare trousers can be rolled so that the weight of the canoe does not cause too much pressure on the back of the neck and shoulders. Although one person can carry a canoe with comparative ease, it is likely that on any camp-sponsored canoe trip there are two campers assigned to each canoe. When there is any wind, it is best to have another pair of shoulders and hands to steady the load and help lift it. A relatively easy two-person portage is to rest the bow seat on the back of the neck of the other. This method is good only for short hauls, however. The idea of taking turns at packing the canoe can also be tested. When the portage is a long one, it is better to carry a load part of the way and return for whatever is left. The empty-handed return allows for some recuperation. Constant portaging develops stamina, and the individual is soon capable of carrying loads without feeling tired or overburdened. For further information on canoeing, consult Chapter 20.

Tracking. When working into rough water or against a rapid current, it may sometimes be impossible to paddle the canoe. For this reason, it is a good idea to attach two ropes, at least 50 feet long, to the bow and stern of the canoe. *Tracking* consists of towing a loaded or unloaded canoe upstream or downstream. The canoe can be guided by means of manipulating the tracking lines at either bow or stern. Thus, the canoe can be turned away

USE TWO OR MORE CANOES. CANOES MUST BE ABSOLUTELY PARALLEL. LASH CENTER BEAM FIRST; IF THWART IS MISSING, PASS LASHING AROUND THE HULL. LASH THE CENTER CANOE AND THE TWO OTHER BEAMS WHEN LASHING THE PLATFORM. WITH HEAVY LOADS AND CHOPPY WATER, LEAVE CANOES OPEN FOR BAILING, OTHERWISE PLATFORM CAN BE SOLID.

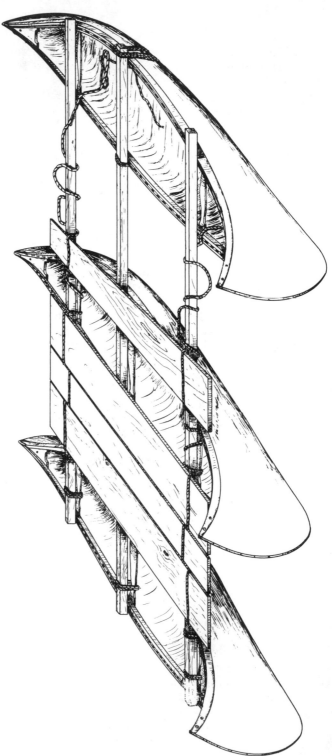

FIGURE 18-2. Canoe catamaran is useful for ferrying supplies.

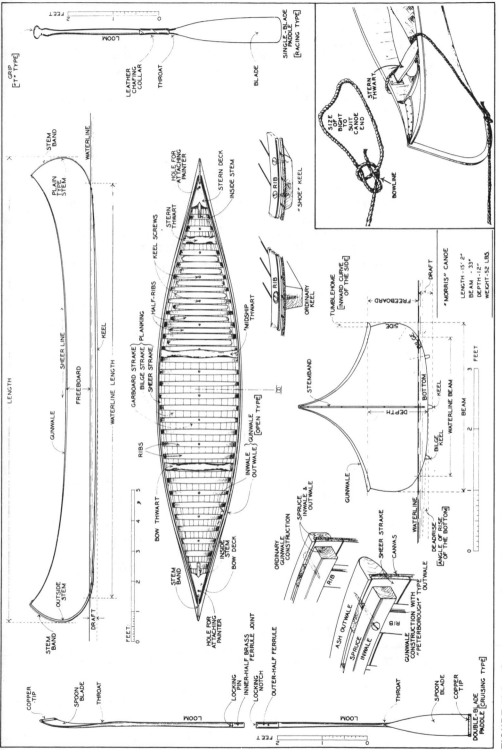

FIGURE 18-3. Canoe nomenclature (insert shows towing bridle).

301

from or toward the shore. By playing out the line or hauling it in, the canoe can be maneuvered around any obstacle. Of course, there must be enough space along the bank of the waterway for an individual to walk. When two campers are canoeing, both may take part in the tracking or one may remain in the canoe and paddle while the other walks along the bank with the line.

Embarking.   Getting into a canoe either from a landing, beach, or dock can damage the canoe and inadvertently drench the would-be canoeist if care is not taken. The best technique for boarding a canoe from a sandy beach or sloping ground is as follows. Two individuals pick up the craft at its center of balance, the center thwart, and carry it stern first and by a hand-over-hand feeding along the gunwales. The bowsman steadies the bow between his legs, while the stern paddler walks down the center of the canoe to her stern position. She will hold onto the gunwales for support while getting to her place. As the stern is heavier because of the added weight of the paddler, the bow will rise slightly. The bow paddler may now enter the craft and push off from the shore.

Where there is a dock or landing, parallel embarkation is necessary. If one person is using the canoe, he may snub the canoe to a mooring place and grasp the far gunwale at the center thwart. Holding the canoe fast to the dock, the camper may then enter the canoe from a crouched position and take his place toward the stern. By releasing the trail line or painter, he is free of the dock. When two campers use the canoe, one may steady it while the other climbs aboard. The embarked paddler steadies the canoe by holding it against the dock as the other camper enters. The occupants are then in position to begin paddling. When landing the canoe, the reverse procedure from embarking is followed.

Safety precautions.   The canoe is thought to be a very unstable craft. This is a myth; in competent hands, the canoe is one of the safest and most seaworthy of all watercraft. Its extreme buoyancy makes it literally unsinkable. Nevertheless, as in any other sport, some precautions must be taken in canoeing. The ability to swim is of chief importance, but this skill alone does not guarantee safety. Several other conditions must be met. A camper must acquire canoeing skills before he is allowed to participate in any trip. Safety procedures should be deeply ingrained in every camper who aspires to out-of-camp excursions.

1. Mastery of all canoeing strokes is essential.
2. Always paddle from a kneeling position except when the water is exceptionally calm or smooth.
3. Never attempt to exchange paddling positions in a canoe. Land first and then shift positions.
4. Carefully distribute the weight in the canoe. Keep the weight low and centered. Trim the craft by equally distributing the weight from bow to stern and side to side.

5. When loading a canoe, load from the middle toward the ends. When unloading, the reverse procedure is the rule.

6. Unless absolutely necessary, it is better not to take a canoe out on rough water during high winds. In meeting high winds or waves, head the canoe either directly to or away from the waves. When caught alone in high winds, it is best to shift the paddling position to the middle of the canoe.

7. If the canoe is overturned by broadside waves, do not leave the canoe (Fig. 18-4). The canoe supports as many people as are paddling it.

8. Attach tracking lines or painters to secure the canoe when mooring.

9. Carry an extra paddle. (See also Chapter 20.)

Horseback Trips

Camps located in pack-horse country can provide campers with the unique experience of horseback trips. Although the acquisition of horses, stables, and gear is expensive for the camp, there is little doubt that the capital returns on the investment are worthwhile to all concerned. In areas of the country that do not normally favor this type of activity, or if the camp had decided not to make the monetary investment in horses and equip-

FIGURE 18-4. Always stay with the overturned canoe.

ment, horseback trips are still possible. The horses and equipment can be rented from a reliable outfitter, who will probably also send along a wrangler or horse handler. Horseback trips can either be of the pack or riding variety.

On horseback trips, light gear is carried, much as that which campers take for a hike. Instead of traveling on foot, however, the horse provides the transportation. Such trips can last one or more weeks, depending upon the amount of feed carried and the terrain over which the trip is planned. The horse can easily carry a rider and 50 pounds of food and gear. The equipment will consist of bedding, tarpaulins for shelter, a few tools, changes of clothing, and perhaps a few more essential items that can be packed because of the extra load-carrying capacity of the horse. The horses must be well fed, cared for, and given a certain amount of shelter from foul weather. The trip must be made where there are known water holes.

Pack-horse trips are somewhat different from horseback-riding trips. If the camp has the outfit, there should be at least one pack horse for every two campers. The trip is much slower than the horseback-riding trip because pack-horse trips normally cover rough terrain. Such outings may be away from camp for periods of up to one month at a time. For this reason, only mature campers who have exceptional wood-craft and camping skills, as well as the ability to ride and manage horses, are capable of taking advantage of this opportunity. The supervisor should be a counselor who is expert with horses, and specifically one who has been or could be a horse wrangler.

Packing.   In order to pack the horse most efficiently and effectively, it is best to use some stout, padded material placed over a saddle blanket. The packsaddle may be of fairly rigid construction but so designed as to fit only the padded back of the horse. It should have small edges or shelves on which the packs can be hitched or attached. Ordinary harness gear holds the entire kit if the harness has rings for a breast and breeching strap. A waterproof packcloth to protect the supplies during inclement weather is also necessary. All supplies can be strung across the packsaddle and tied down. Perhaps the safest and surest technique is to pack the supplies on the ground in two bundles of equal weight. With the horse tethered and harnessed, the two packs are simultaneously placed onto the packsaddle and lashed to it. This maintains balance and ensures the comfort of the horse. The bundles should be made so that they can be tied high on the saddle. Part of the weight thus rests to the rear of the withers. The soft part of the bundle should be against the horse, and the entire pack should be as flat as possible to prevent any back-and-forth movement.

Safety precautions.   As in all trips out of camp, certain rules should be observed for the health and welfare of the participants. Although the gait will probably be a walk, the speed of the group should never be more than the pace that the poorest rider can maintain. When riding hilly terrain, the rider should lean forward to free the horse's hindquarters, thereby giving him greater leverage and walking capability. Saddles should be designed to allow for the greatest ease in riding. For pack or horseback trips of any extended duration, the rider must learn to ride well up toward the withers. There should be a vertical line between the rider's eye, knee, and toe. Sitting in this position takes weight off the horse's loins and permits him a much smoother pace. The rider should always move with the horse, not in an opposite direction. Kindness and gentleness are vital in handling horses, and relaxation is part of riding. The rider should sit erect, guide the horse with neck reins, and enjoy the pleasant sensation of travel by horse. (For further information about horseback riding, consult Chapter 19.)

chapter 19

Motor and Perceptual Skills

Although the residential camp should be oriented toward outdoor living, there is a distinct and necessary place for the programming of a variety of motor skills. One of the chief purposes of providing the opportunity to participate in motor skills at camp is to assist the normal growth and development of each camper. Motor-skill activities are enjoyable means of developing fitness, stamina, strength, and agility. The promotion of neuromuscular coordination, cardiovascular vigor, and good functional health are significant outcomes of athletic motor-skills activities.

Motor skills also often promote a more positive social outlook; skills in sports and games tend to stimulate children and encourage them to participate in wholesome physical outlets. Skill promotes the desire to take part in group activities. The camper who has these skills is likely both to be more adept at social-group interaction and to receive positive responses as a result of his ability to compete with his peers.

All children require physical activity if they are to attain normal growth and development. The child is built for motor skills. The power of muscles, the leverage of bones, and the range of movement accorded by joints are designed for these functions. The structure of the human organism requires that it perform in ways that take advantage of the musculo-skeletal form. Through vigorous activities, the structure of the body and its integrated organs becomes more efficient. The individual becomes able to perform activities that require both large and small muscles, specific coordination, and an evenness of action that is acquired from prolonged practice.

No camp should attempt to modify a distinct camping situation to bring organized team, individual, or dual competitive games to the outdoor environment. There is no need for the highly organized city-type athletic activity. There are so many appropriate motor skills that fit in well with the camping experience that any artificial injection of the typical scholastic athletic program is a questionable practice. Although some special camps are organized around a specific athletic activity, these are less to be considered camps than intensified sports-training centers. There are also some camps that have no competitive athletic contests whatsoever, but generally, almost all camps provide some form of motor-skill experience as one part of a comprehensive and balanced program.

For camps that have a relatively short season, particularly institutional or agency operations whose camping period may be from 1 to 2 weeks long, there is little that can be done in terms of intensified nature science, tripping, or wood-craft activities. However, several outdoor-oriented motor activities can easily be offered. Such experiences are different from those familiar to the urban youngster and are particularly suitable for the camping environment. Activities adapted for ease of instruction and mastery can have carry-over value. Although some activities require 8 to 10 weeks of practice and supervision for the skill to be acquired, others can be taught within 2 or 3 days and can be enjoyed almost from the onset of instruction. As skill is acquired, the activity becomes even more satisfying.

Whatever the duration of the camping season, the program of activities should be sufficiently balanced and varied to provide a comprehensive range of experiences to meet the goals for which the camp was established. Factors such as camper age, sex, maturity, interests, needs, and capabilities must therefore be considered if the program is to be effective. The motor skills that should be included in the camp program are those that approximate experiences that will be useful to the hiker, stalker, or woodsman. There is no need to list individual, dual, and team activities that any city child knows well; some of these activities may have a place in camp, but that place should not be prominent. Activities of this type might be spontaneously initiated, and they should not be prohibited. However, the camp's motor-skills program should stress activities that are consistent with outdoor living.

ORGANIZATION OF MOTOR-SKILLS ACTIVITIES

The success of any series of programmed motor skills depends upon organizational methods, competent guidance, and supervision. Counselors with some general knowledge of sports and games, as well as counselors with highly specialized skills, are invaluable to the production of a soundly planned and satisfying program. The counselors assigned to motor-performance activities should have a genuine enthusiasm for, and a good degree of skill in, the activities that they are teaching.

Among the factors to be considered when grouping campers for motor activities are age, sex, height, weight, maturity, interests, and current level of skill. Although there are variations within age groups, the following developmental characteristics influence participation in motor-skill activities and should be recognized by counselors to whom planning responsibilities are assigned.

Ages 4 to 6

The growth rate is much slower during this stage than at any other time between infancy and adolescence. Children may want to expend a great deal of energy, but they tire rapidly and must rest. During this stage, large-muscle development is most pronounced. Children enjoy activities that require a great deal of running, jumping, hopping, skipping, and climbing. However, coupled with tremendous energy output is a relatively short attention span. Children not only tire easily, they are also easily bored. Activities must therefore be fast, exciting, and quickly finished.

By the time the child is 5 years old he has some skill at ball handling and throwing. Individual differences account for skills, which range from poor to outstanding. Motor skills show an increasing degree of sophistication by the age of 6. The child enjoys social activities and cooperates in games that require chasing, dodging, tagging, and rhythmics.

There are hundreds of activities that children enjoy learning and performing during these years. Some are traditional, ethnic, or simply exploratory. The elements of suspense, rapid movement, simple rules, ease of understanding, and some competition characterize most of them. Line, square, and circle games can be used to maintain individual and group interest. Suggestions for typical games follow.

Little Brown Bear

The children stand in line as though they were on the edge of the woods. A little brown bear lives in the woods. The children wish to go through the woods to the opposite side. They face the little brown bear crouching a short distance in front of them. In her wee voice she asks, "Are you afraid of the little brown bear?" The children answer no and run to the opposite side of the woods, or play space. The little brown bear stands up on her hind legs and chases them. She tags as many as she can. Those whom she touches are her helper bears. The little brown bear then squats before the group, with her helpers in a line beside her. The little brown bear asks the question again. When the answer comes, all the bears chase the remaining children as they run across the play space, and the game continues until all the children become little brown bears. The last child tagged becomes the little brown bear for the next game.

Traffic Police

The children stand in line as if on the curb ready to cross the street. One child is chosen to be a police officer. He stands on the opposite side of the playing area. He calls "green light" and faces the opposite direction from the children, who move forward. He suddenly calls "red light" and then turns toward them. The children must stop immediately. If the police officer sees any child move his feet, that child is sent back to the curb. The police officer continues to call, and the children move forward, or stop, according to the signal. The first child to touch the outstretched hand of the police officer is the new police officer.

Skyball

The players are divided into two teams. Facing one another, they stand on either side of a line marked on the playground. One player, throwing the ball high, tosses it to the other team. If a player on the opposite team catches the ball before it touches the ground, she scores a point for the team. The player who is able to place both hands on the ball first throws it up high to the other team. Each team is careful not to cross the dividing line. The game continues in this manner until 5 points are scored by one team.

Ages 7 to 9

The growth rate of boys and girls is slow and steady at this time. There is a decided integration of the sexes up to about 8 or 9 years of age, and boys and girls frequently play together without difficulty. After age 9, however, there is an equally strong preference for separation of the sexes. There is a need for group or peer acceptance, although individual achievement is a vital factor for motivation. Strong physical movements are noted; vigorous activity predominates. There is a desire for excellence, and the practice of various motor skills seems to come to the fore. One significant feature is participation in team or group activities in which cooperation is necessary. Youngsters at this age want to excel and tend to seek approval from some authority figure—in this instance, the counselor. Physical ability, lengthened attention span, and greater endurance enable participation in activities that have more complex rules and require more time. Games still must be relatively short, but the rest factor is no longer as restricting as before. Lead-up activities for the more highly organized team games should be scheduled.

Among the activities enjoyed by this age group are relays, jumping games, self-testing exercises, hiding and running games, and ball-handling games. The following are some examples.

Circle Chase

The players stand in a circle formation and number themselves around the circle from 1 to 4. The leader then calls one of these numbers. If the leader calls "two," all the players with this number run around the circle once, each player attempting to tag the number-two runner in front of him. All the players who are tagged step into the center of the circle. After each number has been called, the players in the center are counted. The group with the fewest players tagged is the winner. The game is played again with everyone participating.

Gathering Sticks

Two base lines are marked at opposite ends of a playing space at least 100 feet long. This space is divided by a middle line. Six Indian clubs are placed on each base line. The players are divided into two equal teams and are scattered on each side of the center line. On a starting signal, the players attempt to run across the center line into the other team's area and pick up an Indian club without being tagged by an opponent. If a player successfully obtains an Indian club, she may walk back and place it on her base line. Any player who is tagged by an opponent in the opponent's play area becomes a prisoner and must stand on her opponent's base. Her teammates rescue her by running to her if they can avoid being tagged by an opponent. After being rescued, the player may walk to her own side and continue playing. Whenever a prisoner is caught, her teammates must rescue her before they can pick up any clubs. At the end of the playing time, the team with the most Indian clubs on their base line is the winner.

Hook On

Each player selects a partner, joins inside hands with him, and places his other hand on his hip. Partners stand in a play area approximately 5 to 8 feet from the next couple. One player is chosen to be a runner and another to be a chaser. The chaser runs after the runner trying to tag him. The runner keeps from being tagged by hooking arms with another player's partner. The player who is left without a partner in this group of three becomes the runner, and the chaser continues after him. If a runner is tagged while running from the chaser, he becomes the chaser, and the chaser becomes the runner.

Ages 10 to 12

Most children between the ages of 10 and 12 continue to demand vigorous activity. Their muscular development, motor coordination, and stamina are quite good. They are therefore intensely interested in activities that permit them to exhibit skill, talent, and endurance. During these ages, great stress is placed upon participation in competitive team activities. Boys particularly like experiences that require strength and agility for good performance, such as stunts, tumbling, and gymnastics. Girls, on the other hand, frequently show no interest in or desire for such participation. The early-maturing girl is inclined to view such activities as unfeminine.

Corner Dodge Ball

The game is played on a 40-foot square. In each corner and in the middle of the field, a 10-foot square is laid out. The camper groups are divided into several teams of 7 to 9 members each. Each team has a chief who stands in the center square facing the direction in which he intends to throw. Each chief has a rubber ball or volleyball. Each team stands in one of the corner squares. When the counselor signals, all teams run counterclockwise to the next square. As they run, the chiefs attempt to hit players on the opposing teams below the waist with the ball. Players are safe when they are in a corner square. The players who are hit move to the outside of the square and return the balls which are thrown as the chiefs try to hit players. The game is concluded when the players have progressed around the square three times. Teams run only when the counselor signals them to do so. The winning team is the largest number of campers in a square at the end of the game.

Soccer Dodge Ball

The game is played in a circle approximately 25 to 30 feet in diameter. The players are arranged in two teams. One team is inside the circle, and the other team stands on the circle. The team on the circle keeps the soccer ball in play by kicking it, attempting to eliminate the players on the inside of the circle by hitting them with the ball. When a player has been hit, she becomes a kicker. If any player inside the circle steps outside of it, she joins the kickers. The players on the outside must maintain their places. The players within the circle scatter to dodge the ball. The team eliminating the greatest number of players in a given time is the winner. No one is permitted to throw a ball. All balls must be kicked, and they must hit the inner players below the waist.

Ages 13 to 17

The complex changes begun at the onset of puberty and adolescence directly relate to the kinds of physical activities in which this age group participates. Boys are more capable of balancing than are girls. Boys progress and improve this skill, while girls show negligible improvement. Girls seem to exhibit greater perceptual skills; they are more accurate than boys are during this period. Up to the age of 13, girls tend to be more agile than boys; boys easily surpass girls after that age. Boys always exhibit more strength than girls, but the degree of differentiation becomes even more pronounced with maturation. The variations in primary motor skills must be considered by the counselor responsible for the development of the athletic or sports program. Activities suitable to this age group include almost all the standard team, individual, and dual events.

PERCEPTUAL ACTIVITIES

Archery

Archery is a perceptual-skill activity that requires hand–eye coordination in the use of a propelling implement and a missile. Although bow hunting has become popular in the last few years, most participants enjoy the activity by shooting at targets. There are many forms of target shooting. Field shooting requires targets of varying sizes situated at different distances; the object is to hit the target with the fewest possible number of shots. Field shooting, to which camps are ideally suited, necessitates a great deal of space for the targets as well as for safety. Target shooting, on the other hand, has fixed distances from which archers shoot; the object is to receive the highest possible score by hitting the scoring rings in the target.

Archery golf, similar to golf, is played on a golf course or on a specific course designed for archers. The aim is to shoot an arrow from the tee to the green, where a 4-inch straw-ball target replaces the cup.

Clout shooting is long-range shooting at a 48-foot target laid out on the ground. This type of shooting is excellent for teaching the judgment of distances. A number of arrows, usually six ends or thirty-six arrows, are shot from 100 to 200 yards away from the target. The goal, or clout, is in the center of the target, which is ten times larger than the standing 48-inch target. Scores are determined by totaling the points achieved for hitting the scoring rings.

Flight shooting is for distance only. Basically, the idea is to test the strength of the archer and the cast or ability of the bow to hurl the arrow.

No accuracy is involved. In regular flight shooting, the archer stands and draws his bow to the maximum pull he can attain and releases the string. In free-style shooting, the archer may assume any shooting position. Some archers lay down, place their feet on the belly of the bow, draw the string with two hands, and then let fly. Precautions must be taken against danger from stray arrows. As it is not unusual for an archer to shoot an arrow several hundred yards, a long space is required.

Rovers is a game of shooting at any inanimate object on the landscape. Any object—a clump of grass, trees, logs, bushes—constitutes a target. Each archer shoots one arrow at a selected target; the archer who either hits or comes closest to the target receives one point and may then select the next target. The archer with the most points at the end of a predetermined series of marks or period of time is declared the winner. Standard rounds are commonly used for target shooting or in tournament archery competition. The rounds call for shooting a specific number of arrows at each of several fixed distances. Teams usually consist of four archers.

Archery Rules

1. A regulation 48-inch target is used for all competitive and shooting purposes. The target is divided into a center, or goal, 9.6 inches in diameter and colored gold. Around the center are four concentric rings, each 4.8 inches wide; they are colored red, blue, black, and white, respectively. The color values, beginning with gold, are 9, 7, 5, 3, and 1.
2. An arrow cutting two colors is given the higher point value.
3. An arrow passing through the target face or bouncing off the target is given the score of 5 points regardless of where it hit the target.
4. Archers should stand astride the shooting line when shooting.
5. Archers should shoot one end, six arrows, and then all shooters go up to the targets at the same time to score hits.
6. An arrow leaving the bow for any reason is considered to have been shot, unless the archer can reach it without stepping across the shooting line.

Equipment. Archery equipment, or tackle, includes a bow, arrows, quiver, arm guard, and finger tab or shooting glove. The propelling implement, the *bow,* may be of the straight or recurved type (Fig. 19-1). It may be made of wood, fiberglass, or laminate. The bow, particularly if recurved, should be shorter than the individual using it. The *draw weight* of the bow is the number of pounds of pull required to flex the bow to full draw. The average target bow should have a draw weight of between 25 and 40 pounds for males, depending upon age, height, weight, and strength. The average for females is from 20 to 35 pounds. Beginners should start with lighter bows; as proficiency increases, heavier bows can be used.

The majority of fiberglass and laminated bows are recurved or reflex bows. The bow is thickest at the grip or handle. The bow has an upper and lower limb. The part of the bow facing the archer is called the *belly;* that of the opposite side, the *back.* Two *nocks* are situated at the tips of the bow; these are grooves into which the looped ends of the bowstring are placed.

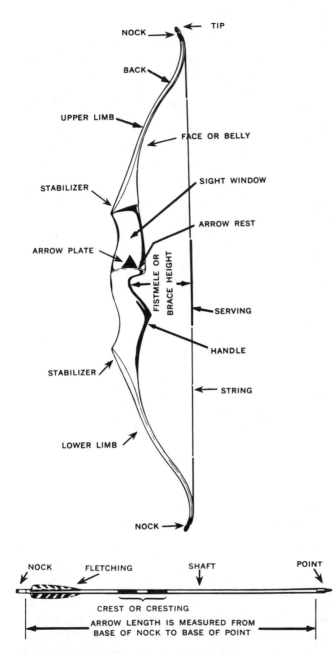

FIGURE 19-1. The recurved bow and arrow.

Some bows have arrow rests and plates that permit the archer to align the arrow and also to protect the flesh between thumb and forefinger from being cut by the fletching as the arrow is released. If there is no arrow rest, the bow hand must support the arrow. Dacron bowstrings are widely used today and are relatively long-lasting. The bowstring has an additional protective covering wrapped around the portion that receives the arrow notch; this is called the *serving*.

An *arrow* is a thin shaft of wood, fiberglass, or metal. It can be hollow or solid. The usual length of the arrow is from 24 to 30 inches, and it is $\frac{5}{16}$ of an inch in diameter. Field, hunting, and fishing arrows are generally longer and heavier than target arrows. The tip, or pile, of the arrow is also differentiated depending upon the target. The main section of the arrow is called the *shaft;* the front, or pointed end, is called the *foreshaft*, or *footing*. The tip is called the *point*, or *pile*. The rear portion of the shaft is the *shaftment*. The feathered end, the *fletching*, is made up of three feathers. The feather set at a right angle to the nock is the cock feather; the other two are hen feathers. The color bands to the front of the fletching are designated the *crest*. The nock at the end of the arrow receives the bowstring. The correct length of the arrow is individually determined and depends upon the arm length of the archer.

All archers should wear some kind of finger and forearm protector in order to prevent blisters, contusions, or welts. A good archer will not hit his forearm with the bowstring, but on occasion the bowstring may snap against the forearm, leaving a welt. If this continues, the skin may be bruised or even broken and lacerated. Leather or plastic guards are attached to the forearm by thongs, straps, or lacing on the back of the arm. Unless the three shooting fingers are well protected by finger tab or glove, they become sore with constant shooting. The tab or glove also permits a smoother release of the string.

Basic Archery Skills

Stringing the Bow   Place the bowstring loop in the bottom nock. Lay the lower curve of the bow over and across the left ankle. The lower limb is then taken under the right thigh. Grasp the upper limb of the bow in the right hand and bend the bow on the recurve. Slip the top loop of the bowstring on the upper nock and release the pressure gradually. Make sure that the bowstring is securely in place before drawing the bow. To unstring the bow, use the same method. Simply bend the bow until there is sufficient slack in the string to allow the loop to be freed from the nock.

Stance   In addressing the target, stand comfortably, head erect, shoulders square, feet slightly separated and approximately 12 to 15 inches apart. The weight is evenly distributed on both feet. The archer's body should be at a right angle to the target. Turn the head in order to look over the left shoulder directly at the target (Fig. 19-2).

Gripping   The bow is held in the left hand by right-handed archers and in the right hand by left-handed archers. Hold the bow so that the grip is against the base of the thumb and the handle is gripped by the thumb

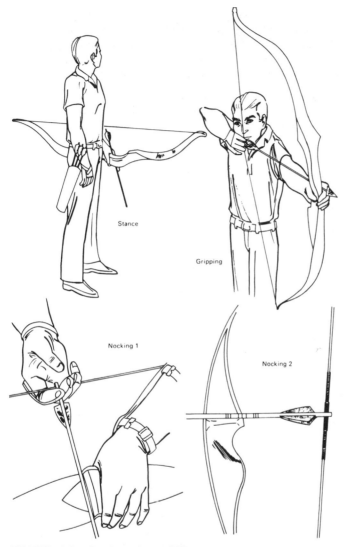

FIGURE 19-2.   Basic archery skills.

and forefinger. The other three fingers can be placed on the grip, but this is not necessary. The palm should be down. By rotating the elbow outward and keeping the palm of the hand facing down, the bowstring can be released from full draw without having it slap against the forearm. The bow arm should be raised to shoulder height (Fig. 19-2).

Nocking   Grasp the bow as just described. Hold the bow directly in front of the hip and horizontal to the ground. With the right hand, place an arrow in the rest and set the arrow nock on the bowstring at the serving so that the cock feather is up or at a right angle to the bowstring. The arrow should be at a right angle to the string. Place the first three fingers of the drawing hand on the string at the first joint. Rest the arrow nock between the first and the third fingers. Rest the fourth finger on the serving. There is no need to pinch the arrow nock between the fingers. The arrow will stay on the bowstring without any pressure if properly seated (Fig. 19-2).

   Drawing   The draw, or spreading the bow, is performed by grasping the serving above and below the arrow nock and pulling it back until the anchor point is reached. The drawing arm is clearly an extension of the arrow (Fig. 19-3). A line drawn through the arrow would continue straight

FIGURE 19-3.   Shooting sequence.

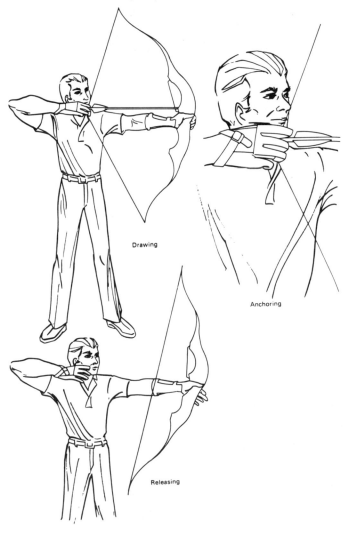

Drawing

Anchoring

Releasing

through the forearm. The elbow is neither raised nor lowered during this maneuver. The body posture should not change during the draw. Muscles in the back rather than the arms should be used to spread the bow.

Anchoring Consistency is fundamental to good shooting. Thus, the archer draws to the same spot each time. Individuals must find their own anchor point, but it is the spot to which the bowstring is drawn for each shot. It is a definite point on the face (Fig. 19-3). Some archers prefer the tip of the nose; others the point of the chin; others the corner of the mouth or the corner of one eye. Wherever the anchor point is, it should remain the same. This prevents indiscriminate shooting or spattering the target with widely placed shots that cannot be corrected. One unvarying anchor point permits shot patterns and corrections to be made for height or wind variations.

Aiming With recurved bows, which have a flatter trajectory than the standard straight bows, it is possible to aim directly at the target without having to compensate for an ascending or descending arc of flight. Re-curved bows can be fired directly at the center of the target from distances of up to 40 yards, although the weight of the bow is a deciding factor in determining point-blank range. As with other bows, there is a tendency for the arrow to drop in flight over long distances, rather than flying on an even level. The aiming point must therefore be moved upward as the distance increases. The reverse is true of shorter distances. When at full draw and anchored, hold the arrow momentarily before releasing it. This action steadies the body as well as the bow and arrow and probably allows a more accurate cast.

Releasing and Following Through Release the arrow by permitting the string to roll off the tips of the fingers as they relax on the bowstring (Fig. 19-3). Do not jerk the string. After the release, the body position is main-tained, although there will be a slight reflex movement of the shooting hand as the string is released. The shooting hand tends to move backward about 1 inch as a result of the loss of tension.

Care of tackle. After shooting, the bow should be unstrung and hung on a rack in a cool, dry storage area. The bow should never be propped up against a wall. The bow should not be flexed nor the string released unless there is an arrow nocked and ready for flight. To retrieve arrows that have been shot into the target, place the hand, palm up or down, against the target face with the shaft of the arrow extending through the first two fin-gers. Grasp the shaft with the other hand as close to the target face as possi-ble and withdraw the arrow with a twisting motion. Draw the arrow straight out in order to avoid bending it. If the arrow enters the ground or some other object, the process is the same. If the arrow penetrates the target to the fletching, draw the arrow through the target from the back. Arrows should be carried so that the feathers cannot be crushed, and stored so that the feathers do not touch; thus, the arrows must be placed in a standing position.

Safety precautions.   Archery ranges should be fairly isolated so that stray arrows do not damage persons or things. The shooting range should be banked at the area of the target butts. This prevents loss of arrows, and also eliminates the possibility of injury to a person inadvertently walking behind the targets. All archers must be cautioned about stepping over the shooting line while others are shooting. To do so is not only a lapse of courtesy, but is also dangerous. The shooting range official or counselor in charge must make this absolutely clear.

Overdrawing can be dangerous because the arrow can be shot into the hand. This can be avoided by making sure that all arrows are of adequate length for the archer's draw. An arrow placed in a 30-pound bow can be as dangerous as any rifle bullet. Archers must be warned to keep their arrows toward the target butts when shooting. The commands of the range counselor must be obeyed instantly; there may be some emergency that the counselor alone sees. All commands should be given loudly and clearly. If a cease-fire is given, all archers, whether at full draw or not, should immediately unnock the arrow. The wearing of protective gear is mandatory for all archers.

Bows, bowstrings, and arrows should be examined for signs of wear from friction or deterioration before any shooting takes place. Injuries from snapped bows can be avoided if tackle is properly inspected. Arrows with feathers that are not aligned or shafts that are warped are potentially dangerous and cause inaccuracies in shooting. Care of equipment, in most cases, prevents damage or injury and permits better shooting performance.

Riflery

Riflery at camp usually involves the sport of target shooting with a small-bore or .22 caliber rifle. The object is to hit a target or series of targets from one or more fixed ranges. The rifle is a clip, tubular, or hand-fed shoulder weapon that is gas or hand-bolt operated (Fig. 19-4). It has a grooved barrel where spiral channels have been cut into the bore so that any bullet fired from the weapon rotates in flight. The rifling effect makes the shot more accurate and overcomes resistance from atmospheric friction.

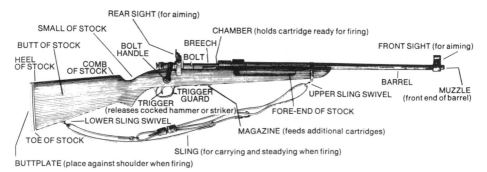

FIGURE 19-4.   A typical .22 caliber bolt-action rifle.

The rifle has four basic sections: the stock, the barrel, the receiver, and the action. The *stock,* of wood or other materials, is the part of the weapon that rests against the shoulder. The *barrel* is the metal part of the weapon through which the bullet is fired. The front of the barrel is the *muzzle,* while the rear is the *breech.* The *receiver* is the metal part of the piece in which the stock is attached. It contains the movable parts of the weapon and permits the bullet to be loaded, locked, fired, and readied for another round. The *action* of the rifle contains those parts that perform the actual movements of loading, cocking, firing, and ejecting the cartridge.

The bolt is a sliding round metal plug that closes the breech in preparation for firing. The bolt contains (1) the firing pin, which strikes and fires the cartridge out of the barrel, (2) the main spring, which forces the firing pin forward, and (3) the extractor, which grasps the shell casing and pulls it out of the chamber after firing. The ejector is a small projection that flips the spent shell-casing out of the chamber after extraction from the breech. The trigger housing contains the parts that release the firing pin in order for the rifle to fire; it includes the trigger, the trigger guard, and the safety, which prevents the trigger from being released accidentally.

The rifle sling is a leather strap arranged to fasten onto the rifle at the rear of the stock and at the fore-end of the stock by means of two metal swivels. The sling can be adjusted to fit the size and length of the arm. The purpose of the sling is not only to enable the rifle to be carried properly, but also to assist in steadying the rifle while aiming.

There are two sights on rifles: the front and the rear. These may be of three standard varieties: front blade sights, beads, and apertures. The blade is simply a thin piece of metal; it may be straight or curved toward the rear. The bead is similar except that there is a small bead of metal at the top of the blade. The aperture sight has a circle around the bead and a small opening through the bead; the whole is encased by a metal ring. Rear sights are either open notch or aperture. The rear sights are attached to the top of the barrel toward the breech. The open sight may have either a V-shaped or a square-shaped notch. The peep, or aperture sight, is one with a small hole set in a casing through which the shooter takes aim. The rear sight may also have screws attached by which adjustments for windage and elevation can be made.

The ammunition for small-bore rifle shooting must have a lead or alloy bullet seated in a rim-fire or center-fire cartridge. The .22 long rifle cartridge is the one most frequently used, although the .22 short is available.

Firing points are spaces approximately 6 feet wide that are intended to accommodate the shooter and the counselor-coach. They are wide enough to permit both the shooter and the counselor to assume a prone position. Any number of points can be used, depending upon the length of the firing line and the number of shooters on the range at any given time.

Shooting techniques. The primary step in learning to shoot is mastering the technique of sighting and aiming. A training aid, called the sighting bar, can be easily and inexpensively made for such practice. It consists of a piece of wood approximately 2 feet in length. At one end of the slat there should be attached a thin, square piece of metal with a hole bored into it near its top. A 1-inch cut is made into the wood 1 foot from the eyepiece; into this is inserted another flat, square metal piece. This second piece of metal becomes the rear sight. An upright piece of metal is drilled into the wood 10 inches from the rear sight. This serves as the front-sight blade. Another slice is made 2 inches in front of this sight, and a target card can then be inserted. Using this device, the camper can be taught how to line up the front and rear sights with the target.

The front sight should be lined up with the rear sight so that the front blade or bead cuts the rear sight precisely in quarters. If a line were to be drawn vertically and horizontally from the front sight to the tip of the rear sight and from side to side, four equal quarters would be formed. When front and rear sights have been aligned, the bull's-eye of the target must be sighted so that it appears to rest exactly upon the top of the front-sight blade or so that the bead covers the bull's-eye.

Positions

Prone Position   Among the four standard shooting positions (Fig. 19-5), the prone position is steadiest and offers the greatest comfort and perhaps the greatest accuracy. The angle made by the body to the rifle is about 30 degrees. Spread the legs comfortably apart, with toes out and heels on the ground. Grip the fore-end of the stock with the left hand; the left elbow should be directly beneath the forestock. Place the rifle butt firmly against the pad of the shoulder. Place the right hand on the small of the stock, with the right thumb along the stock and not around it. Press the right cheek against the upper portion of the stock, with the right eye as close to the rear sight as possible. The index finger of the right hand is in position to squeeze the trigger.

Sitting Position   Sit at an angle of about 45 degrees from the line of aim. Spread the feet comfortably. Bend the body forward at the hips without hunching the back. Rest the left elbow along the left shin or place it against the inner side of the left knee, supporting the rifle. Place the right elbow against the right knee. The heels of both feet should be solidly planted for a steady firing platform.

Kneeling Position   Kneel on the right knee so that the knee makes a right angle with the line of aim. Rest the left elbow below the left knee and well down on the shin. The left knee should be up toward the armpit for maximum support and steadiness. Place the right arm so that it forms a cushion for the rifle butt; place the right elbow comfortably out from the stock. Some shooters wish to hold the right elbow at right angles to the stock or in an elevated position.

Standing Position   The erect body should be at right angles to the target butt. With the left hand, grasp the fore-end of the stock just behind the front sling swivel; the left elbow should be directly beneath the rifle. With the right hand, grasp the small of the stock; the right elbow should be held well up or out.

FIGURE 19-5.   Riflery positions: prone, sitting, kneeling, standing.

Trigger squeeze.   The trigger squeeze is one of the more important factors in accurate rifle shooting. Poor shooting usually results from spoiling the aim prior to firing the rifle. When a shooter flinches at the sound of the rifle being fired, he instinctively jerks the weapon. This throws off the point of aim, ruining the shot. Some campers anticipate the sound of the rifle being fired and flinch before the shot, thereby jerking the trigger. The trigger should be squeezed with increasing pressure so that the shooter is not surprised by the rifle's firing. The aim should be held while the trigger is being squeezed. Some shooters have the bad habit of jerking the trigger just as the sights and target become aligned; this invariably results in poor shooting. The shooter should hold his breath, aim, and deliberately squeeze the trigger. If the barrel of the rifle wavers too much, the shooter should relax and start again.

Safety precautions.   The shooting range should be carefully patrolled and designed so that no one can approach without seeing warning signs or without being seen by the range counselor. When shooting is taking place, there should be a clearly designated signal that all must recognize. A red flag can be used for this purpose. Rifles should be inspected daily. They must be cleaned of carbon and dirt spots in the bore. Daily inspection is also necessary to make sure that chambers and bores are free of obstruction. Rifles should be placed standing in racks with bolts back and chambers open. They should never be rested on their sights or with the bolt underneath.

Rifle-range orders should be purposeful and clear. No camper should be allowed to load his rifle or to begin firing until all shooters are on the firing line and the range counselor is prepared to supervise the firing. Rifles should always be pointed up- and down-range toward the target areas. Ammunition must be distributed only to those who are preparing to fire. At the completion of firing, all unused rounds should be collected and the rifles inspected for clearance before departing the range. Rifles should always be considered loaded. Strict rules apply to those who wish to receive shooting instructions.

Horseshoes

The object of pitching horseshoes is to encircle a metal stake with a horseshoe or, failing that, to pitch the shoes closer to the stake than does one's opponent. Each player pitches two shoes per round. The game can be played in singles (with two players) or in doubles (with four players). To start a match, players usually pitch one shoe to a stake. The shoe that rings or comes nearest to the stake permits that side to pitch first. In single play, each player standing on the same side of the court throws two shoes in succession to the far stake. Both players then walk to the stake, tally the score, and throw the shoes to the first stake. The player who amasses 21 points is the winner. In doubles play, the opposing players stand at each side of the court and pitch in one direction only. Their scores are tallied and their partners on the far side pitch the shoes back. Again, 21 points are needed for a side to win.

The horseshoe court is 50 feet long and 10 feet wide. Two stakes, each 1 inch in diameter, are set into boxes 40 feet apart. The box is a wooden frame 6 feet square, projecting 1 inch above the ground. The box is filled with clay or some other material to a depth of 6 inches. Barnyard, or informal, horseshoe pitching does not require the regulation box. Stakes can be hammered into the ground for play.

The pitching type of horseshoe is an oval-shaped plate of iron or steel with one open end. It should weigh up to $2\frac{1}{2}$ pounds and can be no wider than $7\frac{1}{2}$ inches. The tips of the open ends of the shoe have projecting edges that may not extend more than $\frac{3}{4}$ inch. Shoes are tempered, and their resiliency depends upon their hardness.

Pitching techniques. Horseshoe pitching requires much skill and practice; it is a perceptual skill requiring good hand–eye coordination. There are several methods of holding a shoe to hurl it with some degree of accuracy and control. The most common grip is holding the open end of the shoe away from the body and toward the aiming stake. The index finger is placed on the side of the shoe, but not hooked over the prong. The shank of the shoe rests on the other three fingers, with the third finger acting as primary support. The thumb is on the top of the shank. When the shoe is pitched, it should make one turn and the open end of the shoe should point toward the aiming stake.

A player may stand on either side of the stake, as long as she is within the outer edges of the box, which serves as foot-fault lines. She must be at least 18 inches from the stake. Her feet should be close together, toes pointed at the opposite stake. The right-handed person takes an initial step toward the opposite box with her left foot; the right foot remains in place. The step is taken as the right arm nears the top of the back swing. A correct swing is essential to accurate pitching. The shoe can be held in any comfortable position, chest or chin high. Prior to the swing, the right arm is extended with the shoe pointing toward the opposite stake. The player may actually sight through the open end of the shoe to the top of the aiming stake. She begins the back swing by bringing the right arm downward and backward in a straight line. As the arm swings past the hip, she turns the wrist so that the shoe is released with a turning motion.

The release is made by turning the wrist out and to the right. This causes the shoe to spin and flatten in trajectory; it should thus reach the opposite stake with the open end forward. The player's eyes should be kept on the stake throughout the swing and delivery.

Boccie

In this game, 2 to 8 players are divided into two teams. When 8 people are competing, 2 players from each side are stationed at opposite ends of the court and play alternate frames. Sides match to determine which one bowls first. A player from the side winning the toss initiates the game by throwing the cue, or small ball, from one end of the court to wherever it lands. The same player then attempts to roll or throw one of his game balls as close to the cue ball as possible. His side then retires and does not bowl again until the opposing side gets one of its balls closer to the cue. This procedure is followed until one side uses all of its balls. The other side is then entitled to bowl its remaining balls. Partners play alternately.

All balls must be delivered underhand, although they may be either rolled or tossed. A player must deliver his ball before overstepping the 4-foot mark that constitutes the foul line. The cue ball can be moved by hitting it. Opponents' balls can be knocked away from their position. Rebounds from the side walls are permitted. Any balls thrown out of the court are considered out of play. If the cue ball is hit out of the court, it is returned to the midpoint of the far edge of the playing field. The side winning a point or points begins the next frame. Play is always in the opposite direction from the previous game.

One point is received for every ball that comes nearer to the cue ball than the closest ball of the opponents. Twelve points constitute a game. When the opposing side has 11 points, however, the game must continue until one or the other side has a clear 2-point advantage. A match is the best two out of three games.

Although there is no regulation length or width for boccie, a space 60 by 10 feet is generally used. This space is enclosed by wooden walls, between 10 and 12 inches high. Almost all boccie courts have shallow trenches no more than 6 inches deep at each end of the court to keep the balls from rebounding onto the playing area if they have been bowled too hard. Equipment consists of a cue ball, which is approximately 3 inches in diameter, and one 5-inch boccie ball per player. Some form of measuring device is necessary to obtain the distance of the bowled balls from the cue.

Lawn Bowling

Bowling on the green is essentially a combination of regulation bowling and horseshoe pitching. From 2 to 8 persons can play. In order to start the game, a coin is tossed; the winner bowls first. Thereafter, the winner of each frame has the privilege of bowling first. A frame is completed when all bowlers on both teams have rolled their balls to one end. The player who bowls first is responsible for rolling the cue or jack ball and then his own two balls alternately with those of his opponent. When there are more than two players, the same procedure is used, with one team's player rolling his balls alternately with his opposite number.

The object of the game is to get as close to the jack as possible. The jack may be hit by a bowled ball, as may an opponent's ball. For each ball rolled closer to the jack than an opponent's ball, 1 point is scored. The basic game is 21 points, but any previously decided number of frames or period of time may also constitute a game.

Croquet

Croquet is played with a mallet that can be held in one or both hands. The object of croquet is to hit a ball with the mallet through a series of wickets in a specified sequence. Play begins by hitting a ball through two wickets on one side of the court, then through the right near wicket, the center wicket, the right far wicket, and a set of double wickets, to the far stake. The player then returns the ball down the court on the opposite side from the original course.

A player has one shot or hit at the ball with her mallet to get through one or more wickets. A player may receive one additional turn for hitting a stake or going through a wicket. She receives two additional shots for hitting an opponent's ball. However, she is permitted no more than two shots after a given shot. A player is permitted to shoot until she fails to pass through a wicket, misses a stake, or fails to hit an opponent's ball. The same procedure holds true for other players, who follow in turn. As many as 4 players may compete in a match, either as opponents or in doubles combination.

A player may choose to knock her opponent's ball out of position. She must first hit her opponent's ball. She may then place her ball adjacent to her opponent's ball and use either a carom or croquet shot. In the former, the player simply hits the opponent's ball out of position while endeavoring to hit her own into an advantageous position. In the croquet shot, the player places her foot upon her own ball, to hold it securely, and strikes her ball with her mallet, thereby sending her opponent's ball in whatever direction she wishes, to a certain disadvantaged position. In doubles play, one partner may elect to move her partner's ball to a more advantageous position using the same technique.

A ball is considered to have passed through a wicket if a straight edge laid across the two wires on the side from which the ball came does not touch the ball. If a player plays a wrong ball, her turn is taken by the next player, and her own ball may be placed in any spot on the court. All misplayed balls must be returned to the places from which they have been wrongly taken. Players must play in proper order. If any player goes out of turn, the strokes stand or must be played over at the discretion of the opponent.

The standard court for croquet is 60 by 30 feet. A 30-inch line from the boundary is inscribed all around the court; this is the playing line. Stakes are placed just outside of this line, equidistant from the sidelines. The stakes should be about 2 inches in diameter. The wickets are of wire, about $\frac{1}{4}$ inch thick, and should extend at least 10 inches from the ground. The arch formed by the wire should be no more than 5 inches wide. The 9 wickets are placed so that two, one mallet's-head length apart, are situated directly before both stakes. Two additional wickets are placed approximately halfway between the center wicket and the paired wickets. The equipment for croquet consists of wooden balls and wooden mallets. The balls are striped with various colors to permit easy identification. The mallet has a handle no less than $2\frac{1}{2}$ feet long, and a cylindrical head 12 inches long and 3 inches in diameter.

Horseback Riding

There are a variety of horseback riding activities, but camps are usually concerned with teaching skills in handling a horse for the pure fun of riding, for pack-horse trips, or for steeplechasing or jumping. The chief objectives in riding are enjoyment, comfort, and relaxation, for the horse as well as for the rider. The horse does not necessarily enjoy being ridden, but he should be comfortable and relaxed. With knowledge of fundamental riding skills and the basic characteristics of the horse, an introduction to riding can be offered. It is essential to have qualified instructors who can demonstrate technique and teach the novice or advanced rider by constructive supervision.

Horses can be ridden in the riding ring or on the trail. It is safer and easier to learn in a ring, where there is less danger of distracting the horse. Trail riding should be permitted only when the camper has mastered basic riding skills and knows how to handle his mount. Attention to increased skill should be pursued in the ring, but riding on the trail is ample reward for having practiced the fundamental techniques (Fig. 19-6).

The horse.   The novice must familiarize himself with the characteristics of horses if he is to gain control of the mount and make him respond to commands. Horses are easily excited and stimulated by movements; despite their great strength, they are rather timid. But since the horse can become confident when surrounded by familiar objects and people, it learns to associate security with the good rider. The horse has a good memory and learns to connect particular movements with related commands or pressures. It learns that leg pressure means one thing, a tug on the reins means something else, and that verbal orders or pressure on the sides of the neck require compliance. Most horses respond eagerly to good treatment and perform whatever is in their capacity to do.

FIGURE 19-6.   First time up, but well schooled in the basics. (Courtesy: Crane Lake Camp, West Stockbridge, Mass.)

The horse is a gregarious animal but also has social likes and dislikes that may threaten the rider's safety, and the rider should always anticipate possible trouble from the most innocent sources. The horse's vision permits it to see in almost any direction without turning its head; this peculiarity of vision sometimes causes it to start in fright at objects that would not ordinarily frighten it. The horse's hearing is acute; sudden loud noises can startle it into precipitous movement. The good rider uses his voice to distract the horse from objects that might frighten it, calm it when it is startled, and give it commands to which it will respond. Anticipation of what the horse is likely to do in any given situation results in a more secure seat for the rider.

Equipment.   All riding horses wear two pieces of equipment: the saddle and the bridle. The *saddle* is made of leather with felt padding and is constructed so that it forms a well-built seat for the rider. The saddle is built up around a curved metal form called a *saddle tree*. The *pommel* is the forward part of the saddle top; it curves upward so as not to rub the horse's back and cause sores. The *cantle*, the back part of the saddle, forms the seat for the rider. The *stirrups* are metal pieces that permit the feet to slip in and out easily without passing all the way through. The stirrups are attached to the saddle by means of leather straps with holes so that the stirrups can be easily adjusted to the rider. The *girth* is a wide leather or canvas strap that passes under the horse's belly and holds the saddle on.

The *bridle* is any gear that is placed over the horse's head. The *crown piece* is placed on top of the head and behind the ears to hold the bridle up. The *brow band* is attached to the crown and runs across the forehead just under the ears; this prevents the bridle from riding up over the horse's neck. The *cheek straps* assist in adjusting the bridle. The *throat latch* prevents the bridle from being pulled off. The *cavesson* slips over the horse's nose and prevents the animal from holding its nose too high. Most bridles have one *bit,* usually a snaffle which acts on the corners of the horse's lips. The reins and cheek straps are attached to the bit by large rings at each end of the bit. The reins are attached to and control the action of the bit. The bit is placed in the horse's mouth to control its speed and direction.

Riding techniques.   Good horsemanship is a combination of balance, poise, skill, and movements of the arms, hands, and legs together with the use of the voice to regulate the horse and have it perform in a manner acceptable to the rider. Most horses are trained by the reinforcement system—that is, by reward and punishment. Pressure on the reins or with the legs against the horse's body is painful; the release of such pressure constitutes a reward. When the horse performs correctly, pressure should be released immediately.

All the horse's movements come from its hindquarters. Pressure against the horse's flanks tell it in what direction to move and at what speed. The hands assist in controlling the direction to be taken and also act as a brake. When the reins are pulled taut, the horse will stop; if the reins are held loosely, the horse will continue to move forward. If the horse has been trained to obey commands by means of pressure carried by the reins against the neck, it will move either right or left, depending on the signals the rider gives it by neck reining. The rider should shift his body weight in order to tell the horse whether to slow down, go faster, or jump. Talking to the horse gives it confidence, gets it used to the sound, and may eventually be used to give verbal commands that the horse will understand and obey. The shifting of body weight is the easiest way to have the horse follow directions. The use of leg pressure and finally hands on reins are increasing degrees of punishment for the horse.

Mounting   To mount the horse, stand on its left side facing its rear. Grasp both reins in the left hand, short, but not tight. Place the left hand, holding the reins, on the horse's withers, about 10 inches beyond the saddle. Place the left foot in the stirrup. Place the right hand on the pommel of the saddle. From this position, use the right leg as a spring and jump off the ground. Use the hands on the horse's withers and pommel to hoist the body into an erect position, standing with the left leg in the left stirrup. Swing the right leg over the horse's back without hitting it, and let down into the saddle. Put the right foot in the stirrup.

Sitting   To take the correct position on the horse, sit upright in the deepest part of the saddle. The legs should be hanging straight and loose. Sit on the pelvic bones with the weight well forward. Using the toes to find the stirrups, slip feet into the stirrups. The ankle should be flexed so that the sole of the foot can be seen from the ground. The heel should be lower than the toes, but the legs should be straight and not permitted to move forward. The rider should not be able to see her feet from her position in the saddle. When the rider is well seated, she should be able to rise in the stirrups, leaning slightly forward, without having to depend on her arms for balance.

Pick up the reins and hold them loosely. Hold the snaffle rein between the little finger and the ring finger, across the palm, and between the thumb and forefinger. The fingers should be relaxed. Hold the hands approximately 3 inches in front of the saddle and a comfortable distance apart.

Walking   Once the rider has mounted and adjusted his position, the next step is to walk the horse. Gain the horse's attention by lightly squeezing its sides with the legs. Lean forward in the seat and release the pressure on the reins so that the horse can walk. As soon as the horse has begun to move, relax the legs. If the horse refuses to move, prod it by kicking it firmly behind the girth. As the horse moves forward, relax the arms and allow them to follow the horse's head as it walks. To stop the horse from a walk, shift the weight slightly to the back. Squeeze the legs lightly and draw back slightly on the reins. The horse should stop.

Trotting   The trot is a gait in which the two diagonally opposite legs of the horse move simultaneously. Posting is the only comfortable action that the rider can make while the horse is trotting. To post, move up with the horse by standing in the stirrups, and then sit down as the horse moves down. Tell the horse to move from a walk to a trot by the same method used in getting it to move from a stopped position. Shorten the reins by several inches, as the horse holds its head higher for trotting than for walking. Lean slightly forward and squeeze the flanks. When the horse begins to trot, relax the legs.

Cantering   The canter is a gait in which the horse's hind feet strike the ground separately while its forefeet hit the ground almost simultaneously. When the horse canters, the rider must keep his seat. To begin the canter, shorten the reins and squeeze the legs together. Lean slightly forward from the hips and relax the hands so that the horse can move out.

Galloping   The gallop is an extended canter. The rider's buttocks are completely out of the saddle and his body is well forward with the hips flexed. Relax the legs, knees, and ankles so that movements coincide with the horse's. The hands should be about halfway up the horse's neck, but not resting on the neck.

Dismounting   Dismounting can be accomplished from a halt or, in an emergency, when the horse is still in motion. The dismount is performed in almost the same way as the mount, except that everything is done in reverse. The reins are shortened and held in the left hand. The rider removes his right foot from the stirrup and swings it over the horse's rump so that he is standing on his left leg with his foot in the stirrup. He then places his right hand on the pommel and leans slightly forward so that the weight of his body is on his hands. Taking the left foot out of the stirrup, he slowly slides to the ground, pushing away from the horse. To dismount a moving horse, the rider takes the reins in his left hand and removes both feet from the stirrups. He leans forward and places the weight of his body on his hands. He then swings his right leg over the horse's back and pushes away with both hands, still holding onto the reins, and drops lightly to the ground, facing the direction in which the horse is moving. This vault out of the saddle, if practiced, will become one continuous movement. It is a valuable skill if the rider ever begins to fall from the horse.

chapter 20

Aquatic Activities

The aquatic program can almost be said to characterize the modern residential camp. Some experts even suggest that no camp should be situated on land that does not have a water source adequate for the development of a comprehensive aquatic program. A swimming pool can accommodate only a few of the activities that constitute a balanced and varied aquatic program. It has proven such a successful and popular camp activity that no camp can afford to be without some semblance of this program. In some camps, the entire program is centered around the aquatic facility.

The typical camp's aquatic program reflects a range of activities: recreational and competitive swimming; plain and fancy diving; boating, canoeing, and sailing; skin and scuba diving; lifesaving and water-safety instruction; synchronized swimming; fishing; water skiing; and surfing. The water pageant, another aspect of the aquatic program, is discussed in Chapter 22.

The aquatic program offers the opportunity to learn an activity that will enhance the camper's satisfaction and give him a lifelong recreational skill. At the same time, the camper is learning a survival technique that will be useful in certain dangerous circumstances. Participation in aquatic activities contributes to the camper's physiological growth and development because it promotes cardiovascular conditioning and fitness. Aquatics offers the camper a choice of experiences in which to learn and attain advanced levels of motor skill. The camper's need to belong, to socialize, and to achieve mastery is enhanced through such activity. Participation is not restricted to any age group. Swimming, for example, can be taught to the youngest campers.

ORGANIZATION OF THE AQUATIC PROGRAM

Camps have developed many schedules for the effective use of the water-front. The type of aquatic facility necessarily varies with the environment; depending on the resources available, the program may concentrate on in-structional swimming and competition, water pageants, and shows; boating, canoeing, sailing, surfing, and water skiing; or any combination of these activities. The program director must determine the most suitable activities for the water resource available. The answers to the following questions will significantly influence the choice and scheduling of activities:

1. What is the camp's philosophy?
2. What is the water-resource capacity? Is the facility artificial, natural, a sea-coast, a lake, a river?
3. How many campers are to be served? How many can use the waterfront at the same time?
4. What affects will daily atmospheric changes have?
5. What is the distance of any residential unit to the waterfront facility?
6. How many supervisory and instructional personnel are available at any given time?
7. How is the rest of the camp program organized?

All these factors must be appraised because they have a definite bear-ing on the type of program that can be offered. The schedule for instruc-tional swimming must make maximum use of qualified personnel at the times they are available. The aquatic program should be integrated with all other aspects of the camp program so that no conflicts result. Positive relationships with other parts of the program should be amplified; however, each phase of the program is valuable for its contribution to the camper. No one program should be permitted to strip counselors or specialists from other activities.

Scheduling

The waterfront or facility must be used efficiently, so activities must be scheduled. To the extent that all campers do not have the same water skills, there must be a testing period at the start of the camp season. Testing can be performed on a routine basis as campers are assigned to various phases of the program. It is best to examine swimmer proficiency by bunk or unit. Standard tests are administered, and campers are classified on the basis of skill level. When all campers have been classified according to indi-vidual swimming ability, a general schedule may be put into effect.

Periods can be of the instructional, general, unit, or bunk variety. The schedule should be arranged so that at least one general camp swim and several instructional swimming periods can be offered each day. The all-camp swim is usually the last afternoon activity, between 3:30 and 5:00 PM. The activity may last for 1 to $1\frac{1}{2}$ hours, depending upon temperature and other activities scheduled for the evening or during the day. If two general swims are scheduled, the most typical time allotment is 45 minutes to 1 hour before lunch, and 1 hour before supper. The waterfront schedule can be arranged so that there are at least three and perhaps four 1-hour instructional periods, beginning at 9:00 AM. The daily schedule would then include instructional swimming from 9:00 to 10:00 AM and from 10:00 to 11:00 AM. At 11:00 AM the general swim would begin. The waterfront would again be open to instructional swimming from 1:30 to 2:30 PM, 2:30 to 3:30 PM, and 3:30 to 4:30 PM, followed by a general swim from 4:30 to 5:30 PM. Additional waterfront activities could occur during the early evening hours. Dry-land drills for lifesaving, swimming, and other water-related activities could also be scheduled. If the waterfront is lighted for night use, older campers can be scheduled for specific instructional skills in synchronized swimming, competitive activity, and water shows.

SWIMMING

The aquatic program cannot be limited to any one phase or approach. For this reason, every level of skill must be taken into account in each category of the program. The desirability of each camper attaining some degree of skill in swimming should not be underestimated. Successful achievement in learning other water-related activities is also a main objective of the aquatic program. When the program concentrates on the instructional element of aquatics, it may fail to take advantage of the many facets of a well-rounded program. The recreational feature of free swimming without structured classes must have a place in the schedule. But all aspects of the program depend on the camper's ability to swim.

Swimming Instruction

Swimming instruction is given on three levels: beginner, intermediate, and advanced. Beginning swimming emphasizes introduction to the water (Fig. 20-1). Basic patterns of water movement must be established, and self-confidence in an unfamiliar element must be developed. Gradual immersion and games, including bobbing, blowing bubbles, bending over to pick up objects, learning to open the eyes underwater, and breath holding, are often initially employed to overcome innate fear of the water.

When the child has mastered these experiences, flotation is introduced. This is taught in shallow water by having the child inflate his lungs, hold his breath, and attempt to sit on the bottom; because the individual is buoyant, the attempt naturally fails. With practice, this method becomes the basis for a tuck float, prone float, back or supine float, float with glide, and finally pushing off from the bottom or some stabilized side and performing the prone float and glide. Once this skill has been attained, almost 50 percent of the barriers to learning how to swim have been overcome. Once this primary skill has been learned, other techniques for breathing, body position, arm and leg movements and coordination, and the elementary swimming strokes can be taught.

FIGURE 20-1. Beginners learn to swim at the camp pool. (Courtesy: Crane Lake Camp, West Stockbridge, Mass.)

Intermediate swimming emphasizes progressive skills. From elementary forms of swimming strokes, there now emerges the orthodox stroke pattern necessary for true propulsion through the water. The intermediate group is taught orthodox back, breast, side, and crawl strokes with emphasis on form, style, efficiency, and practice. Entry into the water from some type of diving position is also taught at this level; the camper learns how to jump and then dive into the water from any stationary dock or float.

Advanced swimming involves progress in mastering all stroke forms, with coordinated movements of arms, legs, breathing, body position, and alignment. Style and endurance are practiced in advanced classes. As the camper's competence grows, additional activities such as stunts, competitive swimming, fancy diving, and lifesaving techniques are added.

Teaching Techniques

Instruction in any phase of swimming requires that the teacher build self-confidence in the camper. Those who have never been in or near the water fear that something bad will happen when they go in. For the fear of water to be overcome early and finally, patience and kindness are essential. A matter-of-fact voice and easily understood directions are necessary if successful learning is to take place. The camper must have everything explained before he even enters the water. The instructor must be prepared to take as much time as necessary to bring the camper along slowly but surely. Every step must reinforce those that have been performed and those that will come. The camper must be convinced that he cannot fail; he must be successful at each trial along the way. This can be accomplished by providing an easily attainable objective during each practice session. At first these objectives may be blowing bubbles, opening the eyes under water, counting fingers under water, breath holding, or picking up objects from the bottom. As the camper progresses and begins to float, the goals become increasingly difficult, and success will continue to develop the self-confidence. When strokes have finally been learned and actual locomotion is possible, the goals focus on distance covered, discipline of form, or other equally valuable standards in efficient swimming.

The dry-land drill is an excellent preliminary device for teaching swimmers correct body position and arm or leg motions. Each stroke can be learned without ever getting into the water by analyzing movements and then drilling. With this method, the camper has already made a habit of using the correct movement sequence when he finally does apply himself to the water.

Backstroke.   The backstroke is performed from a supine position. The legs perform a flutter kick, with the power being generated from the hip and thigh. The leg is flexed for a whip-like action. The ankles are relaxed and turned inward. The body is flat, and the head is erect with eyes staring upward. The arms are used alternately. If the swimmer starts with his left arm, it is brought up from the side in either a flexed or straight position. The arm sweeps the water in an arc that brings it to a 45-degree angle from the shoulder line. The palm of the hand is down. The arm is then pulled to the side and the same procedure is repeated with the other arm.

Sidestroke.   The sidestroke is an extremely relaxing stroke, although it is most effective for rescue work. The swimmer, on her side, flexes her knees so that the topmost leg advances while the bottom leg moves back. The top knee moves toward the chin and the bottom knee moves toward the back of the head during the flexed aspect of the kick. For locomotion, the legs are moved in a slightly circular position. The top leg moves up, around, and then vigorously down. The bottom leg moves up, back, around, and then vigorously down. The two legs are thrust together, one atop the other, without actually touching; hence the term scissor kick.

The arm movements are quite simple. The starting position for the arms is an extended one. The foremost arm (either right or left, depending upon the side on which the swimmer is swimming) is extended straight ahead, but approximately 3 inches under water. The rear arm extends to the rear and lies parallel with the legs. The arms are recovered by flexing them and having the fingers of the hands meet almost under the chin. The stroke is taken by thrusting both arms in opposite directions so that the front arm is extended once again and the rear arm pushes through the water until it reaches a point of maximum extension. The procedure is then repeated. The swimmer begins the stroke in the glide position; that is, the arms are extended and the legs are held together. The legs are flexed and the arms are recovered simultaneously. The legs execute the scissor kick, the arms thrust away simultaneously, and the swimmer moves through the water in a series of smooth glides.

Breaststroke.   The breaststroke is performed in a prone position. The arms and legs work simultaneously in the following sequence. From a glide position with arms and legs extended, the arms are pressed down against the water and pressure is exerted so that the stroke is made by separating the two arms down to a point just at the shoulder line. The head is lifted during the stroke to breathe. The arms are recovered by flexing them, and the hands are brought together in a prayer attitude just beneath the chin. The legs are flexed in such a position that the soles of the feet may be brought together. The kick can be either a whip-like circular motion of the knees or a simple pressure by the soles of both feet against the water as the legs are thrust out, around, and then brought together. Arm recovery and leg flexion are performed simultaneously. The arms are thrust out together as the legs take the kick. The result of this movement is a prolonged glide. The only friction is caused by lifting the head for a breath at each arm stroke.

Crawl.   The crawl is performed from a prone position. The legs execute a flutter kick while the arms alternately rotate. The head is turned slightly to either the right or the left, depending upon the swimmer's convenience; the mouth is cupped so that breath may be drawn in. The arm stroke occurs from an extended position. The body is held in a plane position, with the upper body slightly higher than the legs. There may be a very slight arch in the back. The right arm is dropped until it reaches a position to the rear and parallel to the thigh. It is recovered by lifting it almost straight up with the elbow leading. When the arm has cleared the water, it is again extended. The hand is low, the wrist is higher than the hand, and the elbow is higher than the wrist. The thumb should be lined up with the nose. The arm is relaxed so that it can enter the water at an angle which permits the hand to catch approximately 6 inches below the surface. Since the first 6 inches of water from the surface down add nothing to the swimmer's forward locomotion, it is wasted effort to press upon it. The hand should be placed into the water so that all effort is expended in an effective pull. As the right arm pulls and recovers, the left arm repeats the exact movement. The cyclical stroke continues alternately throughout the crawl.

The flutter kick is executed by driving the extended legs up and down against the water. Power is generated from the hip and thigh. The ankle is relaxed and turned inward. There are 6 to 8 kicks for every complete arm cycle.

Dry-Land Drills

Flutter kicks can be taught by having the campers sit on the edge of the dock or pool, or on the sand. The campers can lean back on their hands while they raise their legs. The drill consists of separating the legs vertically and kicking in an up-and-down pattern to get the feel of kicking with the entire leg from the thigh. Many beginners develop the negative habit of kicking with a flexed knee; they merely thrash the water into foam, waste energy, and move slowly, if at all. Campers must practice relaxing the ankle and letting it turn inward of its own weight.

The frog or whip kick for the breaststroke can be taught from the same position as the one just described. The campers are instructed to bend their knees and place the soles of their feet together. On signal, they spread their legs horizontally and then bring both legs together. When this has been mastered, the campers flex their legs and separate them outward by circling them slightly as they bring them together while keeping their feet turned out. In the whip kick, the knees are brought together and the legs are dropped to a vertical position and then circled vigorously together.

The scissor kick is practiced while resting on one hip, the forearm of one arm, and the hand of the other arm. If the camper is on his right side, then his right forearm will be down and his left hand will placed in front of his hips as an additional support. The legs are flexed so that the top leg moves up and forward. The bottom leg moves up and backward. During the kick sequence, the legs are simultaneously circled forward and backward and then brought together vigorously without actually touching.

Arm movements are plotted in precisely the same manner. For crawl and backstroke, the arms are circled alternately in the appropriate manner. For the backstroke, the camper stands erect. The two arms are held up over the head. The right arm begins by descending directly to the right side; the right wrist is turned so that the little finger of the hand is outward. As the right arm is moved up and back to its former position, the left arm descends to the side. The movements are repeated until the camper understands the pattern.

The crawl stroke is taught by having the campers bend forward from the waist until their hands can rest on their knees. The head is raised. The two arms are extended to the front on either side of the head. The hands are relaxed so that the wrist is limp. The thumb lines up with the nose. The wrist is higher than the hands; the elbows are higher than the wrists. The right arm drops from its extended position to the thigh. As the arm is pulled slightly beyond the thigh, the head is turned to the right and the mouth is cupped to the right. The right arm is then recovered by lifting it straight up, with the elbow leading. As the right arm is extended, the head returns to its original position and air is expelled through the mouth and nose. As the right arm is extended, the left arm drops and the stroke is repeated.

The breaststroke is performed from a flexed position. The campers bend at the waist, arms extended at the sides of the head. The stroke begins be separating the two hands and pulling out and down at an angle of approximately 45 degrees. The stroke stops when the arms reach a position in line with the shoulders. To recover the arms, the hands are circled and brought up beneath the chin and then thrust straight out to their original extended position.

The sidestroke is performed with campers standing erect. The right arm extends up and the left arm extends down. The arms are flexed and the hands are brought together under the chin. The right elbow is held up; the left elbow is down. The arms are simultaneously separated and thrust out to their original extended positions. The movement is repeated. The arms move simultaneously, but in opposite directions.

Water Drills

Kicking may best be practiced while holding on to a stationary object such as the side of a pool or dock. For the flutter kick, the left hand grasps whatever handhold presents itself while the right hand is placed down and flush along the side of the object. This elevates the body and permits it to assume the correct position for kicking. The kick is then initiated. Campers should be taught to kick with good vertical separation of the legs. Kick boards can also be used. Campers should be instructed to kick from between 12 to 15 inches beneath the surface of the water with their heels only. This produces the fountain effect from which the flutter derives its name.

The backstroke kick, or back flutter, is performed in exactly the same manner, except that the campers are on their backs. They may rest their necks on whatever lip is available and grasp the side with both hands. The elbows are pointed straight up and will flank the head. The body is elevated to the correct kicking position. There is a slight arch in the back. The legs are moved from the hips and thighs, with a slight bend in the knees to produce a flexible action. The ankle is relaxed and is turned in by water pressure. Good vertical separation of the legs should produce an effective kick.

The breaststroke kick is performed first on the back. The body is brought into position in the manner just described. The knees are flexed and the soles of the feet are brought together. The legs are then thrust vigorously outward, circled, and brought together with a snap. Assuming a prone position, as for the crawl flutter, the knees are brought together, the legs are dropped to a vertical position and then circled and brought together vigorously.

The scissor kick is performed much the same way as it is during dry-land drills. If the camper is on his right side, the right arm is dropped and the hand placed flush against the side of the stationary object. The left arm is lifted out of the water with the elbow high, and the hand grasps whatever handhold is available. The head is turned so that the camper looks back over his left shoulder. The knees are flexed with the top leg forward and the bottom leg backward. The kick is taken by stepping forward and around with the top leg and backward and around with the bottom leg. The two legs are brought on top of each other without touching. There must be a conclusive snap to the process of closing the legs in order to generate power for forward locomotion.

After these preliminary drills, the instructor may have the campers practice kicking across the pool or crib area. The camper takes a deep breath, extends her arms, pushes off from side or bottom, and simply kicks until she reaches the required distance. This drill should be continued until the kick is well executed and the action becomes smooth. The less effort put into the kick, the more energy is conserved and the greater the efficiency of the kick. When the camper is proficient in the kick, arm strokes should be added. Combining arm and leg movements in short drills with some form of water game to maintain the child's interest will stimulate attention and hasten progress. It cannot be too greatly stressed that patience, simple directions, clear explanations, and kindness are absolutely necessary in all phases of instructional swimming.

Recreational or General Swimming

Free swims, where many or all units of the camp use the waterfront area for any reasonable type of aquatic play, are in the best tradition of recreational activity. During the instructional phase of the aquatics program, constant drilling, repetition, and correction are mandatory if skill development is to progress. In recreational swimming, however, the camper is free to move about the water with abandon. Naturally, good safety practices must be observed, but boisterous play, splashing, tag games, racing back and forth—everything that gives enjoyment—is permissible.

Recreational swimming is enhanced by providing equipment that enhances fun. Slides can be installed, and odd-shaped rafts can be anchored in the swimming area to provide imaginative play for swimmers. Diving and jumping contests to see who can make the highest jet of water can be part of this activity. There is no reason that canoes, rowboats, surf boards, and even sailing craft cannot be used at this time, provided that the campers using them are skilled, have passed the advanced swimming course, and are thoroughly checked out. Recreational swimming can also include practice for pageants, stunts, games, races, water polo, water basketball, and many other water experiences.

BOATING, CANOEING, AND SAILING

Instruction in handling small craft can be an important asset to any camp. Many children have the opportunity to learn how to swim and dive, but few are given the chance to handle small craft. Although sailing is becoming extremely popular along seacoasts and in inland regions where lake or river access permits it, only a small percentage of the total population has learned to sail. The following section treats only equipment and methods, and the role of small craft in the aquatic program (Fig. 20-2).

Boating

Rowing is the easiest form of boating that can be included in the camp program. Rowboats are used on ponds, lakes, coastal waterways, and rivers. Rowboats provide a relatively safe means of transportation on waterways, even for unskilled swimmers. Rowing requires little demonstrable skill and is learned within a few minutes by the beginner. However, certain aspects of rowing demand a high degree of skill and therefore necessitate instructional assistance and a good deal of practice before the camper becomes

FIGURE 20-2.   Kayaking is an excellent water sport. (Courtesy: Crane Lake Camp, West Stockbridge, Mass.)

proficient in this method of water travel. Boating is useful for recreational experience, lifesaving, and competitive activities. For anyone who fishes, rowing is a requisite skill. Rowing is also used in water rescues. Skilled boat handling may prove invaluable in beating through high surf.

Rowing is the propelling of a flat- or round-bottomed boat along the surface of the water by means of oars (Fig. 20-3). Oars are long, rigid, wooden blades made of spruce or ash. They are rested on or inserted into oarlocks or rowlocks, which become the fulcrum for maneuvering. The oarlock may be a U-shaped metal device that is fastened to the gunwale on both sides of the boat. The rower sits facing the rear of the boat on a seat or thwart situated in the approximate middle of the craft. The rower moves the boat by dipping the blade of the oar into the water at an angle so that the blade is toward the front of the boat. The rower pulls the handles of the oars to his chest so that the blade moves toward the rear. The boat is thus propelled by means of leverage.

Techniques.   The rower sits exactly in the middle of the thwart and places his legs on whatever footrests are appropriate. Keep the legs straight and the feet braced against blocks. The back should not be bent while rowing, and the shoulders should be square. Bending at the hips is permissible, but not at the waist. Each oar is grasped as close to the end of the handle

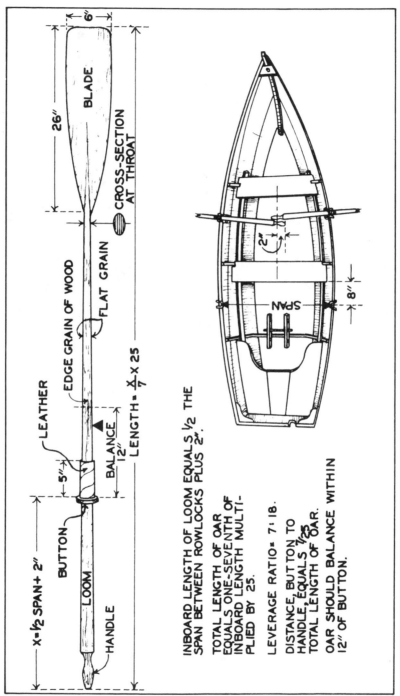

6″

BLADE

26″

CROSS-SECTION
AT THROAT

FLAT GRAIN

EDGE GRAIN OF WOOD

LENGTH = $\frac{X}{7}$ × 25

LEATHER

BALANCE
12″

5″

BUTTON

X = ½ SPAN + 2″

LOOM

HANDLE

2″

SPAN

8″

INBOARD LENGTH OF LOOM EQUALS ½ THE
SPAN BETWEEN ROWLOCKS PLUS 2″.

TOTAL LENGTH OF OAR
EQUALS ONE-SEVENTH OF
INBOARD LENGTH MULTI-
PLIED BY 25.

LEVERAGE RATIO = 7:18.

DISTANCE, BUTTON TO
HANDLE, EQUALS $\frac{7}{25}$
TOTAL LENGTH OF OAR.

OAR SHOULD BALANCE WITHIN
12″ OF BUTTON.

FIGURE 20-3.   Rowboat nomenclature.

as possible, with fingers on top and the thumb underneath. The blade of the oar is perpendicular to the water.

To perform the stroke, the body should bend forward with flexion at the hips. Hold arms directly in front of the body. The oars should have a slightly forward angle to them so that the top of the blade is advanced. The arms are raised so that the oars are dipped into the water at about a 45-degree angle to the side of the boat. The blades are pulled through the water in a wide, shallow sweep toward the stern. The pulling is done with back and shoulder muscles, flexing at the hips until the rower regains his upright position. Keep the elbows close to the sides of the body.

The stroke should be a steady and even pressure. At the end of the stroke, there is a final dig that supplies the impetus for, and aids in, the recovery. At the end of the stroke, the body should regain its upright position. Feathering the oars helps them to lessen air resistance as they are returned toward the bow for another stroke. If a blade tops the water, it will hardly upset the rhythm of the stroke. To feather, raise the blades high enough so that they clear the water easily; however, they should not be so high as to splash into the water at the end of the recovery.

Backing water is accomplished by using the push stroke. This stroke is the direct opposite of the pull stroke. Oars are slipped into the water toward the stern of the boat with the hands at the chest, elbows flexed. By pushing away from the chest and straightening the arms, the oars are forced through the water from rear to bow.

Alternate arm rowing can be used for either back or forward propulsion. In the forward movement, the arms are held in a flexed position; the body does not bend at the hips. The hand merely rotates over the wrist. The strokes are short and rapid. This form of rowing is useful when careful steering is required. The reverse motion is used for the push stroke. Instead of pulling toward the chest, push away, wrist over wrist.

Direction can be changed smoothly and quickly by slipping one oar and either pulling or pushing with the other. For very rapid turns in a limited space, one oar can be pulled while the other is pushed. Thus, to turn to the right, pull on the left oar and push on the right, both strokes being completed together.

Landings alongside a dock or a boat can be made by approaching the object at an angle. Approaches should be made into the wind or current whenever possible. When the bow of the boat is close to the object, the near oar should be slipped or pulled out of the water and into the boat. The outer oar is backed so that the boat swings up alongside the dock.

Safety precautions. The dangers of boating can be overcome by using common sense and maintaining control. All campers who want to participate in boating should be qualified swimmers. At the very least, the camper who uses a rowboat must be able to maintain herself in the water. Rowboats should never be overloaded with passengers. The boat may be capable of accommodating two or more persons, but it is wiser to leave a space vacant than to risk the possibility of overloading. Horseplay on boats should be forbidden; it is dangerous and can result in capsizing or swamping the boat. Passengers should keep their respective seats. If changes must be made, the boat should be landed at the nearest shore. Seating arrangements can be changed, if absolutely necessary, by trimming the craft at each stage of the transfer. Individuals who change seats must crouch in order to maintain a low center of gravity. As the individual moves from one place to the other, she grasps both gunwales and steps to the rower's seat. The rower shifts her weight to one side as the passenger slips to the other side of the thwart. The rower then vacates her seat and executes the same procedure to the vacant spot while the new rower shifts her weight to the middle. One other common-sense regulation should be observed: If a boat is swamped or overturned, it will stay afloat, although awash. Passengers should remain with the boat, which will maintain their weight.

Canoeing

Canoeing is a method of water transportation in an open, elongated, narrow, light-in-the-beam craft that is propelled by means of paddling. Good canoeing requires skilled handling of the craft and an ability to use stroke techniques for rapid maneuvers as well as ease of paddling. Endurance, knowledge of the canoe's potential, manipulation of the craft under varying circumstances, safety precautions, personal conduct in the event of mishap, and care of equipment are all part of the knowledge necessary for the camper who wishes to use the canoe (Fig. 20-4). (See Chapter 17 for a discussion of landing, loading, and carrying of canoes.)

Techniques. Canoe strokes vary inasmuch as proponents of some stroking positions or methods profess to find particular paddling angles or movements more suitable than others. There are several strokes and techniques that are known and held in common by nearly all canoeists, however. Agreement has also been reached on the most efficient positions to be taken by paddlers (Fig. 20-5). Although most novices use the seats in a canoe for paddling, these high perches are not at all useful except for occasional rest, and then only when the water is calm. The ideal position for paddling is on one or both knees. The paddler kneels on the bottom of the canoe, resting a part of his weight against the seat thwart, but with more of his weight pitched forward on his knees. This position is the safest to take in a canoe, because the canoe will afford a steadier ride when the center of gravity is lowered. Cushions or knee pads eliminate discomfort. The one-knee position requires that the leg away from the paddling side be thrust out and braced against the canoe bottom.

Whether the paddler strokes on the right or left side of the canoe makes little difference. The technique for the stroke remains the same. The upper hand is usually away from the side on which the paddle is placed in the water. The upper hand grasps the grip of the paddle, and the lower hand grasps the lower part of the shaft a few inches above the flare. The stroke should be taken in the most comfortable and natural manner possible. By using the paddle as a lever—that is, with the lower hand acting as a fulcrum and the upper hand pushing forward against the grip—a great deal of force is exerted and the canoe is sent skimming over the water. The pad-

FIGURE 20-4. Learning the fine points of the canoe. (Courtesy: Donna Richardson.)

FIGURE 20-5. Proper trim of canoe under various conditions.

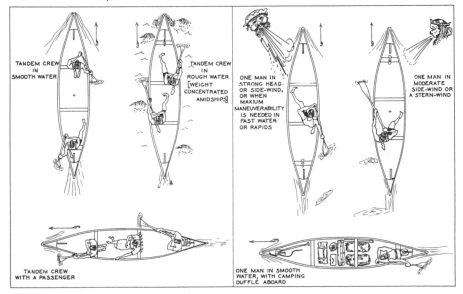

dle should be held as close as possible to the canoe side without scraping or dragging it against the canoe. The lower hand should be close to the water without actually dipping into it. At the completion of any stroke, it may be necessary to remove the paddle from the water to recover for the next stroke. The paddle should then be feathered; that is, the blade of the paddle should be turned so that its flat side is parallel to the water. This allows recovery and cuts air resistance. The more important strokes are described next (Fig. 20-6).

The J-Stroke   The J-stroke is always used by the paddler in the stern. It is effective in counteracting the bow's tendency to swing away from a straight course. Its name is derived from the course that the paddle takes as the blade is pulled through the water. The stroke is begun by reaching as far forward with the paddle as is comfortable, with the blade approximately 1 foot from the canoe's side. The paddle is levered from front to rear, and the blade is permitted to turn so that, at the end of the stroke, the back of the blade is turned away from the canoe. The blade travels in a tight arc away from the canoe and is jerked clear of the water for the recovery.

The Bow Stroke   The bow stroke can be used from any position in the canoe. Insert the paddle into the water at a comfortable distance and then draw it to the stern with the blade at right angles to the canoe side. Another stroke is started by feathering the paddle forward and replacing it in the water.

The Full-Sweep Stroke   This stroke is valuable when one person is paddling. The canoeist is usually kneeling at or near the center of the canoe. Place the paddle as far forward as can be reached, and sweep it around in

FIGURE 20-6.   Canoe paddling strokes.

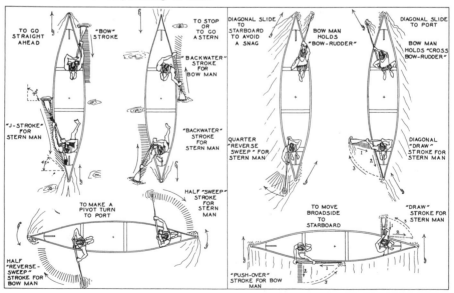

a 180-degree turn from front to rear. The stroke is used to pivot the canoe away from the side on which the paddle is dipped. The recovery is made by feathering the paddle and returning it to the front with the lower end of the blade down.

The Quarter-Sweep Stroke   The quarter sweep is used to veer the bow or stern away from some point or object in the water. Place the paddle as far to the front as is comfortable and sweep the blade through the water to a position where the entire paddle is at right angles with the side of the canoe. When two paddlers are in the canoe, the craft can be quickly turned within its own length by this method.

The Backwater Stroke   The backwater stroke is nearly the reverse of the bow stroke. When it is used, the canoe will be propelled backward, or its forward motion will be slowed and finally halted, or it will veer toward the side on which the stroke is being performed. The stroke is executed by cutting the blade into the water a comfortable distance to the rear of the hip. Then lever the paddle through the water from back to front as close to the side as possible.

The Draw Stroke   The draw is accomplished by reaching out with the paddle at a comfortable distance from the side of the canoe, dipping the blade full length into the water, and then pulling or drawing the canoe to the blade. Just before the blade reaches the canoe's side, turn the blade sideways and feather outward. Then begin the next draw.

The Underwater Stroke   The underwater stroke is used for stalking game. It is a silent stroke and does not give much speed. Begin the stroke by dipping the entire blade underwater and levering it through the water with the blade at an angle of less than 90 degrees. Rotate the grip of the paddle on every stroke to avoid riffling the water. The recovery is made by cutting the paddle through the water with one-third of the blade exposed.

Sculling   Sculling is a useful stroke for pulling the canoe to one side quite rapidly. It is performed by manipulating the paddle so that it cuts a figure-8 through the water. Hold sternward the paddle as if to make a draw stroke, with the blade parallel to the side. The pressure comes from the draw phase of the stroke. This is an extremely short stroke; the lower arm does almost all the work, while the top hand and arm serve as guides.

The Push Stroke   The push stroke is the opposite of the draw. It is used to move the canoe away from the side on which the paddling is being performed. Place the paddle into the water as close to the side of the canoe as possible and in a vertical position; by extending both arms, the paddle is pushed away from the canoe. The upper hand pulls down and toward the canoe while the lower hand acts as a fulcrum.

Sailing

Sailing entails the propulsion of some form of flat-bottomed or keeled craft by means of wind power against spread canvas. A body of water that is at least 4 feet deep is required. There are many kinds of sailing craft, but camps usually use boats with one mast and one or two sails, such as the sailing dinghy and the sloop. The following discussion is based on the sloop, because it is most frequently used at camps.

The sloop has one mainmast with two sails. The mainsail is a triangular sheet attached to the mast on one side and to the boom or lower spar at the bottom. The second sail, or jib, a relatively small triangular canvas sheet, is forward of the mast. It is attached by lines rather than to wooden masts or spars. The sloop may come equipped with a retractable center board or keel. The keel can be used only where the water is deep enough. It provides additional stability to the sailing craft. Fundamentally, all sailing is the same; the nautical terms that have been handed down for a thousand years remain constant. The only variation is in terms of the equipment, the size of the craft, and the number and dimensions of the sails.

Terminology is quite significant to the sailor, and it is necessary to learn the correct terms to designate parts of the boat (Fig. 20-7). The ability to give and obey orders when under sail make the difference between a smooth, enjoyable ride and an uneven, and perhaps disastrous, one. Almost all sailboats require a 2-person crew. The skipper steers the craft and handles the mainsheet, while the mate tends the centerboard and the jib sheet. All directions aboard a boat are indicated by port (left), and starboard (right), aft (back), and forward (front). The open space is called the *cockpit* and the remaining surface around the open section is called the *deck*. Forward of the cockpit is the *mast*, to which is attached a horizontal spar called the *boom*. There are generally three guy wires supporting the mast; these are called the port and starboard *sidestays* and the *forestay*.

Techniques.   It is essential that the wind be brought to bear at the most efficient angle for use in propulsion. To obtain maximum forward momentum, a boat must follow a zigzag course—that is, sailing on alternate tacks at right angles to each other. As the wind fills the sail, part of the pressure is exerted against the sail to push the boat forward. The remaining pressure forces the boat sideways. As the sail fills, low pressure is created on the opposite side, forming a vacuum. The boat moves into this low pressure space and sails, as continued pressure is exerted against the sheets. It is impossible for a sailboat to sail into the wind. For this reason, the best course to follow when the wind is against the bow is at a 45-degree angle left or right of a course to windward.

The three basic positions are (1) *beating,* also called sailing to windward, tacking, pointing, sailing close-hauled, or sailing on the wind; (2) *reaching,* or sailing off the wind; and (3) *running,* or sailing to leeward, or running free (Fig. 20-8).

Beating   When the wind comes straight across the bow or to one side of the bow, the boat must be kept moving and the sails filled while the skipper keeps a course as close as possible to the direction from which the wind blows. The best angle for beating is 45 degrees to the wind. The centerboard will be down; the jib is trimmed in close, but not flat; the mainsail is trimmed close so that the end of the boom is directed at an angle toward the boat's stern, rather than straight back.

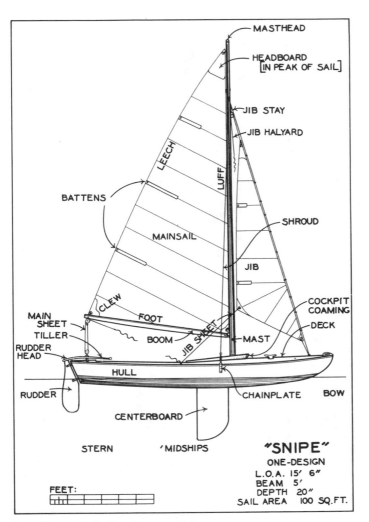

FIGURE 20-7.   Sailboat nomenclature.

Reaching   This occurs when the wind comes directly to the side of the craft at a 90-degree angle to the boat. A close reach is any point of sailing between close-hauled and sailing at 90 degrees to windward. A broad reach is any point of sailing between 90 degrees to windward and running before the wind. Sails should always be trimmed in relation to the sailing position. Sails are best used when they do not luff or flap in the wind, and are slacked off.

Running   When a sailing craft moves in the same direction as the wind, it is running before the wind. With the wind blowing from directly astern, the mainsail is positioned at right angles to the wind. If the water is fairly calm, the centerboard can be pulled clear of the water. This permits

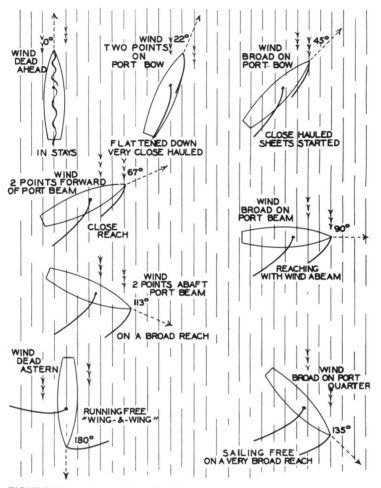

FIGURE 20-8.   The points of sailing.

the boat to move through the water with the least amount of friction. When the boat is running, the skipper must be constantly attentive in order to prevent accidental jibbing. If the direction of wind varies and the skipper has not been alert to the change, a jibe may occur; that is, the mainsail may shift from one side of the boat to the other. Such a condition puts excessive strain on the boat and is dangerous to all aboard. However, an intentional jibe can save precious seconds in a race, or can be performed as the wind changes direction from the stern. When this maneuver is adroitly performed, it is a swift and impressive procedure. To jibe the boat, the centerboard is lowered. The crew trims the mainsail in while the skipper steers the boat off wind until the boom swings over to the other side. The mainsheet is slacked off quickly and evenly, the course is resumed, and the centerboard is lowered. The jib will be reset on the opposite side. The skipper and crew normally shift their weight to the windward side in order to keep the trim.

Getting Away Getting away from dock or mooring is not particularly difficult. There are some details that must be considered, however. First, the skipper should decide on his initial tack by noting the wind direction. The mainsail should be hoisted first, then the jib sheet. Depending on wind direction, the boat will sail to the wind. The bowline must be cast off and moved away from the dock so that the correct side of the boat is presented to the wind. The tiller is pulled over so that the boat clears the dock. The skipper trims the mainsail while the crew trims the jib.

Docking It takes a high degree of skill to maneuver a boat to a dock. The general procedure is to come about directly into the wind so that the boat comes to a slow stop and gently touches the dock. Wind direction and speed must always be taken into account during docking. The boat may be running before the wind as it nears the dock. The centerboard should be lowered to permit easy maneuvering. The boat must be sailed parallel to the dock and at least two boat lengths away from it. The boat should be brought about so as to head into the wind while coming alongside the dock (Fig. 20-9). The sails should be trimmed so as not to catch the dock. When the wind direction is across the dock, the approach to the dock should be on the side away from the wind and close-hauled. When the dock is fewer than three boat lengths away, the ship should be pointed into the wind while the main and jib sheets are let go.

After sailing. The ship must always be left in good condition. It should be clean and ready for other sailings. All sails should be lowered and battens removed. The sails should be stowed in bags. Damp sails should be laid out to dry. All traces of salt should be removed from the sails. All halyards should be fastened, leaving a little slack. Loose equipment must be secured, and the centerboard should be pulled up. The boat must be securely tied to the dock or mooring. The sailor must always consider the possibility of foul weather and secure the boat to ride it out.

SKIN AND SCUBA DIVING

Skin diving, or free underwater swimming, is performed without any attachments to the surface. The diver pursues some object of interest, or simply explores what others have never seen. The basic pieces of equipment for skin diving are a mask and faceplate, swim fins, and a breathing tube. If the diver has an unusual capacity and can stay submerged for several minutes at a time, he may not even want the snorkel. The faceplate and snorkel permit the diver to swim slightly beneath the surface and observe the bottom. The fins enable the swimmer to attain high rates of speed and swim for long distances without too great an effort. When the skin diver reaches a point that seems worthy of exploration, he performs a surface dive and

FIGURE 20-9. Manipulating a model to learn tiller and sailing positions as the wind shifts direction.

submerges to investigate it or to collect specimens. The length of the dive is restricted by the diver's ability to withstand water pressure as well as to hold his breath. Some trained divers have attained a depth of more than 100 feet. Almost any body of water of sufficient depth and clarity offers a challenge to the skin diver.

The self-contained breathing apparatus carried by the scuba diver allows him to remain under water and travel exceptionally long distances. Divers may operate under water on a tank of oxygen for periods up to 1 hour, at depths of 30 to 50 feet. The ability to remain under water for prolonged periods of time, coupled with a high degree of weightlessness and mobility, has attracted thousands of enthusiasts to this form of aquatics. With scuba gear, the diver can fish, photograph, explore, and collect specimens of underwater life and minerals.

Equipment

Several pieces of equipment are essential to any form of diving. The mask, or faceplate, is the most useful item. The mask is usually made of soft rubber and fitted with unbreakable glass plates. Good masks have a wide stainless-steel band holding the glass in place. The mask encloses the eyes and nose but leaves the mouth free for breathing. The mask can be molded to fit facial contours. The paramount function of the mask is to ensure a watertight seal. A strap holding the mask to the head should be attached to the front end; the mask is then more evenly pressed against the face and the insertion of a snorkel under the strap is permitted without breaking the seal.

Swim fins are also vital to the diver, as they increase forward speed considerably. Swim fins should be selected on the basis of the diver's swimming ability. Experienced divers and swimmers want a rigid fin that provides more power per kick; less-strong swimmers probably select a flexible fin that reduces push but enables the diver to use less effort. Fins with adjustable or fixed rubber straps at the back of the heel tend to be less useful than those with enclosed heel guards that are designed for one person's exclusive use.

The snorkel, or breathing tube, is a device used by divers for scanning the bottom while cruising on the surface. The head does not have to be lifted for air. The snorkel itself is a J- or U-shaped tube with a mouthpiece on one end that can be twisted to fit the mouth regardless of the tube's angle. The upper end of the tube should be flexible, so that it will not be torn out of the diver's mouth if it strikes some object.

There are other accessory units that divers can use, such as knives that float if dropped, spears, and spear guns for fishing. Insulated rubber suits can be worn. The diver probably requires some kind of wet or dry suit in cold waters. In the temperate waters of the lakes on which many camps are located, suits may not be necessary.

For scuba diving, underwater breathing apparatus of the closed- or open-circuit variety is vital. The inherent dangers of the closed-circuit apparatus make it useful to experts only. The open-circuit apparatus, by far the most popular, is used by camps. One or more tanks of compressed air are attached to the diver's back by means of a harness. The harness includes two shoulder straps and connecting straps across the chest, waist, and crotch. A demand regulator attached to the compressed air tank is used to supply on demand whatever volume of air the diver requires. The volume equalizes the air pressure within the diver and the surrounding pressure. In the single-stage system, only one operational phase is required. It reduces the high-pressure air, and, on demand, the air is supplied at the same pressure and volume as the surrounding pressure. In the two-stage system, the high pressure is reduced in one stage. The next stage is accomplished under a low pressure of approximately 100 pounds per square inch. In all two-stage systems, the diaphragm activates the low-pressure stage, which regulates the appropriate amount of air to be released to the diver for internal and external equalization.

A weighted belt is generally used to balance the diver. The lead weights counter the natural buoyancy of the body and the equipment. The belt has a quick-release that permits it to be dropped if necessary.

Protective suits are worn by divers if the water is cold, as it usually is when diving to depths of more than 50 feet, particularly in the sea or in unprotected waters where the sea has access. The dry suit is watertight; warm underclothing worn under it keeps the diver comfortable. The dry suit can be worn in very cold water, although any tear will reduce its effectiveness. If water gets into the suit, it seeps into the layer of insulating air around the underclothing. The wet suit is usually made of foam rubber or neoprene. It fits closely, although a small amount of water is permitted to enter the suit to be warmed by the body. The suit insulates the body from outside cold water. The thickness of the suit determines the degree of insulation. Tears are easily repaired, and rips do not cause a loss of buoyancy or any loss of warmth in other parts of the suit.

Techniques.   The diver should be well trained in swimming skills. Swimming with fins requires little instruction, but a good deal of conditioning is necessary for efficient use. Stamina should be gradually developed until the swimmer can propel herself over long distances without becoming fatigued. To use the mask properly, the diver must learn to adjust the pressure inside it by exhaling slightly through the nose. In order to get rid of any water that gets into the mask, the diver pushes in on the part of the mask closest to the surface and exhales through the nose. The air that is trapped in the mask pushes the water out at the bottom. This skill should be practiced in controlled situations by removing the mask under water and replacing it.

Breathing through the snorkel is performed through the mouth. The diver must learn to inhale, pause, and then exhale. Breath holding when diving retains air in the breathing tube and prevents water from entering. It is important that sufficient air be retained to permit a forceful exhalation after returning to the surface, so that any water is expelled from the snorkel.

The air pressure in the ears should be equalized regularly during each dive to prevent discomfort. The diver must practice moving her jaw and swallowing during the dive. This may not be effective, however, and the diver must then compress her mask against her face and blow hard through her nose. A characteristic popping sound occurs as the pressure in the ears is equalized.

Scuba diving is much more complicated than skin diving because of the variety of physical and physiological problems that the diver must recognize before he is equipped to perform at any depth, but particularly if he wishes to swim in open water. Knowledge of the physical laws as they apply to diving is necessary to prevent accidents. Perhaps the most important of these laws is Boyle's law, which states that the volume of a confined gas varies inversely with pressure at constant temperature. This means that when the diver, breathing compressed air or gas, is coming to the surface, he must continually exhale or else suffer the probability of ruptured lungs.

The scuba diver must be able to clear both his mask and his regulator. With the two-stage regulator, the mouthpiece is removed and raised slightly higher than the regulator. This causes air to escape from the mouthpiece. The face is then turned toward the surface, and the bubbling mouthpiece is inserted into the mouth. The head is then turned in the direction of the hose to drain excess water to that side. A forceful exhalation pushes the remaining water out of the exhaust vent. The single-stage regulator requires a brief puff to clear the water from the mouthpiece.

Campers must practice adjusting the equipment and using the regulator. Beginners must be required to breathe with the apparatus on land before entering shallow water for continued practice. Clearing the mask is an essential skill that must be mastered. Buddy breathing—that is, two divers breathing from one tank underwater—must become a routine skill. Progressively prolonged periods of diving to greater depths should be practiced. Lifesaving skills, including treading and floating with tank on, and the removal and replacement of equipment when underwater, must be stressed.

Safety precautions. No diver, especially at camp, should ever be permitted to dive alone. The buddy system should always be used. All gear must be thoroughly checked for leaks, damage, or wear to suit, fins, masks, or tanks. Diving should be performed only when the individual is in good physical condition. Rough water, tides, and currents must be avoided. A quick-release buckle should be a feature on all pieces of equipment. The diver should always exhale while ascending, never hold the breath while surfacing, and breathe normally while scuba diving. The tank should undergo a certified inspection and be filled at a recognized air station.

Campers should not overexert themselves when under water. They must be aware of potential hazards before diving and remain calm. Slow, deliberate movements are more likely than rapid ones to release one from a dangerous situation. The camper should never swim in water that is colder than 70° F unless an exposure suit is worn.

LIFESAVING AND WATER-SAFETY INSTRUCTION

Material on new concepts and techniques of lifesaving and water-safety instruction can be obtained from agencies such as the American Red Cross and the YMCA, which are devoted to organizing and arranging the dissemination of this material. But since lifesaving and water safety often play a key role in the program of the modern camp, an indication of their function at camp is required here.

Every camper should receive some instruction in water-safety procedures. This instruction should be offered early in the season as a basic part of information about the rules for the use of the aquatic facility. Water safety includes using swimming and diving areas, keeping them in proper condition, using counselor lifeguards and buddy checks, and the like. Water-safety practices are designed to eliminate hazards in the aquatic area.

Lifesaving classes can be offered in two categories to advanced swimmers: junior lifesaving for campers under 15 years of age, and senior lifesaving for those over the age of 15. Lifesaving courses are geared to the concept that a person is in trouble and might drown. The courses are therefore primarily concerned with the victim's immediate situation in relation to the nearest assistance. A rescuer does not have to swim to rescue a victim if other aids are available. The distance between the victim and the shore will guide the rescuer's efforts. If a victim is well offshore and a lifeboat is within 100 yards of the rescuer, the best approach is to run to the boat and row to the rescue. Running would take no more than 12 seconds, and the boat could be launched immediately. Another 30 seconds would be needed to row the distance, and then the rescue could be made from the boat. If the rescuer were to swim out as fast as he could, he might reach the victim in less than 30 seconds, but then he would have to recover the victim and tow him all the way back. It is therefore better to use some aid—reaching poles, ring buoys with lines attached, surfboards, small craft—and to actually swim to the rescue only when these are unavailable (Fig. 20-10).

Swimming rescues are classified as (1) entries into the water by jumping, running, or diving followed by (2) front, rear, or underwater swimming approaches; (3) blocks and parries; (4) releases including front or rear strangle, and right, left, or both wrists; (5) carries, including cross chest, head, hair, or tired-swimmer; and (6) shallow water carries, either camel-back or fireman's carry. Finally, there must be practice in the recovery of submerged victims and in resuscitation.

Lifesaving Techniques

The approaches in swimming rescues are from the front, rear, or under water. The camper must be taught to keep his eye on the victim when making the approach, to reverse his position while maintaining correct distance, to contact the victim in the proper manner, and to level off for the tow to safety. In underwater approaches, the victim must be turned so that towing can be accomplished.

Once contact has been made with the victim, without conflict, the rescuer must then tow or carry the victim to safety by using a variety of carries. The cross-chest carry is useful to control the victim's panic-stricken thrashings. Arm and leg movements must be effective, and the victim must feel absolutely secure in the position. Generally, cross-chest carries are used for short distances only. The hair and head carry are properly used when the victim is unconscious and the distance to shore is quite far. The techniques for these carries require that certain arm and hand positions be maintained and that the victim's face be held clear of the water. Leveling off from a vertical position requires a quick reverse by the rescuer and contact with the victim so that an initial movement to shore can be made while putting the victim into the proper position for a carry. The rescuer can correctly position the victim by engaging the victim's wrist with the rescuer's hand, palm and thumb down, and pulling the victim toward the shore while simultaneously turning him. Leveling off is performed by cupping the hand under the victim's chin, thumb extended along the side of the head, and putting the elbow of the cupping arm into the small of the victim's back. This forces the victim into a supine floating position. A carry maneuver is then applied to tow the victim.

If, because of an error of judgment, the rescuer finds himself being attacked by the victim, a series of blocks, parries, or releases can be used. In executing the block, the rescuer keeps his arm outstretched and rigid, fingers spread against the upper part of the victim's chest. In some cases it might be necessary for the rescuer to spread his fingers against the base of the victim's throat to hold off his attempts to climb on the rescuer's head and shoulders. The parry is used to ward off a front strangle attempt in

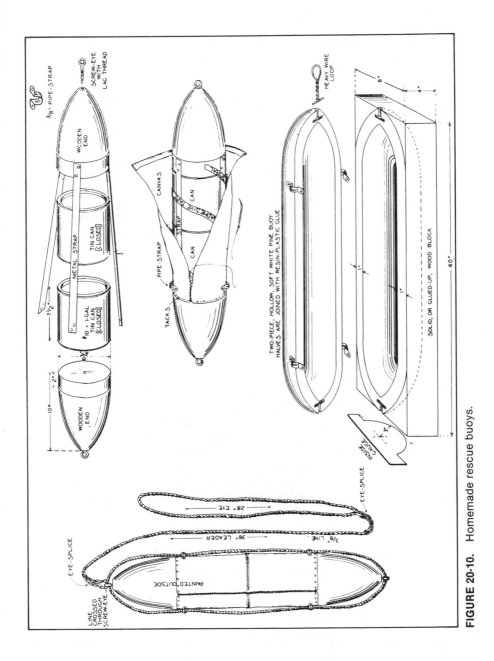

FIGURE 20-10. Homemade rescue buoys.

combination with contact so that the rescuer comes up behind the victim for a leveling-off procedure and carry. The block and turn is a combination that stops the victim and uses his own momentum to turn him around so that leveling off and carry can be applied.

In the event that the victim actually grabs the rescuer in a front head-hold, the rescuer should turn his head aside, tuck in his chin, and push himself underwater. The victim will probably release his hold and try to fight his way to the surface. In any event, the rescuer will place his hand between his own face and that of the victim's, hooking his thumb under the lower jaw. He will grasp the elbow on top at a point just above the elbow joint and push the victim away with both hands while maintaining contact. The leveling-off procedure is then carried out as the victim's arm is held by the rescuer's hand. The rescuer's arm becomes the fulcrum for leveling.

In the rear strangle, the rescuer turns his head to the side, tucks his chin in, and swims down by using his arms to submerge. Once underwater, the rescuer applies pressure to the victim's hand and elbow, bringing the victim to his front by leverage. The victim is then brought to the surface and leveled off at the same time. A carry can then be used. If the victim grasps one or both wrists, the rescuer should bring his hands close together and grasp the victim's wrist. He then takes a breath, forces the victim beneath him, places his outer foot against the victim's outer shoulder (that is, on the side opposite the direction in which the victim will turn), and straightens out his leg. The victim will lose his grip and be able to be turned and leveled off in one swift movement. A carry can then be used.

For shallow-water carries, either fireman's or camel back, the following sequence proves adequate. In shallow water, the rescuer stands alongside the victim and places one hand over the near leg and under the far knee. The other hand should be under the victim's neck. The rescuer submerges to a squatting position and rolls the victim over his shoulders in a prone position. The victim's hips should be squarely above the rescuer's neck. The rescuer can then stand and, with the victim draped across his shoulders, move shoreward. The camel-back carry requires that the rescuer drape the victim's arm over his neck and simultaneously reach over the victim's upper back to support his trunk and head out of water. The rescuer then turns his back on the victim, brings him against his own hips, and wades to shore in this position. With proper balance and applied leverage, any victim can be carried for relatively long distances without discomfort to the rescuer.

SYNCHRONIZED SWIMMING

In synchronized swimming, strokes and patterns of movement are performed to some accompanying rhythm or music. Skill in standard swimming techniques and stunts, an ability to coordinate one's movements with those of others, and practice are all needed. Without a thorough knowledge of basic strokes, the endurance to go through the routines, and the skill to adapt easily to variations, a camper cannot contribute to the group's progress. For those who are just beginning to learn swimming in sets and simultaneous stroking, the group should move no faster than its slowest member. When advanced swimmers rehearse, however, any individual who cannot maintain the pace retards almost all activity. Teamwork, swimming style, and stamina are the three key factors for synchronized swimming.

Techniques

Standard swimming strokes form the foundation for all variations and stunts performed in synchronized swimming. The form of strokes should be consistent. Extensive practice is mandatory until all have acquired the degree of skill necessary to maneuver into various positions. Stroking should be rhythmic, powerful, and relaxed. The standard strokes are used to cover water space and for transitions. For synchronized swimming, some variations are noted. There is an absence of normal breathing techniques. The head is held above water so that performers can see others and keep time. The body position in the water is lower than would normally be considered good practice, in order to avoid undue splashing. Combinations of strokes or variations on arm recoveries can be used to heighten the action or express emphasis. Body positions can be changed, directions can be changed, or the entry of the hand into the water can be modified.

The primary body positions are those of pike, tuck, and layout. In the layout position, the body is extended and aligned from head to toe. The prone or supine position can be used. Sculling can assist in maintaining a relatively stationary attitude. In the pike, the hips are flexed to a right angle. The knees are locked and the toes pointed straight up. The back pike requires that the hips be flexed at an acute angle, with the straight legs being brought closer to the chest. The toes are pointed and the ankles are at the surface of the water. In the tuck position, the knees and hips are flexed. The legs are drawn tightly to the chest, with the head held close to the knees. A flat scull is used to rotate the body. Tucks are executed near the surface of the water.

Sculling, used for support or locomotion, is merely pulling and pushing against the water alternately. The flat scull is performed by placing the hands, palms down, on the surface of the water and maneuvering them in a figure-8. The flat scull is used to maintain a stationary position. A standard scull performed at the waist will propel the body in the direction of the head. When it is used with arms extended above the head, the body moves toward the feet. With the reverse scull, the body moves in the opposite direction from that taken by the standard scull.

Stunts

All stunts are based on the standard positions, strokes, and sculling. Among the typical stunts are marlin, somersault, porpoise, kip, ballet leg, and dolphin. A marlin is a back layout with the arms extended at shoulder level. To move in one direction, the swimmer presses and swings the opposite arm under water toward the leg in the desired direction. The body should roll from back to stomach while the extended arm is swept under water. The roll is continued until the body position returns to a back layout at a right angle from the original position. The marlin is a transition move-ment and can be used to reorient an entire formation. Somersaults can be executed from either a tuck or pike position, front or back. In the tuck, the hands are used to complete the somersault. The porpoise is simply a pike surface-dive. The kip is begun from a back layout position to a tuck posi-tion. The body is rotated as it would be in a back somersault. The arms, with palms facing outward, press up toward the shoulders. The legs are held vertically, and the body is balanced in an upside-down position. The arms are then extended toward the bottom, and the body drops in the vertical position. The dolphin begins in a back layout. By sculling, the swimmer pulls herself under the water in a complete circle until her body returns to a back layout on the surface. The ballet leg starts from a layout position. Either leg is flexed at the knee and hip, holding the other leg in extension. The flexed leg is then raised to a vertical position, while the trunk is ex-tended on the surface and the head and shoulders are aligned. The vertical leg is then flexed and returned to its original position beside the extended leg. The other leg can then be raised in the same manner. An advanced stunt is the double dolphin, where both legs are raised simultaneously.

Synchronized swimming requires a good deal of practice on land as well as in water. A series of drills should be designed, remembering that the movements are geared to be observed by an audience. Thus, if the audience is seated at water level, surface stunts and formations are effective. If the audience is situated above the water, then underwater sequences as well as surface formations will produce excellent results. The type of accompani-ment is also important to the patterns that will be used. Analysis of rhythms will assist in choosing and developing the patterns and movements that can be used to best effect. All water movements must be appropriate to the setting, the accompaniment, the skills of the participants, and the safety of the performers.

FISHING

Fishing, although a part of the aquatic program, should be a part of camp life in general (Fig. 20-11). It combines the excitement of competition with the peace and quiet that solitude brings. It offers opportunities for explora-tion, physical conditioning, and concurrent hobbies. From the sport of fish-ing for food and fun there have developed several competitive activities that add to fishing skills. Among them are fly, bait, and spinning activities and casting games that require hand–eye coordination and much practice.

A location for the teaching of casting skills is easily selected. Selection of equipment, conservation laws, fish and game laws, dress, boat handling, and safety factors can be discussed almost anywhere. Any open space, whether on land or water, offers an adequate area for conducting classes and practice sessions. Members of the fishing and casting class fall into at least three categories: beginning, intermediate, and advanced. Beginners have never cast before and have probably never gone fishing. Intermediates may have done some bait casting, but their skills are limited and they still

FIGURE 20-11. Life imitating life (the fish is on the left). (Courtesy: Clara Barton Camp for Girls with Diabetes, North Exford, Mass.)

have difficulty with the equipment. Advanced campers have had fishing experience and have some degree of skill; they no longer have difficulty with the equipment, but rather need practice to improve their skills.

Optimally, all three groups will receive instruction and demonstrations of casting techniques; however, it is neither necessary nor good practice to force the more highly skilled campers to hold back for less-skilled ones. Once the groups are sorted out and the better casters have been identified, they can be assigned to some area where they may progress more rapidly. Inexperienced campers who obviously need more assistance should be grouped together. The station method of instruction can be quite useful here. As their skills increase, campers move to another section of the practice area, where they receive additional instruction in more complicated movements. In this manner, campers can move as quickly as they are able through the various stages to advanced techniques. Another method, rotating campers to different stages of instruction at the end of definite time periods, can also be used.

Equipment

A sufficient number of satisfactory rods and reels should be available for campers' use. Many campers bring their own fishing tackle to camp, but such tackle is usually of the bait-casting variety. The camp can provide casting equipment of good quality so that each camper can have individual equipment during the group practice period. Eight or 10 outfits, including rod, reel, lure, line, and target, should meet equipment needs.

Bait-casting tackle.   Bait-casting rods are generally made of fiberglass. They are durable and not damaged by moisture. They are strong and flexible, varying in length from 4 to 6 feet. Some rods come in several pieces for easy dismantling and carrying. The reel is a vital part of the equipment. The bait-casting reel has a revolving spool to pick up the line. The spool is geared to revolve four times for every turn of the handle. The narrow spool is recommended for beginners. Preferable to silk lines are nylon lines, which are waterproof, require almost no care, and are extremely durable. All lines should be selected by weight and should be at least 75 yards long.

Fly-casting tackle.   A rod of medium action that bends evenly is recommended for beginners. The best length for all-purpose use is approximately 8 feet. A good rod has at least 7 and perhaps 8 guides to the poles for the line. The windings that secure the guides must extend no less than $\frac{1}{8}$ inch beyond the foot of the guide. The grip should be of good-quality cork and at least 7 inches long. The single-action reel is preferred to the automatic by most experienced fly casters. The weight of the rod and reel together should be about $1\frac{1}{2}$ times that of the rod alone. The line is considered the single most important element in fly casting. The weight of the line is dependent upon the action of the rod. Flexible rods require a lighter line than do rigid rods. Most poles require a line of between 6 and 8 pounds. The weight of the line beyond the rod is the only weight that assists in the cast. Of the three types of lines—level, double taper, and torpedo—the level line is most commonly used.

Spin-casting tackle.   The spinning rod is made specifically for spinning reels. The rods are usually between 6 and 7 feet long. The butt of the rod is either straight for open-faced reels or curved inward for the closed-faced type. The open-faced reel is mounted on the underside of the rod. The closed-face type, recommended for the beginner, is mounted on top of the rod. A bail attached to the front of the reel wraps the line around the reel when the handle is turned. Nylon line is best for spin casting; it should be no more than 8 pounds test.

Skish.   Skish bait-casting employs regular tackle and serves to sharpen accuracy and improve technique when the fisherman cannot go fishing. In skish, the caster attempts to place his plug on a 10-inch target anywhere from 40 to 80 feet away. The caster has two chances at each target. Skish, which can be performed either inside or outside, is a perfect rainy-day activity for those who are learning how to cast.

Casting Techniques

For fly casting, the rod should be held firmly, but without tension, with the reel down. The fingers should be around the handle with the thumb along the side or the back of the grip. The line is held by the casting hand between the fingers and the rod handle. It is the line, rather than the lure, that is cast in fly casting (Fig. 20-12). The cast should be made with a minimum arm movement, the forearm and wrist moving like a hinge. About 20 to 30 feet of line are stripped from the reel and laid out in front of the caster. The tip of the rod should be raised to take up slack. The line is loosely held in the left hand. The rod is lifted until the line is straight. The fly then lands on the surface of the water and the rod is held diagonally to the water. The rod is snapped to a vertical position and the line is permitted to follow around until it is behind the caster, with its weight bending the rod slightly. The forward cast is begun immediately; the rod is whipped

FIGURE 20-12. Dry practice by flipping a plug: (a) ready position, (b) initiating the backswing, (c) most rearward position, (d) whipping forward.

forward until it reaches the original forward diagonal position. For greater distance, the line is released as soon as the fly starts to move forward. Just before the fly settles on target, the rod is raised to remove any slack and prevent the line from splashing into the water. The pickup must then be started slowly in order to remove the line from the water as quietly as possible.

In bait casting, the rod is held with the reel handle up and the thumb pressing lightly against the crossbar of the reel. The fingers are spread comfortably over the handle with the index finger around the fingerhook. In bait casting, unlike fly casting, the bait is thrown and the line follows it. The cast is overhead, and the wrist does most of the work. The rod tip is lowered until the rod is nearly parallel to the surface and then snapped to a vertical position by the wrist and a negligible movement of the forearm. At the vertical position the rod is stopped, although the weight of the lure will bend the tip of the rod backward. The forward cast begins immediately, with the rod tip pointing at the target upon completion of the cast.

The spin cast is similar to bait casting. The chief difference is the control of the line during the cast. When using an open-faced reel, the grip of the rod is taken with the finger holding the string close to the rod to prevent release on the back swing. The bail is open so that the line is free to run when the finger is straightened. As the rod is snapped forward, the finger is straightened and the line is freed. With a closed-face reel, the line is freed by pressing the release button with the thumb.

Safety Precautions

There is almost no danger in practice casting, but there is a certain hazard when participants use hooks. Barbed hooks may be necessary for fishing, but it is inadvisable to use them in practice sessions. Before casting with a plug, the participant should always make sure that the area is clear so that no one will be hit accidentally. When fishing from a boat, the same rules apply as for water and boat safety.

chapter 21

Indoor Activities

Every camp is affected by weather conditions that simply prevent the normal outdoor activities. But the indoor activities to which counselors resort during inclement weather provide as many opportunities for meaningful and enjoyable experiences as the outdoor activities. Some summer rains are light and may not prevent outdoor activities if campers are properly dressed. With slight modifications, a variety of activities can be continued under shelter, without going indoors. Riflery, hobbies, preparation for special events, art, crafts, dancing, dramatics, trip planning, and motor-skill activities can all be carried on. In fact, counselors can use the time that is usually taken up in active camping experiences to discuss new and useful concepts for improving the program.

Campers, particularly the younger ones, may become anxious during heavy rainstorms. If thunder and lightning accompany the storm, the apprehensiveness of young children may be manifested in depression, crying, or insecurity. The counselor can counteract fear by explaining these natural phenomena; at the same time, he can use the opportunity to encourage campers' interest in meterology specifically or in nature science generally. The campers can make a game of counting the seconds it takes to hear thunder after the flash of lightning has been seen.

Rainy days are too often filled with activities to which too little thought has been given. Activities suited for indoor spaces should be planned as meticulously as the daily outdoor program. Many activities can be planned for small or large groups, and for small or large indoor areas. The opportunity to produce a variety of enjoyable experiences, develop latent talent, and maintain campers' enthusiasm should not be overlooked.

RAINY-DAY ACTIVITIES

Almost any activity that holds campers' attention during one or more days of rain is worth doing. The counselor should always plan ahead for rain. If the camp has several facilities that can be used for large groups, it may be necessary to pool talents and resources. It is not unusual for the counselor and his bunk to be left to their own devices, however. Any of the following are appropriate rainy-day occupations.

Campers can make a bunk log, which is a scrapbook of adventures, achievements, and historical facts about the camp, unit, or bunk. It requires cutting out pictures, describing activities, drawing illustrations, and pasting. Younger campers particularly enjoy making a log. Perhaps the group has decided to refurbish the interior of its cabin, but has put off such plans because the weather was too nice; here is an appropriate time for decorating. Campers can plan for parties, trips, skits, and stunts at this time. An indoor scavenger hunt for items that are relatively difficult to find can create enthusiasm and help pass the time. Other suggestions are as follows:

1. Arrange a bunk display of cartoons of the campers.
2. Play charades.
3. Compose a bunk cheer or yell.
4. Draw and paint.
5. Work on hobbies.
6. Hold a quiz program.
7. Hold a speech competition.
8. Learn a bunk song.
9. Listen to the radio or records.
10. Make puppets.
11. Organize a comb-and-whistle band.
12. Practice camp-craft and wood-craft skills.
13. Practice first aid procedures.
14. Practice lifesaving dry-land drills.
15. Play quiet games.
16. Read.
17. Rehearse a skit or play for presentation at the next unit meeting.
18. See to the care and maintenance of camp equipment.
19. Set up a silhouette theatre.
20. Sing.
21. Tell stories.
22. Stage a talent show.
23. Write a bunk newspaper for distribution at supper.
24. Write letters home.
25. Write short stories.

Storytelling

One of the best rainy-day activities is storytelling. Storytelling is an ancient art, undoubtedly as old as spoken language. Long before they could read or write, humans communicated their deeds, doubts, and dreams through the spoken word, creating in the process a body of oral literature—

fables, myths, ballads, legends, folktales. From age to age, the storytellers of one generation passed their tales on to the next. The most gifted among these storytellers not only refined and polished their tales, but also defined and developed the art of telling a story.

Skilled narrators were accorded honor and respect by their peers, for everyone enjoys the magic of a superbly constructed story told with consummate skill. Listening to the storyteller was one of the few forms of recreational activity for early peoples. The stories were more than entertainment, however; they were the means of transmitting the ideals, beliefs, concerns, and aspirations of members of the adult community to each other and to the younger generation. The storyteller, then, was teacher as well as entertainer.

In the present day, storytellers no longer serve such an important and prominent role, having been largely supplanted by the printed word. Nevertheless, storytelling is still greatly enjoyed. The function of the present-day taleteller is essentially the same as that of his more esteemed predecessor: to bring to his audience a meaningful experience that is at the same time entertaining. His success depends upon the story chosen and the way it is told.

Choosing the story. A major consideration in the selection of stories is the age of the listeners. Stories suitable for young children do not appeal to older children, who have more sophisticated tastes and interests. Consequently, the listeners in any one group should be approximately the same age. If there is a wide range of ages in the group, however, the storyteller would be wise to choose stories that appeal to the older campers, for it is generally easier to capture the attention of the younger children with a story that is beyond them than to hold the interest of the older ones with a story that seems beneath them.

It is difficult for an inexperienced storyteller to judge which kinds of stories most interest each age group. Children's interests are shaped by a number of factors, including mental ability, background, and maturation, so that in any age group, many interests are found. Nevertheless, certain general interests common to each age level have been identified, and this knowledge can be used as an index to the kind of literature that appeals most to each age group. Information about the age appeal of various types of literature can come from a librarian or from the references listed in the Bibliography.

Regardless of the age or interests of the listener, the most appealing story is the one that "tells" well; effective telling of the story is ensured by its superb construction. Such a story has a clearly defined conflict; the action builds swiftly and directly to the climax and resolution of the conflict; its characters are sharply delineated in a few brief lines; all details superfluous to the plot are omitted. The theme of such a story is subtly conveyed; it is never forced by means of a contrived plot.

The story should appeal to the teller, because when a story gives the teller pleasure, she enjoys sharing it with others, and her delight is conveyed in the telling. Enthusiastic reception by her audience is virtually guaranteed. The novice storyteller best insures success with her own enthusiasm for sharing a story she loves with her listeners.

Telling the story.   Preparation for the actual storytelling begins with a thorough reading of the story. During the reading, give thought to the sequence of action in the plot, the qualities of the characters, and the prevailing mood of the story. This reading, in effect, is an identification of the qualities that are unique to this particular story. The entire story should be read several more times, enough to fix the pattern of the story in mind.

It is helpful to give each new plot development a label that is easily recalled, and then memorize these labels in their proper sequence as a guide for repeating the story. This technique is very helpful for stories that are long or have complicated plots. Even with short stories, it is better not to memorize the story word for word, for if the storyteller forgets the exact wording, he may falter completely. Even if he recovers and proceeds with the story, some of the magic has been lost from his storytelling. Frequent reading of a story plants certain phrases in the mind, and the storyteller should employ these to advantage in giving an original flavor to the telling. This is entirely different from deliberate memorization. Some stories, however, because of the charming and unique style in which they are written, must be told from memory to do them justice; Kipling's *Just So Stories* are an example. Storytellers who cannot memorize such stories for retelling should read them aloud.

In telling the story, the teller should visualize the setting and the characters as he is verbalizing these details for the listeners. This technique greatly enhances communication, for it helps the teller to create the special emphasis and tone needed to make the pictures of the story some alive for the listeners. Moreover, it influences the rate of the telling, so that there are well-timed pauses that allow the listeners a moment to see the scene before turning their attention to the next words.

After having thoroughly planned how to tell it, the storyteller should practice telling the story aloud. This allows him to hear how it will sound to his audience. If a tape recorder is available, recording the practice presentation is the best way of hearing how it sounds; speech mannerisms or poor speech habits that detract from the telling of the story can be detected and eliminated. Aside from these special problems, the storyteller should listen carefully for clarity in enunciation and variety in pitch and pace.

Ideally, the story is told in a voice that is naturally pleasant, with good diction, sufficient volume, and variations in pitch and speed suited to the mood and action of the story. Pleasure in listening to the story depends first of all upon being able to hear and understand the words that are spoken. Beyond this, pleasure is derived from emotional involvement and identification with the characters engaged in the story's conflict. The storyteller must therefore increase or decrease the tempo of his storytelling, and raise or lower the pitch of his voice, as required by the action or mood of the story at a particular point.

In storytelling, the story is told, not acted. Facial expressions and small gestures with the hands are natural accompaniments to telling a story and enhance the listening experience. Except in those cases in which the story-teller has genuine acting talents, however, actions beyond this should be restricted; they subtract from the storytelling rather than add to it.

Language that is characteristic of a certain kind of story should be retained for the unique flavor it gives the story; but unless such words can be understood from the context in which they are used, they may cause problems in interpretation. The storyteller can usually overcome the prob-lem by interjecting a brief explanation of the term or phrase. If the story-teller thinks, or knows from experience, that there are a number of obscure words in the story, he should discuss them briefly before telling the story.

The storyteller should make every effort to control the environment for the storytelling; this is essential for the novice who has not yet learned how to hold an audience despite distractions. A quiet spot where the chil-dren can be comfortably seated is the best choice. The space should be large enough to allow the children to be seated a comfortable distance from one another and still see the storyteller easily; a semicircular grouping usually works well. A pleasant grassy area away from the distractions of other camp activities, and a similarly quiet and comfortable area indoors (a library or reading room) for rainy days are ideal sites.

Much storytelling at camp occurs spontaneously. Counselors know that a good story is an effective antidote for numerous camp woes, ranging from temperamental flareups to homesickness. It also has a marvelously calming effect upon restless campers during rest hour and before "lights out." In these circumstances, the storyteller cannot, of course, be selective about the environmental conditions; he must rely entirely on his storytell-ing skill to capture and hold the children's attention. Needless to say, he should choose the most popular story in his repertoire.

To the romantic, the camp fire glowing against the evening sky seems the ideal setting for telling stories; for the storyteller, it is actually one of the most difficult. The camp-fire storyteller must contend with sudden crackling bursts of fire, smoke that stings the eyes and throat, and the shift-ing of bodies nearer to or away from the warmth of the fire. In addition to these distractions, he labors against the disadvantages of the darkness and the customary circular seating around the fire, which make it difficult for him to be seen and heard. The storyteller's main defense against the hazards of the situation is his choice of an appealing story and his own effective rendition of it. As well, he should make certain that the fire is laid and tended by someone who can control it effectively.

Whether at the camp fire or in the reading room, the storyteller must take a comfortable position in order to be perfectly relaxed during the storytelling. As long as everyone in the audience can see his face, he may sit or stand, but he must be comfortable in that posture. Otherwise the air of relaxation and easy enjoyment that should permeate the storytelling at-mosphere is difficult to maintain.

Reading the story. There is a tendency to substitute story reading for story telling in the belief that it is equally effective and much easier to do. A well-read story is certainly preferable to a poorly told one. The preparation for reading a story well is only slightly less than for telling it, however; the process is identical with the exception of the memorization involved. The book in the hands is an obstacle that is likely to interfere with the communication between reader and listener. Each time the reader looks from the children to the book, her hold on the audience is threatened. For this reason, story reading is generally much less effective than storytelling. The reader can reduce this distraction by planning the transitions from audience to book carefully so that they are made at the least important places in the story, or at places where breaks might most naturally occur. The same technique applies to showing pictures in the book to the audience.

Storytelling records.   If a good phonograph is available, storytelling records can be used to give variety to the programs and to introduce children to the beautiful speech of some of the world's finest storytellers. Only a machine in perfect working order should be used so that there is no distortion of sound. It is usually necessary to introduce the children to the listening experience with a few pertinent remarks about the storyteller and the high points of the telling. Toward this end, play the record through a time or two before presenting it to the children.

THE CAMP NEWSPAPER

Work on the camp newspaper, whether as a member of the editorial staff, or as a feature writer, illustrator, printer, or distributor, leaves a lasting impression and is a continuing source of satisfaction to the participants and the readers. Many camps put out a weekly newspaper; others publish papers once or twice during the season. Regardless of how often the newspaper makes its appearance, however, it is eagerly awaited. Every camper wants to see his name in print. All activities that occur at camp are excellent sources for a story, feature, or comment. As with other camp activities, democratic procedure in the paper's operation ensures the greatest readership, enjoyment, and sense of belonging and achievement. The most successful paper is one that has many children contributing to its pages and offers wide latitude for editorial discretion. The camp newspaper is a primary source of information about new activities. Letters to the editor offer an outlet for pent-up frustrations and emotions, thus alleviating them. The camper who feels that what he writes will be published may take a greater interest in the camp.

One counselor should be assigned to advise the newspaper staff and assist in the makeup of the paper itself. Without interfering with the prerogatives of a reporter or editor, she should discourage any writing that is untruthful, slanderous, or otherwise unbecoming. She should help her staff report the news and make it interesting. She should be constructive without being dictatorial.

The newspaper staff varies according to the ages of the campers. Required are a managing editor, several feature editors, and reporters of specific activities, such as sports, aquatics, shows, and socials. Bunk reporters, who write articles dealing with the activities of each bunk, might also be included.

Everything that happens at camp—everything that concerns the campers, counselors, and the staff in general—is news. Every camper should be encouraged to submit items of whatever length he chooses. The paper must appear when it is scheduled; as with most papers, yesterday's news is stale. A camp newspaper is operated for the enjoyment and satisfaction that the camper receives from contributing something creative to it and reading it. Those who staff the paper should still have time to do all the other things that campers participate in. Work on the paper is fun coupled with a sense of responsibility. The paper is produced indoors, although news gathering is a task that requires all-weather recording. On rainy days, the news staff may work to produce a "Wet Special," but this is optional. The counselor's leadership and guidance makes work on the camp paper one of the most stimulating and worthwhile experiences in a camper's summer.

INDOOR GAMES AND STUNTS

Even when campers are forced to remain indoors because of inclement weather, physical activity of many types can still be undertaken. Children of all ages find outlets in other activity forms, but younger campers generally prefer physical movement. There are hundreds of excellent motor-skill experiences that require relatively little space and can easily be played indoors. The counselor should have a complete repertory of tricks, stunts, self-testing exercises, and games that hold campers' attention and permit them to find needed release through action. The following are among the indoor games:

Hot Potato   All players sit in a circle, except the one who is It. A ball (the potato) is rapidly passed from one player to the next while It tries to tag the player with the object. If a person is tagged while holding the object, he becomes It.

Hot and Cold   One player leaves the room while another player selects an object in plain sight of those in the room. The one who left the room returns and tries to guess the object. When she is far away from the object, the players clap softly. As she comes nearer the object, the campers clap louder, thereby helping the player to find it. When the player finds the object, she selects someone to take her place.

Swat the Bag   Suspend a bag of candy or peanuts by a string. Blindfold one camper and give him a fly swatter. Turn him around three times. Give him three tries to hit the suspended bag. If he fails, choose another camper for the same attempt. When the bag breaks, the group scrambles after the goodies.

Run Home   The campers, with their hands at their sides, stand in a circle. A leader walks around inside the circle. She places her right hand between two campers and says, "Run home." The leader stands with arms outstretched, while these two campers run in opposite directions around the circle. The camper who touches the leader's hand first is the leader in the next game.

Slap Jack   The campers form a circle. One child runs around the outside of the circle and tags another as he runs. The one tagged immediately leaves his place and runs in the opposite direction. The object of the game is to return to the vacant place first. Whoever succeeds wins and remains in that place. The one left out becomes the runner for the next game. For variation, the players may place hands on opposite shoulders, bow, or clasp hands as they meet.

Back-to-Back Change   All children except one are in couples, standing back to back with elbows locked and scattered over the playing space. One player is the caller and calls, "Back-to-back change." Each player must find a new partner, hook elbows with her, and stand back to back. The player who fails to find a partner is caller for the next game. If a player fails to find a partner three times, she must choose someone else to be caller.

Opposites   Players are seated in a circle. The camper who is It moves about in the center of the circle and suddenly stops in front of any player, touches some part of his own body (such as his nose), and says "This is my eye." The player confronted must point to and name the opposites on his own body. Thus, if he can touch his eye and say "This is my nose" before It counts to ten, he becomes It. If he fails, It continues and tries to trick another player.

Poison Penny   The players sit or stand in a circle while music is played. The leader starts a penny around the circle. It must be passed as rapidly as possible. When the music stops, the holder of the penny drops out. If music is not available, a whistle can be blown. If the group is rather large, several pennies can be used.

Pippety Pop   Players stand or sit in a circle. The player who is It takes his place inside the circle. He points his finger at a player and says either "pippety pop" or "poppety pip." If he says "pippety pop," the player at whom he is pointing must say "pip" before It has completed saying "pippety pop." If "poppety pip" is used, the player must say "pop" before It can complete his words. The first syllable of It's word must be given by the players addressed. If It succeeds in saying his words before a player responds correctly, they exchange places.

Self-Testing Activities

A number of these activities call for counting seconds; the recommended method is to say "thousand one, thousand two, thousand three," and so on. In order to make balancing tests meaningful, the counselor must determine whether or not the camper is performing the tests satisfactorily.

1.   Stand still, with feet together. Close both eyes. Hold the position for 10 seconds without moving. The counselor gives signals to start and stop.

2. Holding the left foot in the right hand behind the right leg, hop around on one spot in a circle three times without losing balance.

3. Clasp hands on head, step forward with left foot, and kneel onto the right knee and return to a stand, without moving the feet from the first position.

4. Stand. Kick the right foot up so that the toe becomes at least level with the shoulders, without falling over.

5. Jump into the air, clap the feet together once, and land with feet at least 2 inches apart.

6. Jump into the air and make a half turn to the right or to the left, landing on the same spot (but facing about) without losing the balance—that is, without moving the feet after they first hit the floor.

7. Lie flat on the back on the floor and fold the arms on the chest. Raise the trunk to a sitting position without unfolding arms, bending knees, or moving heels.

8. Fold arms behind the back, kneel onto both knees, and get up without losing balance or moving the feet about.

9. Stand on the left foot. Close the eyes. Hold position without moving for five seconds. Start and stop on the counselor's signal.

10. Stand with both feet together, bend down, and extend both arms down between the knees without losing balance. Hold position for five counts.

11. Take full-squat position with arms together in front of the body, fingers touching the floor. Spring up onto both heels, with toes up, swinging both arms at sides horizontally, legs straight, and feet about 18 inches apart. Repeat this three times rhythmically.

12. Jump into the air and clap feet together twice, landing with feet at least 2 inches apart.

13. Jump into the air and make a full turn left or right, landing on the same spot and not losing balance.

14. Stand on the left foot with the right foot extended forward off the floor. Squat on the left heel without touching the right foot or the hands to the floor, and stand without losing balance.

15. Hold either foot in the opposite hand and jump through the loop thus made.

16. Stand on the left foot, with eyes open, for 5 seconds without moving. Start and stop on the counselor's signal.

17. Walk in a straight line, placing the heel of one foot in front of and against the toe of the other foot. Place each foot on the floor five times (that is, step two times) without losing balance. Begin with the left foot.

18. Stand with hands on hips; go to full-squat position with heels off the floor, keeping the trunk straight and perpendicular. Return to a standing position slowly without losing balance, bending the trunk forward, or moving hands.

19. Jump into the air and slap both heels with both hands behind the back.

20. Walk backward in a straight line for ten steps, placing the toe of one shoe against the heel of the other. Look at the feet, but do not lose balance or walk a crooked line.

21. Touch the tips of the fingers to the floor without bending the knees.

22. Stand on the left foot, place both hands on the floor in front of the left foot, raise the right leg and extend it behind, touch the head to the floor, and regain the standing position without losing balance.

23. Take a front-leaning rest position—that is, rest on the floor supporting the body by both hands and feet with arms and body straight. Bend the arms,

touching the chin to the floor, and push up again to straight arms two times in succession. Do not allow knees or waist to touch the floor. (Girls should push up once.)

24. Kneel on both knees, extend the toes out flat behind, swing the arms and jump to the feet without rocking back on the toes or losing balance.

25. Fold arms on chest, sit down cross-legged, and get up without unfolding the arms or having to move the feet around to regain the balance.

26. Stand on the left foot, hold the right foot against the left knee, place both hands on hips, shut both eyes, and hold the position for 10 seconds without shifting the left foot on the floor.

27. Stand on the right foot. Grasp the left foot behind the right knee, touch the left knee to the floor, and stand without touching any other part of the body to the floor or losing balance.

28. Take a squat-leaning position with elbows out—that is, squat on the heels with hands on the floor in front of the feet, and place the knees well over the elbows and rock forward onto the hands, raising the feet off the floor. Hold position for 5 seconds.

Relay and Ball Games

If the camp has a recreational center or lodge, or uses the central dining facility as a multipurpose room, physical activities requiring larger spaces than are ordinarily found in the cabin can be offered. There are hundreds of tag, relay, circle, and line games, and no equipment is necessary to play them. The games are fast and exciting, and provide many chances for each player to participate. They can be organized at a moment's notice and maintain interest, especially among younger campers. If enough space is available, ball games can be enjoyed by the youngest and oldest campers.

Ankle-Worm Relay　Arrange any number of players into equal teams. Place the teams in parallel columns 6 feet apart on a common line. Players should have equal distances between them. Establish a finish line 30 feet in front of the starting line. Have all players sit down with knees flexed so their feet are close to their buttocks. Have each player reach back and grasp the ankles of the players to his rear. At a given signal, the players raise their buttocks from the floor and move forward, retaining the ankles in the grasp. The team that completely crosses the finish line first without having its column broken wins. Any team breaking its column is immediately eliminated from the race.

Arm-Roll Relay　Teams form parallel lines 10 feet apart. The players of each team stand shoulder to shoulder with arms raised forward and curved so that all of the arms together form a trough. Give the first players of each team a ball. At a given signal, the first player in the column rolls the ball down the trough of arms. The other players of the team roll it toward the foot of the line. The last player receives it, carries it to the head of the line, and rolls it in the trough toward the foot of the line. After throwing the ball, the player takes the position at the head of the line with her arms held forward. Each player carries the ball in turn until all have run. The team that arrives at its original formation first wins.

Balance Relay   Teams form parallel columns with the first player in each column standing on the starting line. A board, approximately 8 inches square, is given to the first player. At a given signal, the player places the board on his head and walks to the finish line and back, then hands the board to the next player, who repeats the process until all members of the team have performed. After the board is placed on the head, a player may not touch it unless it falls off, in which case the player may not move until he places the board on his head again. The first team to complete this process wins.

Other Relays   Participants walk backward to the turning point and then back to team. Participants skip to turning point and back. Participants travel on all fours. Participants duck (bear, crab) walk and back.

Ankle Throw   Players try to throw an object, such as a baseball or a knotted rag, over their heads from behind by using their feet.

Here I Bake   Players join hands in a circle. One player inside the circle is captive. She endeavors to get free by trickery and force. Touching one pair of clasped hands, she says, "Here I bake." Passing around the circle, she touches another pair of clasped hands and says, "Here I brew." Suddenly, in the place least suspected, the prisoner whirls around, jumps at the two clasped hands, and tries to break through. As she does so, she shouts, "Here I mean to break through." The prisoner endeavors to catch the players off guard. The two players responsible for allowing the captive to break through draw straws to determine which one becomes the next prisoner.

Human croquet.   Eleven players take the position of stakes and wickets as placed for regulation lawn croquet (see p. 325). The players acting as wickets spread their legs. Ample distance between wickets should be allowed. The stakes stand upright. At the whistle, two contestants leave the opposite stakes and crawl on all fours between the legs of the wickets in the direction that croquet would normally be played. The object of the game is to race the entire course and be the first to return to the starting stake. One variation of this game is to permit team members to begin the circuit at 30-second intervals. The team whose members are first able to complete the circuit wins.

Streets and alleys.   From 10 to 30 campers can play this game in an enclosed space. The object of the game is for It to tag the runner as quickly as possible, for the runner to evade It, and for the other players to change rapidly from streets to alleys when a signal is given. As streets change to alleys, the course of It and the runner is modified. All players are arranged in several lines, one line behind the other. When the players in each line join hands and face the leader, they form streets. When they face right from this position and join hands with the players on either side of them, they form alleys. At the beginning of the game, the players form streets. One player is chosen as runner, another as It. Both of these players are in different streets. At the Go signal, It chases the runner. As the chase continues, a designated person calls "Alleys" or "Streets," and the rows change. The runners must also change their direction. It and the runner may run only in the aisles or outside the lines. They may not break through any joined hands. It may tag the runner only when he is in the same aisle or outside the group lines. When It finally tags the runner, two new players are selected for the It and runner positions.

Quiz Games

Quiz games are interesting indoor activities. These games are organized along popular seasonal game rules. Thus, a football quiz would have questions graded in terms of yardage gained, field goals kicked, and touchdowns scored. A basketball quiz would be scored in terms of offensive baskets and foul baskets. The quizzes themselves should cover a wide range of subjects.

Quiet Games

Card games, dominoes, jigsaw puzzles, checkers, chess, and Chinese checkers are quiet games played by one, two, or more persons seated around a game board. There can be just as much excitement and competition generated by these games as by any motor-skill activity. Emotions can be aroused by making a clever move, amassing property, falling into a well-laid trap, or taking a trick. Other games that require pencil and paper or other minor supplies also fall into this category. They may not require a game board, and their rules of play may not be as carefully stipulated as the rules of the foregoing games, but they can be performed in confined spaces and are less strenuous than full-fledged physical activity. Some examples follow:

Buzz One of the players starts the game by saying "one," the next says "two," the next "three," until the number seven is reached, at which time the word "buzz" is substituted for seven. The subsequent player says "eight," and so on up to the multiples of seven, fourteen, twenty-one, twenty-eight, and so on. On each of these multiples of seven, the word "buzz" is substituted instead of the number. The word "buzz" is also substituted in any number in which the digit seven appears, as in seventeen, twenty-seven, thirty-seven, and so on. The number seventy-seven becomes "buzz buzz." When seventy is attained, the counting proceeds in the following manner: "buzz one," "buzz two," "buzz three," and so on. Whenever a player says a number instead of "buzz" or says "buzz" at the wrong time, he must pay a forfeit and start the game over by saying "one." The game can also be played by dropping the player who misses from the game. Where this is done, the player retains his seat, but sits in silence. The game then becomes even more confusing for those who remain active.

Bull Board Play is like shuffleboard. The court is never longer than 20 or 30 feet. If a disc or puck slides into the bull head, it cancels all previous scores. A trip around the world can be played by requiring the players to get the numbered spaces in order. A player gets three attempts in this instance. As long as she is able to get the spaces consecutively, she continues to play. Landing in the bull head is considered seasickness, and the player must begin from the start. The numbers in the nine blocks represent the magical 15. Any added column will always make 15. This game can be played with wooden or linoleum discs 3 or 4 inches in diameter, which the players throw or toss at the target. In this method of playing, the tossers must stand at least 10 to 15 feet from the bull board.

Battleship   This game can be played by two or more individuals or groups. Each player or side has a sheet of paper containing three charts. The first chart indicates shots taken at enemy ships. The second chart registers hits on personal ships. The third chart registers opponents' shots. The shot charts each contain 100 squares. Each player (or side) locates his (or their) ship on the first chart as follows: four consecutive spaces or squares for a battleship, three squares for a cruiser, and two each for two submarines. The ships may be located horizontally, vertically, or diagonally. A player is not allowed to see the location of an opponent's ships. Each player in turn shoots a volley of seven shots at his opponent's ships, being allowed three shots for the battleship, two for the cruiser, and one each for the two submarines. For example, the first player calls his shots as follows: "I am shooting at A1, B2, C3, D4, E5, F6, G7." As he shoots, player 1 locates his shots by volley in the second chart by using the number 1, meaning volley 1. At the same time, player 2 marks the figure 1 in each place called by player 1 in the chart where his ships are located. Player 1 asks whether he hit anything. Player 2 must answer truthfully but does not tell where the hits scored. Player 2 shoots his volley in the same manner and asks the same question. On the second round, players use the number 2 to indicate volley 2. This is significant because it helps to locate the enemy ships. When a ship goes down, the player loses the shots going to that ship.

Chase the Rabbit   The players stand or sit in a circle. A rag, ball, or handkerchief is started around the circle. Players must pass the rabbit from hand to hand as rapidly as possible. A second item is started around the circle; this is the hound. Players continue to pass both items as rapidly as possible, trying to catch the rabbit on the one hand while simultaneously trying to let the rabbit escape capture.

Calendar Toss   A calendar containing large numbers is placed on a table. From a line approximately 8 feet from the calendar, players must pitch bottle tops so that they fall on the calendar. Each top scores the amount of the number on which it lands. If the top touches two numbers, it scores the amount of the higher one. Each player has three throws each turn.

Coffeepot   With an It out of the room, the other players select a word representing some activity. It returns and asks any question of the players, passing from one to the other around the circle. It uses the word "coffee-pot" to denote the activity until It guesses what the activity is. The next It is the one whose answer gave the first It the clue to identify the correct activity.

The Moon Is Round   Players sit in a circle. The leader stoops, and with his left hand outlines a face on the ground or floor, saying, "The moon is round, it has two eyes, a nose, and a mouth." The other players must stoop and perform the same action. If they do not use their left hands, they have failed because they did not imitate the leader. A variety of odd movements, throat noises, or facial contortions are variations that the leader can employ.

Testing the Cloth   All players sit in a circle facing the center with elbows linked. All players pull at once in order to break the circle. When a break is made, the two players at the point of the break drop out of the game. The circle is renewed and the process is repeated until the circle can no longer be broken.

Talking Tournament   The players stand back to back. At a given signal they face each other and talk furiously on any subject for a specified length of time. Other players vote on the best orator.

Twenty Questions   One players writes down the name of any object anywhere in the world. The slip is folded and placed in sight of all. The other players, in order, ask twenty questions and must guess the object by the twentieth question. Questions can be answered only by "yes" or "no" or "I do not know." The player naming the object selects the next topic.

Uncle Ned Is Dead   Players are seated in a circle. One player begins by saying to the player on her right, "Uncle Ned is dead." That player asks, "How did he die?" "By closing his eye," the first player answers and closes one eye. Player number 2 turns to the player on her right and repeats the conversation. This continues until all players have one eye closed. Then the first player starts the game again by turning to the player on her right and saying, "Uncle Ned is dead." In reply to the question, "How did he die?" she answers, "By closing his eye, with his face awry." When that statement has made the circle, the third statement is, "By closing his eye, with his face awry, and his foot up high." The fourth statement is, "By closing his eye, with his face awry, his foot up high, and waving goodbye." Each successive statement is completed with an appropriate grimace, posture, or motion and maintained to the end. After the fourth round the leader shouts, "He's buried!" and the game ends.

Who's Missing?   One player leaves the room. A second player is chosen to hide. All players change positions. When ready, the player who left the room is recalled. He gets three guesses to discover the missing player. When he does guess, a new It is chosen.

Who's Got the Whistle?   One player is blindfolded while the others form a circle around him. One player, with a whistle, slips up behind It and softly blows the whistle. It must catch the whistler and identify him by touch. If It catches and identifies the whistler, the latter becomes It. If not, another player takes the whistle and tries to elude It.

Find the Leader   Players stand or sit in a circle. One player is chosen to leave the room. A leader is selected. The person who left returns. The leader starts any motion that appeals to her and is imitated by the other players. It tries to find the leader by guessing or spotting the player who begins the various motions. Players should make an effort not to be too obvious in their observation of the leader, who gradually changes the motions that they follow. It is allowed three guesses, and if she guesses correctly, she may be It again, until she has had three turns.

Fruit Basket   Players are seated in a circle and count off by 4s. All the number 1s are lemons, and 2s oranges, the 3s apples, and the 4s grapes. One player is selected to be It and stands in the center of the circle. It names two fruits, such as oranges and apples, whereupon the fruits named change places on the circle. It tries to get a place in the scramble. The player left without a place becomes It. Any combination of fruit may be called. If It calls "fruit basket," everyone changes places.

Chinese Fingers   Two players or more may play. In large groups, pairings are necessary so that there are always two players for each match. Players count one, two, three and put out their right hands simultaneously, either closed or with one or more fingers outstretched. At the same time they call a number that they believe will be the number of fingers out for both hands. The player who guesses the correct number of fingers, or the nearest to it, scores one point. Five points constitute a game.

ARTS AND CRAFTS

Art at Camp

Camp is a natural place for encouraging self-expression through art. The camper's every experience may inspire graphic or plastic creativity. Camps should provide excellent instruction in several art forms. If the camp offers art classes, campers who have not previously had the time or the inclination to draw or paint may become interested. Art activities can be held outdoors as well as indoors, but because they generally require little space and can be performed by one individual intent upon his material, they are here considered an indoor activity.

Perhaps the best advice a counselor can give to any camper who wishes to express himself in art forms is to remind him to be alert to the countless aesthetic forms that surround him at camp. The counselor should also suggest that the interested camper carry a sketchbook in which he can record his daily experiences. His sketches can later be translated into paintings or drawings that will recapture memories of a grand summer for years to come. Like all other programmed activities at camp, art instruction can be included in the schedule. Nevertheless, any camper who has the talent and desire to go beyond what is offered in the courses should be encouraged to do so.

Crafts at Camp

Crafts are a camp mainstay. There are many crafts activities that offer the camper the chance to make some object—decorative, utilitarian, or a combination of both—with various materials (Fig. 21-1). Crafts are enjoy-

FIGURE 21-1.   Inkle loom weaving at autumn camp. (Courtesy: Leona Gwaz, Camp Schade, Connecticut.)

able and satisfying partly because of the end product. The range of ideas and materials that can be used is almost inexhaustible. A list of possible camp projects should indicate the scope of a crafts program. A second list of some skills needed for the construction of objects indicate how much the camper can learn through an interesting program.

Projects

basket and raffia work	embossing	needlework
beading	enameling	papier mâché
block printing	fly making and tying	pottery
cardboard construction	kite making	soap carving
carving	leather crafts	telescope lens grinding
cement craft	metal work	weaving
crepe paper craft	modeling	wicker work
dyeing and batik	mosaics	woodworking

Skills

beading	carving	chipping
bending	cementing	cutting
beveling	chasing	drilling

dyeing	lacing	splicing
embossing	lashing	stippling
etching	planing	tooling
filing	polishing	twisting
firing	sawing	tying
folding	sealing	weaving
grinding	sewing	whittling
hammering	shaving	
joining	soldering	

The crafts program must be integrated with the total program; it should not be a solitary experience having no relationship to other activities. Many projects can supplement and extend the experiences obtained through dramatics, music, art, motor skills, and other activities (Fig. 21-2).

PUPPETRY

Puppetry has a strong appeal for young people. In the hands of an artist, its entertainment value is tremendously magnified. But even if the individual is not particularly adept at voice modification or modulation, the ma-

FIGURE 21.2.   Craft skills are an important camp learning experience. (Courtesy: Crane Lake Camp, West Stockbridge, Massachusetts.)

nipulator can produce any number of exciting and amusing poses, actions, or gestures. Puppetry is a group activity combining art, crafts, drama, and music. An introduction to dramatics, it offers an outlet for the talents and efforts of campers regardless of age or ability. Campers who ordinarily shy away from acting forms are drawn to puppets and derive a great deal of satisfaction and pleasure from them. Perhaps this is true because the puppet operator is behind the scenes and performing before an audience at the same time. This unique combination can encourage even the most reserved or inhibited camper to try his talent.

Puppetry at camp is usually most successful if introduced during another activity rather than as a separate experience. Picking up natural objects around camp—pine cones, for example—may provide a point of departure for introducing puppets. Puppetry is a natural outgrowth of any of the dramatic forms including storytelling, role playing, or reading. Puppetry requires the construction of puppets before dramatic material can be introduced. Making the puppet is at least as important as producing the puppet show later. Puppets can be easily made using wood blocks, potatoes, rubber balls, paper bags, socks, crepe paper, papier-mâché, or sticks. Various simple craft techniques used for making puppets are described next.

Making Puppets

Finger puppets. Materials needed include tongue depressors, cotton balls, cotton swabs, scrap material, construction paper, rubber bands, colored pencils, scissors, crayons, and paste. With cotton, cloth, construction paper, or any other material at hand, paste or draw the hair on the top of the tongue depressor. Using crayons or colored pencils, draw the face of the finger puppet. Arms can be made by pasting cotton swabs across the back of the tongue depressor, or they can be cut from construction paper. Cut pieces of scrap material to dress the tongue depressor in appropriate clothing. Costumes can be created from construction paper or cloth pasted to the tongue depressor. Children's drawings or pictures cut from newspapers or magazines can be pasted to the tongue depressor and also used as puppet figures. A rubber band around the finger and the waist of the puppet figure secures the puppet. A jersey loop used for making pot holders can be used in place of a rubber band. Move the figure back and forth or from side to side for action. (See Figure 21-3.)

Stick puppets. Materials needed include paper bag, newspaper, paint, brushes, sticks, rubber band, construction paper, glue, and scrap cloth. Fill a paper bag with crumpled or torn strips of newspaper. Tie the bag to the end of a Y-shaped stick or branch, putting the Y part of the stick up into the paper bag. Paint a face on the bag or cut features out of construction paper and glue them to the bag. Dress the figure in construction paper, crepe paper, or scrap material. Make the arms from another stick, crossing the center stick approximately one-third down from the top. Secure arms to the main stick with a rubber band. This puppet can be held in the hand. Only the head and shoulders are attached to the stick; the rest

FIGURE 21-3. Construction for finger puppets.

of the body falls away for movement. If cloth is used, stuff the body with newspapers. (See Figure 21-4.)

Crepe paper puppets. Materials needed include crepe paper, cotton batting, a small amount of lightweight cardboard paste, scraps of colored cloth, construction paper, needle, thread, and scissors. Take a 9-inch square of crepe paper and fill it with cotton batting to form the head. Use a card-

FIGURE 21-4. Construction for stick puppets.

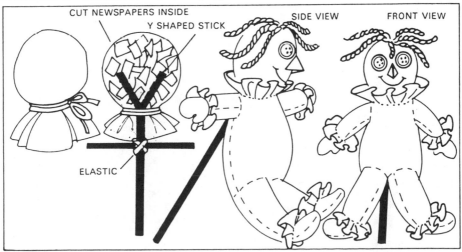

board cylinder for the neck. The cylinder should be large enough to permit passage of the index finger. Cut excess paper away from the cylinder, leaving enough to cover the neck. Cut features from colored construction paper and paste them on the head. The costume consists of a piece of crepe paper or colored cloth about 10 inches long and 15 inches wide. Gather the width of the paper or cloth around the neck and sew it to the cardboard cylinder. Slash holes for the middle finger and thumb to come through for arms. Finish the project by adding construction-paper ears, hair, and eyebrows. (See Figure 21-5.)

Paper bag puppets. Materials needed include a No. 7 paper bag with square bottom, a pencil, ribbon, crepe paper, construction paper, paste, and scissors. Open the bag completely before planning the features. Indicate features lightly in pencil. Do not place the eyes too high; there must be room for a forehead. The mouth should be placed approximately halfway down the bag with a piece of ribbon or crepe paper. The features, cut from colored construction paper and pasted onto the bag, should be large. Make a nose that stands out. Hair can be added with strips of paper. Eyelashes can be added by fringing a piece of paper and bending the fringes back so that they stand away from the eyes. (See Figure 21-6.)

Paper bag animal puppets. Materials needed include two paper bags, scissors, paste, and construction paper. Use two bags. Open one bag completely. Cut diamond points A and B one third of the way down the bag. Cut the two back corners, C and D, 1 inch further down, to tip the head slightly forward. Fold the two side pieces inside the bag. Fold the top pieces up and the bottom piece down. Place the top-folded edge over the first bag 1 inch from the top and paste in place. The piece extending beyond the top can be used for ears if they are cut round and folded down the center.

FIGURE 21-5. Construction for crepe paper puppets.

FIGURE 21-6. Construction for paper bag puppets.

For nostrils, notch the bag at point E. If the animal's ears extend from the side, use the two side pieces instead of folding them under and fold the top piece under. Use construction paper to make animal's features. (See Figure 21-7.)

Papier-mâché puppets. Materials needed include newspaper, wheat paste, water, and tin cans. Roll one sheet of newspaper into a ball. Take another sheet of newspaper and cover the ball, which becomes the head, by twisting the ends to form a neck. Place the head in a tin can to hold it upright. Cut a strip of newspaper about 4 inches long and 3 inches wide.

FIGURE 21-7. Construction for paper bag animal puppets.

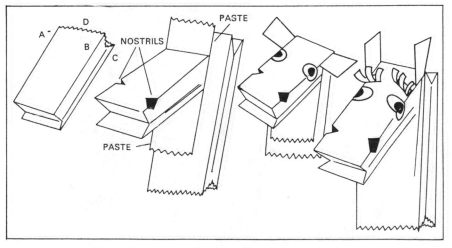

Fold it into a long strip and glue to the head where the nose should be. (See Figure 21-8.) Cut many strips 1 inch wide and 1 inch long. Mix the wheat paste with water until it is paste. Dip the strips of paper into the wheat paste, covering both sides. Wipe the excess paste back into the paste dish. Paste the strip onto the head. Continue to paste on strips in order to cover the head with three layers. If possible, make the first layer black and white paper, the second layer comic papers, and the third black and white again; this makes it easier to cover the whole puppet head completely with each layer. Cover the nose and smooth down all wrinkles. Let the head dry completely before painting. Do not let any of the wheat-paste strips cover the jar or can holding the head. Paste strips about 1 inch down the neck, but do not paste over the end of the neck. When the head is dry, push fingers up into the neck and pull all the papers out. The head will be a solid, uncollapsible shell.

Brushes, poster or tempera paint, cotton, yarn, paste, and cloth or fur are needed to decorate the papier-mâché puppets. The head must be completely dry before paint can be applied. The surface where the hair is to be added should not be painted, because paste does not stick well to a painted surface. The face paint must be dry before any other decorations are added. Cotton, yarn, or fur can be used for the hair, or it can be painted on with poster paint. (See Figure 21-9.)

Scrap cloth, an old sock, a needle, thread, buttons, scissors, and glue are needed to make a body for the papier-mâché puppets. When using the sock, cut the toe off halfway to the heel and save it. Cut the toe in half and sew up the sides of the two pieces, leaving an opening at the end. Turn inside out to form the arms. Cut two holes for the arms and turn the body of the sock inside out. Sew in the arms. Glue the top of the sock to the neck just under the chin. Decorate the puppet's costume with buttons, lace, ribbons, or colored patches. (See Figure 21-10.)

FIGURE 21-8. Construction for papier-mâché puppets.

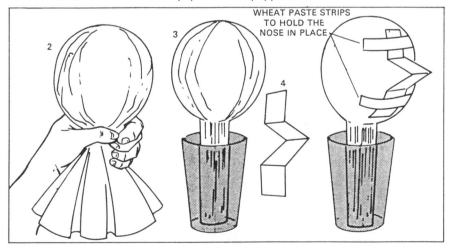

FIGURE 21-9.   Decoration for papier-mâché puppets.

Talking puppets.   Materials needed include light cardboard, scissors, a rubber band, a stick, and glue. Bend the cardboard at one third of its length. Glue, tack, or staple to a 16-inch stick one third of the way down. Attach the rubber band by cutting two 1-inch slots into the top and bottom of the cardboard. Secure one loop of the rubber band around the tab made by the two slots. Tie string or coarse thread, not less than 16 inches long, to the tab on the bottom flap. To cover the face, use tag board or heavy paper as long as the cardboard and about an inch wider. Bend corners and fold down as shown in Figure 21-11. Trim the mouth with scissors. Make a nose out of creased paper cut 1 inch into the crease. Bend the flaps to glue

FIGURE 21-10.   Construction for body for papier-mâché puppets.

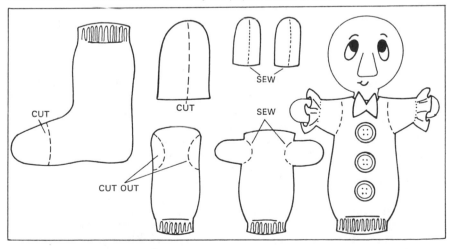

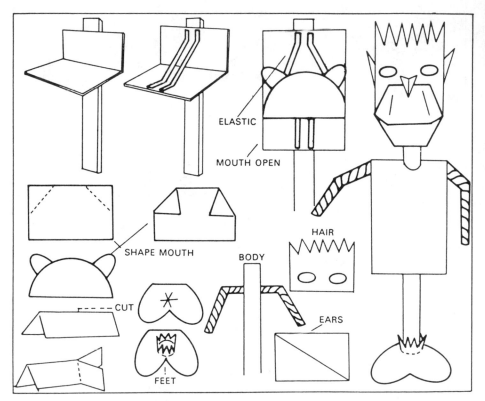

FIGURE 21-11.   Construction for talking puppets.

them. Make ears from a square piece of paper cut diagonally. Make the upper face from a square piece of cardboard, with hair cut from the top in short pieces. Add eyes. Cut a slot in the bottom center of the square to help fit the face onto the stick. Make the body from a tube of rolled paper, and the feet from heavy cardboard; make the arms from rolled paper. Either glue or staple the arms and legs to the body tube. To dress the puppet, make a poncho of cloth or crepe paper bound around the middle with a string.

Wire puppets.   Materials needed include a show box, drawing paper, stiff wire, construction paper, crayons, scissors, cotton, and masking tape. Cut an opening into the top of the show box so that the wire puppets can be lowered into it. Cut an opening into the cover of the box so the puppets can be seen by the audience. Construct scenery using indoor or outdoor backgrounds for the figures. There should be some scenery toward the front of the stage to create a three-dimensional effect. With crayons or pencil, draw the play's figures. Figures must be in side as well as front view. When the figures are completed, cut them out and tape their backs to the wire, which should not be bent before pasting the figure onto it. Lower the puppet onto the stage through the opening in the top of the show box. The feet should touch the floor of the box and the wire should then be bent horizontally. When the figure is being moved around the stage, the person moving the puppet will find it easier to keep the puppet's feet on the floor, giving more realism to the puppets. Construct curtains from construction paper or cloth. (See Figure 21-12.)

Counselors who supervise or direct a puppet theatre should observe the following techniques.

1. To distinguish which character is speaking when more than one puppet is on stage, the puppets should move around and make gestures when speaking but should remain still at other times.
2. Each puppet's voice should be different.
3. Speech should be loud and distinct.
4. The puppet's every action should be exaggerated and dramatic.
5. The camper who makes the puppet should operate it.
6. Puppets operate best in profile, turning forward for their speeches.
7. The dress or puppet costume should be long enough to cover the operator's hand and wrist.
8. The hands of hand puppets should be used for hugging, slapping, handshaking, and other gestures.
9. Campers should be encouraged to use their own language rather than memorizing set speeches.
10. To hold the audience's interest, puppets should make direct appeals to the audience, asking questions, advice, and so on.
11. To retain interest between acts or when the show is delayed, let the puppets peep out from behind or beneath the curtain and make remarks to or about the audience. Song leading by puppets can also be attempted.
12. Let the puppets introduce themselves, or let one of the performing campers do the announcing.

FIGURE 21-12. Construction for wire puppets.

13. To produce certain effects, it may be necessary for an announcer to set the scene or briefly narrate the action.

14. Puppets are used primarily for entertainment, but they can also be used to teach safety, good manners, good health practices, and so forth.

15. The puppets should come off the stage at the sides (wings), not in view of the audience.

16. Discussion about lines, costumes, action, sets, and props should be encouraged to promote camper cooperation and cohesiveness.

MUSIC, DANCE, AND DRAMATICS

Although the performing arts can be effectively demonstrated in the outdoors, and there are many excellent opportunities for producing plays, concerts, and dances in outdoor settings at camp, these activities naturally lend themselves to indoor environments. The experiences afforded by participating in the performing arts are enhanced if they are combined. Separately, they contribute much to the individual's pleasure and satisfaction; combined, the arts are striking in their ability to emphasize and supplement every facet of a stage production or entertainment. How much more intense are the words of a play if there is background music to carry the action! Dance, when appropriate to the piece, greatly heightens the quality of a performance. This section gives a brief explanation of the opportunities to encourage the performing arts in camp life, along with suggestions about the leadership necessary to inculcate appreciation of these arts. The camp may employ a specialist in each of the performing arts, but every counselor at camp should have some knowledge of the performing arts, as well as some experience either as participants or organizers of this type of activity.

Music

Singing is perhaps the most universal of all musical sounds. At camp there is plenty of singing—from the first night, through all the days, to the final "Auld Lang Syne." Campers returning from previous seasons often remember their favorite camp songs—the knock-and-boost songs used to parody other bunks, the camp-fire songs, or songs written especially for "their" camp to the tune of well-known melodies. Singing songs should be encouraged at almost any time during the day or evening. Opportunities for singing arise in the dining hall, around the all-camp council fire, and at community sings held before some special event. Soloists may perform at scheduled or nonscheduled times. Songs that depict action or work, spirituals, hymns, ballads, rounds, and singing games leave an indelible impression on the camper's mind and heart. For some unexplained reason, the songs one learns as a camper seem to remain over the years. What former camper, although he may have forgotten everything and everybody at the camp he attended so long ago, does not recall sitting in front of a blazing camp fire and raising his voice to join with the others in songs? The sound of music is heard from reveille by bugle to taps at night. On rainy days, some of the best moments are passed in singing four-part harmony (Fig. 21-13). Campers do not need special training or an ability to read music.

FIGURE 21-13. Music at camp. (Courtesy: Crane Lake Camp, West Stockbridge, Massachusetts.)

The ability to carry a tune or maintain the right pitch is more than sufficient to admit the camper to the world of song and music.

Camp songs. Camp songs are most effective when they tell about the camp or about a specific unit at the camp. At the start of the season, counselors should teach their bunks a song that will identify them in the camp from that day forward. The camp should acquire a series of songs, whose verses can be very simple and set to borrowed tunes, to be sung at reunions, on any occasion, or as an introduction to the camp.

Camp songs have several things in common. They are easy to sing; their lyrics are uncomplicated. There are no dramatic shifts to the music, and the beat is easy to follow. Some camp songs are traditional folk tunes that almost everybody knows before coming to camp. Other songs are learned at camp; they should be appropriate to the camp and acceptable to all who sing them.

Instrumental music. Instruments for making music should be available to campers. Accomplished musicians might bring their own instruments to camp; their practice and solo performances greatly enhance the music program. However, campers do not come to camp to do the things they ordinarily do at home; they can always play in the band or sing in the chorus at school. Music at camp should be thought of as a natural expressive outlet. Much of it should be spontaneous. This does not mean that there cannot be instruction in singing or in playing instruments; it does mean that compulsory, scheduled sessions must be held to a minimum or eliminated. Music is a natural outgrowth of the way campers live. Singing a song while hiking is a method of preventing fatigue as well as a way of keeping spirits high. Playing a guitar during rest periods provides not only singing practice, but also the pleasure of appreciation for bunk members.

Dance

Dancing of all types—modern, folk, square, and social—has a significant role in camp life. Folk and square dancing are traditional favorites at most camps. Social dancing is reserved for coeducational groups, but circle, round, and ethnic dances are always received with a great deal of enthusiasm. Sometimes a project that has nothing whatsoever to do with dancing can stimulate interest in a special form of dancing. An art or crafts project can result in an investigation of the culture of a particular national group.

Often, dancing simply happens spontaneously; many a new dance has been introduced to a group of campers who were waiting around for mail call. The council fire activity may give rise to Indian dancing, which in turn may lead to folk and square dancing because of the pioneer carryover between the two. Campers enjoy costumes, and nothing delights the male camper more than masquerading in full Indian regalia. Some ethnic dances are strenuous and require not only rhythm but also a high degree of skill and endurance.

Counselors should watch for opportunities for promoting dance activity. When campers must stay indoors because of inclement weather, a phonograph with square and folk-dance records enlivens the atmosphere, especially if the counselor has any knowledge of calls. With a lively barnyard tune and a simple call, children are ready to forget their fears and join right in. Girls appear to have a built-in receptivity to dancing that is not as strong in boys; but when the campers are all boys, and the counselor knows what he is doing and participates along with his campers, an acquaintanceship with music and dance may soon develop into a routine demand. As with most activities that need rhythm, folk and square dancing do not require any instrument for supplying a beat. Many camp songs are adequate for this form of dancing. While it is wonderful when a guitar, banjo, fiddle, or piano can be played, if the campers can sing and clap their hands in unison, they can dance.

Perhaps the easiest square (or round) dance that can be taught in the least amount of time is the "Oh, Johnny" dance, which can be taught in a square or a circle. How it is taught depends upon the number of campers involved. If there are so many campers that there is not space to form squares, then arrange campers in circles. Terms are very important in teaching square dancing. The caller calls out these terms so that the dancers know what to do. Here are some frequently used terms:

Do-si-do is a back to back figure; you and your partner first face each other and then pass and circle one another by passing right shoulders.

Allemande left is accomplished by turning your back to your partner, facing the person to the rear, and extending the hand that is called—in this case the left—and walking around your new partner until the original position is reached.

Grand right and left entails extending the called hand to the person in the rear and walking past that person, alternating left and right hands as you continue around the circle or square.

Honey, squaw, taw, your own all refer to your partner.

Corner, the girl you left behind you, neighbor refer to the person to your left.

Circle the ring indicates that as many dancers as are in the figure join hands and walk, skip, or two-step around the circle in the direction called.

Honor your partner means that boys bow, girls curtsy.

Promenade is walking with your partner counterclockwise around the circle.

Swing means to whirl your partner or neighbor once around in four steps.

The "Oh, Johnny" square or circle, performed to the song of that name, is called in the following manner:

Now you all join hands and circle the ring (circle left).
Stop where you are, give your honey a swing.
Swing that little girl behind you.
Swing your own, if you have found that she's not flown.

Now allemande left with the girl on your left.
Do-si-do with your own.
Now you all promenade with the sweet corner maid,
Singing Oh, Johnny, Oh, Johnny, Oh!

Dramatics

Dramatics does not necessarily involve a formal production with memorized roles. It can be the outgrowth of any daily camp experience. The desire to act out a part is sometimes stimulated by hearing a story, experiencing an overnight hike, or discovering some historical fact. Participation in dramatics can be most satisfying. Imagination can be given full sway. How the camper feels can be woven into the creation of a character. Improvisation, mimicry, and pantomime all have significant places in life. A rainy day may be just the key to unlock a hidden desire to act out a role. When campers are confined to quarters and are bored with other activities—although this is rare if the counselor has planned systematically—the idea of "putting on a show" is bound to please.

Dramatics should be an integral part of life at camp, related to other activities such as games, music, dancing, art, crafts, storytelling, and reading. Some of the most appropriate forms of dramatics for camp are developing a story for stage presentation, song skits, pantomimes, stunts, puppet shows, charades, and blackouts. Theatricals that require too much time for rehearsal, memorization of lines, costuming, and stagecraft take up too much of the camper's day. At camp, the best dramatic activities are the easiest to prepare, present, and stage. For young campers, fairy tales, myths, legends, and pioneer stories all lend themselves to dramatization. Some of these can be performed without any staging or rehearsal, impromptu, if the children are familiar with the story and its characters. Characterizations of campers, counselors, and other staff members are another form of dramatics. Particular phrases associated with a person or a distinctive movement, stance, or walk can be mimicked without hurting that individual's feelings.

A shadow play.   Shadow plays are excellent vehicles for carrying out a simple story line. One of the classic shadow plays is "The Operation." The presentation is easy to stage, requiring few props. All one needs are a bed sheet strung in front of the players, a table, and a lamp. The sheet is pinned or tacked to the ceiling of the cabin or wherever the performance is to take place. The light from a small lamp will provide the necessary illumination to throw the shadows of the players on the sheet. Sound effects can be made by ripping paper at the appropriate moment, sawing on a board, banging a hammer on a board, and making a popping sound (either by sharply patting the hand against an open mouth or by snapping the index finger across the inside of the mouth against the cheek). The operation can also be enhanced by playing recorded music—for example, Von Suppe's "Poet and Peasant Overture"—and fitting the actions to the tempo.

The action consists of one camper (the surgeon) working over another (the patient), who is stretched out on the table. First the surgeon holds a butcher knife against the sheet to indicate the scalpel. The more exaggerated the instruments appear, the better the skit. Anesthesia is administered by "hitting" the patient over the head with a large mallet. The surgeon proceeds to operate by "slicing" the patient from head to toe, with newspaper being torn to simulate the sound of cutting. The surgeon then reaches into the "body" and removes shoes, bananas, a length of crepe paper, and other objects. He then saws off both "feet"; this is performed by placing two overshoes on the table beside the patient's feet. The saw is silhouetted against the sheet, and the sound-effects person simultaneously saws a piece of wood. Once the shoes are dropped to the floor, the surgeon moves to the patient's head. The light must be brought quite close to the patient's head in order to throw a sharp shadow on the sheet. The surgeon opens the patient's mouth and looks inside. The first time he bends over the patient, his nose should appear to go into the patient's mouth. The second time, the surgeon bends his head down alongside the patient's head so that it appears to the audience that the surgeon's head disappears into the patient's mouth. Variations of this can be performed with the hand and then the arm. The climax of the skit comes when the surgeon inserts a huge forceps into the patient's "mouth" and withdraws a giant tooth, whereupon the patient gets up and congratulates the surgeon.

chapter 22

Special Events

Every camp needs to inject something special into its program from time to time. There is little question that nearly all campers find activities that interest them in the daily schedule. Nevertheless, there are always a few campers whose participation must be stimulated by something out of the ordinary. Special events allow many campers to assist in an operation involving all of the resources and age groups of the camp. Complete involvement is achieved because the successful integration of many activities necessitates full camper cooperation in presenting skills, talents, and knowledge. The special event enlivens the atmosphere and makes the daily program more attractive. It can be either closely related to the regular program or a complete change from it.

CLASSIFICATIONS OF SPECIAL EVENTS

The variety of special events is limited only by the imagination of the counselors and campers who plan these projects. The following categories are guides to the possibilities that should be considered in planning these events.

1. *Demonstrations of acquired skills.* Skills that campers have learned are presented; activities may include archery, canoeing, synchronized swimming, camp crafts, wood crafts, and folk, square, or round dancing.
2. *Exhibitions.* Things that campers have collected during the course of the season can be exhibited and explained.
3. *Performances.* This category includes dramatic presentations, concerts, tableaux, water shows, or ceremonies performed before an audience.

4. *Tournament competitions.* Field days, swimming meets, orienteering, canoe or sailing races, archery or riflery contests, and fishing rodeos are included here.

5. *Mass group participation.* Any activity practiced in small groups, such as folk and square dancing, talent shows, singing, gymnastics, and stunts, can be performed by all campers at the same time.

6. *Social activities.* Parties, visits to or by other camps, banquets, and dances are included in this category.

7. *Spectacular displays.* These include pyrotechnical displays on July 4th, pageants, parades, carnivals, and circuses.

8. *Traditional activities.* Traditional camp activities include camper–counselor day, all-camp fires, visitors' day, color war, recognition evening, and themes for specific occasions.

Descriptions of Special Events

Appropriate posters and the camp newspaper announce that a costume party is coming up. Publicity might be created that teases the campers with mysterious messages. Clues can be posted on bulletin boards around the camp for at least one week prior to the event itself; each day a new clue or more information concerning the special event can be distributed. Small handbills can be passed out during meals.

The Pirates' Party can either be an indoor or an outdoor activity. As decorations often play an important part, suitable arrangements for decorations should be made well before the date of the event itself. Palm trees, seashore scenes, a fortress with a cannon, a full-rigged pirate ship, barrels, rope, and seaweed all suggest a pirates' cove. Signal flags, along with the skull-and-crossbones motif, are also colorful decorations.

Costumes can be created from tattered shorts, colored cloth, bandannas, buccaneer hats, earrings, toy sabers, and pistols. Crepe paper can effectively trim sashes, belts, boots, sleeves, and collars. Stage makeup gives the pirates a swarthy look. Evil scars and other disfiguring marks can be applied with wax and tape.

Activities include the assignment of campers to various pirate dens as they arrive at the pirates' cove. Each den will have a pirate chief who will lead the group on the treasure hunt at the appropriate time. A short skit to introduce the idea of the treasure hunt can be supplied by having "Captain Blood" appear at a specified time to address the assembled campers; he may indicate the scope of the hunt and provide the first clue. The pirate dens, with their designated chiefs, are allowed to participate at the sound of a pistol shot—simulated by bursting a paper bag or a balloon, or by firing a blank from a starting pistol. There can be any number of checkpoints and clues, but in the interest of maintaining camper attention and excitement, it is best to have no more than 6 map references from which additional clues pointing to the treasure are gained. The final clue should direct campers to the pirates' cove where the treasure has been hidden. The clue must be specific enough to make it fairly easy for the returning pirates to capture the loot. The first group to capture the treasure divides up whatever is inside the chest.

The treasure chest usually contains candy bars wrapped in gold and silver foil, items designed to look like jewelry, or objects that might delight the camper, such as tickets allowing the camper to select any 10-cent item at the camp store. Once the treasure is found, a dance with refreshments can be held, or perhaps a pirate movie. Of course, there could be many more activities, such as water fights, sailing contests, water pistols at 20 paces, and game activities adapted to represent pirate conduct.

Hobby Carnival

This event offers each camper the opportunity to display individual skills, talents, collections, and knowledge. Novice sculptors, painters, mineral collectors, taxidermists, and leaf and insect collectors may all display their work. Exhibitors can belong to a club or can enter as individuals. The carnival facility must be well planned if each entry is to be displayed to equal advantage. No one hobby or group should have a paramount position. All materials necessary for the proper display of each hobby should be coordinated. Cases, shelves, wire for hanging, easels, volleyball standards, tables, sheets, spotlights, crepe paper, posterboard, and other required supplies should be made available to those who wish to show their hobby. Each booth or stall should be constructed and lighted so that the objects can be displayed effectively. If the camp has a photography club or photography enthusiasts, they can take pictures at the carnival.

The Living Calendar

The idea of the living calendar is to suggest a theme for each week at camp and to have one special event each week based on that theme. Thus, campers have some idea of what is coming up and may consider taking part in previously unfamiliar experiences. To be useful, the living calendar must be organized and presented within 1 week of the opening day. If the camping period is 8 weeks long, each week can be represented by the themes that follow. Backdrops should be planned ahead of time.

1. *Potpourri Week.* A camper sits before a map of the camp, surrounded by equipment representing all the activities to be found at the camp.
2. *Indian Week.* A camper dressed as an Indian poses in front of a backdrop that suggests a tepee, a birchbark canoe, and archery equipment. Indian ceremonial costumes and headdresses may surround him.
3. *America Week.* A camper, dressed as Uncle Sam, sits before a flag. Mock firecrackers can also be used to signify Independence Day.
4. *Pirate Week.* A camper, dressed as Captain Kidd, sits before a background that depicts a treasure map.
5. *Nature Week.* A camper dressed as a pioneer scout sits in front of a lean-to or other shelter, with a reflector fire in the foreground. This depicts camp-craft and wood-craft skills to be acquired.
6. *Circus Week.* Dressed as a clown, a camper poses before a backdrop illustrating a Big Top or midway.
7. *Colors Week.* A camper, dressed in the camp's colors, sits before a backdrop neatly divided into the two colors of the camp.

8. *Roundup Week.* Dressed as a cowboy, a camper poses in front of a backdrop showing part of a rodeo. Lariats, saddles, rifles, and other paraphernalia can heighten this concept.

Fishing Rodeo

The fishing rodeo is a tournament that integrates all activities related to fishing: fly tying; bait, spin, and fly casting; spear fishing; and boating. It is a test of skill, patience, and some luck for the campers who wish to compete. Categories, which cover an entire day, can be chosen from the following possibilities: longest fish caught, heaviest fish caught, fish taking the longest to land, largest fish caught of a species, greatest total number of fish caught, largest number of fish of a species caught. This rodeo serves several purposes. It provides competitive activities for anglers, encourages more campers to try various forms of fishing and casting, and permits those with a high degree of casting skill to try themselves with specific lines, reels, and poles against fighting fish.

Rules must be set for the regulation of the tournament. Only campers are permitted to enter the rodeo. There is a definite time limit in which fish may be caught. All fish must be caught by using some kind of rod and reel, unless the competitor is entered in the spear-fishing contest. The rodeo might also include a water polo match between several bunks or a simulated bucking bronco contest with scuba gear worn by the horse (camper) and rider. An aquatic show might also be included, with decorated watercraft and a demonstration of synchronized swimming or fancy diving. The grand finale of the evening could be a gigantic fish fry of all the fish caught during the rodeo.

Carnival or Circus

The entire camp community can participate in the summer circus or carnival. The camp's central open space can be the midway, where stalls or booths are erected, or real tents can be used for each exhibit, display, or show. Each bunk takes responsibility for putting on one skit, stunt, or display, or for making a float to be used in the grand march. A variety show and talent contest, with campers in costumes, can be presented in the center ring (Fig. 22-1). Small fees can be charged to enter the midway attractions, with the proceeds going to some worthy cause previously agreed upon by the campers, or entry can be free. The number of carnival games and midway attractions that can be created is almost unlimited, and most of the participants will suggest ideas. The following suggestions give an idea of the possibilities:

archery targets	block chopping contest, using an ax on a log 10 inches in diameter
artist to sketch portraits or cartoons	
balloon throw for distance	card toss for accuracy
basketball or volleyball roll	fortune teller
bearded lady	frog-jumping contest

FIGURE 22-1.   Costumes are part of the camp carnival. (Courtesy: Leona Gwaz, Camp Schade, Connecticut.)

headless man or woman
hog- or duck-calling contest
hoop toss
jugglers
log sawing
magicians
mirror booth

nail driving
penny toss
pie-eating contest
shooting gallery
water-pistol to extinguish candles
world's strongest person

The circus can be indoors, outdoors, or both. Circus acts require a ringmaster to introduce each new performance. A music director should accompany each act with appropriate music. A tape recorder or record player with loud-speaker attachment is an excellent substitute if a music director is not available. A director of clowns is also necessary.

Areas for the audience should be roped off to keep spectators from crowding the performance area. Benches, bleachers, or chairs can be used, or the campers can sit on the ground. The center rings can be constructed of wooden boards that form the edge of the circle, or the circles can be marked on the ground with lime. At the time set for the circus performance, the ringmaster, suitably garbed, runs into the arena and requests silence from the audience. He then announces the grand entrance. A musical overture, a typical circus march, accompanies the performers' entrance. The parade is made up of all circus and carnival performers, who line up outside if the circus is to be held indoors or underneath a large tent. If the entire presentation is outdoors, performers should be lined up out of the audience's sight. The order of entrance follows the program, although it is best to place the clowns at the end of the procession. All performers march once around the arena, bowing and waving to the audience. Then the parade exits the way it came in.

Animal acts are essential to the circus. Animals can be made as a part of arts-and-crafts activities. Animal heads can be made of chicken wire over which papier-mâché is placed; after the papier-mâché dries and hardens, it can be painted with inexpensive paints. For the performance, lions and tigers are guided by a tamer; they can jump through hoops, sit up and beg, roll over, climb on boxes to form pyramids, roar, and snarl at the tamer. Bears wrestle with their trainer, perform a dance, sit up, and go into the audience for food. Seals play automobile or kazoo horns that can be fastened to a small platform. At the conclusion of their musical number, the seals roll over, clap their flippers, and bark. Seals can also balance balloons on their noses by holding the strings in their teeth. They can be rewarded with paper fish. Elephant acts are always crowd pleasers; the elephant stands on his hind legs, climbs onto a small platform, steps over the trainer who is down on the ground, and dances.

Clowns are an integral part of circus routines. They must be clever, original, and alert to use every situation to comic advantage. They provide the comedy effects and maintain the attention of the audience during act changes. Clowns are always in motion. They can play a pantomine baseball or football game by exaggerating their movements or performing them in slow motion. They can play a musical selection using a bicycle pump as a trombone, two pan lids for cymbals, a washboard with wooden spoon for a stringed bass, a kettle with spoon for a drum, kazoos, a stretched rubber band for a guitar, and strings tied to two pieces of wood for a harp. The ringmaster announces some minor masterpiece and the clowns pantomime, "playing" their instruments as a record player plays some short, famous symphonic work. Among the clown performers are tramps, hayseeds, clowns with their clothing on backwards, police, and firefighters. A clown giant can be played by someone who is very tall, by a counselor, or by a camper who can balance himself on stilts.

Refreshments are an essential part of any circus presentation. Supper for the campers may consist of circus-type food; hot dogs, sandwiches, peanuts, popcorn, lemonade, milk, candy apples, and ice cream can be served from refreshment booths.

Water Shows

Water shows, like other special events, are designed to combine the interests, talents, and skills of many campers, as well as to integrate a variety of camp activities into one unified presentation. Under the direction of the waterfront instructor, each participant is offered a chance to learn and perform skills in aquatics, synchronized swimming, music, lighting, costum-

ing, makeup, staging, and production. The planning requires intense cooperation. Each participant can contribute something valuable to the production. Water shows provide opportunities for swimmers and divers of all
degrees of skill to demonstrate their achievements. The show itself can be
an incentive for the camper to try a little harder to attain a particular level
of skill. Almost all water shows include some of the following acts: synchronized swimming by 2 to 10 campers; contests involving one swimmer with
flippers and one without, swimming without using the arms or hands; comedy swimming; plain, fancy, and comedy or clown diving; competitive swimming; and pageants.

The well directed and produced water show should reflect the camp's
objectives. The concepts used are the same as those for staging any play.
The opening number should be colorful, but not overpowering. At least
half the cast should be introduced in the first number. The show is made
up of at least one act from each of the categories just mentioned. The modifications inherent in this type of program are unlimited, and such presentations are particularly adaptable to the needs of camps. Pageants that tell the
camp's story or a regional legend are very effective. The overall production
should have some central theme introduced by the opening number and
reinforced with each successive act, building to the grand finale. Numbers
should seem to blend, although costumes of different colors and different
stunts should be apparent in each act. The entire show should be fast-paced,
colorful, enjoyable, and even more important, satisfying to the participants.

A water show can combine land activities with water events. Dances,
skits, trampoline acts, bathing-beauty contests, free exercise, and other performances can be held on land. Suitable music for each act, adequate stage
lighting to emphasize certain activities, and appropriate props that carry
the action of the show should be considered in any water-show production.
If the water is clear enough, the water ballet numbers can be staged for
greater effect with underwater spotlights or with surface spots.

Small-craft activities can also be included. The craft may maneuver in
procession, permit the inclusion of special effects, transport players to and
from various points, stress certain entrances, and generally be used as an
integral part of the show. The water show, if it is well staged, integrates many
of the camp's activities—dramatics, dance, music, art, crafts, games, stunts,
and aquatics. The show's theme can be based on some aspect of camping
or nature. Whether behind the scenes as technicians, script personnel, or
riggers, or out front as performers, many campers can enjoy the satisfaction
of being a part of the show. Self-confidence, self-expression, and simple
pleasure at belonging to this group are some of the significant outcomes of
this type of endeavor.

EVENING ACTIVITIES

The time after supper and before bedtime offers the opportunity to bring
the campers and staff closer together. It is a quiet time, although there are
occasions when the evening activity will be vigorous. The evening is a time

for relaxation and slowing down after the full program of the day. The evening program has an outstanding effect on the campers' impressionistic minds. Campers may forget much of the hiking, fishing, nature study, and crafts that take place at camp, but they almost always remember the songs, legends, and ceremonies set around a blazing fire.

Evening programs are limited only by the ingenuity, imagination, and knowledge of the staff members who plan them. Evening events must be considered an extension of the camping day. Short-term camps must produce a great variety of evening activities that have little continuity and can be produced without great expenditure of time or effort; if the camp period is 1 or 2 weeks long, there simply is not enough time to prepare complex activities that have continuity. But in a season of 2 months, intricate and detailed activities that stress progression in a series of evenings can be planned.

The evening program should reflect the philosophy and orientation of the total camp program. If the heart of the program is wood crafts, for example, a continuation along these lines should be evident in the evening. Evening events should be planned with the total camp schedule in mind. They may prepare the way for coming activities and assist in publicizing other facets of the program. As with other elements of the program, the campers should have some hand in planning what they do in the evening. But the program staff is well advised to surprise the campers occasionally with a spontaneous show.

Evening gatherings can be thought-provoking and stimulating for the camper. They may elicit the camper's suggestions for and participation in future events. Evening activities should be scheduled around bunks and unit enclaves, with special events programmed for the entire camp. Some evening experiences can be planned with hobby or interest groups in mind. At the bunk level, the counselor is in the best position to draw upon individual camper skills, knowledge, and talent for spontaneous or planned performances. Such activities give the camper a chance to exhibit skills that boost his personal confidence and status among his fellows. No one camper should be permitted to dominate the evening activities; all must be allowed to offer their ideas. The counselor should be judicious in her selection of material for presentation. She must remember the timid or nonaggressive camper whose latent talents require encouragement.

Most evening activities should be held outdoors. They should be fairly simple in scope and structure. Intensive rehearsal for evening activities is usually unnecessary. There is little that has to be staged in the evening. Nothing is more impressive than a camp fire around which campers are gathered to roast marshmallows, yams, or frankfurters, sing, or take part in some council ritual. Nearly every evening is enhanced by the long shadows thrown by flickering flames. Still, there is time for stunts, skits, pantomimes, storytelling, ceremonial pomp, and quiet reflection, and even for individual contests, challenges, dances, and games. Evening activities, like all camp activities, should be chosen and planned for the contributions they can make to the learning, enjoyment, and growth of each camper.

HELPFUL REFERENCES

Annual Catalog of Selected Camping Publications (Martinsville, Ind.: American Camping Association).

Archery

Athletic Institute (ed.), *Archery: A Sport for Everyone* (North Palm Beach, Fla.: The Athletic Institute, 1984).

McKINNEY, W.C., *Archery* (Dubuque, Iowa: Wm. C. Brown, 1985).

PSZEZOLA, L., *Archery*, 3d ed. (New York: Saunders, 1984).

Backpacking

BRIDGE, R., *America's Backpacking Book*, rev. ed. (New York: Scribner's, 1981).

DOAN, M., *Hiking Light* (Seattle: The Mountaineers Books, 1982).

FLEMING, J., *Games and More for Backpackers* (New York: The Putnam Publishing Group, 1983).

FLETCHER, C., *The Complete Walker*, 3d ed. (New York: Random House, 1984).

GREENSPAN, R. and H. KAHN, *Backpacking: A Hedonist's Guide* (Chico, Calif.: Moron Publications, 1985).

HARGROVE, P. and N. LIEBRENZ, *Backpacker's Source Book*, 2d ed. (Berkeley: Wilderness Press, 1983).

HART, J., *Walking Softly in the Wilderness: The Sierra Club Guide to Backpacking*, rev. ed. (San Francisco: Sierra Club Books, 1984).

McNEISH, C., *The Backpackers Manual* (New York: Times Books, 1984).

MEIER, J. F., *Backpacking* (Dubuque, Iowa: Wm. C. Brown, 1980).

RETHMEL, R. C., *Backpacking*, 7th ed. (Piscataway, N.J.: New Century Publications, 1984).

WOOD, R. S., *The Two-Ounce Backpacker: A Problem-Solving Manual for Use in the Wilds* (Berkeley: Ten Speed Press, 1982).

Boating and Sailing

BROWN, R. (ed.), *Boater's Safety Handbook* (Seattle: Mountaineers Books, 1982).

FARNHAM, M. H., *Sailing for Beginners* (New York: Macmillan, 1986).

FENWICK, D. C., *Boatman's Bible* (Summit, Pa.: TAB Books, 1985).

FRANZEI, D., *Sailing: The Basics* (Camden, Me.: International Marine Publishing, 1985).

HALSTED, H. F., *Boating Basics* (Englewood Cliffs, N.J.: Prentice Hall, 1985).

Camping

ANGIER, B. and Z. TAYLOR, *Camping-on-the-Go Cookery* (Harrisburg, Pa.: Stackpole Books, 1983).

ARNOLD, E. and J. LOEB, *Lights Out! Kids Talk About Summer Camps* (Boston: Little, Brown, 1985).

ARMSTRONG, W., *Camping Basics* (Englewood Cliffs, N.J.: Prentice-Hall, 1985).

BAIRSTOW, J., *Four Season Camping* (New York: Random House, 1982).

BATES, J. D., Jr., *Fishing: An Encyclopedia Guide* (New York: Dutton, 1985).

Boy Scouts of America, *Camping* (North Brunswick, N.J.: Boy Scouts of America, 1984).

CLARK, E., *Camping Out* (New York: Putnam's, 1986).

COWAN, D., *Campfire Nights* (New York: Bantam, 1984).

DISLEY, J., *Orienteering*, 2d ed. (Harrisburg, Pa.: Stackpole Books, 1979).

GOODRICH, L., *Decentralized Camping* (Martinsville, Ind.: American Camping Association, 1982).

GOULD, J. M., *How to Camp Out* (New York: Walking News, 1982).

KRAUS, R. G. and M. SCANLIN, *Introduction to Camp Counseling* (Englewood Cliffs, N.J.: Prentice-Hall, 1983).

KROLL, S., *Breaking Camp* (New York: Macmillan, 1985).

LANSING, A. and A. GOLDSMITH, *Summer Camps and Programs: Over 250 of the Best for Children Ages 8 to 18* (New York: Crown Publishers, 1983).

MADDOX, I. (ed.), *Campfire Songs* (Charlotte, N.C.: East Wood Printing/Fast & MacMillan, 1983).

MATTSON, L., *Camp Counselor* (Whiteface Woods, Cotton, Minn.: Camping Guideposts, 1984).

MITCHELL, A. V. and J. F., MEIER, *Camp Counseling*, 6th ed. (New York: Saunders, 1983).

MITCHELL, G., *Fundamentals of Day Camping* (Martinsville, Ind.: American Camping Association, 1982).

RIVIERE, B., *The Camper's Bible*, 3d ed. (New York: Doubleday, 1984).

Camp Administration

American Camping Association, *Camp Standards with Interpretations* (Martinsville, Ind.: American Camping Association, 1984).

BALL, A. B. and B. H. BALL, *Basic Camp Management* (Martinsville, Ind.: American Camping Association, 1982).

FARLEY, A. P., *Perspectives on Camp Administration* (Martinsville, Ind.: Project Stretch and the American Camping Association, 1982).

GOLDRING, D., *The Camp Health Manual* (Martinsville, Ind.: American Camping Association, 1984).

KNOLL, A. P., *Food Service Management* (New York: McGraw-Hill, 1976).

WILKINSON, R. E. *Camps: Their Planning and Management* (St. Louis: C.V. Mosby, 1981).

Canoeing

ANGIER, B. and Z. TAYLOR, *Introduction to Canoeing* (Harrisburg, Pa.: Stackpole Books, 1981).

CROWLEY, W. (ed.), *Rushton's Rowboats and Canoes* (Camden, Me.: International Marine Publishing, 1983).

DAVIDSON, J. W., *The Complete Wilderness Paddler* (New York: Random House, 1982).

DRABIK, H., *The Spirit of Canoe Camping* (Minneapolis: Nodin Press, 1981).

ESSLEN, R., *Back to Nature in Canoes: A Guide to American Waters* (New York: Vanguard, 1985).

EVANS, J., *The Kayaking Book* (Lexington, Mass.: Stephen Greene Press, 1983).

HARRISON, D. and J. *Harrison, Canoe Tripping with Kids* (Lexington, Mass.: Stephen Greene Press, 1982).

JOHNSTONE, B. D., *Guide to Canoe Camping* (Martinsville, Ind.: American Camping Association, 1980).

OVINGTON, R., *Canoeing Basics for Beginners* (Harrisburg, Pa.: Stackpole Books, 1984).

RICHARDS, G., *The Complete Book of Canoeing and Kayaking* (North Pomfret, Vt.: David & Charles, 1981).

SANDERS, W., *Kayak Touring* (Harrisburg, Pa.: Stackpole Books, 1984).

SHAVE, N., *Canoeing Skills and Techniques* (Wolfeboro, N.H.: Longwood Publishing Group, 1985).

Crafts

BLOOD, C. L., *American Indian Games and Crafts* (Danbury, Conn.: Watts, Franklin, 1981).

BODGER, L. and D. EPHRON, *Crafts for All Seasons* (New York: Universe Books, 1980).

BRANDT, K., *Indian Crafts* (Mahwah, N.J.: Troll Associates, 1985).

DONDIEGO, B. L., *Crafts for Kids* (Summit, Pa.: TAB Books, 1984).

DUBANE, J. and D. FRIEND (eds.), *Kid Crafts* (New York: Simplicity Patterns Co., 1984).

EVARD, G., *Homespun Crafts From Scraps* (Piscataway, N.J.: New Century Publications, 1983).

FORTE, I., *Nature Crafts* (Sacremento, Calif.: Incentive Publications, 1985).

JOHNSTON, D., *The Wood Handbook for Craftsmen* (New York: Arco, 1983).

MONTGOMERY, D. R., *Indian Crafts and Skills: An Illustrated Guide for Making Authentic Indian Clothing, Shelters, and Ornaments* (Bountiful, Utah: Horizon Publications, 1985).

RICH, V., *Crafts for Fun* (Valley Forge, Pa.: Judson Press, 1986).

WANKLEMAN, W. F. and P. R. WIGG, *One Hundred One Arts and Crafts Projects* (Dubuque, Iowa: Wm. C. Brown, 1985).

WOLFE, M., *Easy Crafts for Children* (Cincinnati: Standard Publishing, 1985).

Hiking

DANIELSON, J., *Winter Hiking and Camping,* 3d ed. (Glens Falls, N.Y.: Adirondack Mountain Club, 1982).

DROTAR, D. L., *Hiking: Pure and Simple* (Washington, D.C.: Stone Wall Press, 1984).

ELMAN, R. and C. REES, *Hiker's Bible,* rev. ed. (New York: Doubleday, 1982).

RUTSTRUM, C., *Hiking* (Merrillville, Ind.: ICS Books, 1980).

Horseback Riding

BROCK, A., *Riding and Stable Safety* (North Pomfret, Vt.: David & Charles, 1983).

CONDAX, K. D., *Riding: An Illustrated Guide* (New York: Arco, 1983).

EDWARDS, E. H., *From Paddock to Saddle* (Bridgeport, Conn.: Merrimack Publishing, 1985).

GORDON-WATSON, M., *Handbook of Riding* (New York: Knopf, 1982).

MORTIMER, M., *The Riding Instructor's Handbook* (North Pomfret, Vt.: David & Charles, 1981).

OWEN, R. and J. BULLOCK, *Riding* (New York: Arco, 1985).

PERVIER, E., *Horsemanship: Basics for Beginners* (New York: Arco, 1984).

PERVIER, E., *Horsemanship: Basics for Intermediate Riders* (New York: Arco, 1984).

PERVIER, E., *Horsemanship: Basics for Advanced Riders* (New York: Arco, 1984).

SANDERS, R., *Horsekeeping: Riding, Handling, Training* (New York: Sterling Pub. Co., 1983).

SOLOMON, D. S., *Teaching Riding: Step-by-Step Schooling for Horse and Rider* (Norman, Okla.: University of Oklahoma Press, 1982).

WALL, S. H., *Invitation to Riding* (Greenville, N.C.: S7S Publishing, 1984).

Knots

BIGON, M. and G. REGAZZONI, *Morrow's Guide to Knots for Sailing, Fishing, Camping, and Climbing* (New York: Morrow, 1982).

CASSIDY, J., *Knots for Squares and Others* (Stanford, Calif.: Klutz Pres, 1985).

FRY, E.C., *The Book of Knots and Ropework* (New York: Crown, 1983).

GIBSON, C. E., *Handbook of Knots and Splices and Other Work With Hempen and Wire Rope* (White Plains, N.Y.: Emerson Books, 1985).

HIN, F., *This Is Knotting and Splicing* (Boston: Sail Books, 1983).

MARCH, B., *Modern Rope Techniques* (New York: Hippocrene Books, 1983).

WHEELOCK, W., *Ropes, Knots, and Splices for Climbers,* rev. ed. (Glendale, Calif.: La Siesta Press, 1982).

Nature Study

DAVIDSON, N., *Astronomy and the Imagination: A New Approach to Experience of the Stars* (New York: Methuen, 1985).

DEJONGE, J., *Bats and Bugs and Snakes and Slugs* (Grand Rapids: Baker Books, 1981).

DUNN, J., *Astronomy for the Younger Set* (New York: Vantage Press, 1984).
HESS, L., *Secrets in the Meadow* (New York: Macmillan, 1986).
JUNEK, J., et al., *First Nature Watch* (San Diego: Wright Group, 1986).
OLESKY, W., *Nature Gone Wild!* (New York: Julien Messner, 1982).
RUSSELL, F., *Watchers at the Pond* (Boston: David R. Godine, 1981).
TESTA, F., *If You Look Around You* (New York: Dial Books Young, 1983).
WARD, A., *Experimenting With Nature Study* (North Pomfret, Vt.: David and Charles, 1986).
WELCH, M. M., *Close Looks in a Spring Woods* (New York: Dodd, Mead, 1982).

Rock Climbing

BARRY, J., *The Great Climbing Adventure* (Newbury Park, Calif.: Interbook, 1986).
HYDEN, T., et al., *Rock Climbing Is for Me* (Minneapolis: Learner, 1984).
KELLY, J., *Survival: A Guide to Living on Your Own* (New York: McGraw-Hill, 1980).
LOUGHMAN, M., *Learning to Rock Climb* (San Francisco: Sierra Club Books, 1981).

Shooting

HUMPHREYS, J., *Learning to Shoot* (North Pomfret, Vt.: David & Charles, 1985).
JARRETT, W. S. (ed.), *Shooter's Bible, No. 77* (South Hackensack, N.J.: Stoeger Publishing, 1985).
KLINGER, B. (ed.), *Rifle Shooting as a Sport* (Cranbury, N.J.: A. S. Barnes, 1981).
MARCHINGTON, J., *Shooting: A Complete Guide for Beginners* (Winchester, Mass.: Faber & Faber, 1982).
REES, C., *Be An Expert Shot With Rifle, Handgun, or Shotgun* (Piscataway, N.J.: New Century Publications, 1984).
WIKINSON, F. (ed.), *The Book of Shooting for Sport and Skill* (New York: Crown Publications, 1980).

Water Safety

DONAHUE-GANDY, M. M., *Teaching Basic Aquatics . . . Especially to Those Who Have Difficulty Learning* (Citrus Heights, Calif.: M. M. Donahue-Gandy, 1984).
VERNIER, J., *Swimming* (Wolfeboro, N.J.: Longwood, 1985).

Appendix A:
Films and Film Strips

Adventures at Day Camp. Produced by the Girl Scouts of the U.S.A., Audio-Visual Aids Service, 830 Third Avenue, New York. 16 mm sd. film.

Archery Fundamentals. Bailey Films, Inc., 6509 De Longpre Avenue, Hollywood, California. 16 mm sd. film.

Axemanship. Produced by the Boy Scouts of America, Visual Education Services, National Council, New Brunswick, New Jersey. 16 mm sd. film.

Backpacking. Produced by the American Camping Association, Bradford Woods, Indiana. filmstrip.

Be Water Wise. Produced by Norwood Films, 926 New Jersey Avenue N.W., Washington, D.C. 16 mm sd. film.

Beginning Skin and Scuba Diving. Produced by the Society for Visual Education, 1345 Diversey Parkway, Chicago, Illinois. filmstrip.

By Map and Compass. Produced by International Film Bureau for Cawley, 19 Fairmont Avenue, Ottowa, Canada. 16 mm sd. film.

Camping. Produced by the American Camping Association, Bradford Woods, Indiana. filmstrip.

Camping: A Key to Conservation. Produced by Indiana University Audio-Visual Center, Bloomington, Indiana. 16 mm sd. film.

Camping Education. Produced by the March of Time, Rand McNally Company, Box 7600, Chicago, Illinois, 16 mm sd. film.

Camp Happiness. Produced by Purdue University Audio-Visual Center, Lafayette, Indiana. 16 mm sd. film.

Camp Site Development. Produced by the Girl Scouts of the U.S.A., Audio-Visual Aids Service, 830 Third Avenue, New York. filmstrip.

Camp Site Selection. Produced by the Girl Scouts of the U.S.A., Audio-Visual Aids Service, 830 Third Avenue, New York. filmstrip.

Camp Time, Any Time. Produced by the Girl Scouts of the U.S.A., Audio-Visual Aids Service, 830 Third Avenue, New York. 16 mm sd. film.

Camping and Recreation Programs for the Handicapped. Produced by the Audio-Visual Center, Indiana University, Bloomington, Indiana, 16 mm sd. film.

Collecting Insects. Produced by the JAM Handy Organization, 2821 East Grand Boulevard, Detroit, Michigan. filmstrip.

Easy in the Saddle. Perry-Mansfield Motion Pictures, Steamboat Springs, Colorado. 16 mm sd. film.

Explorer Leaders Basic Training. Produced by the Boy Scouts of America, Visual Education Services, National Council, New Brunswick, New Jersey. filmstrip.

Finding Out About Rocks. Produced by United World Films, 1445 Park Avenue, New York. 16 mm sd. film.

Fly Fishing for Trout. Produced by New York State Department of Commerce, Film Library, 40 Howard Street, Albany, New York. 16 mm sd. film.

Health and Safety in the Out-of-Doors. Produced by Visual Sciences, Suffern, New York. 16 mm sd. film.

Learning About Insects. Produced by Encyclopedia Britannica Films, 1159 Wilmette Avenue, Wilmette, Illinois. filmstrip.

Let's Take a Walk in the High Country. Produced by Gateway Productions. 16 mm sd. film.

Let's Go Troop Camping. Produced by the Girl Scouts of the U.S.A., Audio-Visual Aids Service, 830 Third Avenue, New York. 16 mm sd. film.

Life on a Dead Tree. Produced by Film Associates of California, 11014 Santa Monica Boulevard, Los Angeles, California. 16 mm sd. film.

Paddle a Safe Canoe. Produced by Aetna Life Affiliated Companies, Information and Education Department, 151 Farmington Avenue, Hartford, Connecticut. 16 mm sd. film.

Shooting Safety. Produced by the Ohio Department of Natural Resources, Information and Education Section, 1500 Dublin Road, Columbus, Ohio. 16 mm sd. film.

Sport of Orienteering. Produced by International Film Bureau for Cawley, 19 Fairmount Avenue, Ottowa, Canada. 16 mm sd. film.

The Environmental School. Produced by the National Audio-Visual Center, General Services Administration, Washington, D.C. 16 mm sd. film.

The Scout Trail. Produced by the Boy Scouts of America, Visual Education Services, National Council, New Brunswick, New Jersey. 16 mm sd. film.

This is Camping. Produced by the Audio-Visual Center, Indiana University, Bloomington, Indiana. 16 mm sd. film.

To Light a Spark. Produced by the Audio-Visual Center, Indiana University, Bloomington, Indiana. 16 mm sd. film.

What Makes Weather? Produced by Central Scientific Company, 1700 Irving Park Road, Chicago, Illinois. 16 mm sd. film.

Appendix B: Typical Camp Counselor Contract

Camp Fresh Air
Memorandum of Agreement

Name _____ Date _____
    Last   First   M. I.
Address _____ Telephone No.: _____
Age _____ Date of Birth _____ Social Security No.: _____
    (as of June 1)
For employment during the season _____, beginning _____
and ending _____, I understand that my responsibilities include both general and special:

General

Being responsible for a part of the routine of camp, maintaining discipline and proper deportment at all occasions and in all areas of camp, assisting others who are in charge of special camp functions, and adjusting my personal habits and actions to the customs and policies of Camp Fresh Air, as outlined in the second part of this agreement. I will attend the five-day orientation period before the opening of the camp season.

Special

Special duties assigned to the above named are the responsibilities of _____ as described in the job description.

Remuneration

In consideration of the faithful and loyal performance of the above-mentioned duties by the above-named individual, Camp Fresh Air agrees to remunerate him/her bi-weekly for eight (8) weeks: Salary: $_____.

This contract is non-negotiable upon applicant's signature.
Accepted in all above terms: _____

Employee signature

_____.

Date

_____

Parent/guardian signature (under 18)

_____

Executive director

Special duties, responsibilities, and time commitments must be clearly understood before signing this agreement.

If you have any questions, write or call Sandy Green, executive director, 10 Bartlett St., Somewhere, Connecticut.

Customs and policies

The camp aims to build health, character, and citizenship and therefore endeavors to secure for its staff, men and women of sterling character, high ideals, strong personality, and special ability. The campers are in their formative years and are so impressionable that they readily absorb the prevailing spirit of the environment and often acquire the ideals and habits of those they admire. The camp desires its staff members to realize the serious responsibility they assume for the molding of young lives.

The serious responsibility assumed by the Executive Director for the welfare of the campers and staff members justifies her expecting from those associated with her the same devotion of duty that motivate her. The camp has earned the reputation among citizens of New Britain/Berlin for reliability in carrying out its announced program, for safeguarding its campers both morally and physically, and for adhering to its high ideals.

The camp endeavors to avoid the employer–employee attitude in its relationship with staff members. Preferring that the spirit of co-workers and comradeship should prevail, it asks them to conform with the custom of the camp as to their personal habits and their social relationships within the camp circle.

Male staff members shall not visit within the assigned quarters of the female staff members and the reverse shall also be true. Social relationships with other staff members shall be limited to the employee's free time. The camp does not tolerate any use and/or possession of illegal drugs. Visitors shall absent themselves from the camp, and all staff shall have reported for duty by the designated curfew hours.

The camp includes as standard practice ceremonies of patriotism, e.g., the Pledge of Allegiance, singing of the National Anthem, religious activities, e.g., grace before meals and worship services on Sunday, when camp is in session. Disruption of these practices will not be tolerated.

I have read and do agree to follow the above policies for being a staff member at Camp Fresh Air.

_____   _____

Date   Signature

Appendix C: Organizations Associated with Camping

American Alliance for Health, Physical Education, Recreation, and Dance
  1900 Association Dr., Reston, Va. 22091
American Camping Association
  Bradford Woods, Martinsville, Ind. 46151
American Canoe Association
  Box 248, Lorton, Va. 22079
American National Red Cross
  17th and D Sts. N.W., Washington, D.C. 20006
American Whitewater Affiliation
  Box 1483, Hagerstown, Md. 21740
American Youth Hostels, Inc.
  National Campus, Delaplane, Va. 22025
Association of Private Camps
  55 West 42nd St., New York, N.Y. 10036
Boy Scouts of America
  North Brunswick, N.J. 08902
Camp Archery Association
  200 Coligni Ave., New Rochelle, N.Y. 10017
Camp Fire, Inc.
  4601 Madison Ave., Kansas City, Mo. 64112
Canadian Camping Association
  1806 Avenue Rd., suite 2, Toronto, Ontario, Canada M5M 3Z1
Christian Camping International
  Box 400, Somonauk, Ill. 60552
Funds for the Advancement of Camping
  Suite 1126, 19 S. La Salle St., Chicago, Ill. 60603
Girl Scouts of the U.S.A.
  830 Third Ave., New York, N.Y. 10022

Isaak Walton League of America
  1800 Borth Kent St., suite 806, Arlington, Va. 22209
National Campers and Hikers Association
  P.O. Box 182, 7172 Transit Rd., Buffalo, N.Y. 14221
National Camping Association
  353 West 56th St., New York, N.Y. 10019
National Recreation and Park Association
  3101 Park Center Dr., Alexandria, Va. 22302
National Trails Council
  P.O. Box 1042, Saint Charles, Ill. 60174
Project Adventure
  P.O. Box 157, Hamilton, Mass. 01936
United States Canoe Association
  617 South 94th St., Milwaukee, Wis. 53214
United States Orienteering Association
  The Broadmoor, Colorado Springs, Colo. 80906

Appendix D:
The Food Groups

The Basic Seven Outline

Group 1:   *Green and yellow vegetables.* These foods provide carotene, riboflavin, iron, and calcium. In this group are asparagus, string beans, celery, lettuce, kale, green peas, wax beans, spinach, carrots, pumpkin, yellow squash, yams, and corn.

Group 2:   *Citric producers.* These include oranges, grapefruit, lemons, limes, tomatoes, tangerines, pineapple, rutabaga, cantaloupe, strawberries, raspberries, cabbage, cauliflower, and brussels sprouts. These foods, to a greater or lesser extent, provide ascorbic acid.

Group 3:   *Starches, minerals, and other nutrients.* These include potatoes, vegetables, and fruits.

Group 4:   *Milk and milk products.* These foods supply proteins, vitamin A, riboflavin, and calcium.

Group 5:   *Meat, poultry, fish, and eggs.* This group provides proteins, thiamin, niacin, riboflavin, and iron.

Group 6:   *Bread, flour, and cereals.* These foods provide proteins. Enriched whole grain foods supply thiamin, niacin, riboflavin, and iron.

Group 7:   *Butter and oleomargarine.* These foods furnish vitamin A.

The Right Foods List

Milk. For the growing child, $\frac{3}{4}$ to 1 quart daily; for others, 1 pint or more.

Leafy green or yellow vegetables. One or more servings daily.

Tomatoes, oranges, grapefruit. One or more servings daily.

Potatoes, other vegetables, or fruit. Two or more servings daily.

Eggs. At least three or four each week.

Lean meat, poultry, fish. One or more servings daily.

Cereals and bread. At least two servings of whole grain products daily.

Fats, Carbohydrates, and Water.

The Four Broad Foods Group

Milk Group

Foods

Milk: fluid whole, skim, evaporated, dry, or buttermilk; part or all of milk may be derived from source other than fluid whole milk.

Cheese: cottage, cream, or cheddar type.

Ice cream: cheese and ice cream may be replaced by part of milk, amount being based on equivalent calcium content.

Quantity

Daily whole fluid milk (8-oz portions):
　　Children: three to four portions
　　Teenagers: four or more portions
　　Adults: two or more portions

Meat Group

Foods

Beef, pork, veal, and lamb
Poultry and eggs
Fish and seafood

Quantity

Two or more servings daily
Three oz lean cooked meat, without bone
Three oz poultry or fish, without bone
Two eggs

Vegetable-Fruit group

Foods

All fruits and vegetables—oranges, grapefruit, cantaloupe, honeydew, Persian melon, watermelon, strawberries, raspberries, blueberries, apricots, cherries, peaches, plums, nectarines, bananas, tomatoes, broccoli, carrots, summer squash, spinach, yams, string beans, green peas, lima beans, wax beans, and so on.

Quantity

Four or more servings daily
One $\frac{1}{2}$ cup of fruit or vegetables
One banana, orange, or potato
One $\frac{1}{2}$ grapefruit or cantaloupe

Bread-Cereal group

Foods

All breads and cereals that are whole-grain, enriched, or restored—especially breads, cooked cereals, ready-to-eat cereals, corn meal, crackers, macaroni, spaghetti, noodles, rice, rolled oats, and flour.

Quantity

Four or more servings daily

One slice of bread

One ready-to-eat cereal

One $\frac{1}{2}$ to $\frac{3}{4}$ cup of cooked cereal, rice, and so on.

Index